The Information Revolution and Developing Countries

The Information Revolution and Developing Countries

Ernest J. Wilson III

The MIT Press
Cambridge, Massachusetts
London, England

This book was set in Sabon by SNP Best-set Typesetter Ltd., Hong Kong. Printed and bound in the United States of America.

Library of Congress Cataloging-in-Publication Data

Wilson, Ernest J., III.
The information revolution and developing countries / Ernest J. Wilson III.
   p. cm.
Includes bibliographical references and index.
ISBN 0-262-23230-8 (hc. : alk. paper)
1. Information technology—Economic aspects—Developing countries.
I. Title.

HC59.72.I55W55   2004
303.48′33′091724—dc21

2002043177

10 9 8 7 6 5 4 3 2 1

Contents

Acknowledgments

More so than most, this book would not have been written without the close cooperation and cheerful instruction of many, many colleagues around the world in Africa, Asia, Latin America, as well as Europe and North America.

Financial and material support for various pieces of the research were given by the School of Behavioral and Social Sciences at the University of Maryland, the Leland Initiative of the United States Agency for International Development (USAID), the Hewlett Foundation, and the Markle Foundation. I wish to thank various collaborators who over the years as this book was being written provided insights and resources that allowed me to investigate the real-world dynamics of the information revolution, including K. Y. Amoako and his team at the United Nations Economic Commission for Africa (UNECA) in Addis Ababa; Jacques Diouf, director-general of the United Nations Food and Agriculture Organization (FAO) in Rome; the Global Information and Communication Technologies Department (GICT) leadership team at the World Bank Group and the International Finance Corporation (IFC), including James Bond, Carlos Braga, Elkyn Chaparro, Carl Dahlman, Nagy Hannah, Bruno Lanvin, and Jean François Rischard. My Markle Foundation colleagues Zoe Baird, Karen Lynch, Julia Moffett, and Fred Tipson also provided useful dialogue as well as support over the years. Colleagues and programs at the RAND Corporation helped sharpen my argument, as did fellow researchers at Canada's International Development Research Centre. Lane Smith of the USAID Leland Initiative was a valued colleague as well.

Colleagues at the Global Information Infrastructure Commission (GIIC)—including Ambassador Diana Lady Dougan, Carol Charles, Russell Pipe, Robert Rogers, and Joe Young, as well as our many private-sector colleagues like Koos Becker, Bowman Cutter, Denis Gilhooly, Masanobu Kato, Minoru Makihara, and David Olive—were unstinting in their suggestions and guidance over many years. A year-long consultancy with the Global Business Dialogue (Electronic Commerce) (GDD(e)) and the opportunity to interact with dozens of business leaders around the world also provided access to their strategies and priorities. Carter Eltzroth was a helpful guide through this process.

For my work on Brazil, I wish to thank Carlos Afonso, Ambassador Rubens Antonio Barbosa, Antonio Botelho, Ivan Moura Campos, Thomas Case, Ken Conca, Caio Tulio Costa, Eduardo da Costa, Marcelo Lacerda, Professor Carlos Luceno, Rodrigo Mesquita, Simon Romero, John Stebbins, Tadao Takahashi, Ricardo Tavares, and Rubens Vaz da Costa. A special thanks to Eduardo and his colleagues of the "Gang of Four" for agreeing to meet for a whole day in Rio to share the details of Brazil's early experiences with the Internet and to provide their comments and interpretations. They also read through parts of the Brazil chapter and made helpful suggestions.

For the Ghana chapter, my good friend Nii Quaynor submitted to endless interviews around the world and provided steady guidance not only on Ghana but on many other global ICT issues as well. Minister Edward Saliah and then Minister Ekow Spiro-Garbah were also generous with their time, as was P. V. Obeng. Others in Ghana at nongovernmental organizations, in the private sector, and in government, many of whom requested anonymity, were also supportive.

For my chapter on China, I was helped by several institutions. Especially helpful was a seminar organized by the Chinese Academy of Science, which provided invaluable information about the evolution of the Internet in the Middle Kingdom. The engagement of participants like Dr. Qiheng Hu was crucial to my understanding of China's Internet history. Mao Wei and his colleagues at the Computer Network Information Center provided excellent advice and support, as did associates at the Chinese Academy of Social Sciences and the China Reform Forum. Entrepreneurs like Jian Shen, Edward Tian, Edward Zeng, Charles Zhang, and Michael Wan took time out of their busy schedules to submit cheerfully to interviews, as did Peter Zhang of the China Electronic Commerce Association. Government officials like Gao Hongbing, Lu Xinkui, and Song Ling were also helpful. In Hong Kong, Taylor Fravel, Peter Lovelock, Fred Tipson, Zixiang (Alex) Tan, and John Ure provided an excellent early orientation to the subject. Other scholars like Fan Xiang, Will Foster, Guo Liang, Margaret Pearson, Tony Saitch, and Mao Wei were extremely helpful. Conversations with my former University of Michigan colleague, the late Michel Oksenberg, were also valuable, as were my talks with Duan Qing.

Colleagues who read parts of the manuscript and provided comments include Nagy Hanna, Brian Kahin, Nanette Levinson, and George Sadowski.

I have benefited greatly from ongoing conversations with a variety of experts, including Izumi Aizu, Bai Akridge, Raymond Akwule, Derrick Cogburn, Peter Cowhey, John Daly, Wilson Dizard, William Drake, Frank Fukuyama, Nancy Hafkin, Virginia Haufler, Yuki Imamura, Shumpei Kumon, Robin Mansell, Bruce McConnell, Richard P. O'Neil, Sean O'Siochru, Francisco Rodriguez, Olivier Sagna, Lane Smith, Robert Valantin, George Vradenberg, and my Center for International Development and Conflict Management (CIDCM) colleague Kelly Wong.

Research assistance was provided by 'Dayo Adekson, Ryan Barbera, Bidisha Biswas, Terah R. Gaertner, Nicole Millson, Duan Qing, Xie Shiqing, and Ivani Vassoler. I wish especially to thank Malik Ernest Wilson for helping me edit much of this manuscript and pushing me to move forward at a time when I was wallowing in detail. My editor at MIT Press, Robert Prior, was always available for understanding and advice.

The excellent staff of the CIDCM at the University of Maryland was supportive and capable in so many ways, from arranging visas to retrieving the latest version of a chapter on my H drive.

With so many excellent people giving so much good advice and support, there should be no errors of fact or interpretation. Alas, some may remain despite my colleagues' good efforts, and for these I alone am responsible.

The usual disclaimers about family tolerance and support are especially relevant here, since Francille Rusan Wilson and Malik and Rodney all contributed materially to this project and were always there for the unconditional shoring up that all authors badly need.

Introduction: Why This Book Now?

Books get written for different reasons. This particular book grew from my fascination with the complexity of the global information revolution and my frustration with the limits of existing explanations. Too many either had the details right but ignored the big picture or painted a big picture with inadequate supporting details. And all too often they interpreted technology as an independent driving force remaking the world in its image. I set out to create a framework that would overcome these and other deficiencies.

This book aims to provide a clear, consistent analysis of the major trends and transformations of the information revolution, while rooting these explanations in national and societal structures and dynamics. To account for these transformations, I develop a model I call *strategic restructuring* (SRS), which links the massive changes we see taking place around the world today with local-level initiatives of individual information activists, especially in developing countries. SRS locates the dynamics of information and communication technology (ICT) change in self-interested actions by individual women and men pursuing strategies they believe will advance their material and ideological interests.

Research always brings with it some surprises. The biggest surprise in my research was discovering the hugely important influence of the individual men and women who are making the global information revolution. As I traveled back and forth to Brazil, China, Ghana, India, Malaysia, South Africa, and other nations, I came to realize that the massive structural changes that constitute the information revolution—such as shifts from public to private ownership or from monopoly to competition—are being driven on the ground by local information champions who struggle daily to overcome local apathy as well as entrenched opposition to the revolutionary reforms they propose. These information revolutionaries struggle individually and collectively in groups to press these changes. If this book is successful, it will give voice to these agents of change and capture some of their own unique perspectives on the revolution they are making.

Yet these individual reform efforts always take place within a dense and rich structural context of tangled social, political, and economic relationships that are simultaneously local, national, regional, and global. Capturing both the structural and the individual elements of the information revolution is a goal of the strategic restructuring model. It is the interaction of the two that creates the revolution.

Agency is especially important for those engaged in trying to produce these transformations, as well as for those trying to understand and explain them. In any period of big societal changes, individuals and groups want to know how much freedom of action they have under the new circumstances. "How much maneuverability do I have?" they ask. "Do I have some freedom to use the new technologies to become more productive, more innovative, more free, and more powerful?" Being poor and powerless, most of the world's people have far fewer choices than those who sit astride powerful and rich institutions in rich and powerful countries. One purpose of this book is to explore the tremendous opportunities for innovation and for personal and collective advancement that the information revolution might offer and yet to identify the very real structural, institutional, and cultural constraints that foreclose options for the wider spread of information and communication technology resources.

In this light, *The Information Revolution and Developing Countries* is targeted to the engaged scholar as well as the thoughtful practitioner. Some of the issues that this book analyzes are the real-world strategic and policy issues that practitioners must resolve—such as how to pursue Internet diffusion, privatization, and regulatory reform and thereby reduce the digital divide—and it does so through the theoretical lens of the strategic restructuring model.

Recognizing constraints also means recognizing the incomplete views that most observers bring to the information revolution. If where one stands on an issue depends on where one sits, then it makes a difference if the observer of the revolution comes from a private organization, the public sector, or a nonprofit organization. In writing this book, I have benefited from working in senior positions on information and communication technology issues across a wide variety of institutions and sectors—with private firms and international ICT trade groups like the Global Information Infrastructure Commission and the Global Business Dialogue (Electronic Commerce); with international organizations like the World Economic Forum, the United Nations Economic Commission for Africa, and the World Bank; and with nongovernmental organizations like the Markle Foundation and the Center for Democratic Technology. I have also been fortunate to work with a number of governments, including that of South Africa. In the United States, I am privileged to serve on the Board of Directors of the Corporation for Public Broadcasting. I have worked on the National Security Council at the White House and in the U.S. Information Agency on international communications issues. Moving among these institutions and many countries has given me great respect for the unique perspectives that their experts have developed. These experiences have also taught me that cross-sectoral cooperation is a determinant of successful ICT reforms and wider diffusion of ICT resources around the world and that any single view point—whether of government officials, business executives, NGO leaders, or university professors—cannot adequately represent the global information revolution.

In chapter 1, the reader is introduced to the real-world challenges of the information revolution and the strengths and weaknesses of researchers who have tried to explain these far-reaching changes. While experts agree that economic structure is the single most important factor shaping ICT outcomes, nonetheless there are surprising ICT differences among countries with similar economic structures. Why should this be so? And precisely how do various factors—including structure—shape these outcomes?

Chapter 2 offers a modified structural analysis—the *strategic restructuring (SRS) model*—that I believe answers the puzzle. This analysis fills in the missing elements of other approaches by unifying structural, institutional, and political and policy factors into a single framework to account for different diffusion patterns around the globe, especially in developing countries.

In the chapters 3, 4, and 5, I apply the SRS framework to the politics of Internet expansion in Brazil, Ghana, and China. Each chapter follows the same format—it begins by analyzing national structures and then reviews the institutions, politics, and public policies (and private strategies) that directly shape ICT diffusion.

Chapter 6 takes up the difficult and widely discussed topic of the *digital divide*, redefining it conceptually, providing a rigorous comparative analysis of its extent, and then exploring its multiple relationships with economic performance. With these basic empirical facts and the causal relations established, chapter 7 returns to the political economy framework of the earlier chapters and analyzes the ways that various individuals, institutions, and groups—especially leading private-sector firms and business associations—have interacted on the global scene to structure the worldwide debate on the digital divide and to promote some solutions while setting aside others.

Finally, chapter 8 draws together the insights of the earlier chapters to assess the utility—and the limits—of the strategic restructuring model for explaining the information revolution.

In these turbulent times ICT ministers and moguls come and go. Institutions change their names and responsibilities, bandwidth expands, and prices fall. Some names, responsibilities, and price levels cited will certainly change before this book is published. But the basic ICT structures and dynamics will change little.

One conclusion is clear: understanding the realities requires diverse and multivariate analyses across ICT systems. I hope this book will challenge some of your own assumptions about the global information revolution and provoke you to rethink your ideas about the momentous times that lie ahead.

The Information Revolution and Developing Countries

1

Puzzles to Be Solved

In the twenty-first century, the capacity to communicate will almost certainly be
a key human right. Eliminating the distinction between the information-rich and
information-poor is also critical to eliminating economic and other inequalities
between North and South, and to improving the life of all humanity.
—Nelson Mandela, TELECOM 95, October 3, 1995

Introduction

Spreading outward like ripples on a lake, fundamental changes are
spreading throughout the world, driven in part by information and communication technologies. These changes are widespread and affect our
most personal interactions among friends and families as well as global
corporate business practices. We see changes in the structure of employment patterns, in the volume and velocity of capital flows, and in the
reach of world commerce—in the most advanced countries, information-
related services and activities now employ more people than any other
industry. Utilizing new digitalization techniques, physicians are transforming the medical profession. Changes have deeply affected global
culture as images of foreign nations are beamed into our homes. Taken
in the aggregate, these changes are momentous enough to suggest our
arrival in a new information age.

Although these momentous changes are occurring, they are neither
universal nor uniform. The citizens of the highly developed, fully wired
countries, primarily in northern Europe and North America, have
entered the new digital century with simple, affordable, and almost universal access to the Internet—in their homes, their offices, their brief-
cases, and their cars. Concomitantly, most people in the world have never

used a telephone. As South African leader Thabo Mbeki says, there are more telephones in Tokyo than in all of sub-Saharan Africa.

This book explores the world of the as-yet unwired and unconnected, the underwired and the underconnected, and examines their efforts to participate in the global information revolution. Their eventual membership in the global information society and the possible redefinition of that society by the five billion people who live outside the West will be momentous. This transition will have material consequences for future global growth, modern governance, and military strategies. One Japanese communication expert who is working with developing countries signs his Internet messages, "Helping to write the history of the future."

As countries leave behind the familiar certainties of the industrial and agricultural worlds, they are stepping into uncharted technological territories. Joseph A. Schumpeter (1943) foresaw that the transition to a mature capitalist society would result in the simultaneous occurrence of widespread creation and widespread destruction. Information and communication services will create new patterns of winners and losers, reshaping the distribution of wealth as communication technology becomes a prerequisite for economic success. New forms of conflict and cooperation will ensue. Access to databases and software production will be as globally determinative as stock in Chrysler, Mitsubishi, or Shell. Foreign investors are seeking richly educated populations, not just rich mineral deposits. Minds are needed more than mines.

The new information and communication technologies (ICTs) have the potential to bring growth and equity to the world's developing countries. The great risk in this transition is that the new technologies might fail to live up to their expectations and that ICT might become a great and powerful engine of *inequality* rather than a tool for greater global and national equity. This book is designed to achieve four basic purposes:

• *To advance a detailed critique of the "technology first" information revolution analysis.*   I argue that the information revolution is as much an institutional and political revolution as it is a technological one and that it occurs within particular structural and cultural contexts. Much of the current writing on information and communication technologies

(ICTs) in developing countries overemphasizes technology to the detriment of other factors such as politics.

• *To describe developing countries position in the emerging global information society* and what the local experts in Brazil, Ghana, and China—whose views are often unavailable—feel about ICT.

• *To analyze real-world policy challenges facing senior government officials in developing countries.*

• *To provide an alternative analytic framework for describing and understanding the information revolution.* Statistics alone about Internet growth and telephones per thousand have not adequately advanced our understanding; neither have casual accounts of an author's favorite story from his latest trip to India or Africa. This book provides an overarching analytic framework in which empirical findings can be situated, examined, and evaluated.

The Strategic Restructuring Framework and an Unconventional Definition of the Information Revolution

A Definition for North and South

The *strategic restructuring (SRS) framework* I put forth is built around a particular definition of the information revolution (Wilson 1987). SRS seeks to capture the richness and variety of the information revolution while avoiding monocausal simplicities. It uses a modified structural approach as its platform, examining individual initiatives against the backdrop of economic, political, and social constraints. ICT is defined not as machinery but as a scarce and valuable resource that people compete for and that benefits those who can maneuver themselves to avoid its downside risks. In this respect, information technology is not just a benign application like mobile phones, distance education, or Internet telephony. Instead, ICT is like land or capital, which has differential impacts when diffused differentially across nations and social groups. Some groups are more likely to gain access than others. The information revolution is the process through which these new resources are produced, distributed, and consumed across the globe. Because the new ICT resources have the capacity to empower certain individuals and groups (such as private entrepreneurs or activists from nongovernmental organizations) and disempower the authority of other groups (such as telecom operators and political dictators), they always receive a mixed reception wherever they spread—from China to Chiapas. Some individuals try to promote the spread of ICT aggressively, often via a liberalized mode of diffusion where the state takes a back seat to NGOs and small companies. But managers and beneficiaries of large, state-owned ICT monopolies who understand that liberalized ICT diffusion will threaten their social status and power seek to block the liberal diffusion of these new resources and to maintain control of ICT distribution through their own reliable channels. The particular mix of liberal versus controlled distribution is largely a function of who gets to write the new rules of the game in the ICT sector—the liberal challengers or the conservatives. As I demonstrate in chapter 2, tracking this process is the purpose of the strategic restructuring model.

Complex social, political, and economic interactions operate simultaneously across macro, meso, and micro levels. The strategic restructuring framework seeks to capture the variety of these dynamics for information and communication. This model consists of four causal variables—structure, institutions, politics, and policy—that can account for many of the cross-national patterns we see in new technology diffusion.

The SRS model also encompasses distributional and equity outcomes. I argue that too many accounts of the information revolution tend to privilege technological innovation and to minimize politics. These accounts are driven implicitly or explicitly by the persuasive technocratic logic of Moore's law or Metcalfe's law about the positive sides of ICT innovation and diffusion. Less attention is paid to the exponential *costs* of being unconnected. This distributional concern sits at the core of the SRS framework.

Not everyone agrees with this way of framing the information revolution. Others do not believe that Internet diffusion is worth all the fuss and attention it has received. When traveling in South Africa or South Asia, I have discovered very different views on the importance or lack of importance of the information revolution. Some intellectuals and policy makers in the global South have tended to dismiss ICT as a luxury the poor cannot afford, a far cry from the obvious imperatives of clean water, health care, or education (personal communications: India 1999, South Africa 1998). Still others claim that the current global arrangement of ICT helps strengthen the economic dependence that has been characteristic of the South's relations with the North for centuries. The nature of this arrangement imports Western values and dictates the image that less developed countries have of themselves (Sprague 1994). Other ICT experts in the North dismiss poor countries as strange exotica that are fundamentally irrelevant to global ICT diffusion. Others believe that the information gap is "their" problem and therefore not relevant for northern concern. These beliefs are either said outright or implied by what is omitted.

I argue that these arguments are incorrect on several accounts. Creating greater access to information and communication services is everyone's problem and everyone's opportunity. Citizens, policy makers, and business people must pay attention to developing countries' information revolution.

The Importance of ICT Diffusion

Understanding the basics of the information revolution and developing countries is urgent for the global South. Economically, advances in information and communication technologies are contributing to a wave of change that is sweeping around the world like a tidal wave, pushing men and women selectively to create new relationships and new forms of organization that facilitate their use of new technologies. Countries that anticipate and respond innovatively to these new threats and opportunities will excel during the coming decades; those that fail to anticipate and innovate will perform poorly. Leaders who fail to seize ICT opportunities may produce the same results as leaders who failed to build factories or railroads in the early stages of the industrial revolution. Some developing countries' elites understand the urgency of their condition. According to a senior government official in China that I interviewed for this book, "Because China was so inward looking, our people missed the industrial revolution of the last two centuries. Because we were so slow to catch up, it set us back 100 years behind the West economically and militarily. We don't want to miss the revolution this time" (Ministry of Information Industries senior official, personal communication January

2000). And according to the Federal Industry Minister of India, Murasoli Maran, "We have missed the industrial revolution, but we do not want to miss the ICT revolution that is sweeping the world" (Maran 1999).

A strong, flexible, and modern national communication system has become a requirement for capital investment, both foreign and local. Transnational corporations regularly report that a modern national information infrastructure is at least as important as low taxes and low wages for where they will invest. In the modern period, inadequate information infrastructures have halted investment, productivity, and high wages, leading to less development (World Bank 1999). One businessman claimed that "There is probably no single more important infrastructure that will help Brazil become more competitive and more economically viable than telecommunications. It is a precious opportunity that fully exploited will put Brazil back where it should be in the world economic scene" (Romine 1998, 1).

One of the ironies of the new globalized world is that strengthening local cultures requires interaction with the international culture. Every country and culture wishes to protect its national heritage and values from external influence, but in this new networked world, defending basic values means having the wherewithal to produce and project one's culture, which in turn requires a sophisticated multimedia infrastructure. Yet at least in the short term, building such an infrastructure increases access to foreign content—precisely what many cultural nationalists want to avoid. Robust and extensive national information infrastructures must be constructed to achieve these cultural and political goals.

Developing countries face tremendous difficulties, including a dearth of money, technology, and training. But perhaps the biggest challenge faced by these countries is that these problems come in a tightly bound *political* package. One of the most unexpected conclusions that I've drawn from my visits to dozens of countries is that in developing countries the information revolution is viewed as a highly political affair and not as a technical challenge. The people introducing the Internet to Egypt or China succeed by constructing an explicit political coalition. These coalitions and their constituencies must believe they will benefit from introducing new technologies, so the leaders advance their technopolitical reforms through education, propaganda, bureaucratic maneuvering, and monetary rewards.

People in developing countries care about their own information revolution. But why should Westerners or northerners care? In brief, the reasons are commercial, political, and social. The question is *economically* important for the future growth of ICT markets for European, Japanese, and North American companies and hence for employment and corporate earnings in the North. Between 1990 and 1996, China was the fastest-growing market in the world for telephone mainlines, with an increase of 690 percent (AEA 1997, 106). Over the same years, in the United States Internet hosts grew by 44 percent, while in Malaysia they grew by 375 percent, and in China computer use rose by 528 percent (AEA 1997, 104–109). Developing countries are also a growing source of international competition for Western industries. Thailand, Korea, Brazil, India, and Taiwan contend with Western private firms in their home markets and around the world. In addition, less expensive, imported ICT goods keep down the inflation rates of developed countries. The choices made by ICT elites in developing countries may also shape the evolution of hardware and software globally. Some "free-software evangelists believe the key to the success of open-source software is getting the support of poorer, developing nations. There are efforts in China, Argentina, and many other countries to pass laws that would require governments to look at free alternatives before purchasing technology" (Cha 2001, E01).

The spread of information and communication technologies is already affecting global *politics and security*. Most countries have an interest in promoting a smooth, conflict-free transition from an industrial society to an information society. Yet by their nature, these new media destabilize traditional cultural and political practices. The terrorist attacks in New York, Washington, D.C., and Pennsylvania in September 2001 point to the high costs incurred by society when sophisticated networked fanatics are willing to use all forms of ICT to pursue violent goals, provoking calls for counterstrategies of "swarming" and network war (Arquilla and Ronfeldt 2001).

Even before the 9/11 attacks, the Pentagon and U.S. intelligence agencies were worried that the potential threat of hackers, terrorists, and others from poor countries against the United States' basic information infrastructures could be significant. The terms *cyberwar* and *cyberterrorism* have been added to the national security lexicon. The eruption of anti-Western terrorism in late 2001 reflects the unstable brew of new media and foreign values meeting discontent and alienation.

ICT may also be contributing to the *growing gap between rich and poor*. The World Bank reports that the wealth and income gap is not improving between the world's richest and poorest. At the growth rates shown between 1980 to 1993, for example, India would take decades to reach the United States' gross domestic product (GDP) per capita. Most economists generally agree that changes in technology are the greatest contributor to the wage gap. Wealth and income gaps are already substantial in many ways:

• The three richest people in the world—Bill Gates, Warren Buffett, and Paul Allen (the first and last are Microsoft multibillionaires)—have total assets greater than the combined GDP of the forty-three least developed countries.

• Of all the patents in the world, 97 percent are held by industrialized countries.

• More than eighty countries have a lower per capita income today than a decade ago.

By studying the monumental shifts in other societies, we gain a better perspective on the *changes in our own society*. Such comparisons require us to reexamine assumptions, helping anticipate future changes. Culturally, we may be on the verge of a renaissance like the one that transformed Europe in the sixteenth century, as world music, world dance, and world literature become widely available. Slowly and inevitably, northerners will become consumers of southern content. This cultural element reminds us that cyberspace is an unfamiliar world that is without clear boundaries and that, like the real world, is not culturally homogenous. Whether bounded by AOL or China.com, cyberspace reflects specific spatial and cultural distinctions. Yang Guobin's (2001) work compares Chinese-language Web sites in terms of the construction of a unique global Chinese cyberspace and points to the creation of other cultures' public spaces. In my experience, North Americans often erroneously assume that the cyberspace they create is somehow universal, a belief reinforced by Americans' own indigenous culture and their current influence in creating and distributing digital content. Those in the unnetworked world are more likely to realize that today's cyberspace remains partial, incomplete, and culturally bounded. Cyberspace is not as socially, ethnically, or culturally segregated as real space, nor is it as polyglot as some enthusiasts claim.

According to the bible of North American cyberculture, *Wired* magazine: "A while back I wrote about race and the Internet and how few minorities, especially African Americans, are online. The column sparked intense discussion. . . . One of the most interesting messages came from . . . Scotland. . . . One mistake I consistently make is to forget the global nature of this medium. In language, political symbolism, and subject matter, I too often assume that the World Wide Web is part of the U.S. media for North American institutions to define and control" (Katz 1998).

After the column appeared, the columnist, Jon Katz, received a note from Scotland that said, "You missed the real problem. By the end of the next year [1999], there will be a new minority on the Net—Americans." The writer pointed out that in less than five years, more than half of all Internet users will be non-English speakers: "What's new is that middle America is going to get its collective nose rubbed in the fact that there exist people who do not share the core assumptions of American daily life." For Katz, the staggering implication of the message—that U.S. Netizens will become a minority presence on the Web—"reminds us just how radically we in the United States may have to rethink our notions of culture, communications, and politics."

Not Fewer Borders: More Borders
Cultural borders, like territorial borders, define most of our lives. On a trip to China to meet with cyberentrepreneurs, I was struck by cyberculture's new connectedness. Before going to China, a colleague pointed out that the United States and China actually share a border—a border in cyberspace. At the time I smiled and took it as a metaphor. But once in Beijing, I became aware that from culture to commerce, the United States and China are cheek to jowl in a new, exciting, and potentially

troublesome relationship. The United States, a relatively cloistered, iso-lated nation, has gone from having two borders to having two hundred. These borders are unexplored, are undemarcated, and have few effective treaties. Cultural exchanges and pen pals between North and South is one kind of transborder exchange. But the "Love Bug" computer virus attack in May 2000 is another. For good and for ill, the wired networked nations of the world all share common borders. We now have two hundred reasons to care about the information revolution in developing countries. The Internet has brought more borders, not fewer.

Finally, the eruption of terrorism in September 2001 underscores the fact that people around the world are intimately linked together through the infosphere: television and the Internet tie us all together. The media show us how rich or poor we are relative to others. They exalt or debase our cultures. If resentment builds, the new technologies, whether TV or the Internet, provide us the means to express our frustration and to direct it against others.

What Is a Developing Country?

In his essay "National Information Infrastructures in Developing Economies," Eduardo Talero (1997, 287–288) describes "less developed country" as a term of convenience denoting "the group of countries in which the fight against poverty, malnutrition, infant mortality, illiteracy, gross social and income inequality, poor administration of justice, inef-ficient government, and environmental degradation is most pressing. The term does not imply homogeneity in any other respect or that other economies have reached a preferred or final stage of development." This definition reminds us that while Rio, Rabat, and Pretoria are in many ways first-world cities, the surrounding countrysides in Brazil, Morocco, and South Africa are economically and politically underdeveloped. Developing countries have many differences, but they share these impor-tant commonalities that differentiate them from developed nations.

The conditions of underdevelopment have widespread and determi-native impacts on the development of a national information infrastruc-ture (NII):

• Southern populations are severely bifurcated between poor and rich, and the poor find it nearly impossible to bridge the gap.

• Countries in the South are more likely than their northern counterparts to lack trained ICT workers.

• Countries in the South are likely to possess weak and inexperienced institutions and systems of economic governance that subvert the indigenous efforts to manage technological innovation and change (and to "leapfrog" the ICT gap).

• Countries in the South are likely to be ICT consumers—importers of hardware, software, and content.

• Countries in the South have sharp sensitivities to cultural autonomy and cultural threats.

• Poor countries are less knowledgeable about and are less engaged in the forums where the rules of the global information society are being written and enforced.

More on the Meaning of the Information Revolution

The underdevelopment of ICTs in poor countries is propelled by general drivers of change. The information revolution can be conceptualized as a set of independently turning gears that must mesh properly for the machine to function. At least four gears must be present and moving to support radical social changes—digital technologies, commercial leadership, institutional integrity, and political coalitions.

The central technical gear consists of information and communication technologies—specifically, *digital technologies*. *Digitalization* is the conversion of information into zeros and ones, a universal language that can be used for broadcasting, publishing, Internet or other forms of communication. The move from analog to digital data representation has expanded our ability to process and distribute information quickly, flexibly, and cheaply. Digitalization and technical convergence in turn enable a highly distributed, networked architecture to link once-separate applications that are now able to communicate with one another and in some instances to become one another. This networked quality promotes the central, powerful aspect of these new networks—their interactivity. Ultimately, these networked architectures are meant to link people. The importance of the information revolution, after all, is not about machines talking to machines but machines helping and connecting people.

For the technical gear to transfer its potential power to consumers, there must be parallel changes in the *commercial leadership* gear. Unless the companies in the business of providing ICT services and goods change, the potential power of the technologies remains only latent. Boundaries between the three main businesses—computers, communication, and content—are dissolving, and a small but growing multimedia industry has slowly emerged. At first, commercial leaders and entrepreneurs simply seized new technologies and tried to make them work, but eventually they discovered that they had to reorganize the company itself to capture the technologies' full potential. Under growing pressure to deliver services and goods in different ways and more cheaply, smart companies adapt, others lose market share, and some go out of business. The most farsighted commercial executives saw opportunities early on. They reorganized their internal business processes, management structures, and relations with customers and suppliers so that their companies could take full advantage of the new technologies. The most conservative executives saw the technology as a threat or as a way to do old things slightly better.

The technological and commercial gears could not transfer their potential power beyond the narrow confines of a few labs and a few firms without substantial shifts in the third gear—*institutions.* Institutions link the whole process together and include everything from intellectual property laws that allow companies to capture a revenue stream from patented commercialized technologies to more visible institutions like effective regulatory agencies or functioning capital markets. At the core of the information revolution is a critical shift in institutional incentives and public policy that creates a friendly environment for commercial and governmental actors. Noncommercial institutions also spread the revolution, from universities and research centers to nongovernmental organizations (NGOs) that in many countries helped incubate the real "information revolutionaries" described below.

Finally, knitting all these disparate elements together is a factor that is often forgotten by most academic analysts of the information revolution but that in my experience is essential for any revolution—*political coalitions.* It is virtually impossible for the technical, commercial, and institutional gears to mesh and turn efficiently unless the politics is right. If the politics is wrong, especially in developing countries, then the other three elements will not function. Politics includes leadership, doctrine, ideology, and the conscious and strategic use of power to pursue consistent ICT reforms. Leaders need to reward the reformers and punish the opponents of reform. Without local political leadership, the information revolution cannot move forward. Leaders must be willing to press changes in the face of institutional rigidity, technological backwardness, and political resistance. In China, India, and Ghana, local public and private leaders have stepped forward to build political constituencies and coalitions, to provide intellectual and policy justifications, and to mobilize against the opposition. Without politics and political leadership, the information revolution simply does not occur. While conducting my research and travels, I came on such individuals, whom I term *information champions* or *information revolutionaries* and whom I describe in detail in chapter 2.

These four main gears—technical, commercial, institutional, and political—together make a revolution and can block the revolution if they are not present, well oiled, and closely coordinated.

Moore's law states that information processing costs fall exponentially as efficiency increases. Yet for many countries, the impact and spread of Moore's law is limited not for technical reasons but because other equally powerful laws take precedence—such as Michel's iron law of oligarchy or Weber's laws governing the relationships among charismatic, traditional, and legal-rational authority structures. Moore's law applies in regions with a particular combination of property rights and institutional authority. It relies on flexible, efficient institutions and innovation-friendly policies that support new tools and techniques.

A final point (to which I return later) is partly conceptual and definitional and partly empirical: is the information revolution also a social revolution? The evidence from developing countries indicates that change has occurred within a relatively small number of industries—communication and information. (Several similar industries together constitute a sector.) The practices, the institutions, the norms and expectations, and a thousand other things have changed substantially inside this sector. There is certainly an information and communication revolution. In business processes in the private sector, we see big changes. However, the empirical evidence does not support the claim that we are also living in the midst of a social or political revolution of the type experienced by France in the late 1700s, by China in the 1940s, or by the developed world over many, many years by the agricultural and industrial revolutions. Societal changes (beyond the handful of communication and information industries) are not nearly as radical nor as far reaching, especially when we look beyond the narrow band of mostly northern nations where these changes have progressed the furthest. Some claim that we are only about 5 per cent of the way into the information revolution. Widespread revolutionary changes may well come in the future. But they are not yet in our present, especially in developing nations. The evidence simply does not support the view that the information revolution has become a full-fledged social revolution. We are best advised to be skeptical until the empirical evidence is in.

This book makes the case that the information revolution is not simply a technological or economic revolution but an institutional revolution as well. Indeed, unless the institutional revolution leads the way, then developing countries cannot achieve the full benefits of the information revolution and risk being left behind in the agricultural and early industrial worlds of the past, while the Group of Seven nations rocket into the information society of the new millennium. Already, some in Africa, in their most pessimistic moments, are asking if that troubled continent has already missed the train leaving the station and will be mired in conflicts and underdevelopment forever.

The Africans may not be far from the mark. Since institutions are much weaker in poorer countries, a revolution that is mainly institutional and not technical is not easily achievable. Their future is worrisome indeed.

The Big Story

People tell very different stories about the information revolution and its coming impact on the developing world's 4.5 billion women, men, and children. Some say that the new information and communication technologies will allow countries to bypass or leapfrog critical stages of technological and social development. According to these people, the populations of developing countries can capture the benefits of the dramatic global changes by leapfrogging old, outmoded technologies and entire economic stages (Singh 1999) . Many point to Moore's law—that information processing costs fall exponentially as efficiency increases—to note that because computing power doubles and technology prices drop by half every eighteen months the new technologies are able to reach into previously unwired areas. Cheaper ICT services create a cornucopia of new services, new opportunities, and new wealth for individuals and communities (Price and Noll 1998). According to one expert from the World Bank, the new information and communication technologies can help people fight poverty, reduce the isolation of rural areas, educate children, support lifelong learning, create efficient, accountable, and transparent governments, increase economic reforms, monitor and protect the environment, promote small and medium-sized enterprises, and participate in global trade (Talero 1997).

Similarly rosy scenarios characterize the World Bank's *World Development Report* (1998/1999, 3): "The remotest village has the possibility of tapping a global store of knowledge beyond the dreams of any one living a century ago, and more quickly and cheaply than anyone imagined possible a decade ago."

One author notes that "the Internet is viewed as an 'escalator from poverty' for individuals and nations." He writes that the Internet allows people at the periphery of population centers to overcome the limitations of their locations (Kowack 1997, 53). Peter Schwartz (Schwartz, Leyden, and Hyatt 1999), CEO of Global Business Network, says in *The Long Boom* that the global system as a whole will experience a long rise in income and well-being for the next twenty-five to fifty years, driven in part by new ICT developments.

The spectacular episodes of ICT successes are well documented—from female Bangladeshis who hawk cell phone time to rural doctors who use new ICTs to save lives. One story reported that "in the mountains of Laos and Burma, yak caravans employ mobile phones to call ahead and find the best route to take during the rainy season to bring their goods to market; and in China, a little girl's life was saved when her doctor posted her symptoms to an Internet discussion group and received an immediate answer" (ITU 1998).

The people who tell this story marshal convincing evidence showing that ICT progress is being made in developing areas. The International Telecommunications Union (ITU) points out that telephone penetration in countries like India and China is on the rise (ITU 1985). The widely cited Maitland report (ITU 1985) warned of a growing digital divide, and the ITU points out that "At the time the report was published, almost three billion people, more than half the world's population, were living in countries with a teledensity below one (i.e., one telephone per 1,000). This situation has improved, so that by the end of 1996 less than 800 million people were in the 43 remaining economies with a teledensity of below one. The world's two most populous nations, China and India, graduated in 1993 and 1994, respectively" (ITU 1998, 10).

The Other Story
Another story about the information revolution is captured by the 1999 Human Development Report for the United Nations Development Program (UNDP), which claims that "The Internet is contributing to an ever-widening gap between rich and poor which has now reached grotesque proportions" (1999, 24).

Referring to the same ICTs that others see as evidence of phenomenal growth, the UNDP insists that "many who most need access cannot obtain it. An invisible barrier has emerged that true to its name, is like a world wide web, embracing the connected and silently, almost imperceptibly, excluding the rest." To buttress their story, people highlight facts (UNDP 1999, 24).

• There are more telephones in Manhattan in all sub-Saharan Africa.

• The industrialized countries hold 97 percent of the world's patents.

• In Cambodia, there is one telephone per 100 people; in Monaco, there are ninty-nine telephones per 100 people.

• Tanzania spends four times more on repaying debts than on education.

Inequality between northern and southern countries is growing, particularly in terms of ICTs and wealth, as I demonstrate in chapter 6. Francisco Rodriguez and I (Rodriguez and Wilson 2000) document an emerging ICT gap and construct indicators using a basket of ICT applications, such as Internet access and cell phone ownership. We discovered that while ICT use is growing in the nation-members of the Organization for Economic Cooperation and Development (OECD) by about 23 percent annually, the same ICT applications are growing by only 18 percent in the non-OCED nations. We should also remind ourselves that 99.5 percent of Africans and 98 percent of Latin Americans are not connected to the Internet. Even in Brazil, the eighth-largest economy in the world, 96 percent of the population remains unconnected to the Internet. Which world, or whose world, is being transformed?

These two very different ICT stories have two different estimates of the impact of ICTs on developing nations. One story is optimistic about the distributional and developmental impacts of the information revolution. The other is much more cautious and indeed pessimistic about ICT's distributional impacts and conjures up a world of political conflicts and economic shocks.

Adding More Information and More Confusion

As I demonstrate in chapters 3 to 5, these twin stories fail to capture the full complexity of the information revolution. Other stories reach us through a cascade of aggregate figures: 300 million Internet connections, 1 million new telephones in China. For many, the global numbers are a familiar story we read in newspapers and journals. They provide a useful bird's-eye view of the revolution but miss the finely grained realities where most people live their lives. None of the many conversations I have had over the past several years were aggregate: they were with individuals who had faces and families and dreams.

Some of these ICT dreams were hopeful, others were not. One teacher in Butare, a town in southcentral Rwanda where ethnic battles pitted political forces against one another, told me, "Yes, I was there, and I heard Radio Mille Collines." He was referring to the state-owned radio station that was used to manipulate massacres in Rwanda (personal communication 1999):

The Hutu radicals, who were in power then [1993], had decided that they needed to consolidate their control. So Hutu who opposed their radical ideas, and of course Tutsi people, were targeted for elimination. And these people used the radio broadcasts to do it.

You see, radio in Rwanda is very powerful! It is the most powerful medium in the country, since we have so few telephones, and literacy is so low that people don't buy many newspapers and they are expensive for the poor. Rwandans have always been used to listening to radio. The scary thing about the Radio Milles Collins managers is how well the radicals knew the medium. They didn't just have special programs about killing people. It was more dangerous and more terrible than that. Instead, after they played a favorite piece of really popular music and before they would read the news, they would read an announcement that said, "We've heard there are some Tutsi people staying at so and so neighborhood and so and so address. Why are they still there? Someone should get them and teach them a lesson. And now, after this commercial, we go to the news."

This hate radio became so important for the Hutu government that the radicals went outside the country to recruit disc jockeys and radio personalities who had been very popular with the people in the past so they could get their genocide message out to their listeners. It was very well organized; and it could not have been done without the media. Yes, I'm embarrassed to say it, but radio was a tool for genocide in my country.

The aggregate, macro-level cannot tell us who advocates for these new technologies, who opposes them, what purposes they're used for, and under what circumstances they're developed. To answer these questions requires additional analysis.

Filtering the Information Revolution: Blind Men and the Elephant

Confronting the challenges of sorting through stories, anecdotes, and aggregate statistics brings to mind the proverbial blind men who touch and describe an elephant. Each feels something different. Each experiences a limited localized animal, and no one captures the full reality of the animal as a whole.

Another popular metaphor describes the search for information as an attempt to drink water from a fire hose: the problem before was too little information, and now it is too much. But this is only partly true. On some topics in some countries, there is an information flood; on others, there is a drought.

Many filters are being used to sort through the information revolution's stories, data, and trends. These filters generally interpret change from different perspectives (Alford and Friedland 1986). Each focuses on different problems and operates at different analytic levels, whether macro, micro, or meso. Each differs in its imputations of cause and effect.

Each filter, paradigm, or theory tells us whether relations among nation-states, social institutions, and firms will most likely be conflictual or cooperative.[1]

Scholars also reach different conclusions based on the regions where they work. Those who report on ICT developments in East Asia tell of aggressive entrepreneurial adaptation, technological innovation, and supportive government officials. Scholars reporting on East Africa tell ICT stories about bureaucratic inertia, hobbled institutions and entrepreneurial deficits. Within Asia, people working on mainland China have one narrative, and people working in Thailand have another. Extrapolations cannot automatically be made from one country to another.

As other scholars have noted, the information revolution is occurring during a massive and unprecedented acceleration of globalization (Vogel 1996; Friedman 1999). *Globalization* refers to two types of world changes—quantitative and qualitative. Because of the acceleration of cross-border flows, global transactions now affect more people in more countries than ever before. The speed, scope, and depth of cross-border flows have all increased. These transactions are occurring in all sectors, whether commerce or culture. Qualitatively people also feel these flows more deeply in their professional and personal lives, in part through the spread of mass media.

The analytic frameworks that I review are drawn mainly from English-speaking literature, although substantial literatures also exist in continental Europe and Japan that have unique regional and national features. For example, the *Scandinavian Journal of Information Systems* has published widely on the discipline of information systems: "Research contributions from Scandinavia often have special features because they are created as part of societies with long traditions for democracy in the workplace, with an openness to debate and conflict, and with a strong tradition for design of artifacts" (Mathiassen 1999, 434). Even this relatively culturally homogenous region has no single research tradition but a mixture of technical, social, and political traditions (Mathiassen 1998). Japan's tradition draws heavily on intellectuals like Masuda, who helped coin the expression "information society" as early as 1969 (Masuda 1981). The French-speaking intellectual tradition has joined the globalization debates, and a critical discourse concerning the information revolution and American power is carried out regularly in *Le Monde Diplomatique*. Some of these discussions promote the use of the French language and the minimization of the hegemony of the English language. The debate is truly global.

Yet all the leading ICT paradigms suffer from monocausality. Too many reduce their subject's complexities into bite-sized, consumable chunks. Neoclassical economics tries to squeeze ICT into ready-made demand-and-supply categories. State-centric models concentrate mainly on government policies, regulations, and pronouncements. Technological determinism is widely used and is both appealing and misleading.

The Power of the Technodeterminist Paradigm

Writing with only slight hyperbole, John McDermott (2003, 59) says in the *New York Review of Books* that "if religion was formerly the opiate of the masses, then surely technology is the opiate of the educated public today, or at least its favorite authors. No other single subject is so universally invested with high hopes for the improvement of mankind generally and of Americans in particular." This quotation captures today's ICT arguments. Core technologies are claimed to be the matrix around which the new information society is forming. David Lyan (1995, 67) identifies a more scholarly and open-ended version of this thesis and a second "view popularized in many media and policy accounts [that] stresses the major changes for the better that follow in the wake of ICT. This popular version may well be buttressed by the 'findings of social science.'"

Technological determinism provides an explicit starting point into ICT and society and a clear and compelling logic. The starting point for this analysis is technology. The analyst begins by describing the technology's component parts and its overall properties and tracing the technology's recent evolution. With its importance established, the analyst insists that the technology's internal properties may reshape key aspects of the surrounding society. This may include everything from organizational hierarchy to economic productivity to the spread of civil liberties. If a technology is found to be inherently distributed and participatory, then the analyst claims that the technology should necessarily reshape the society to be less hierarchal, less centralized, and more participatory. If the technology is judged to be highly individualistic (as the Internet is often claimed to be), the new technology will increase individualism and perhaps alienation. Most of the intellectual energy in this paradigm goes into describing technology, not society: impact flows *from* technological innovation *to* new attitudes and behaviors. Such research focuses almost exclusively on the technological infrastructure rather than other social, economic, and political attributes (Masuda 1981).

While this paradigm can in principle reach conclusions that are pessimistic and dystopian, more often than not it judges the impacts of these technologies to be benign or even utopian (Wilson 1999): technology will improve life for individuals and societies; the new ICTs will provide richer choices, enhanced political transparency, and greater educational achievements. Rarely do analysts point out any negative aspects, such as determining the fair distribution of scarce material or political resources.

As Cees J. Hamelink (1997, 23–24) writes, "The gravest problem with the techno-centric perspective is that it ignores the social origins of information and communication technologies. It suggests they originate in a socio-economic vacuum and fails to see the specific interests that generate them. Guided by this perspective . . . policy makers find it very difficult to accept that . . . whether the potential of technologies will be realized . . . depends much more on their institutional organization than on the features of their technical performance."

In much utopian writing, ICTs represent a revolutionary force that can transform societies and individual lives. According to this perspective, the imperatives of technological development determine social arrangements: technological potential drives history (Toffler 1980; Beniger 1986). A technocentric perspective holds that the digital revolution brings more effective health care, better education, more information and diversity of culture. The new ICTs they claim will create more choice for people in fields like education, shopping, entertainment, news and travel.

Technological determinism is not the exclusive province of the global North. Global southerners sometimes also paint with its large brush. Sam Pitroda (1993), a well-known figure in international telecommunication circles and former senior Indian official, has stated that "as a great social leveler, information technology ranks second only to death. It can raze cultural barriers, overwhelm economic inequalities, even compensate for intellectual disparities. In short, high technology can put unequal human beings on equal footing, and that makes it the most potent democratizing tool ever devised."

Social actors—whether individuals, groups, or institutions—take a back seat to these new scientific advances. Social values, social structures, and social groups are background features. One takes as given that the necessary structural requisites are all in place: market structures and pro-technology public policies allow change to sail forward without human agency. By criticizing technological determinism, I do not dismiss technology's importance for key economic and social trends. But I am not alone in viewing technology as an important second-order influence and not the principal variable shaping structures and behaviors uniformly. James Rosenau (2002, 275) write that these technologies are "essentially neutral" (that is, they don't force social outcomes to be good or bad or systems to be open or closed) and that the "tilt" in the outcomes "is provided by people" (individuals and organizations) who infuse values into information, introduce information into political arenas, and thereby render it good or bad. "Starting with the premise of neutrality" enables us "to avoid deterministic modes of thought in which people are . . . deprived of choice by the dictates of information technologies." The neutrality premise compels us to focus on human agency and how it can use information technologies.

We should not define ICT as a deus ex machina but as a neutral enabling tool that may enhance social actors' capabilities. Research indicates that ICTs have demonstrable effects on individual and group behaviors and on social institutions but that these effects are never monocausal or automatic. Instead of one societal impact, ICTs affect distinct groups and subgroups within society in various ways. Information and communication technologies have particular consequences for particular applications, under specified structural and institutional conditions, at particular moments in time, for particular populations.

Robin Mansell (Mansell and Wehn 1998, 410) argues that these technologies "influence, contextualize, facilitate, permit or inhibit courses of action, but not as first-order dynamics that change, transform, foster, impose or shape a course of action." ICT is not a radical independent factor acting as an "unseen hand that somehow gets people, groups, or communities to pursue goals and undertake actions without awareness of why they do what they do" (Mansell and Wehn 1998, 411).

One sophisticated observer of Russia insists that when dealing with the Internet in that country, "it is necessary to adopt a socially and historically specific approach to cyberspace" (Rohozinski 1999, 3). The Internet "is not a single undifferentiated phenomenon whose properties can be taken for granted wherever it appears. It is a technological system that exists within widely varying economic contexts, structures of power and organizational settings. And the role it can play in the construction of democracy depends very much upon the way these factors shape the specific nature of cyberspace in each concrete case" (Rohozinski 1999, 22). Rohozinski (1999, 22) reminds us that prior to the Internet, "The Russian Net [was] built upon the cultural traditions of the *blat* networks," which were used by Russian Net enthusiasts "to extend and empower social networks" by "routing around" the hierarchical dominance of the institutional order, while providing a mechanism for the exchange of much coveted private information. The networks of enthusiasts of various stripes used the technology; the technology did not create the networks.

One can also conclude, however, that ICT has greater independent consequences than suggested by either Mansell's or Rosenau's conception of it. Under certain specifiable circumstances, new ICTs like the Internet can indeed flatten hierarchy, add greater transparency, and empower nongovernmental organizations. But these ICT-enabled changes must occur through systematic interactions with other political, institutional, and economic factors.

Sometimes technodeterminism stands on its own, and sometimes it is imported into other well-known paradigms as they adopt the false or premature certainties of technological determinism. For example, neoclassical economics is a powerful and simplifying paradigm whose enthusiasts may introduce premature certainty in their information revolution analyses. Neoclassical assumptions of efficiency and distribution form the basis of modern policy analysis and are widely used in describing information revolution dynamics and government action, and easily accept techno determinism.

Despite these assumptions, inventions do not float above society but instead grow organically from its institutions and scientific networks. As Anne Wells Branscomb (1994) shows, this holds even for "pure" activities like research and development. Technological determinism suffers from many failures, including the failure to integrate adequately structure and choice. Peter Evans (1995) argues convincingly that this balance of embeddedness in society and autonomy from society allows privileged interest groups to shape computer-sector performance and structure. This is defined as a problem of embeddedness in sociological theory and in the work of political economists like Karl Polanyi (1944). While some theorists undersocialize behaviors and interpret them as entirely atomistic and free, other theorists oversocialize and interpret behaviors as entirely predetermined. Mark S. Granovetter (1997), a leading theorist on these issues, writes that "much of the utilitarian tradition, including classical neoclassical economics, assumes rational, self-interested behavior affected minimally by social relations. . . . At the other extreme lies . . . the argument that the behavior and institutions to be analyzed are so constrained by ongoing social relations that to construe them as independent is a grievous misunderstanding." Granovetter quotes economist James Duesenberry's remark that "economics is all about how people make choices; sociology is all about how they don't have any choices to make." The same might be said of the technodeterminism paradigm as well.

In technological determinism, the actors are machines and software that drive women and men by their strict imperatives. These models do not convey the full range of choices confronting individuals in developing countries. In countless interviews with me, ICT decision makers talked a lot about the difficult issue of freedom of choice—and particularly the politics of choice. These are the issues on which they say they spend most of their time. ICT officials are beset by political problems as much as by technology problems. How will they change a bureaucratic, statist community into a group of ICT enthusiasts? Politics—the deliberate exercise of authority and power by self-interested actors to effect favorable outcomes—must be reckoned with in any model, especially in developing countries. The challenge is to design a framework that takes advantage of technological insights while minimizing its limitations.

The Developmentalist Literature on ICTs

The following approaches illuminate an alternative approach to information and communication technology diffusion in developing countries. Each focuses on links between ICT and development. This section discusses the work of two distinct subgroups—on the one hand large institutional agencies (like the World Bank, the International Telecommunications Union, the United Nations Development Program, the International Development Research Center, and France's ORSTOM) and academic writers on the other.

Analyses by International Institutions

Perhaps the best-known and most productive bilateral agency is Canada's International Development and Research Centre (IDRC), which has for the past decade led the study of ICTs' developmental impacts. Studying technology in its institutional and societal contexts, researchers at IDRC analyze the new technologies' demand and supply sides. They have published work on the costs and benefits of telecenters and case studies of national information infrastructure initiatives in Africa and supported Internet service provider networks in Asia. Their work is sensitive to societal contexts and is a useful corrective for scholars and activists in the field. Additional bilateral commentators on ICT-development issues include the Netherlands' International Institute for Communication and Development (IICD), the USAID's Leland Initiative, and development agencies in France and the United Kingdom.

Some of the most detailed and data-rich writing is by large general-purpose international institutions like the United Nations Development Program (UNDP) and the World Bank. Their mandate is to improve conditions in developing countries. Important work has also been prepared by ICT-specific organizations like the International Telecommunications Union (ITU). All three of these institutions have published massive, thoroughly researched, and influential documents on the information revolution and developing countries. In the pivotal year of 1999, the United Nations Development Program devoted its annual *Human Development Report* to ICT issues, and the World Bank (1999) devoted its annual *World Development Report* to ICTs and development.

These documents share several features. They are ambitious in sectoral and geographic scope. They cover hard infrastructures (i.e., telephones per capita), soft infrastructures ("knowledge institutions"), and the growing importance of electronic trade, private ICT investment, and accelerated education and training. Their substantive sectoral and national coverage is an important contribution. Each volume is rich in useful statistical sets. These volumes performed the difficult task of helping to reset the global intellectual and policy agenda. By making the development community aware of ICT's development potentials, they convinced experts that ICTs were relevant for poor nations.

One of the downsides in the developmentalist approach, however, is that it strains for universality and global coverage and thereby weakens its theoretical focus. These works are written mainly for practitioners and are not theoretically explicit.

Analyses by Academic Writers

Where the main purpose of institutional authors is to advise decision makers about optimal policy prescriptions, the scholarly writers use ICT materials to illustrate broader theoretical arguments. These theoretical arguments grow from a distinctive scholarly discourse defined by a particular discipline's central tenets. Academic economists, for example, gain institutional status not by solving ICT problems but by solving theoretical problems deemed important by the profession.

My experiences with policy-related issues like privatization, energy, and telecommunications have taught me that a product cycle accompanies the study of big, international phenomena and that it has at least four phases:

• "In phase one, the technical phase, a once quiescent technical issue handled in the middle ranks of public bureaucracies is propelled into public view and onto the action agenda of senior policy makers. . . . Typically, the works that dominate this phase are authored by engineers, scientists, or economists whose purpose most often is to explain the most advanced, cutting-edge features of the new technological issue to other like-minded experts" (Wilson 1997, 1). These technical problems require technical solutions implemented by technicians.

• "In the second phase, social theorists take up the issue." With different purposes and audiences, writers and journalists seek new answers to age-old human problems—quality of life, democratic practices, and so forth. As theorists look for answers in the new technology, they usually puff up this phase with hyperbole and utopian or dystopian special pleading. This is neither policy nor social science (Wilson, 2).

• The third phase finds engaged social scientists pursuing nontechnical issues. These analysts attach themselves to the institutional, distributional, and political dimensions that have been previously ignored. Organizations like the former United States Office of Technology Assessment (OTA) (1990, 2) and manifold think tanks discover that "diffusion rates of the new technologies will be shaped by institutional incentives" and that change creates losers and winners. During phase three, nongovernmental organizations are able to break through the "iron triangle" that established interest groups have jealously guarded.

• In phase four, university-based scholars take up the issue. Their purpose is not to guide particular policy makers nor inform the general public but to test long-standing hypotheses using the new technical materials. Once university-based scholars take up an issue, normalization occurs. It becomes domesticated and incorporated into the conventional academic literature.

The most relevant and highest-quality scholarly work has been done by Peter Cowhey (1990), Cowhey and Jonathan Aronson (1993), Brian Levy and Pablo Spiller (1996), Ben Petrazzini (1996), J. P. Singh (1999), and Stephen K. Vogel (1996). These scholars compare two or more countries at a time. Excellent work is also being done on single countries, like Milton Mueller and Zixiang Tan (1996). These authors are compatible and indeed complementary with one another in their general methodology, in their theoretical assumptions concerning cause and effect, and in the societal issues they deem interesting and problematic. These authors help fill some, but not all, the gaps I identified earlier.

These writers decry the apolitical reading of past ICT reforms. The writers recognize the political importance of demand-side private-sector groups and state officials. They assume that reforming wealthy, capital-intensive sectors with substantial constituencies and beneficiaries is daunting and difficult. Unlike other authors, they do not assume a simple, automatic transition from one way of organizing ICT to another.

Ben Petrazzini (1996, 1) writes, "Puzzling and counterintuitive economic reforms are quickly spreading throughout the Third World." J. P. Singh (1999) asserts that "most LDC states are unable to resolve the myriads of pressures they face for telecommunications restructurings to effect accelerated or 'leapfrogging' development. . . . Therefore, telecommunications restructuring initiatives in most developing countries remain slow, piecemeal, and capricious." Jon Guice (1998) points out that the telecommunications diffusion process is neither easy nor automatic, as technodeterminists insist, but requires consistent guidance from multiple actors in an uncertain and open-ended process.

In addition, these authors recognize what might be called a valence problem. When one adds up all the societal political forces that favor reforming ICT imbalances, the combined weight of these liberalizing forces do not seem to add up to the amount of change an informed observer would expect.

Here important substantive differences emerge in these authors' interpretations. Vogel (1996) differs from Singh by suggesting that the senior public officials who actually design and implement liberal telecommunications reforms have considerable political autonomy. He imputes much less power to interest-group pressures and political coalitions than Singh does. This is especially interesting as Vogel describes the reforms in advanced industrial countries like the United States, the United Kingdom, and Japan, where proreform interest groups are stronger than in developing countries. Cowhey (1990), who writes on developed and developing political economies, sides with Singh on this important question.

Levy and Spiller (1996), although economists and not public administration experts, claim that analysts need to understand how newly reformed institutions of the ICT sector, especially regulatory agencies, fit within a country's prevailing institutional and political patterns— everything from hierarchical administrative arrangements, legislative-executive balances, and the historical (lack of) autonomy for independent regulatory bodies.

Through their politically sensitive approaches, these scholars render a great service by overcoming some of the shortcomings in the models identified above—the problems of automaticity and inevitability, the lack of institutional attention, the exclusion of politics, and the inability to view change as open-ended. At the same time, some of the problems I cited above remain, while new ones arise. None of these authors devotes much attention to the growing nongovernmental organizations (NGOs), which have proven so important to the movements toward democratization around the world. NGOs have been an important factor in creating civil society—space slowly carved out from authoritarian control by often-heroic NGO men and women. Their analyses are also weakened because they do not address adequately the political character of the established policy systems of developing countries. ICT politics doesn't start from ground zero with the Internet; it has existed in prior institutional frameworks or political pacts. Most developing countries have had (and probably still have) an "iron triangle" policy network that was able to include and exclude particular interests.

Nor do these studies stray much beyond the telecommunications sector into other industries like radio, television broadcasting, or computing. Cyberspace is not yet on these authors' analytic screens, and yet new ICT sectors are arguably as important as telecommunications for the liberalization of developing countries. These academic writers also fail to address some important theoretical concerns. The continuing question of structure and agency is pursued only indirectly, yet policy makers feel that this is their bottom line: "Given the constraints and opportunities I confront, how much freedom do I have to pursue my interests?" An abiding concern of great intellectuals from Max Weber and Karl Marx through Talcott Parsons and Anthony Giddens, structure-agency is one of the central social science questions. In most accounts of ICT diffusion, we do not find many individuals, whether saints or sinners. The actors are still large institutions or large societal agglomerations (consumers and suppliers). There are few leaders or followers, few policy or private entrepreneurs, few opponents and proponents.

Structure and Beyond

The following structural "law" relating to information and communication technologies and economic development levels is judged nearly universal: *the more developed a country is, the more widely diffused its ICTs will be.* Scholars acknowledge the direct relationship between key aspects

Table 1.1
Telecommunications and Internet Diffusion, by Country

	Population (in millions) (2001)	GDP per capita (2000)	Main telephone lines per 100 persons (2001)	Telephone line (k) (2001)
China	1,296.14	834	24.99	323,846.0
Ghana	20.93	372	2.08	435.9
Brazil	172.56	3,500	38.35	66,176.5

Source: ITU (1998).

of societal structure and key ICT-sector outcomes. If a society is richer, it will have more and better quality ICTs. As societies develop and as individual disposable income grows, individuals and collectivities can better afford services. As incomes grow, people can allocate their disposable income to nonessential services like electricity and telephones. More and more people can afford radios and televisions, and some can even pay for Internet access. Similar relationships hold for other indicators associated with development, such as urbanization and white-collar employment.

Structure Shapes ICT Outcomes
The most appropriate starting point to consider economic structure's relationship to ICT diffusion is a country's wealth. By far the most widely used indicator of societal structure is the level of gross domestic product (GDP) per capita.

Table 1.1 and figures 1.1, 1.2, and 1.3 capture these structural relations for telecommunications and Internet diffusion. There is a positive and direct relationship between GDP per capita and ICT (Internet, telecoms) penetration. Richer countries lie at the upper right of the three figures, and poorer ones at the lower left. The GDP per capita structural law is robust and yet ultimately problematic because it leads us back to the institutional and agency side of the structure-agency debate. The three figures show these structural relationships hold across Least Developed Countries, Less Developed Countries, and Middle Income Countries, although it is most robust among the Middle Income Countries.

Mobile phone subscribers (2000)	Internet users (k) (2000)	Users per 10,000 inhabitants (2000)	Hosts total (2000)
85,260.0	22,500.0	173.70	70,391
130.0	30.0	14.84	17
23,188.2	5,000.0	293.92	876,596

Main lines per 100 inhabitants

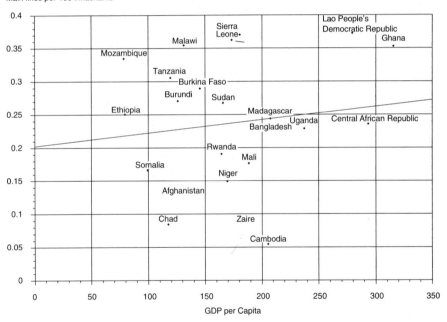

Figure 1.1
Telecommunications Infrastructure in the Least Developed Countries, 1995
Note: Main lines per 100 inhabitants based on 1995 values for main lines in operation and population. Gross domestic product per capita based on most recent available values.
Source: Mansell and Wehn (1998), chap. 2.

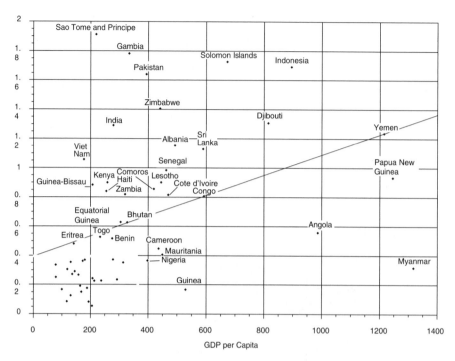

Figure 1.2
Telecommunications Infrastructure in Less Developed Countries, 1995
Note: Main lines per 100 inhabitants based on 1995 values for main lines in operation and population. GDP per capita based upon most recent available values.
Source: Mansell and Wehn (1998), chap. 2.

A study by Kenneth Kraemer, Jason Derrick, and Eric Shih (2000, 54) reached similar conclusions for ICT investments. While there were certainly good reasons to believe that ICT investment (like diffusion) would be determined by a mix of factors (such as education or market performance), the authors found that from a sample of thirty-one developed and developing countries for the period 1985 to 1995, "The only consistently significant determinants of ICT investment at the country level are the level of wealth and the structure of the economy. Other hypothesized factors such as telecommunications infrastructure, education levels, or IT price performance either had no impact or the results were inconclusive due to inadequacy of the data."

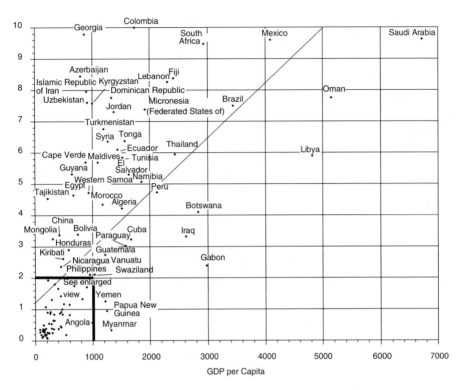

Figure 1.3
Telecommunications Infrastructure in the Middle-Income Countries, 1995
Note: Main lines per 100 inhabitants based on 1995 values for main lines in operation and population. Gross domestic product per capita based on most recent available values.
Source: Mansell and Wehn (1998), chap. 2.

Charles Kedzie (1997) undertakes a similar exercise with ICT diffusion rates and the cross-national incidence of democracy. He claims that democracy is the greatest single predictor of Internet diffusion: the more democratic a country is, the more Internet diffusion it has. While distinctive, Kedzie's analysis is highly structural. His analysis of basic political features of a society is the political counterpart to the OECD's and others' reliance on economic structure as the main explanatory variable.

The relationship between economic structure and ICT outcomes— whether defined as penetration or investment—is clear. Yet this robust structural relationship begs additional questions. The most important is, *why do countries at the same economic level sometimes have different ICT penetration?* As shown in table 1.1, for example, although China's GDP per capita is much lower than Brazil's, it far surpasses the latter in telephone lines. Economic structure explains most of the puzzle (perhaps 60 percent plus of cross-national variation) but not all. What explains the rest? What information are we missing? Is it culture and language? Izumi Aizu (2000), for example, reviews the cultural argument about diffusion in Japan, juxtaposed against economic arguments about pricing and monopoly. He asks, "Do networks evolve differently from one country or culture to another? Do cultural differences affect the course of evolution of computer networks?" What part do education and training, institutions, and pricing policies play?

But there is a second, more fundamental critique of a strictly structural explanation for ICT diffusion. Structure tells us almost nothing about process. Structure alone cannot tell us the ways human beings are driven to fashion unique ICT outcomes to meet their own needs. Even if we consider the spread of the Internet and other ICTs as inevitable, *inevitable* does not mean *automatic*. A structural emphasis leaves us unable to explain group or institutional roles. How do individuals and groups interpret their structural contexts and battle for advantage?

Furthermore, broad structural explanations are not particularly relevant to purposive action or public policy. Structures change slowly, over decades, well beyond the time horizon of most policy makers. Policy makers in poor countries are not helped if they are told that they can increase ICT penetration by growing economically. They need to understand the behavioral, contingent factors that they might affect.

Thus, while the gross domestic product per capita relationship to ICT diffusion holds across most countries, some interesting and important anomalies are worth more detailed examination (see figures 1.1, 1.2, and 1.3). Angola, Guinea, Myanmar, and Papua New Guinea are well below the line. For countries with less than one main telephone line per 250 inhabitants, we find a less clear relationship between gross domestic product per capita and main telephone lines. One of the world's poorest countries, Ethiopia, has $75 GDP per capita, and yet it has more telephone penetration (.25 per 250) than either Bangladesh or Uganda, which have three times the per capita levels ($220 to $245). Ghana has a $330 GDP and a .35 penetration rate (diffusion), while Senegal has a GDP per capita of $450 but a telephone penetration rate of about one per 100 inhabitants. Mansell and Wehn (Mansell and Wehn 1998, 29) points to interesting patterns for poor countries with fewer than ten to thirty telephone lines per 100 population. They find that of the twenty countries above the average, "ten are former socialist countries (Estonia, Latvia, Lithuania, Czech Republic, Slovak Republic, etc.), 7 are island economies (Granada, Dominica Saint Lucia, etc.), and 3 are left over (UAE, Turkey, and Uruguay)." One conclusion is that, "under socialism, relatively more telecommunications infrastructure was constructed. Island countries, in some cases because of their financial and tourism connections, are more likely to construct more extensive networks than other countries of similar incomes" (31).

The determinants of global ICT diffusion are the subject of theorization and analysis by other scholars, including Pipa Norris (2000) and Eszter Hargittai (1999). They concur that GDP per capita is the most powerful determinant of diffusion. Differences emerge, however, in the explanatory weight assigned to factors like education or policy. Norris concludes that social and political factors (such as English-language capability, literacy, or censorship) have secondary impacts. Like Hargittai, who tends to find some residual impacts of policy interventions on diffusion patterns, Norris (2000, 15) concludes that even when controlling for conventional factors, "Scandinavia, North America, and Western Europe still emerged as significantly ahead of all other regions, suggesting that there are residual social or cultural factors that are not being picked up in the model." If we bounce from the aggregate to the national level, interesting pairings provoke our curiosity. China has been adding new lines at a furious clip, faster than the rest of the developing world combined, while India's rate has been slower. The small island economy of Jamaica has roughly the same diffusion rate as oil-rich Venezuela. Chile has more lines than Mexico, while Malaysia scores better than Chile. Colombia outpaces Brazil, as does South Africa. Why should this be?

When we examine the evidence from other ICTs like cell phones, we find broad patterns and interesting anomalies. Some of the world's poorest countries (like Mozambique) have a greater ratio of cell phones to land lines than many developed nations. A strict structuralist model would predict a nearly perfect match between GDP per capita and ICT penetration. Yet interesting and important cross-national ICT differences abound at the same level of GDP per capita.

Conclusion

The brave new world of information and communication technologies is more complicated, messy, opaque, and uncertain than leading policy models suggest. Theoretically, we don't know the precise relationships between cause and affect among economic structure, institutions, culture, and ICT diffusion patterns. We lack a nuanced theoretical understanding of structure and agency. Analytically, we don't know how these patterns emerge in poor countries. We don't know how new ICT markets are created, structured, or maintained. Conceptually, we still don't have adequate definitions of critical terms like *information revolution* or *digital divide* that capture all the richness and variability of developing countries. And in normative policy terms, there is little agreement on how best to maximize diffusion and much disagreement over how to make the inevitable tradeoffs and to implement preferred policies. We don't know where we want to go, and no one has a fool-proof way of getting there.

Perhaps the greatest gap is the wisdom gap—the gap between the information revolution's inherent complexity and our capacity to comprehend it. We need a multidisciplinary and comprehensive framework for analyzing the information revolution. I offer such a framework in chapter 2 and then apply it in the subsequent chapters to three countries and to the international system as a whole.

2

Strategic Restructuring: A Framework for Analysis

Introduction

Chapter 1 identified the analytic challenges that have been created by the global information revolution. The greatest challenge is to frame research questions so that multiple factors could be brought together in a common field of analysis: What is the main cause of global diffusion patterns—economic structure, government policies, or technology? What mechanisms allow these technologies to diffuse? Do diffusion dynamics portend greater equality or greater inequality? Ultimately, why do countries with similar structural and economic features have divergent patterns of ICT distribution?

We have seen several different responses for each of these questions, but the prevailing social science frameworks are limited by their inability to view technology as deeply embedded within social structures, institutions, and practices. They rarely see technology as the product of particular historical trajectories or analyze institutional and political influences on ICT. Many authors failed to convey a proper sense of balance between structural determination of ICT outcomes and individual agents' ability to shape them.

To capture these missing elements, drawing on Giddens (1979) and others, I employ a modified structural approach that insists on the importance of both institutions and politics in shaping ICT outcomes. The framework rejects the assumption that individuals can leapfrog structural or institutional constraints. Both structure and agency are central to large societal innovations like the information revolution.

Why Political Economy, Why Structure? Describing the Framework

The framework I offer links structure, institutions, and policies by drawing on the field of political economy, which directly addresses the gaps in the literatures identified above. From classical political economists like Adam Smith and David Ricardo, to Joseph Schumpeter and Karl Polanyi, to contemporaries like Douglass North, political economists address issues that other disciplines tend to overlook. Central to political economics are distributional issues—who wins and who loses in the process of social change (Schumpeter 1943). In addition, the best political economists focus not only on particular transactions (whether sales in a market or voting in the political arena) but also on the overarching rules of the game that guide all transactions (Williamson 1986). They analyze the rules governing the allocation of scarce resources across different categories of social actors, whether at the international level (nation-states) or the subnational level (classes, elites, and interest groups). Political economy addresses the overarching constitutional question of which societal actors set the rules as the world moves from the older information and communication technology regime of state-run monopolies toward a regime that is more liberal, competitive, and globalized.

Political economists look the issue of power squarely in the eye and explain the power resources that social actors employ to protect and advance their own material or ideational interests. Because political economists assume that human beings are self-interested animals constantly on the search for their own relative advantage, they look for the self-interests behind administrative or technical rationales and try to explain who gets what and why. Finally, good political economists are highly suspicious of the claim that any one discipline or any single model can account for all the interesting outcomes we observe in societies. They pose the metaquestion: what paradigm or what element of a particular paradigm provides the best analytic leverage over a specific problem under particular circumstances?

The down side of this approach is the risk of eclecticism. Broad, encompassing theoretical propositions can be less rigorous, robust, and convincing than narrow ones. But there are tradeoffs in intellectual life as there are in markets and polities. At certain moments in the life cycle of an issue, breadth is especially needed. When confronted with a relatively new phenomenon, conventional models may provide the depth but miss critical new interconnections and nonobvious overlaps among key trends. At such moments, applying the open-architecture metaframeworks of political economy can advance both expert and popular understanding. An open-architecture intellectual approach is especially critical when reviewing the ICT experiences of many countries over a period of years. The brilliant scholar Charles Tilly (1984), in *Big Structures, Large Processes and Huge Comparisons*, demonstrates that big global issues can be handled with care and discrimination by accounting for unique local conditions as well as seemingly universal processes.

Strategic Restructuring (SRS): An Open-Architecture Model

In this section, I introduce my strategic restructuring (SRS) model and the dynamics that drive it. Later in this chapter, I describe in detail the logic, utility, and application of each of the model's components. The model explains outcomes through interactions of four distinct determinants:

• *Structures* (especially social structures but also economic and political structures),

• *Institutions* (that is, persistent patterns of roles and incentives),

• *Politics* (especially elite strategic behaviors), and

• Government *policies* (specifically, a mix of four policy balances— private and public initiative, competition and monopoly, foreign and domestic, and centralized and decentralized).

In social science terms, these are the *independent variables* I select to account for ICT diffusion. The *dependent variable* is the pattern of *technology diffusion* within and across societies. The purpose of the SRS approach is to account for the relationships among the variables and analyze them in detail. Let me elaborate on each, starting with the dependent variable *technology diffusion*.

My conception of what is conventionally called information and communication technology captures the complex behaviors associated with its diffusion. I conceptualize ICT as a potentially powerful new, scarce, and desirable societal resource—like capital or land. When introduced into a particular social setting, it has the capacity to empower and advantage some groups but also to disempower and disadvantage others. Stated more formally, information and communication technology is defined as *a scarce and desirable resource that groups and individuals contend for in order to consume, control, or own for their own purposes.* Individuals and groups that feel they will be advantaged and empowered by the spread of the new societal resource will try to promote it. Others who believe they will be disadvantaged and disempowered by some ICT technologies will tend initially to block and oppose its diffusion, partly through ignorance of its full effects but also through a correct evaluation that their short-term personal and professional status will be compromised.

In the final analysis, people are not really interested in technology: they are interested in the desirable things technology can bring. Most of us are not interested in automotive technology when we visit Beijing; we want to use a taxi, a rented car, a bus, or a pedicab to go from one place to another. Most are interested in depositing our money safely in a bank or ordering something with a credit card; we're not interested in financial technologies. Therefore, the technology to be explained must be intimately linked to the user's particular purposes.

Other definitions of information and communication technologies have merits but tend to ignore these essential societal and political implications. Other analysts define ICT as

• A tool or instrument used concretely to achieve particular tasks,

• A particular industry within the ICT sector (computers, telecommunications, the media, or the Internet),

• The overall ICT industry as a whole, or

• The particular goods and services that ICT can provide (e-mail, voice communications, information storage and retrieval, and so forth).

These definitions are useful for some purposes and not for others. They are not very useful for explaining the diffusion of new technologies through society and to understand their complex interactions with various aspects of society.

The SRS framework explains ICT diffusion in a given country (a dependent variable) through the interaction of the four independent variables cited above (structures, institutions, politics, and government policies). First, structures are examined, then linkages between structures and leading institutions in the ICT and other key sectors, then the political and leadership dynamics in and around those institutions, and finally the key government policies that flow from the politics and directly affect the distribution and use of resources like the Internet or cell phones.

The Explanatory Power of Structure
Structure—the more or less permanent, fundamental elements of society that do not change quickly or easily—include the following:

• *Level of economic development*   Gross domestic product per capita is a widely used indicator in most of the work on ICT and development.

• *Economic structure*   The sectoral structure of a country captures the relative shares of domestic economic production contributed by agriculture, manufacturing, and services (including information) in the national economy.

• *Social structure*   This refers to the class hierarchy of a society—that is, the shares of educated white-collar workers, farmers and peasants, and other classes.

• *Political structure*   This refers to local political culture (for example, participatory or authoritarian, with people seeing themselves as citizens or as subjects) (Bendix 1956).

The structural dimension is the most appropriate starting place for analyzing ICT diffusion. Comparative analysis across many different kinds of nations requires an initial study of the most basic features of the society to avoid producing bad analysis by extrapolating from the basics of one's own society and assuming that others share the same features.

By analyzing the demographic and economic structures of a society, the analyst learns that they shape in decisive ways the most likely *patterns of demand* for information and communication services and goods. For example, a society with a large agricultural sector and many peasants is likely to exhibit a much lower rate of aggregate demand increase for modern ICT services than a society with a large service sector and many white-collar workers who can afford and seek out everything from mainframes to laptops to palm pilots. Rural agricultural societies peopled mostly by peasants have lower demand for high-tech services and seek other ICT services instead.

Analyzing structure also tells the analyst a great deal about the *supply side* of the ICT equation. Some nations manufacture and export hardware or software; other nations neither produce nor export ICTs. Whether a country is an exporter or importer is important for its future development. The production structures will also shape the political forces most likely to coalesce around particular economic policies. Thus, the structure of demand and supply dramatically affects the kind of public policies—and hence the diffusion patterns—most likely to be found in a country.

The Explanatory Power of Institutions

Once a country's economic, social, and political structures are analyzed, the strategic restructuring model turns to a careful analysis of *institutions*. Institutions directly shape the behavior of women and men by providing them with incentives to act in particular ways. Some of the institutions that shape ICT diffusion are centered within the ICT sector, while others operate more widely. Sometimes the institutional base of a country is federal like Brazil, and sometimes it is centralized like China. Some institutions provide positive incentives for innovation and capital investment; others do not. In some countries, institutions tend to centralize political power; in others, political power is dispersed in a federal, decentralized fashion. In societies like China, one powerful, highly institutionalized political party dominates political life and widely shapes social and political behavior, including rules governing access to the Internet. Brazil and Ghana have no such institution, with very different results. Brazil's federal structure has again and again led to distinctive patterns of ICT innovation that do not occur in China or Ghana. Institutional differences affect incentives to use the Internet, the resources available to do so, and the political discourse that surrounds diffusion.

To analyze ICT diffusion in society comprehensively, a minimum first step is to identify the leading institutions with ICT responsibilities. Typically, the most important include ministries of communication or information, state-owned enterprises like the telephone company, regulatory agencies, specialized ICT bodies, and joint public-sector/private-sector institutions. Institutions are important in part because an individual's institutional position substantially shapes his or her substantive behaviors and politics.

The Explanatory Power of Politics
The strategic restructuring model assumes that institutions and structures are important but that people act individually and in groups to spread new technologies through society. Individuals are the social actors who make the information revolution happen. Individual people decide whether to buy computers, to use the Internet, to open an Internet service provider, to develop new local content, or to become a champion of freedom of the media. Individuals staff the institutions and reshape and reform them, even as they are being guided by those same institutional rules. An inevitable tension always exists between structure and agency, and each side is important. Indeed, SRS puts this tension at the center of the model.

Internet diffusion is greatly shaped and, indeed, is largely driven by the strategic decisions of individual elites. The role of farsighted and influential individuals in promoting particular patterns of Internet diffusion is huge, especially in the early years when the institutions that typically should provide guidance, support, and incentives for individuals have not yet been put in place. Yet individuals are largely invisible in today's scholarly work on ICT diffusion.

The strategic restructuring model concentrates on the political behavior of elites. This focus reflects the realities of the ICT sector. To the degree that politics has been involved in that sector, it has been very much elite politics, not mass politics. Furthermore, elites are in a position to rewrite the institutional rules of the game. Concentrating on elites is thus a conceptual and theoretical decision, not a normative one. Elites in developing countries are defined both by their senior positions within formal organizations (like companies, nongovernmental organizations, and government agencies) and by their high educational and professional status. Thus, the strategic calculations of individuals in a variety of institutional settings are driven partly by their positions within formal institutions and partly by their analyses of the broader structures and social dynamics of the society in which they are embedded. They recognize emerging opportunities and threats and respond strategically to those structural and institutional cues. As I describe below, these critical actors are driven by very mixed motives—personal, institutional, professional, and political.

This step of the SRS model identifies the leading individuals or *information champions* who lead the charge for liberal ICT diffusion in a society. These people might be leaders of NGOs, senior government officials, or private-sector entrepreneurs. Without exception, in all countries a small group of information revolutionaries is determined to change the rules and enhance ICT diffusion using typically liberal methods.

But not all individuals are radically committed to Internet diffusion, especially through liberal models. In fact, 95 percent of the people in the world are unconnected to modern networks, and most of them are probably relatively indifferent to new ICTs, given their other priorities. Others are simply opposed. To explain Internet diffusion fully, therefore, it is equally imperative to identify those individuals and groups who oppose rapid ICT diffusion and who calculate that the introduction of these new resources undercuts in some way their own institutional interests as regulators, ministry officials, or telephone company managers. In developing countries, these individuals often form a political bloc or coalition that supports a top-down version of diffusion that might be called *controlled diffusion* rather than *liberal diffusion*. Proponents of controlled diffusion do not adopt liberal diffusion just because they read a compelling brief; more typically changes occur through negotiated settlements spread out over years.

In all countries, therefore, the history of Internet expansion is the history of these two and other groups of elites variously collaborating and conflicting with one another to influence the pace and direction of Internet expansion. Thus, SRS focuses on *interelite bargaining* that occurs at two levels. On the most immediate level of individual transactions, elites bargain over the price of broadband access, the acquisition of ISP licenses, and the availability of foreign partnerships. At the structural level, individuals and groups negotiate over the general rules of the game that govern those particular transactions. Even when individuals are good negotiators, the rules usually determine the price of broadband or relations with monopoly suppliers or foreign partners. These rules are typically institutionalized in laws and regulations. And at particular and unusual moments in history, many of these laws and regulations are challenged by more and more people who are driven in turn by rapid technological and other changes in society. We are at such a moment today. The strategic restructing model is one method of explaining these dynamics.

The Explanatory Power of Government Policies
The final factor that shapes ICT diffusion is the relative balance of certain government policies. Comparative analysis of diffusion demonstrates that the pace, extent, and effectiveness of information and communication technology diffusion can be directly shaped by four government policies—private and public balances, domestic and foreign balances, monopoly and competition balances, and central and distributed balances. These four policy balances taken together act somewhat as an *intervening variable* in the strategic restructuring model. Policy balances lie somewhat ambiguously between the upstream factors of structure and institutions and the downstream element of diffusion. In some respects, the balances are tied to institutions, which can be considered both the product and the producers of the balances. On the other hand, the balances are the immediate constructed outcomes of political bargaining. Policy is the medium through which the elites make their influences most directly manifest, and policies provide very immediate incentives to employ or not employ new ICTs and to employ them in some ways and not others. When a government policy sets Internet service provider prices high, then Internet demand is certainly lowered. Where elites can provide positive incentives for diffusion and where structural conditions are propitious, then Internet diffusion is enhanced. Where these four policy balances are not favorable or set up negative incentives, then diffusion occurs much more slowly than it does in other countries where the policy balances are favorable. As I describe in subsequent chapters, these four balances correspond to

broad political economy categories—*property rights* (private-public balances; domestic-foreign), *efficiency* (monopoly-competition), and *governance* (central-distributed balances). In chapter 6, I turn to another policy dimension—equity—which I refer to as the fifth balance.

The strategic restructuring model leads us to concentrate on the process of rule making and on the societal actors who are most involved. The model pays less attention to final or even intermediate consumers. For example, SRS does not analyze in detail the structure of demand that characterizes different countries. This is not an unimportant matter, since the demographics of demand shape the provision of ICT supplies as well as the kinds of political coalitions that will form within the sector. The demographics of demand is also important because demand or use differs by country or region. The demand structure in developing and developed countries indicates that the Internet is a more elitist technology in poor countries. Thus, in the United States, the percentage of Internet users who in 2000 completed university, some university, completed secondary, and some secondary are 86, 70, 53, and 31 percent, respectively. But in Romania, the same categories are 22, 13, 4, and 3 percent. The top to bottom ratios are three to one in the United States but seven to one in Romania. Among other implications, this means that when we aggregate Internet users by country, "Americans or Swedes are online and interconnected" means one thing and "Romanians or Sri Lankans are connected" means something quite distinct. There is excellent comparative work being done on this subject by a research consortium at the University of California at Los Angeles UCLA and by InterMedia. I return to these kinds of demand-side features in chapter 6.

The Drawbacks of the Strategic Restructuring Framework

All theories and conceptual frameworks have drawbacks as well as strengths. Intellectually, they have various degrees of parsimony, power, conscilliance, and elegance. They also differ in their mechanics—their capacities to be applied in many circumstances by different observers. Some require lots of data (whether numbers or interviews), and others little. Some can be done easily by researchers outside the country; others require the researcher to pursue local details personally.

The strategic restructuring framework has its own strengths and drawbacks. It places a high premium on comprehensiveness and explanatory power over parsimony. A parsimonious theory (such as the theories of Karl Marx or Sigmund Freud) selects one powerful variable, which claims to explain a great deal. Others rely on several independent variables to explain outcomes. Such theories should, however, demonstrate conscilliance—an elegant fitting together of all parts of the theory, especially where they operate at different levels of analysis (macro, meso, micro) (Alford and Friedland 1986).

To be employed properly, the strategic restructuring model requires considerable commitment by the analyst to conduct complementary analyses at the macro, meso, and micro levels. It certainly requires substantial investigations within a country. The model is expensive because it takes seriously the subjective views of the local actors, assumes that different people in the restructuring processes will hold very different perspectives about important ICT-related issues, and insists that the analyst go in and uncover those different perspectives, since they drive behaviors. Different actors bring different meanings to the technologies. In other words, using the SRS model requires a lot of field work trekking about asking a lot of people a lot of questions about a lot of things. SRS analysis cannot be done at arm's length. It is retail analysis. Finally, by concentrating on those with social influence, I choose not to provide as much detail on the general ICT consumption patterns of the population as a whole. That is, I do not detail the demand patterns of various consumers by income, education, gender, and so forth. John P. Robinson, Meyer Kestnbaum, Alan Neustadtl, and Anthony Alvarez (2000) are doing excellent work on this topic, but because it is less directly political, I choose not to do so here.

The Structure and Evolution of the Information Sector

At least since the publication of Daniel Bell's brilliant *The Coming of Post-Industrial Society* (1973), critics have debated the structure of information societies and promoted contending theoretical formulations to describe information sectors and their relationships to the structure of society as a whole. Four years before Bell, a Japanese intellectual, Yoneji

Masuda, published in Japan a remarkably prescient book about sectoral transformations that rings true more than thirty years later (Masuda 1981).

Much of the debate hinges on alternative ways to measure the extent of the information sector and its effects on other economic and social sectors. Certain theorists claim that, in this process of information and communication technology diffusion, industrial society is transformed into a "postindustrial" or "information" society. Scholars have employed various ways to measure the extent of the information sector. The simplest and least satisfying is to describe the "diffusion of computer and telecommunications technologies as the defining characteristic" (Steinfeld and Salvaggio 1989, 7). This is akin to what I call the technodeterminist paradigm and equates ICT diffusion with major societal change. The information society therefore is equivalent to the number of appliances and applications that citizens own in a society. Others, like Marc U. Porat (1977), measure the extent of the information sector in terms of its contribution to employment—that is, knowledge workers as a share of the total labor force. Porat's now-classic multivolume study of the U.S. economy found that half of that country's labor force was employed in information activities by the mid-1970s.

Others concentrate on the consumption of ICT, using such measures as the number of telephone calls per capita or the per capita consumption of newspapers. Another frequently used approach is to analyze the economic weight of the ICT sectors in their contributions to gross domestic product, relative to other sectors like manufacturing and agriculture.

As Charles Steinfeld and Jerry Salvaggio (1989) point out, some critical treatments of the scope of the information society don't fit easily into these categories. Writers like Dan Schiller (1999) insist that the information society is simply the latest expression of voracious modern capitalism, now in a more global and technology-intensive guise. Such writers are as critical of the potential costs of the information society as many other writers are celebratory of its potential contributions. They point to the concentration of ownership and control among global conglomerates and the abuses of civil liberties and even democracy that may result from its diffusion. As citizens' viewing options narrow, content variety is also restricted. The risk is that more and more, content will be produced by mostly U.S.- and Western-based multinational corporations, and cultures in Africa, Asia, and Latin America will be overwhelmed by media materialism. This is the dark side of the information society.

Before we conclude that structural shifts toward a new kind of society are indeed occurring in developing countries, we need to counterpose the concept of an information society against the underlying realities of developing countries. What is the relevance of Bell's formulation of a postindustrial society for people in Africa still seeking an efficient agricultural society? Indeed, does it even make sense to apply a term like *information economy* or *knowledge society* to developing countries? Is the *information economy* a hoax, an intellectual two-step? While many wax enthusiastic about the revolutionary, transformative nature of the new technologies, few have stepped forward to describe these trends or imagine what the structure of an ICT-transformed developing country might look like.

Bell (1973) and Manuel Castells (1998) make an important qualitative argument beyond the usual quantitative balances between economic sectors. Their argument concentrates on science and technology's role in modern society. Both argue, though Castells (1998) more strongly, that the central elements in the information revolution are sectoral shifts *and* the increase and spread of the use of the scientific method of experimentation. The knowledge society is thereby created through the sustained and accelerating application of more knowledge to more societal elements. It is thus defined by the spread of new knowledge practices and a new mind set. This transformation is both cultural and economic.

When sophisticated observers of developing countries use the term *knowledge society*, they tend to do so in cautious terms. These observers are aware that structural shifts are happening in some countries, and although they are aware of the future potentials, they hesitate to predict future outcomes for their own countries. Skepticism about the transformatory role of ICT is rife even in major development institutions like the World Bank, a strong and optimistic advocate of ICT use in developing countries. Other skeptics include insightful intellectuals like Robin Mansell (Mansell and Wehn 1998, 12), professor at the London School of Economics, who insists that "ICTs are best considered as tools," not

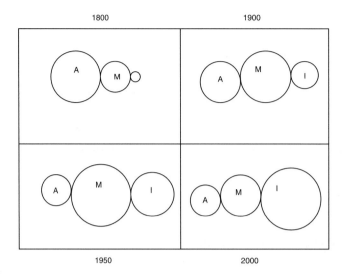

Figure 2.1
The Economic Structure of Group of Seven Countries: Agriculture, Manufacturing, and Information, 1800 to 2000

transformative agents. "These technologies do not create the transformations in society by themselves; they are designed and implemented by people in their social, economic, and technical contexts." For her, ICTs are best viewed as "capabilities," like other capabilities such as education or health. ICTs are not automatic change drivers or societal transformers.

Even with these caveats, the ICT-related structural shifts that are caused are important signposts. Figure 2.1 captures the essence of my structuralist argument. In strictly heuristic terms, it describes the economic evolution of today's Group of Seven countries (the United States of America, Japan, Canada, the United Kingdom, Germany, Italy, and France) from the nineteenth century to the twenty-first. Each circle represents the economic weight of one sector (agriculture, manufacturing, and information) compared with the weights of the others. The larger the circle, the greater that sector's share of gross domestic product (GDP); the smaller the circle, the smaller that sector's contribution. Reducing national economies to three constituent pieces is a simple rendering of a complex reality, but this illustration is meant to be illustrative and not definitive. Serious measurement problems are encountered when a term like *information sector* is retroactively applied to 1800 or 1900.

The figure shows that in the 1800s the economic structure in the G7 countries was dominated by agricultural production. The political elites of the period, from Thomas Jefferson and George Washington to their local counterparts in France and Germany, were all deeply rooted in farming and plantation life. By 1900, factories had sprouted across the United States, and in the United Kingdom cities like Birmingham spewed dark smoke from the steel industry and capital goods companies. In Germany and France, the industrializing trend was the same. Yet agriculture remained extremely important for national life.

Politically, farmers' parties and land-based movements around 1900 were struggling to retain authority in the face of a growing and restive industrial workforce. Industrial elites sought to impose their world view on the still agricultural society. Conflicts erupted over issues like tariffs, money supply, labor laws, and infrastructure support. Some societal elements embraced industrialization and commercial agriculture, other elements supported industrialization selectively, and others mightily resisted all change. Some sought to accelerate industrialization's changes; others sought to slow down reform's pace. Karl Polanyi (1944) captures these contradictory imperatives in his term *double movement*: different interests embrace or reject different restructurings at different times. New groups, new interests, and new political and economic elites emerged, and each tried to influence these restructurings in ways that would benefit them.

By 1950, the balance between agriculture and industry had shifted decisively in the United States and other G7 countries. The industrial buildup associated with military conflict accelerated this restructuring, as industrial innovations and processes became societywide and no longer were confined to a single sector. While still an imperfect transition, given that a significant proportion of the population still lived on farms, Americans were witnessing the supremacy of the industrial sector. The demographic importance of urban populations and the political dominance of urban elites now overshadowed agricultural elites. Services were a rising proportion of GDP as farm work declined and information processing work increased.

Structures, institutions, and laws usually lag behind economic and demographic shifts. In the United Kingdom and the United States, mid-century legislative representation still overrewarded rural constituencies, but this too was rapidly changing. The U.S. Supreme Court's decisions of the early and mid-1960s (*Baker v. Carr* and other reapportionment decisions) reallocated power from rural to urban constituencies. The transition from an agricultural society to an industrial society involved massive institutional restructurings and substantial dislocations. There was, as Joseph Schumpeter (1943) wrote, "creative destruction," although more creative for some and more destructive for others. New patterns of winners and losers emerged, as losers scrambled to protect their material and moral interests by blocking change when they could. Industrial elites sought to restructure market, state, and society in ways that would benefit their material, political, and societal preferences. The motors of change were rising incomes and new technologies, which complemented each other. These two facets combined to increase levels of market demand and consumption. "Business" now included both international and domestic business, and America's share of world markets loomed large (especially after the destruction of much of the industrial base of Europe and Japan). Educational access also widened during this period.

These changes occurred in parallel but not identical ways in the world's advanced capitalist nations. The general trend was toward a modern mass society based on manufacturing, although each country's path to postwar industrial capitalism was unique, as J. Rogers Hollingsworth (Hollingsworth, Schmitter, and Streeck 1994; Hollingsworth and Boyer 1997), and others demonstrate.

In the lower right quadrant of figure 2.1 stands the latest moment in this process of economic and political restructuring. The millennial year 2000 is in some ways the mirror image of 1800. The information economy has ballooned beyond all expectations. Agriculture in today's G7 countries now resembles the information economy in 1800—tiny in economic weight but exercising some political weight. The comparative evidence suggests that the United States is ahead of the pack in its structuring of an information political economy, but the G7 countries as a whole are following this trend (OECD 1999).

Major economic transitions are neither automatic nor frictionless. The lesson of the earlier periods is that we should expect friction and political contention during these periods. The G7 nations did not leap suddenly and effortlessly from pure agriculture to perfect manufacturing. Agriculture is still important in Europe; values associated with rural, preindustrial life remain vibrant and appealing, and institutions like the church and community associations guard the treasured old ways that buffer individuals from market excesses. Even during today's putative transition from industrial society to information society, France's and Italy's most volatile public demonstrations concern agricultural politics. The current transition from familiar institutions to unknown new territories stumbles along in the guise of millions and millions of tiny experiments and tests.

Were we to construct a similar sequence based on figure 2.1 for developing countries, we would discover a vastly different picture. Most developing countries have not reached quadrant four of the figure, and many of the world's poorest countries have not reached quadrant three. The 2 billion people of Africa and South Asia live in countries that look more like quadrant one. Rural agricultural elites dominate the daily political discourse. Literacy rates are low. Social conservatism is high. These are the structural contexts in which information and communication appliances are being diffused. The ways that today's underdeveloped countries experience industrialization is quite different than the ways that European nations experience it. For India and China, industrialization comes on the back of foreign domination and colonialism. Without understanding the extent of economic backwardness and social conservatism in developing countries, we profoundly misunderstand the nature of ICT diffusion.

Structural Perspectives: Take Two

Let me suggest another interpretation of the national economic structures in which ICTs diffuse globally. Social structures and political structures are of course important for ICT diffusion. A country with a large educated middle class, many entrepreneurs, and many young people will have a particular ICT diffusion pattern. The typical social structure of advanced capitalist societies has a long narrow top, a bulging middle class, a solid working-class base, and a relative small layer of very poor people at the bottom. Although each advanced country differs in its details, this is the modal profile for advanced societies. This bulging middle class provides both a large *supply* of knowledge workers to create and distribute new innovations and also represents the *demand* for those products and services.

The typical social structure of a poor developing country has a different structure. The social base of poor peasants and a poor working class is a much larger proportion of society. The modern salariat and petit bourgeoisie is growing, although it is much thinner than in rich countries. More often than not, a huge difference exists between the economic conditions of those at the top and the bottom of these societies. These structural features will also affect diffusion rates. These social structure differences are significant for demand- and supply-side ICT. A large, educated class means more engineers and inventors to supply new ICTs. A large, prosperous middle class means more people to buy new appliances and services.

If the class structure tends to closely follow the sectoral structures described earlier, political structures exhibit greater autonomy across the same structures. By *political structure*, I mean something akin to political culture—that is, the dominant, long-standing lines of political or ideological cleavage and the channels through which power is exercised (Almond and Verba 1989).

In developing countries where democratic participation is shallow and pro-forma, complex ties between patrons and clients often operate with greater force than in the developed world. These ties link powerful local religious and secular leaders with their followers through various combinations of traditional fealty, charisma, and material benefits. These ties are almost always more important than simple market incentives of neutral demand and supply and prove more persuasive than formal voting incentives. These ties are instrumental for shaping the allocation of all scarce resources, including ICT-related resources. These structures mold other political patterns, including institutional centralization and decentralization, unitary and federal arrangements, and presidential and parliamentary systems. Each of these structures is also likely to impact on ICT reform potentials. Ben Petrazzini (1996) makes this argument clearly in the case of telecommunications reform in developing countries, claiming that the more autonomous the government is from social pressures, the more privatization is likely to succeed. India's federal structure of many separate states set inside a relatively democratic polity has slowed the spread of telecommunications reform, even as it has contributed positively to the growth of broadcast diversity. China's heavily centralized, top-down system made it possible for a firmly committed central political leadership to bulldoze through ICT reforms. China has mobilized billions of dollars and built enormous infrastructure projects at breakneck speed. India's slowness and China's speed reflect each country's political and institutional structures. The Chinese political structure also reflects broader historical and cultural patterns of Confucianism and traditional values. The dividing line between economic structures and political and social structures is imprecise.

These features of structure provide several insights for ICTs and less developed countries. Structure reminds us of the slow pace of long-term societal change. Revolutions in social structure do not happen overnight, even today. Changes in developing countries also have earlier antecedents. We can search for insights from these earlier periods even as we recognize that certain fundamentals may vary from one period to another.

This structuralist perspective also demonstrates how different countries have different starting points and how far many countries must travel. A structuralist perspective also raises important questions about diffusion mechanics. As the revolution proceeds, change must be transmitted from one sector (the ICT sector) outward, if it is to spread to become a societywide revolution.

From Structures to Institutions

As important as these structural patterns are, they do not determine every single information and communication technology outcome. Mediating between these broad structures and a particular telephone call from X to Y stands a dense network of interconnected institutions, groups, and individuals that act through a variety of public entities, private companies, and nongovernmental organizations to shape ICT outcomes.

In their sweeping analysis of the embeddedness of institutions in contemporary capitalism, J. Rogers Hollingsworth and Robert Boyer (1997, 2) refer to the "social system of production," delineating "the industrial relations system; the system of training of workers and managers; the internal structure of corporate firms; the structured relationships among firms in the same industry on the one hand, and on the other, firms' relationships with their suppliers and customers; the financial markets of a society; the conceptions of fairness and justice held by capital and labor; the structure of the state and its policies; . . . all these institutions, organizations, and social values tend to cohere with each other . . . into a full-fledged system." And deeply embedded within these institutional systems is knowledge—its production and consumption.

A central tenet of this study is that *the information revolution is an institutional and political revolution more than a technical revolution.* We open ourselves to profound analytic errors if we concentrate on the technical aspects of these epochal changes. The production and consumption of knowledge occurs in a complex institutional system where interactions occur among a variety of actors: The great sociologist Emile Durkheim pointed out in 1897 "Since [social] activity takes place outside each of us . . . , it is necessary to fix, to institute outside us certain ways of acting and certain judgments which do not depend on each particular will taken separately. . . . One can . . . designate as 'institutions' all the beliefs and all the modes of conduct instituted by the collectivity" (quoted in Hechter, Opp, and Wippler 1990, 1).

The word *institution* is used here to refer to concrete organizations with names and addresses, as well as legal concepts such as the institution of property as conventionally defined.

The most important and difficult reforms in the telecommunications and broadcasting industries are not technological innovations. The greatest challenge for corporate leaders and senior government officials is achieving political consensus and reforming rules and institutions.

The importance of effective institutions in the development of societies is beyond doubt. One definition of an underdeveloped society is precisely one whose institutions are underdeveloped and weak (North 1990). Consistently structured institutions are at the core of a national information infrastructure. Institutions structure positive and negative incentives for particular ICT uses. Brian Kahin and I (Kahin and Wilson 1997) refer to the national information infrastructure as a national system that is shaped by technology but that is chiefly a set of interlocking institutions that guide and constrain the behavior of consumers, suppliers, public officials, and citizens. The institutional adjustments that leaders make to accommodate new technologies are imperative for successful ICT use (Mansell and Wehn 1998).

Institutions in Action: Taiwan's Institute for Information Industries

In the mid- to late 1970s, the economic and political elites of the Republic of China grew concerned that the island's future economic performance was tied to a set of industries that were losing their competitive global position. They believed that Taiwan needed to make a leap from one kind of industrial base to another. After a series of deliberations, they decided to target information industries. How would they get from here to there? The consensus was that the existing institutional role players—conventional ministries, state firms, private associations—were not up to the task at hand.

Through a series of interviews I conducted in the republic's capital, Taipei, I found that, in 1979, this coalition created the Institute for Information Industries (III), which Taiwanese officials hoped would help Taiwan make the jump into new ICT areas. The Institute for Information Industries was launched under the sponsorship of one of the most important institutional players on the island, the Ministry of Economic Affairs, so that the prestigious ministry could draw on governmental as well as private-sector resources to achieve new national goals.

The government set out to promote the effective and efficient use of ICT and thereby strengthen national competitiveness. This would be accomplished by research and development, by cultivating ICT professionals, and generally by attempting to facilitate ICT industry development. One of the institute's leaders, Major General Gao, pointed out that "if we are to compete globally, we must apply ICT to all organizations and companies. But not everybody appreciated this need at first. We at III had to go into industry and help them recognize the problem and to introduce new procedures and processes" (personal communication, 1999).

Taiwan has emerged as one of the most successful ICT economies in the world. Gao focused on difficult research and development initiatives, such as software development, but also acknowledged the importance of institutions in promoting ICT trends: "People didn't understand the Internet. But we put together a team to review its implications for the country. We had about twenty people. The team recognized that the Internet could be our window on the world. I thought it could help our companies do business, and I wanted to expand its use. So at the start, we decided not to charge anything for Internet use" (personal communication 1999). In 1994, the Institute for Information Industries spawned the SEED Internet service provider, and the number of users quickly shot up to 20,000. That also was the year that Taiwan created its own National Information Infrastructure Steering Committee to help build the Taiwan information highway.

It is difficult to quantify the contributions of organizations like III. Similar bodies were created in Thailand, India, Malaysia, and other countries within and beyond the region, many of them created in the 1993 to 1996 period, and my interviews with people involved in ICT issues in these three nations and in Taiwan indicate that they had mixed successes and some outright failures.

The history of the Internet and other innovations in the United States has been variously described, and it is generally agreed that the diffusion of the Internet occurred through a succession of institutional innovations from an original research and development activity launched by the United States Defense Advanced Research Projects Agency (DARPA). This activity was then financially and managerially supported by a complicated and rich network of institutions, one after the other, from the United States Department of Defense to universities like Stanford and Wisconsin, followed by the eventual involvement of promotional agencies like the National Science Foundation. This high level of public institutional engagement occurred in a national environment rich in private firms and corporations, and yet government and research bodies launched the revolutionary processes, which were then handed off to private actors and rapidly commercialized (but in the early days remained under substantial government monitoring). The United States enjoyed an environment abundant with efficient and highly interconnected institutions.

Regrettably, many analysts miss the problematic nature of institutions in poor countries. Interested mainly in the technology itself, too many analysts overlook the role that institutions play even in advanced countries. The institutions that enabled the information revolution to occur where and when it did are not present in many developing countries. There are several complementary ways to analyze institutions' impact on ICTs. Finding and using information are social processes with a beginning, a middle, and an end; they are not isolated, one-step activities. The contours of this process are guided, sustained, and blocked by institutions. Within this process, institutional incentives substantially shape the way people will research, invest in, produce, sell, distribute, pay for, and use information and communication technologies. Invariably, these activities occur within the context of one or more institutions, such as universities, research laboratories, and commercial outlets.

The National Research Council (NRC) recognized the sequential and institutional basis for knowledge production and use when it prepared a new methodology to help institutions like the World Bank and others assess a national knowledge system for countries. The NRC described the "institutions that control and regulate the flow and use of knowledge in the economy and society" (NRC 1996, 06). It identified a series of activities that countries engage in—creating knowledge, providing access to knowledge, assimilating the knowledge, diffusing knowledge throughout the economy and society, and using knowledge for social benefit and productive enterprise (NRC 1966, 1–2). In its study of rural areas in Canada, NRC researchers found that the contributions made by institutions to each of these steps were even more important than originally anticipated. Where an institution was weak or failed, that step in the processes failed, jeopardizing the entire diffusion process (NRC 1999).

We also look at institutions and ICT diffusion as a commercial product cycle. The *product cycle* describes the stages that characterize a product's market introduction, its use, and its removal from the market. The product cycle for technology moves through several stages that include research and development, investment and financing, commercialization, production, distribution (wholesale and retail), and product servicing. New products move onto the market as old ones are taken off. This process does not occur in a vacuum, however: institutions bracket each stage in the cycle, advancing or retarding forward movement for the product.

Products never invent themselves, sell themselves, or diffuse themselves. Technology never diffuses on its own. Institutions push and pull innovations through the institutional processes described above. In places like Silicon Valley or Bangalore, we find a succession of interlocking institutions—small startup companies, venture capital firms, industrial parks and company incubators, producer industry associations, downstream marketing firms, and sophisticated buyers. If these institutions do not function well internally or in concert, ICT diffusion will not proceed smoothly. These commercial organizations are, in turn, embedded within a complex set of interacting institutions, laws, and regulations. Tax codes promote and prevent innovation, tariffs protect and promote industries, agencies promote exports and imports protection, patent laws may advance technology investments (Evans 1995). All these institutions and laws have their own trajectories, and each country's ICT path is unique. All institutional environments are not created equal.

Lewis Branscomb, emeritus professor of public policy and corporate management at Harvard University and former chief scientist for IBM, takes the institutional argument one step further. Institutions that meet narrow needs are not sufficient. Also necessary are matters like trust and efficiency: "Functioning economic institutions that trust one another, an infrastructure for information and distribution that is flexible and inexpensive and reliable, an attitude toward the balance of personal reward and collective well-being that is conducive to responsible economic behavior—these are the requirements for science-based development" (Raymond 1996, 2).

Palo Alto and Boston, and later Bangalore, became hotbeds of technological innovation for reasons that have little to do with hardware but
a great deal to do with the unique institutional histories of each site. Universities, research centers, science projects, and customers were available
in Palo Alto, Boston, and Bangalore. These institutions are the incubators of innovation: they provide raw material (both human and material), nurture the incubation process, and even provide jobs that allow
people to buy the new products (Saxenian 1999a).

Leading Institutions in the ICT Sectors

Several clusters of institutions occupy center stage in the ICT sectors of
developing countries. These institutions decisively shape nearly all critical sectoral outcomes. The success or failure of these institutions shapes
the success or failures of the entire sector.

Each institution is closely intertwined into an integrated policy system.
Because the performance of one institution is difficult to separate from
the performance of another, reforming the ICT sector is both complex
and contentious: the *relationships* among many institutions are what
must ultimately be reformed. Fixing one institution will not change the
systems that govern various sectors or significantly alter ICT outcomes.

The interplay among these institutions is critical for the information
revolution's success in any particular country. Intragovernmental relations are important, and equally important are the ties between government and actors like private sector institutions and civil society groups.
In an efficient and balanced ICT governance system, separate institutions
mesh smoothly so that knowledge flows smoothly from where it is produced to where it is needed, either through state or nonstate institutions.
The most sophisticated analyses of economic development point precisely to these partnerships among institutions as the true catalysts
for successful qualitative changes in productivity (Sell 1998). My experiences in the poorest developing countries have shown that the most
difficult step for senior officials to admit is that private-sector interests
have something useful to contribute to the national policy process. Senior
officials often view businessmen as interlopers or as enemies of the
state.

While formally the same, institutions in developing countries are not the same as those in developed countries. Their performance differs substantially. Institutional relativity must be kept in mind when analyzing the information revolution globally. The following are several generally acknowledged features of institutions in developing countries, though each country well differ in the details:

• Power and authority tend to be concentrated at the top, with less consultation between executive officers and subordinates than in developed nations.

• Unofficial patron client ties compete with formal bureaucratic authority relations within and between organizations.

• Overstaffing exists at all levels.

• Underskilled, underexperienced staffs are common.

• Corruption is prevalent.

• Organizational efficiency is low.

Interorganizational features often found in institutions in developing countries include the following:

• Limited relations with customers or clients,

• Risk-averse behavior, and

• Susceptibility to external pressures for employment and contracts.

At least three essential elements of interinstitutional dynamics are important for sustained ICT diffusion:

• First, the *interactive* effects among clusters of institutions are important determinants of ICT performance. Superior institutions operate as nodes of interconnected networks. They are not isolated, freestanding entities.

• Second, institutional features are neither inevitable nor predictable but are highly *path dependent*, reflecting earlier institutional decisions.

• Third, an unpredictable *threshold effect* seems to occur as institutions mature and interact. At some point, a spark ignites ICT potential, and a mature and effective system connects and consolidates. The benefits from these interactions seem to flow from learned experiences, shared substantive knowledge, and trust developed through personal networks and commercial exchanges.

Bangalore Is Not a Miracle City

The "miracle city" of Bangalore, India, exhibits all these interinstitutional elements. Bangalore possesses a rich network of educational, training, and scientific institutions that supply the necessary inputs to its highly touted software miracle. Bangalore's wealth is created from the networked interactions of the men and women who pass through the city's institutions, absorb the city's values, and learn critical development strategies. In this dense, science-packed city, a *critical mass* of entrepreneurs, engineers, scientists, and managers has emerged. These knowledge workers trade e-ideas and e-solutions to e-problems over Italian coffees and strong teas at Bangalore's cybercafes and traditional cafes. Bangalore is not a modern miracle; its success is the result of decades of steady institutional development and political leadership.

Social networks exist prior to technological networks. Young people attend primary and secondary schools, join social clubs, graduate from professional schools, move through religious and civic associations, and make friends who are members of other clubs and groups. They build trust and social capital (Putnam 1999). These dense ties form the social capital on which entrepreneurs and technicians build technical networks. Some locales possess dense sets of institutions conducive to widespread and sustainable ICT diffusion. Other locales do not.

Like its counterparts in Boston and San Francisco, Bangalore's suburbs possessed a rich network of supportive ICT institutions. For a city in a poor, developing country, Bangalore has a wealth of institutions. It claims three universities, fourteen engineering schools, and thirty-seven polytechnic schools. It contains a large number of aeronautics, defense, health, and environmental research centers (Stremlau 1996). High-tech industrial estates abound, including a park of hundreds of acres that houses multinationals like Motorola, Hewlett-Packard, and 3M (Stremlau 1996). Millions of dollars flow in from other developing countries, including Singapore's investments in an information technology park. Bangalore supports a truly extraordinary mix of institutions. Half the number of institutions would be remarkable for a country where the 2000 per capita annual income is estimated at $2,200 (CIA 2000).

Bangalore's dense network of institutions and the educated elites who populate them are not Johnny-come-lately successes. They are the results of a long, consistent *tradition* of engineers and educational excellence dating back fifty years to the period when India was ending its four-hundred year period of British colonial influence. That tradition put the city on the path to a digital future, but staying on that path depended on a series of incremental decisions that were guided by a vision to stay a particular course. The tradition of excellence was reinforced under British colonialism and accelerated after independence in 1948. This city benefited from the vision and leadership of India's first prime minister, Jawaharlal Nehru, who from 1947 to 1964 vowed to make Bangalore "the city of the future." One commentator wrote, "It would be a place where scientists could get away from the multitudes and produce ideas and programs that would guide the nation's ambitious plans to achieve economic and military self-reliance" (Stremlau 1996, 153). Nehru and all subsequent prime ministers put their money where their vision was, pumping resources into the city to make it a true Indian technopolis (Stremlau 1996, 154). The government "spent lavishly in the building of Bangalore's civilian science and technology infrastructure as well as the nation's most sensitive and advanced military and space research facilities" (Stremlau 1996). Nehru structured institutional rewards to entice scientists to live and work in the city. In my interviews in India, people frequently referred to this very consistent, long-term support for information and technology centers based around Bangalore. One keen observer I interviewed noted that successive prime ministers selected large national projects to support, including the national nuclear program and the Indian space program. Typically, a senior science advisor promoted and protected resources flowing to India's scientific institutions, including those of Bangalore. A recent advisor pressed to build the human and the physical infrastructures of the Indian telecommunications industry. Without successive decisions that were made over many years, Bangalore would not have achieved its tremendous success.

Even with this slow, steady accretion of critical institutional, material, and human factors of production, the city of Bangalore did not become a household name among the global ICT crowd until the early 1990s. It first had to pass a threshold point: societal networks, indigenous institutions, and "old boy" networks were not enough. The final ingredient was the spark of steady external demand for locally supplied products and services. Although India has an enormous English-speaking middle class—the largest in the world—India's domestic demand alone was not enough to jumpstart Bangalore's ICT industry. Even today, the forward linkage between Bangalore and the general Indian population is minuscule; Bangalore remains an economic enclave. The missing ingredient was consistent demand for information services. For international businesses, the local industry provided low-cost valued-added inputs. Multinationals started in India with low-level back-office activities that were far down the value chain. A substantial multibillion-dollar business for increasingly sophisticated services and goods emerged later. Combining with Bangalore's rich institutional networks, foreign supply-and-demand elements coalesced, and a modern ICT Mecca was born.

Elites in other cities are eying Bangalore's miracle jealously, seeking to recreate it institution by institution. Privileged by a huge influx of foreign capital and foreign companies, cities like Hyderabad are reaching for similar status. Both cities are promoting themselves as global centers for knowledge-based industries. It is an open question whether other Indian states and cities will successfully create and resuscitate individual institutions and enforce a productive, progressive, interinstitutional governance system (*India Today* 2000). But as David G. McKendrick, Richard F. Doner, and Stephan Haggard (2001) find in their recent study of the hard-drive industry, *From Silicon Valley to Singapore*, global corporations are aggressively seeking location-specific benefits in new places—including strong research universities, specialized labor, and clusters of critical suppliers.

Achieving greater sophistication requires institutional and policy incentives that prompt intimate interinstitutional linkages between demand and supply, design, manufacturing, and customer satisfaction. According to two observers of a proposed ICT plan for another Indian state, Tamil Nadu, "The extent to which the benefits of the 'Information Revolution' are actualized will depend on the success with which countries' regional subdivisions incorporate into policy and initiatives these interlinkages between various components of an ICT strategy. The Tamil

Nadu government's ICT strategy, although progressive and comprehensive, is deficient in its understanding of these interlinkages, and needs to address them to ensure that a flourishing IT industry translates into regional development" (personal communication, 2000).

Silicon Valley and Route 128 Are Not Miracles

AnnaLee Saxenian (1999b) demonstrates convincingly that very similar factors operated in other ICT success stories, like California's Silicon Valley and Boston's Route 128 area, centered in Cambridge, Massachusetts. Both Cambridge and Silicon Valley have important private and public institutions and dense networks that advance and sustain the design, diffusion, and use of innovative new technologies. These include the Massachusetts Institute of Technology and Harvard in Cambridge and Stanford and Berkeley in California.

Popular culture and academic studies remind us that California has outpaced Massachusetts. Saxenian unequivocally attributes Silicon Valley's absolute successes and its relative triumph over the corporate and educational ICT complexes in Cambridge to northern California's unique institutional patterns. She cites the critical importance of high-quality, world-class single institutions like MIT and Stanford. Especially critical are institutional cultures that emphasize mutual problem solving and information sharing among engineers; institutional incentives promoted openness.

Saxenian found that the institutional patterns in old New England were more rigid and hierarchical than they were in young California. New England executives expected tasks to be accomplished in-house and did not oversee as much outsourcing and collective problem solving among different companies as their counterparts in the West did. New England's Puritan traditions were more authoritarian and top-down. The Valley's institutionalized patterns of high interfirm labor mobility prompted high levels of knowledge sharing essential for its success.

Other ancillary institutions were in place in California to provide the essential upstream inputs that the burgeoning computer industry required. These included institutions supplying skilled, smart workers (universities like Stanford and Berkeley) and institutions supplying capital (venture capital firms). New social institutions sprang up to support the "softer" but essential elements of trust across groups, such as the voluntary private-public partnerships that markets require to function effectively.

Beyond the more obvious and visible organizations like think tanks and for-profit corporations are two institutions whose effectiveness helps or hinders ICT diffusion—property and property rights. Economic historians like Douglass C. North (1990) recognize the regular, predictable protection of property rights as the cornerstone of long-term, sustainable economic development. Entrepreneurs and managers seeking sales, investment, and innovation opportunities in the ICT sector simply will not sell, invest, or innovate if they believe that the property rights regime is not adequately specified and enforceable. As risk takers seeking benefits, they need to have confidence that the rules of the game will allow the fruits of their labor to be retained (minus the tax man's share). Confidence comes with reliable, transparent institutions that structure activities and secure core privileges and rights of property—the right to use property however one wishes, the right to the fruits of one's property, and the right to dispose of property. The provision of these fundamentals is a prime responsibility of institutions, whether courts, legislative bodies, or regulatory agencies. In many ways, the right of property is the world's most important institution, yet during the transition from a world of atoms to a world of bits and bytes, the protection of property rights is especially problematic (Negroponte 1995). Deborah Spar (1999) recognizes this point in her argument about the importance of property rights in cyberspace. Cyberrights and intellectual property rights are especially difficult to enforce in poor countries where institutions are weak.

ICTs Affect Institutions

The relationships between institutions and information and communication technologies are reciprocal and iterative. Institutions impact ICTs; ICTs impact institutions. We have argued that political, economic, and educational institutions always have major influences on the sequencing and overall performance of the information revolution. The converse is also true; ICTs are starting to affect the structure, staffing, and performance of institutions in developing countries. The degree and the ways in which these institutions absorb the pounding waves of innovation associated with the new ICTs will greatly shape the position of these countries in the evolving global system and eventually the overall contours and performance of the international system itself.

The conventional wisdom, buttressed by a growing body of empirical work in the West, suggests that the introduction of ICTs like computers and the Internet encourages organizational decision makers to make the following changes within and between modern organizations, *given the right circumstances*:

• Flatten vertical hierarchies within organizations,
• Tilt the desired skill mix toward staff with higher educational levels,
• Regularize and rationalize work routines,
• Increase organizational transparency,
• Reduce some costs (communications) while raising others (hardware), and
• Facilitate the shift toward team management.

In addition to these mainly internal shifts, the introduction of the following techniques may alter external relations between organizations:

• Tighten links with upstream suppliers,
• Tighten links with clients and customers, and
• Tighten links with external competitors and allies.

These claims have been substantiated for some organizations operating under certain societal and institutional conditions. They have not been confirmed for all organizations under all circumstances. As one excellent report from the U.S.-based National Research Council insists, there is no such thing as "the" impact of "information technology" (NRC 1998a). There are only multiple possible impacts of particular applications under particular circumstances in particular organizations.

In general, most case-level analyses of formal organizations have been conducted within the most sophisticated organizational structures within the most advanced sectors of the most economically advanced countries. Most of the research has been done on business organizations in the United States, the United Kingdom, and the Scandinavian countries. Extrapolating to other very different conditions is unwarranted. Regrettably, far fewer analyses of the impact of ICTs on organizations in developing countries have been conducted, and the evidence we do have demonstrates rather different outcomes.

Since modern information technologies are not well absorbed in developing countries, ICT affects fewer institutions and affects them in more shallow ways than their counterparts in the developed world. Penetration is thin, and overall effect is modest. *The ICT-institutional dynamics probably parallel those in advanced countries but with important differences of scope, speed, depth, and impact.* The independent variable will differ between a typical developing and developed country.

Also, the "typical" organization in the "typical" developing country (already a big assumption) differs substantially from organizations in the typical developed countries. The same technology dropped into a modal developing country organization and a modal developed country organization will have very different consequences. Developing country organizations tend to have specialized features, as we saw above.

ICTs will possibly have consistent impacts on most developing country institutions, but some impacts may run counter to conventional wisdom. These institutions are often enmeshed in deep-seated patron-client ties where the ostensible organizational purpose can be displaced or redirected for implicit political, personal, or general-welfare purposes. Government organizations sometimes act as employment agencies of last resort since governments try to keep unemployment rates and the political costs of unemployment low. Personnel downsizing might not result from ICT diffusion if it runs counter to strong political imperatives. Political imperatives may blunt technical possibilities, and ICTs may serve, at least initially, to buttress elite power. Peter Loveluck (1996) makes this argument in his work on the effects of the Internet and other new technologies on the Communist Party power structure in China.

ICTs Affect Organizations and Sectors: Examples

Given the paucity of empirical data on these issues, I draw on my own research and that of others to give a few examples from various sectors and to speculate on possible ICT impacts on organizational structure. The evidence provides a cautionary tale about not reaching conclusions too quickly.

Telecenters in Developing Countries

Data on telecenters have been used to make a variety of points about ICTs and developing countries. One central message of the research on the community-based electronic center is the complicated, nonobvious relationships between core technologies and institutional structures. Telecenters provide one case study of the ways that modern communication technologies can vary substantially between locations.

The most reliable efforts in this area have been done by the International Development Research Centre (IDRC) of Canada. According to Steven Dorsey and Jacqueline Hess (1998, 3, as quoted in IDRC 1999, 121), "The developed world model of personal acquisition and ownership of technologies that facilitate access to and participation in the Information Age is not replicable in the foreseeable future in the developing world. Alternative models must be pursued." Given the low levels of per capita income and of effective demand in developing countries, this conclusion implies that new organizational forms must be found to launch even first-order ICT changes because ICTs cannot be embedded in homes and offices as they are in the developed world.

One institutional innovation is the telecenter. Telecenters are "variously called community learning centers, telecenters, telecottages, cybercafes, etc. [They are] facilities connected to telecommunications networks. They provide a range of public electronic services. At the low end, telecenters provide telephone, fax, and e-mail services. More sophisticated configurations provide Internet connectivity with specialized information retrieval or distance learning delivery" (Elmer 1999). While admitting that "the potential of computer-based technologies for solving problems of sustainable development is tremendous" because telecenters can address both technological access and equitable access, telecenters are still in such "an embryonic state, the impact of telecenters on sustainable development is largely untested. . . . Despite the lack of empirical evidence, however, the telecenter model appears to be a promising option for reducing knowledge gaps within developing countries" (Elmer 1999).

Telecenters have been established based on various organizational models—from fully funded government centers to entirely private-sector entrepreneurial ventures that must earn profits to survive. Ghana has some freestanding telecenters, and South Africa has some attached to municipal buildings like post offices. Telecenters can have large or small staffs. In two nearby villages, the institutional forms may differ substantially. According to researchers Samnel Kyabwe and Richard Kibomba (1999), the ownership and management are community based in one Ugandan village and semiprivate, semipublic in a neighboring village. These different structures attract different customers who use each telecenter for slightly different purposes. Each telecenter affects its community differently.

Given this organizational variability, the core technology package does not seem to completely determine institutional housing. Even though there are few (if any) reliable studies of ICT impacts on poor countries' institutions, especially beyond the more-studied corporate sector, the telecenters undercut the argument that ICTs automatically reshape developing country institutions. The imperatives of technology do not seem to require one best way of institutional design for providing ICT services. The right institutional design is shaped by a variety of factors, including the needs and purchasing power of the potential user population. This holds for smaller freestanding institutions like telecenters, as well as for ICTs embedded within larger, more complex institutions.

ICTs and Changing Organizational Dynamics among West African NGOs

The links between ICTs and organizational structure and performance emerge in interesting ways, as I discovered while leading a team of three senior researchers on a field mission in West Africa sponsored by the National Academy of Sciences. We were charged with designing a framework for assessing the impact of ICTs (especially the Internet) on developing societies. Because these technologies are new to Africa and were commercialized only in the mid-1990s, we quickly realized that we couldn't hope to document ICT impact on society—whether on entrepreneurship, capital accumulation, family structure, or labor patterns—because the ICTs were too new. We thought that we might, however, be able to see some impacts on the organizations that housed and used these tools. After interviewing ICT experts and senior people in government ministries, private firms, trade associations, and nongovernmental organizations, we concluded that at best we could begin to see modest impacts on institutional operations and on budgets of selected organizations, especially those in the NGO sector.

The institutions most affected in our small sample were NGOs that had close ties to overseas donors or NGOs that were local offices of overseas international organizations. Even among information ministries, government agencies in West Africa were rarely connected through intranets or the Internet. When computers were used in government, they were more likely to be employed for word processing or financial accounting. They were rarely networked. Universities were also severely limited by their ICT resources.

The ICT staff members for NGOs like ENDA (Environmental Development Action) or ONG (Organisations Non Gouvernementales) in Senegal and for think tanks in Ghana reported that they were able to substantially reduce communication costs, often by one-third to one-half (NRC 1998b). The local staff also reported closer ties to other like-minded international groups, finding themselves more in the loop and better able to participate in international movements. These ties helped them to be better informed about the ways that global issues affect local interests. They reported greater possibilities for cross-national policy and political campaigns.

We found an ICT diffusion pattern that may have implications for institutional restructuring and performance. West Africa's communication network seems to have diffused in the following manner:

1. Initial ties reached to overseas headquarters, affiliates, and funders;

2. Links were created to the headquarters of other NGOs in countries with similar interests;

3. Ties were made to colleagues in the organization through intranets;

4. Ties were developed with organizational clients; and

5. Links were slowly developed to an organization's field offices in other countries.

This diffusion pattern may indicate how organizations adjust their institutions to these new ICT opportunities and suggests that poor nations are not likely to experience major ICT-prompted institutional changes in the immediate future.

In the more sophisticated nations of the developing world like Brazil or Korea, the Internet and intranets appear to be having move direct institutional consequences that are more in line with what we witness in developed economies. Some leaders in the corporate sector in developing countries are seizing the implications of electronic commerce and committing resources to retooling company operations and structures to take advantage of e-commercial opportunities.

ICTs also seem to be affecting the structure and organization of traditional media. Journalists and activists in developing regions are excited about being better able to meld the low cost of information of the Internet with the reach and accessibility of traditional media like radio or television. Alongside the crumbling state-owned publishing and broadcasting monopolies, one sees the rapid growth of new independent radio and television stations. Some of these are community-owned, others were started by private entrepreneurs, but they all provide new sources of information. To the extent that these changes are diffusing beyond just a small ICT-intensive core, they may be more important for authoritarian and repressive developing countries than for developed countries.

All of this suggests that with the right leadership, vision, and institutional adjustments, some poor countries can begin to reduce political authoritarianism and economic poverty by effectively deploying the right ICTs. This may be true within limits, and some poor countries with poor institutions are making great advances with the Internet, the World

Wide Web, and telecoms. But their leadership's capacity to use ICTs to make quick institutional fixes is still limited, even under the best circumstances.

A New Culture of Communications

I have been struck by the number of respondents I interviewed in Africa, Asia, and Latin America who, on their own, used the term *culture of information* or *culture of knowledge* to characterize the nature of the challenges they face. They report that success is not simply a question of using imported content or hardware. The challenge is for national leaders to foster a new set of attitudes, expectations, and values that encourage people to lean toward the creation and diffusion of knowledge (personal communication 1998).

The term *knowledge culture* suggests a degree of difficulty more daunting than *technology transfer*. The latter is mechanistic and predetermined and minimizes human agency. The former is organic and open-ended and assumes human agency within a particular structural context. India's showpiece city of Bangalore did not become Silicon City because of technology transfers. It developed a special culture nurtured by leadership, institutional development, and the availability of values, attitudes, and behaviors that could support a Silicon City. Just as the indigenous local cultures of Santa Clara and Cambridge could be manipulated by information champions to support innovation, diffusion, and local ICT sustainability, all developing countries must create a local ICT-enabling environment that draws on traditional and modern strengths.

The challenge for leaders is to create a hospitable environment for creating a continuous application of intellectual energy, transforming it into knowledge, and distributing it and redistributing it again to more and more potential users. This is the great insight of Manuel Castells (1998): the information revolution is a process by which institutions, groups, and individuals interact to redesign the production and distribution of ICT services. These interactions cannot be mandated or forced but can be guided and facilitated with vision and leadership.

The Politics of Information and Communication Technologies

Politics is a critical element missing from current ICT diffusion analysis. When politics is omitted, thin, static, and ultimately unconvincing portrayals are presented as reality. I argue that without sufficient national political will and support, a country cannot start or sustain an information revolution.

The classical definition of *politics* is "who gets what, why, and how." Politics occurs in all venues, not simply at the ballot box or the campaign rally. Terms like *office politics*, *bureaucratic politics*, *party politics*, or *big money politics* suggest the wide range of activities in which "who gets what" matters a great deal. And when the services or goods being distributed are scarce, considerable competition and conflict can occur. Information and communication technologies fit easily under the rubric of scarce resources, especially in developing countries.

Politics under the Old Regime

Until recently, the politics of ICT was a rarified and elitist affair. The determination of who got what ICT services was a technical and administrative matter and was not subject to a lot of consistent, high-visibility politicking. At moments, politics seemed to dominate, but on the whole, the politics of ICT lacked the visibility of other substantive policy areas like land redistribution, abortion, or education. The presence or absence of information and communication technologies in developing countries did not mobilize political masses because services were scarce and were not affordable by most people. The politics of ICT in these countries became the politics of patronage. It meant knowing senior people at the relevant ministry, relying on friends at the state-owned telecommunications company, and earning political patronage in the local branch office. From most accounts, politics also meant a lot of bribing. In the Congo, the official waiting list for a telephone line was ten years. The conditions of extreme scarcity set up perverse incentives: customers offered bribes to jump the ten-year queue, but as bribes increased, the incentive to expand service decreased.

The politics of broadcasting or print media differed somewhat but followed a similar pattern. In most developing countries, television and radio stations were owned and operated by government agencies or by families that were dependent on the government. Protests against censorship and state control may have occurred, but they were intermittent and often ineffective. The politics of broadcasting was more open than the politics of telecommunications, but it too was an affair of citizens (or competitors) against a stable and insulated monopoly.

In both telecom and broadcast industries, there were always some implicit pressures on central government elites to guarantee the delivery of public services like telephones. The business community and local governments exerted pressure on national governments to distribute more efficient ICT services. Political tensions were greater in federal states like Brazil and India than in centralized countries like China. Most transactions occurred through elite interactions between the Ministry of Communications, the operating company (usually a state-owned corporation), and other relevant government agencies like the Treasury Department. NGOs and citizens groups were rarely involved in distributional decisions.

Iron Triangles and Policy Monopolies

There are several ways to characterize the old politics of ICT. Scholars like Morton Halperin (Halperin, Scheffer, and Small 1992) refer to these tightly circumscribed interactions as *bureaucratic politics*, where the major players are not political parties or NGOs but big government institutions. Another useful term for these interactions is "iron triangle," where central political elites are linked with legislators and lobbyists into an iron triangle of political action that works to exclude others. Frank R. Baumgartner, Bryan D. Jones, and Michael Macleod (2000) use the term *policy monopolies* to describe particular policy domains that resist pressure from outside groups. Such monopolists make claims for exclusivity based on their expertise in issue areas that tend to be difficult and complicated.

I have found that this tightly circumscribed form of politics is especially characteristic of a certain type of policy issue that I term an *e-issue* (Wilson 2000). E-issues include the politics of energy, the politics of the environment, and now the politics of e-commerce and e-government. E-issues are characterized by their technological and cognitive complexity and their sudden appearance on the agenda of senior policy elites. These forms exist in developed countries and are especially elitist affairs in developing countries. Leon Lindberg (1977) points out that, because of the expertise of these elites, their hierarchical control, and their ability to mobilize resources, interorganizational coalitions can generate dominant policy outcomes. They can increase their individual and collective resources and eliminate conflict and cooperation by controlling the agenda and excluding other actors.

Thus, the politics of ICT in developing countries was rarely a populist affair, nor was it politically neutral. Powerful forces that could penetrate the iron triangle were heard; less powerful voices remained excluded. For the most part, who got what and when was determined by elites in capital-intensive and urban-based units that included both public actors and a few private ones.

At its heart, the politics of the information revolution, therefore, involve established elites that operate within iron triangles and that are pressured by newcomers to alter their substantive policy positions (on issues like state ownership, monopolies, and skewed distribution) and to restructure their engagements with outsiders. Sometimes state elites change their tunes quickly, but most often they do not. It is still an empirical question as to whether and to what extent organizational and substantive changes have occurred in any given country. The overall global trend is decisively toward restructuring substance and access, but national and sectoral patterns and the paths to them are quite idiosyncratic. Figure 2.2 shows two paths that countries might follow as they move toward greater competition and private ownership.

It should be kept in mind that between the mid-1960s and late 1980s, the old individual national ICT regimes existed in a much more restrictive and constrained global political environment. The World Bank and other international bodies supported domestic state-owned monopolies. Most countries in Latin America and Africa were military or civilian dictatorships, and Asia was not much better. Repressive political economies discouraged popular mobilization for greater communication. Debt-blasted economies meant middle-class growth was sluggish. If iron

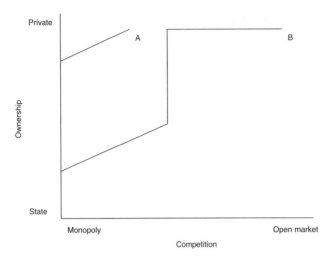

Figure 2.2
Different Paths to ICT Reform
Source: World Bank (1999).

triangles governed ICT, iron triangles governed many areas of public policy.

A Politics of Transition

I agree with Steven K. Vogel's (1996) characterization that the liberal reforms of telecoms in the 1980s and 1990s were the work of senior elites within the state—the president or prime minister's office and the ministers of communications and information and their staff. Interest groups and outside reformers may have proposed change, but the state elites actually selected alternative actions. As Vogel demonstrates, however, state elites that liberalized deliberately robbed themselves of some of their formal powers in telecoms.

My research findings also agree with Peter Cowhey (1990) that the substantive changes in policy toward greater liberalization reflected new patterns of political mobilization among a variety of important economic actors, particularly in the business sector. The outsiders' own political clout grew relative to the state's, and their incentives to push their public-sector counterparts to do new things or do old things in new ways was decidedly greater by the end of the growth spurts of the

1990s. Confronted by growing competitive pressures, business elites had both the motives and means to press for liberalization. A slow accretion of people into the middle classes of the developing world also added some demographic heft to businesses' demands. The old regime of rules and regulations rested on an often implicit coalition of state-owned telecommunications supporters and through the political inaction of the unserved classes. Although public ICT policies are in the first instance crafted and designed by a small group of technocratic elites, the sustainability of policies and programs rests largely on coalitional and constituency bases. Unless and until substantial elite political realignment occurs, major policy changes will not occur. When they do occur, they will not be easily sustained until a new coalition is crafted.

Peter Cowhey makes a parallel argument to explain the "big bang" of telecommunications liberalization in advanced capitalist countries (Cowhey 1990). He claims that deregulation in the United States resulted in large measure from the slow crumbling of an old political coalition built on AT&T's telephone monopoly position. Based on the technologies and commercial conditions at the time, the policy and institutional arrangements of the old regime worked well through the early 1980s. After the technological changes of the 1980s, however, globalization and hypercompetitiveness began to alter coalition members' calculations. Especially notable was the pressure on earnings of large ICT consumer corporations that felt compelled to lower basic costs to remain globally competitive. Cowhey demonstrates that at the same time other corporations (MCI and Sprint most notably) began to challenge the domestic, quasi-public, AT&T monopoly. The combination of an outsider coalition of would-be suppliers, anxious customers, and ideologically supportive legislators and jurists undermined the old monopoly rules in the United States. These trends were visible globally, as when the United States pressed Brazil to eliminate barriers in its domestic information processing markets.

What Cowhey (1990) and J. P. Singh (1999) underestimate in the 1980s and 1990s is the constant direct external pressure felt by developing countries to change their domestic regimes. Among the international constituencies for liberal reforms in developing countries, none was more relentless in its push for change than the World Bank. The World Bank's ICT impact varies by precise issue area and country. India resisted Bank blandishments more than Mozambique and Ghana. Poor African nations proved more vulnerable than wealthier Asian ones. The Bank had been the biggest single lender for telecommunications infrastructure to developing countries. Many poor countries relied heavily on Bank staff workers to substitute for their own thin technical expertise. Staff and consultants did everything from providing policy guidance to designing placement of telephone lines.

The Bank's role is discussed in greater detail in chapter 7. Let me say here that Singh and others who draw conclusions based mainly on the experiences of large Asian countries minimize the determinative role of the Bank in the diffusion of liberal reforms in other poor countries. The Bank played the role of a powerful and consistent member of the core ruling coalition that determined policy priorities in Africa, Asia, the Caribbean, and Latin America. Bank Structural Adjustment Programs (SAPs), backed by big conditional loans, shaped decisively the reform agenda in Africa and the Caribbean, often in great detail. Telecommunications was often a major component, as in Ghana and Senegal. Although Singh (1999, 195) and I disagree on the relative weight of Bank influence, we agree on its political role. He writes of India, "After 1991 it is safe to argue that an 'international' liberal coalition continued to strengthen in India comprised of large business users, domestic and international businesses engaged in the Indian market, multilateral institutions like the World Bank and the WTO, and foreign governments. Large users, in particular, lobbied the Indian government fiercely through their service organizations." Singh insists on modeling these international actors as interest groups that do have impacts upon domestic political processes (Singh 1999). For poor countries, these institutions often had determinative impacts (as I argue in chapter 7) that went beyond ICT issues. As countless scholars have demonstrated, when the debt crisis and global stagnation led developing country economies on a downward spiral for a decade or more, the international financial institutions stepped in aggressively to press orthodox financial and economic reforms across the board, including in the telecoms sector.

Personal Politics: A Mixture of Motives

In much of the ICT literature, actors' motivations are seen as an exogenous variable determined outside the model. Underlying these analyses is the basic assumption that ICT actors share identical concerns—to see ICTs diffused rapidly. Yet human motivations are more complicated than they are portrayed in the models. Outside the world of technology determinism and neoclassical economics, women and men are driven by many motives and rarely act on one dimension alone. Because societal actors respond to more than one set of incentives, by factoring in multiple motivations, we gain a better appreciation for the limits and possibilities of the information revolution in poor countries. Based on my own observations, several important motivations are at work among central-state elites in their restructuring of the information and communications sectors:

• To meet the goals and responsibilities of the institution in which the elites work;

• To promote and advance the use of modern ICT technologies and services;

• To preserve (and if possible extend) their current institutional authority and privilege;

• To protect the interests and authority of the current regime in power;

• All other things being equal, to allocate the ownership, control, consumption, and other benefits of reforms and new technologies first to NGOs, private-sector groups and individuals who support the regime;

• To protect the nation (and regime) from overseas threats to its political sovereignty, cultural integrity, and economic opportunities; and

• To delay or block the introduction of new technologies that threaten to empower their political opposition.

This list reflects the imperatives and priorities of those closest to the incumbents in power, whether political or institutional.

The incumbents are most often the defenders of the status quo, but other political actors have different priorities and motives. Most frequently, the more progressive and indeed radical innovators who challenge the status quo have the following goals:

• To advance the interests of their countrymen by helping to bring them greater access to the new networked technologies like the Internet;

• To advance their own interests by moving into a position to influence the future evolution of the technologies and the services they provide;

• To do battle with the forces of state control at every level to achieve wider ICT diffusion (or when appropriate, to ally with the state to promote diffusion); and

• For survival's sake, to refrain from overly antagonizing the prerogatives and authorities of the current regime in power (unless necessary to achieve goal 1).

In other words, the same base and exalted motives that drive human beings in other sectors of the political economy drive them in the ICT sectors. At the end of the day, the information revolution is fought over the allocation of scarce resources and the rules and practices that guide those allocations. These fights over rules and practices occur among individuals and groups seeking to advance their ideational and material interests. They do not occur among technologies or even among large aggregates (like "society"). The actual path of diffusion in any country reflects the negotiations among elites with these varied interests.

The Politics of Information Champions

Employing a modified structural framework helped me uncover an interesting if unexpected political reality of the information revolution—the influence of deeply committed local information and communication technology innovators and groups. Although my ICT research began by investigating economic and political structures in developing countries, its most surprising finding was the major role played by individuals. The interactions between the structural level and the individual level proved to be intriguing. In every country I studied, individuals and groups championed new ICTs and aggressively pressed to change the old statist rules and practices. These individuals kept "intruding" into the research that was tailored to institutions and structures, and I was forced to adjust my methods in response to the new findings.

The individual biographies of these information champions make fascinating reading, as do their insights into the processes of social change, available through what C. Wright Mills (2001, 5–6) called the "sociological imagination," which allows one "to grasp history and biography and the relations between the two in society" and to "understand the larger historical scene in terms of its meaning for the inner life and the external career of a variety of individuals." Two aspects of these information champions seem especially salient—the personal characteristics of each individual and the characteristics of the surrounding social networks they collectively constructed.

The Personal Characteristics of Information Champions

Information champions are generally individuals who press the existing rules, procedures, and institutions to encourage the wider distribution of ICT services by introducing innovative technologies and practices. They are similar to what Everett M. Rogers (1995) calls "early innovators" and appear early in the process of social innovation in a variety of institutions—public, private, and civil.

Exactly who saw ICT opportunities on the horizon that others did not see? Who were the first information champions? For my research, I used a reputational technique to answer this question and learn about these individuals. I accumulated names from diverse sources, including published reports, well-known ICT institutions, and overseas nationals. I constructed initial lists and conducted interviews with people who in turn provided additional names during the interviews. In every case, I asked interviewees to name the top five or ten most influential individuals involved in Internet diffusion in their country. Once identified, I interviewed many of the top champions and found that they shared similar features.

Each information champion showed common features of education and training. Most early innovators were *educated abroad*, often in the United States, and many worked overseas for several years. While abroad they were exposed to the whiz-bang gizmos and enhanced services of the new technologies. They were exposed to these new applications in a cultural and institutional context that encouraged and rewarded experimentation and change. These individuals were also trained in *technical fields* like electrical engineering and computer science.

Second, the early innovators shared certain attitudes and values. After years abroad, these wanderers typically returned home to their country driven by a compelling _sense of duty_ and because they recognized unique _opportunities_ to do something socially important and personally rewarding. Personal wealth was rarely their top priority. Respondent after respondent reported the twin motivations of duty and opportunity, especially those who returned in the early to mid-1990s before the Internet's commercial possibilities were fully visible. Most champions demonstrated an almost _missionary zeal_ about the work they were doing and the benefits it could bring their people. This helps to explain why many of the leading Internet innovators left lucrative jobs and comfortable conditions in the Western world to return home and labor under difficult circumstances.

A dominant theme in the information champions' professional and personal lives was their sense that they were participating in a _global social movement_ of great significance. During graduate school and their early professional lives, these individuals interacted with similarly minded people around the world, as well as with citizens of their host country. They also attended international conferences by organizations like the World Internet Society, where the zeitgeist of benevolent globalism was in the air.

The champions saw themselves as a part of a global trend, but they were driven by local imperatives: they thought globally and acted locally. In dozens of conversations with information champions from many countries, I grew to understand that they were deeply motivated by a kind of nationalist altruism. Their greatest enthusiasm was for bringing these powerful new technologies back to their own countries. Like earlier modernizers in eighteenth- and nineteenth-century Europe described by Alexander Gerschenkron (1962) and others, these individuals were driven by the recognition of the tremendous potentials of the technologies and the difficult realities of their country. These individuals saw the digital divide firsthand before it became a fashionable term in the West. Like Russians returning to St. Petersburg from Paris in the 1800s, they knew the advanced state of the new technologies and the extreme backwardness of their own populations.

The *social backgrounds* of the information champions were also similar. A disproportionate number of those I interviewed came from middle-class families, their parents often professionals who worked in the fields of medicine, teaching, law, or engineering. Individuals from very rich or very poor backgrounds were conspicuously absent. Their parents seemed to enjoy a kind of professional autonomy, a taste for which they passed on to their children.

While demonstrably civic minded, these early information champions possessed a mix of *altruism and idealism* and *political pragmatism.* Whether they learned their pragmatism from their practical training as scientists and technologists, from a professional ethos, or from local conditions or whether it was inherent in their personalities, the information champions recognized that some very practical political steps were required.

Whatever idealistic naïveté the champions might have maintained abroad was typically dashed when they returned home and confronted the institutional and political realities of the telecommunications and broadcast iron triangles. In the early 1990s (and still today in many developing countries), the local telecommunications sector leaders were uninformed about the Internet's possibilities. To the degree they knew about cell phones, the Internet, and pagers, they were often extremely suspicious or outright opposed to their diffusion. In nearly every conference, consultant's report, newspaper interview, or conversation of the period, the Internet innovators decried the deeply held conservatism of telecom managers and ministerial officials. The innovators had few illusions about the opposition of the anti-innovators. The senior officials of the monopolistic, hierarchical, centralized state-run telephone companies shared none of the positive excitement over the capacity of the Internet to destroy hierarchies, promote competition, and promote distributed outcomes. They were, after all, in the monopoly business.

The information champions shared a final feature. Confronted with huge institutional and political barriers to rapid and effective ICT diffusion, the champions came to share a set of *well-defined policy goals.* They knew what was required to make their technology dreams a societal reality. They were not driven by strong political ideologies of left or right, and most eschewed a clear ideological position. They relied on pragmatic reasoning about what policies were required domestically and internationally and about how to employ solutions. For Chinese, Brazilians, and Jordanians to use the Internet, the price must fall. For the Internet's price to fall, the state-run monopolies must lower their prices. For the state-run monopolies to lower their prices, they needed competition, more private-sector pressures, and more consumer demands. In other words, state monopolies had to change their structure and behaviors. Who would do the restructuring? Some information champions became information revolutionaries when they realized that collective action was required to restructure the old and invent the new. This was a process of building informed constituencies as much as redesigning information technologies.

The information champions built constituencies around the world. Their views reflected similar institutional and policy realities—ignorance, suspicion, and opposition. These individuals reached similar conclusions about the institutional changes that were necessary to advance their cause: they needed to rebalance the structures of ICT subsectors, especially the balances between public and private, domestic and foreign, monopolistic and competitive, and centralized and distributed administration. Adopting these "radical" positions moved some beyond analysis and research to advocacy. Information revolutionaries were bent on radically and actively restructuring old rules and regulations to make way for the knowledge society. The revolutionaries were pushy activists who didn't take no for an answer, and they allied themselves with nongovernmental organizations or other institutions in their countries that would help them advance their cause.

In one developing country after another, we see waves of committed ICT missionaries returning to their communities with the new tools of an information age. Most wanted to "do their own thing"—to stay in touch with friends, to chat online, to build computer labs in their local colleges, and sometimes even to start their own companies. Many of these individuals found that even to "do their own thing" required getting the local state monopolies to provide infrastructure support and services, whether leased lines or new telephones. Since in many instances the traditional suppliers were hostile to such ideas, many ICT enthusiasts became ICT champions who grew into information revolutionaries.

For these people to be personally successful, they were going to have to change their governments, which required that they band together with others. Some of these individual features were not unique to the ICT sector, as Rogers (1995) shows.

The Social Network Characteristics of Information Champions

The information champions' recognition of the political nature of their goals and their need for kindred spirits led small groups of like-minded people to come together to pursue common goals. They overcame the substantial initial barriers (Olson 1971), and their strong beliefs in modernity and later, their selective benefits, maintained the networks. These social networks were a kind of social capital that created trust across individuals and institutions. The collective actions of these individuals created new, actionable knowledge, which they and others use to innovate in ICTs, as occurred in Silicon Valley.

These ICT champions were especially visible in value-added subsectors like mobile telephony, paging, and the Internet. ICT champions were less visible in the reforms of existing large-scale, state-led broadcasting and telephone monopolies. The clear successes of the Internet champions reflect the newness of the technologies. The new value-added services expanded into a relatively empty social space devoid of dense institutional architecture. The mandarins of the old services were comfortable with long-term clients, protective of their constituencies, and linked closely to their upstream equipment suppliers. The underpopulated political and institutional terrain of the new technologies was, by contrast, available to smaller, politically weak, and institutionally innovative groups. Because the new distributed networks encountered no existing Institutes of Internet Policy or Ministries of Paging, they were able to develop unhindered. As one ICT revolutionary noted, "For years we were so small that we were beneath their radar screen." Government officials therefore did not initially bother them. Economic barriers to entry for new, smaller firms also were low. So new entrepreneurs needed neither political capital to break the barriers erected by the political elites nor high levels of financial capital. By the time the Internet appeared on the radar screens of senior officials, it seemed like small potatoes when compared to the billion-dollar players in telephone land lines and satellites.

As I interviewed the early ICT instigators in developing countries, several salient dimensions emerged from our discussions. The initial ICT coalitions were similar in size, coherence, group initiative, and group membership. Members shared individual traits and also group traits. In each country, the initial networks that formed were relatively small. These people got to know one another when searching for advice on technical matters or attending promotional events. Small groups are easier to maintain than large ones (Olson 1971).

The size of the country did not greatly affect the size of the founding group. In a country of 1.2 billion people, the consensus on the list of the top ten innovators is remarkably consistent. When one inquires in a small country like Senegal, the lists provided by interviewees are also quite consistent. The small initial networks were constructed by people who were technically trained and occupied overlapping professions in different institutions. The early institutions tended to be research centers, universities, and selected government ministries like education or science and technology.

There were some interesting differences among the initial ICT coalitions, as well. The coherence of the networks in various countries differed substantially, reflecting the incentives for individuals encapsulated in their particular institutions (universities, government ministries, and firms) to break out from their organization and cooperate across them to form mutually supportive networks. In some countries, champions created clubs of like-minded people; the founding of a local chapter of the Internet Society is a good indicator of group cooperation (or in some instances, like Thailand, of internal group conflicts). Senegal formed close-knit networks of advocates, some of whom came together to create a new publication that would serve the community. In other settings, individuals were socially aware of each other, met occasionally, but didn't create an autonomous separate group outside their institutional homes. In some circumstances, these were not groups but individuals who were similarly situated in a variety of institutions and networks and who held common values, pursued common goals, used similar strategies, and acted in parallel ways to achieve their goals. These should be characterized as more of a dispersed, informal network of convenience than a formal organization. I return to this idea of intermediate bodies in chapter 7.

The similar *membership structure* of the groups proved a curious feature. In countries where a collective did emerge, as in Morocco and Brazil, it often included one or two people from technical universities, one or two people from NGOs, and someone from a relevant ministry or parastatal body. Someone always had close personal ties to the office of the president, prime minister, or top communication officials. This feature proved important in moving the Internet reform agenda forward.

The original impetus for cross-institutional communication came from many sources. In most developing countries that I visited, a small group of people began to meet in the late 1980s and early 1990s in informal meetings, whether in Moroccan cafes or Senegalese universities. Distinctions can be found between top-down network initiatives (which occurred in places like China) and bottom-up network initiatives (which occurred in places like Senegal).

A country's structural and institutional features don't automatically translate into particular organizational forms for the networks of champions. But substantial cross-level consistencies exist. For example, the behavior of the information revolutionaries in China very much reflects the top-down, highly authoritarian structure of the Communist Party system and its closely controlled statist institutions. The regime simply does not permit autonomous interest groups to operate. Instead, the Internet champions' interactions occurred in a series of special state commissions and joint research and ministry initiatives, with the state-owned ICT corporations and the state security bureau taking growing roles. In Brazil, the highly federalized institutional structure, combined with an unequal economic structure, is reflected in the high mobility of the same small group of champions across many different institutions in a relatively short period of time, often in different regions.

While economic structure and institutions set broad common parameters for individual behavior and group dynamics in these countries, considerable individuality exists within each national political culture. Senegal and Ghana are both poor, agricultural-based economies with semidemocratic political structures, and yet substantial differences are found in each of its ICT communities. Reflecting elite structure and culture, as well as a French colonial heritage, the Senegalese research, commercial, and governmental innovators were in close and consistent cooperation. In Ghana, the intersectoral interactions were less frequent, less inclusive, and less cooperative.

It is still early to make the leap from describing emerging social networks to concluding that a particular network configuration shapes performance outcomes. Greater system heterogeneity, however (more members across more institutions, such as universities, firms, government, and NGOs, with greater communication) does seem to produce greater technology diffusion and sophistication. I describe these national systems in greater detail in subsequent chapters.

These patterns of innovation and elite political interaction demonstrate a number of features that scholars have noted in other contexts. In his study "Understanding the Role of Leadership in Economic Policy Reform," Joe Wallis (1999) points out that major policy paradigm shifts of the type I am describing occur when performance anomalies occur that "shouldn't" occur according to elite expectations and past performance. His review of the experience of structural adjustment programs finds that poor performance in one area occasions questions and a search for quick fixes. Policy makers begin with ad hoc experimentation to eliminate the anomaly (as was done by the World Bank when it led economic reforms in developing countries) until it becomes apparent that a piecemeal approach is not fixing the problems. The problems are then recognized as being systemic, and officials reluctantly turn to comprehensive alternatives that they hope will be more effective. This was very much the experience of ICT policy diffusion.

Under these conditions, new leaders *might* emerge who are driven by their formal roles and their policy ambitions. These new leaders might advocate the reconstruction of public policy on the basis of a new paradigm, provided that the paradigm is both coherent and authoritative. Wallis (1999) points out that, in patrimonial states that rely on strong patron-client ties, these changes will almost invariably threaten well-entrenched and influential groups that benefit directly from the current state of affairs and that actively oppose reforms. Based on his analysis of policy changes in New Zealand, Wallis concludes that these dynamics are best described through a "conspiracy theory" that captures the combative, strategic, and occasionally secretive behaviors of conspiracy groups.

This conclusion comes close to my understanding of cyber-revolutionaries. Wallis (1999, 42) defines the conspiracy group as having "shared goals among two or more with shared substantive views." These individuals provide "coherent policy leadership" that is highly focused, and they are "willing to use their own authority and political skills to overcome and circumvent the resistance to reform generated by special interest groups; to bring bureaucrats in line; to lead public opinion by taking firm positions on contentious issues." Wallis also emphasizes, quite correctly, the collective nature of the reform project. Rarely does one person achieve all that is required. He notes that a division of labor is involved in the provision of leadership so that not every individual needs to fulfill every task required.

Within this political context—where a handful of innovative ICT activists struggle to effect substantial reform—others have identified complementary patterns. Everett M. Rogers's (1995) rich and suggestive sociological work on patterns of innovation across a variety of different sectors finds that the process of innovation and diffusion is marked by the engagement of different groups of individuals. He, too, has analyzed the personal characteristics of each group, their attitudes toward risk, their salient values, their communications behaviors, and their personal relationships. His pioneering work remains useful in the study of ICT diffusion, although in a later study on ICT diffusion in the banking industry he modifies his earlier conclusions somewhat by insisting on the importance of minimal threshold levels needed for those technologies to achieve rapid diffusion. Drawing on observations of innovation in a variety of activities, Rogers finds that at the start of the innovation process a few individuals are willing to assume the high risks associated with employing new technologies. Typically, this group of innovators constitutes only 2.5 percent of a given population. Later, other groups— early adopters (10 to 15 percent), early majority (33 percent), late major-ity (33 percent), and laggards (10 to 20 percent)—are eventually willing to try out the new techniques. By then the risks are lower since some of the bugs have been worked out, but the rewards may also be lower.

Rogers's (1995) work on patterns of innovation is often cited as evidence of a universal diffusion pattern, and it is persuasive. It is also quite suggestive of what may be occurring among information champions or information revolutionaries, who seem to overlap with the innovators. Jeffrey C. Fine and Jaeques Rostenne (1998, 5) have applied this approach imaginatively to East Africa:

> Empirical studies indicate that Innovators tend to have a much higher than average level of entrepreneurship, income, and often, but not necessarily, formal education. Innovators' two most distinctive traits are that they crave innovation and that they are "outsiders." They are not part of any establishment or in-crowd. Consequently, they are less affected by social risks, ranging from social isolation to ostracism and downright opposition, which are associated with transgressing accepted behavior and embracing innovations. Also, Innovators see change as a means of self-fulfillment. In terms of diffusing innovations, Innovators constitute a critical catalyst that must be present but managed with care. Innovators will often volunteer to assist in the process of diffusion. However, their outside status can severely limit their usefulness beyond the very first stages of the process.

As useful as Rogers's (1995) approach may be, it is derived mainly from U.S. experiences in a few sectors, and one should not blindly extrapolate from it. We know that many of these ICT innovations are carried by private-sector elites. We know that entrepreneurial activities in much of the developing world occur within a complicated social mosaic marked by sharp ethnic boundaries. Given these societal boundaries, Rogers's pattern of innovation may not necessarily hold in countries where one ethnic group dominates the public sector and another the private. We don't know if these new communication and information technologies will remold these diffusion patterns in new countries in new ways, either to accelerate or retard their diffusion.

The Contributions of Leadership and Vision to the Information Revolution

Understanding leadership is especially important in the current conditions of radical change within the global information and communication technology industries. During periods of major structural change, such as the one we are experiencing, the contribution of good leadership is substantially magnified (as are the costs of bad leadership) (Minitrom 1997). Leadership means appealing to others to convince them to follow a route to a particular set of goals. In this author's interview with Robert Galvin, the visionary leader of Motorola offered a concise and insightful definition of leadership in the ICT field. Drawing on his many years of experience, he noted traditional features like charisma and knowledge but stated that the most important task of the leader is "taking people to a place they didn't know they needed to go." This simple formulation captures the heart of leadership. Implicit in Galvin's formulation is this: "and providing the means to let them get there." Leadership involves mobilizing resources to achieve strategic ends. Effective leaders provide the psychological and professional bridges between previous period of certainty and later periods of wider agreement.

Many years ago the "father of organizational sciences," Chester Barnard, defined organizational leadership as "the indispensable social essence that gives common meaning to a common purpose, that creates the incentive that makes other incentives effective, that infuses the subjective aspects of countless decisions with consistency in a changing environment" (Barnard 1989). A number of well-known examples of this kind of leadership come to mind in the ICT field. William Hewlett and David Packard's innovations in organizational structure and incentives for their new company made them wealthy and set new organizational standards for the growing semiconductors industry. Andrew Grove, Intel chair, realized that institutions needed to change in order to use technology effectively and that change would arise from visionary and consistent leadership. John Chambers at Cisco has led his company from a traditional to a virtual organization. His company was restructured, but it could be restructured only with a visionary leader at the helm.

Leadership in ICT is important the world over, from Tata in India, to Koos Becker and Thabo Mbeki in South Africa. The top leadership of Lee Kuan Yew and then Goh Chok Tong in Singapore gave the world its very first ICT vision in 1992, before U.S. information champions crafted their own. After observing the United States and developing countries, I noted that five distinct types of ICT leadership emerged from my research—promotional, issue, ideological, structural, and political. Each of these leadership traits is important, and they tend to be complementary, not exclusionary. Although analytically they are distinct, in the real world they blend together: they rarely are all demonstrated in the same person. But successful ICT initiatives, in companies or countries, manage to identify leaders to pursue all these aspects.

Promotional Leadership
The leader promotes the general idea of the importance of the global information revolution to his or her followers. The message from the leader is, "Pay attention to these big new changes in ICT. They are neither ephemeral nor hype. They will affect your life in a variety of ways." This is where vision enters to link the call to arms with broader needs and goals. A senior leader who is not an official within the ICT sector but carries broad political responsibilities is often the person to fill this role. The prototype for this ICT leader may be U.S. Vice President Al Gore, who for years was consistent in his call for an information superhighway. South African President Thabo Mbeki played a similar role in his country, and Prime Minister Dr. Mahathir bin Mohamed has radically reformed Malaysia's ICT sector through his personality, his control over resources, and his constant repetition of ICT's importance for all Malaysians. This kind of leadership is especially important early in the reform and diffusion process.

Issue Leadership
Certain leaders stake out a particular position on one or two ICT issues (such as distance education, privatization, access, or universal service) and push them forward relentlessly. Others may take opposing views. The leader presses his case forward, publicizing the superiority of his position. The tenacity of Brazilian telecoms Minister Sergio Motte is legendary, as was that of the Pate Dewang Mehta, executive director of the Delhi-based National Association of Software and Services Companies (NASSCOM), who pressed tirelessly for greater government support for software. His slogan was, "The Indian government must go from red tape to red carpet for its ICT companies," and he believed the government had, for the most part, heeded the private-sector leadership on this

issue. Minister Hu Qili in China became known as a bull dog who aggressively pushed for competition and diversification, and he pushed these themes constantly.

Ideological Leadership

Ideological leadership frames important ICT concepts. For example, if ICT is defined as an economic issue, it will mobilize one constituency, creating a particular kind of agenda. If ICT is defined as a matter of national sovereignty under assault, other constituencies and institutions are mobilized. This work of defining the issue is done by government officials and senior people in the research and scientific communities (such as those in MIMOS Malaysia) or by intellectuals in the popular press. Will leaders frame ICT issues so that citizens view them as directly relevant to their other concerns? These are issues relevant to ideological leadership.

Structural Leadership

Structural leadership is one of the most important and least understood aspects of ICT leadership and one of the most difficult aspects of leadership to achieve. This form of leadership seeks to redefine the rules of economic structures to make them fit current national needs. This happens in the ICT sector as in other markets and sectors. Such rules include whether ICT ownership will be a public or private monopoly or open market? As older structures collapse during a period of transition, control over the writing of new rules is up for grabs, and each party seeks to redefine them in its favor. Collectives typically provide this kind of leadership, whether specially appointed blue-ribbon commissions, interagency task forces, or political parties. Often, the top leader in the country must step forward and provide adequate political protection to allow individual and collective leaders to act without their restructuring initiatives getting blasted out of the water. The Chinese "informatization" strategy is one example.

Political Leadership

To advance ICT visions and truly bring about favorable ICT conditions, leaders must establish constituencies and coalitions in support of their positions. Political leadership in the ICT sector means explaining to particular constituencies how their conditions will improve by following the path the leader creates and then actively mobilizing them. The effective political leader will also be able to maintain a coalition to mobilize his constituency.

Leadership and Vision

Closely related to ICT leadership is ICT vision. Vision has proved important in explaining why some countries and companies move forward in the information revolution and others stagnate. In the ICT context, vision is a body of arguments or doctrine that conveys effectively and coherently the ways that ICT services can advance the core values and goals of a given group, institution, or society. An ICT vision describes the present, offers an attractive image of the future, and provides a way for people to move successfully to that future. An ICT vision is not a vision of freestanding technology. It does not emphasize shiny new toys but suggests ways that people can use the application of new tools to solve basic organizational tasks or broad national objectives. In other words, an ICT vision advances a broader societal and institutional agenda through the use of information and communication technologies.

A vision is not a one-time event but is a message conveyed repeatedly in speeches, articles, and manifestos over a period of time. Vision provides a matrix for making sense of a complicated and chaotic world. A strong vision has emotive as well as analytic content. Successful visions are eventually diffused through a society or group as more and more people embrace the vision and come to alter their behavior based on that vision.

There are two excellent examples of linking an ICT vision to social imperatives: Prime Minister Dr. Mahathir bin Mohamed in Malaysia and the back-to-back presidents of South Africa, Nelson Mandela and Thabo Mbeki. In my research in these two countries, I found that the considerable success of the two governments in diffusing ICTs lay in part in the visions of the countries' leaders. While quite different in many respects, Mahathir and Mandela (and later Mbeki) mobilized important constituencies to support ICT innovation by appealing to social cohesion and prosperity goals. The risk of social collapse and chaos was not an idle threat as interethnic warfare was fresh in the minds of both populations. If ICTs could be defined in a way to show their strengths in creating jobs and bringing people together, the information revolution would be supported (Wilson 1999).

The great scholar of business, Alfred Chandler (1977), found that successful leaders used their vision and strategy to redesign institutional structures to become more effective instruments of competition. In reviewing years of business activities, he found that vision, strategy, and institutional change were closely linked and, indeed, noted memorably that *structure follows strategy*. In the information revolution too, vision, strategy, and structure are closely linked.

The Four Balances in ICT Sector Relationships

The information revolution occurs when a significantly powerful and politically coherent segment of the national state leadership groups decides that political, economic, and social conditions require a rebalancing of long-standing ICT sector relationships. This is in large part a shift or reconstruction of core policy balances. The recent history of ICT industries suggests that four major balances appear and reappear—the balances between private and public sectors, between monopoly and competition, between domestic and foreign ownership, and between centralized and distributed administration. Although other issues are important, these four balances constitute the building blocks of policy stability and are central to all industries. Other issues, such as intellectual property rights, are important but relevant mainly to firms and policy makers in one or two subsectors. These four balances usually must be established before other important issues can be settled. A stable policy environment for computer software production requires the relevant parties to sort out the role of the state, the status of foreign investors, the nature of competition, and the government's organization. As a rule of thumb, these four building blocks constitute about 80 percent of what is important to know about developing countries.

Table 2.1
Shares of Private Sector Participation in Developing Countries

Telecom Operator	Percent in Developing Countries
No private operators	19%
Other private operators	24
Fully or partly private incumbent	57

Source: ITU (2002).

Private-Public Balances
The shift between private and public is at the heart of the Information Revolution. It alters the sources of sectoral ownership, control, wealth, innovation, power and authority. This shift in sector dynamism and initiative moves power from senior civil servants to senior corporate managers. Most countries now permit private sector participation in the telecoms sector (see table 2.1).

The technical and economic arguments about the relative benefits of public and private initiatives should not mask the raw interests that lie just below the surface. From World War II to the present, the ICT sectors in developing countries were controlled by senior officials in government ministries and government-owned enterprises. Senior officials in publicly owned institutions like the World Bank controlled global money. These state-based entities and their intergovernmental networks were authoritative and unchallenged. They had particular constituencies and formed a cross-national coalition to ensure regime functioning and longevity. Senior government officials had the decisive say in investing billions of dollars of capital or purchasing billions of dollars of ICT equipment.

Supporters of state control have long made several arguments about its benefits, arguments that were especially prevalent after World War II. First, the absence of local investors to supply pools of capital to telecom and broadcasting development presented a genuine problem for poor countries. Since the capital required for these networked technologies was so large, only government had the financial wherewithal to build the infrastructure. Building these networks also demanded substantial planning and organizational sophistication, for which government had a distinct advantage.

The broadcasting industry was a means for nation building and creating a sense of unity among polyglot populations; government ownership could create a greater sense of unity than commercial operations. The telephone system and broadcasting were too strategically important to the national economy to be left to the private sector. All these arguments seem to buttress and be buttressed by the capital-intensive, large-scale nature of the technology. In very practical terms, these arguments were wrapped into a final ideological justification that the state had a moral and political obligation to provide basic services to its citizens. The state could be relied on to act for the good of the community, providing services that others could not. Through the actions of the International Telecommunications Union, the World Bank, and others, the international regime supported these principles materially and ideologically.

To what extent have these underlying conditions changed? The slow and steady rise of larger middle classes in many developing countries has led to more investors, more entrepreneurs, and more management talent. Big changes in the technology mean that investments have become less large and lumpy; small and medium-sized companies are now starting Internet service providers or other ICT businesses. Global broadcasting has made national borders more porous so the rationale for state monopolies has diminished. The leaders of the international regime press hard for much more space for private initiatives, and private firms are investing billions abroad, eclipsing the World Bank and other government agencies. Political shifts are also occurring. As middle classes grow, they become more aggressive in asking for things their global counterparts want—public services like power and communications and a say in governing their lives (Inglehart 1990).

People in developing countries no longer accept that the central state is the first and the final protector of the public interest. Instead, private actors are now active in promoting public interests. The new trends, including the poor performance of state-owned enterprises, have thrown earlier assumptions into question.

Our understanding of the relationship between states and markets in modern capitalist economies has become much more sophisticated over the past several years, moving away from either/or generalities. A more nuanced understanding of the wide range of activities that governments do to support or undercut markets is now the norm. Students of government-market relations like Peter Evans (1995) and J. Rogers Hollingsworth, Philippe C. Schmitter, and Wolfgang Streeck (1997) point to the variety of roles that states can play, from monopolistic direct ownership and control of production to more arm's-length regulatory and informational activities that promote and protect private entrepreneurs. Governments also use a wide variety of tools to achieve those goals. In addition to ownership and operational roles, governments set policy guidelines, regulate economic activities, and set and protect property rights. Governments effect their will not only by issuing direct commands but by exercising their authority more subtly through incentives given to producer and consumer firms, individuals, government agencies, and civil society groups.

Monopoly-Competition Balances
The early market for telephone services was originally quite competitive, reaching at one time more than 500 companies in the United States alone. As the industry consolidated, telecoms came to be defined as a natural monopoly, especially in poor countrie, which (the argument went) had so few human and material resources on the supply side that they shouldn't be wasted through unnecessary competition. Parallel telephone lines and competing companies seemed wasteful in countries that had only a few dozen trained engineers. On the demand side, poor populations were often scattered across the countryside and hard to reach economically. With commercial ventures, they might be ignored completely. Governments were at least rhetorically committed to enhancing equity and could pressure a monopolist company to use its revenues to cross-subsidize the poor. In return for being granted a monopoly, the company was obliged to serve poor populations. The balance in favor of a state monopoly was backed by a powerful international regime and local elites.

Conditions have changed enough to drastically undercut old rationales. Research on ICT and other sectors indicates clearly that increased competition has the greatest positive impact on sectoral efficiency and innovation. The experience of much of East Asia suggests that government's insistence on rigorous interfirm competition makes more difference than whether a firm is private, public, foreign, or domestic.

Domestic-Foreign Ownership Balances

Domestic-foreign ownership balances are heavily freighted with political and symbolic significance. This is especially so for developing countries, which often feel the victims, not the beneficiaries, of past foreign interventions. One African intellectual put it this way: "When the Europeans first got to Africa, we had the land and they had the [holy] book. But it didn't take long before they had the land and we had the book." The concern this time around is that the foreign powers will get the land, the book, the television station, and the telephone company.

Among developing country elites, the desire for new technologies and content is inevitably tempered by their experiences of colonialism and neocolonialism. At least since World War II, most developed and developing countries held telephone, water, electricity, and broadcasting as the "commanding heights" that had to be protected from foreign influences. It was feared that foreign takeovers would bring highly deleterious effects, whether economic, political, or cultural. These effects were thought to include cultural alienation and corruption, appropriation of national economic resources, and reduction of national security. Since small poor developing countries, and some larger ones as well, had small local entrepreneurial classes, any opening to the private sector meant bringing into the country a flood of foreign companies and their suspicious behaviors and interests.

Most people I interviewed recognized the need to invite foreign capital into their country to some extent to gain access to the know-how needed to create a knowledge society. Foreign capital brings exciting content, produces up-to-date software, and also brings jobs. Work done by Rodriguez and this author (Rodriguez and Wilson 2000) indicates conclusively that more investment in technology alone does not automatically correlate with economic growth and yet that without foreign investment and without access to foreign markets growth and development are hindered. This does not eliminate, however, the sharp political concerns.

Centralized-Distributed Administration Balances

Under the old ICT regime, sectoral responsibilities were concentrated in a very small number of government bureaus and enterprises. A ministry had responsibilities for policy setting, regulation, property protection, and monitoring. The state-owned enterprises carried out the operational tasks required to achieve government's broad goals. In point of fact, the state-owned enterprises were often the tail that wagged the governmental dog, since they possessed far more technical expertise and money than the ministries.

The centralization in the ICT sectors seemed to fit perfectly with the technological imperatives and authoritarian political trends of the 1970s and 1980s. Democracy and decentralization were not pushed onto the world's political agenda until the late 1980s with the wave of democratization that swept the world during that tumultuous and change-filled decade (Huntington 1991). The rise of indigenous bourgeoisies and bourgeois democracy gave political impetus to open up once-closed bureaucracies. Newly mobilized grassroots groups demanded greater institutional transparency and accountability. As new governments came to power and as old ones implemented reforms, responses often came in the form of decentralized systems of governance, including reformed economic sectors. This somewhat distinct trend (closely tied to globalization) intersected with trends toward cheaper, more portable, and more powerful communication technologies. Together they made decentralized institutions much more likely and created a better fit between reformed institutions, new technologies, and liberalizing political and economic trends.

One of the most dramatic changes in the balance between distributed and centralized administration of the sectors is the growth of regulatory agencies around the world. Decentralization's growth is captured in figure 2.3. I describe this radical innovation in sectoral governance in more detail in the appendix to this chapter.

The Balances Are Political

To be sustainable, these policy rebalances are accompanied by parallel restructurings of the country's underlying political coalitions. Such restructuring typically requires a group of aggressive reformers to

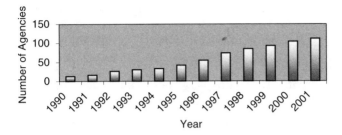

Figure 2.3
Regulators on the Rise
Source: Petrazzini (1996), ITU (2002).

actively take on and ultimately take apart the old coalitions. It also requires that reformers seek out, encourage, and create a new political coalition that will support the new policies. Unless this elite realignment occurs, major policy changes will not be sustainable. Even liberal reforms that push back the state from direct ownership need the full complement of proreform political coalitions to support the changes, proreform politicians to write new rules, proreform spokesmen to popularize changes, and proreform policy intellectuals to publish justifications for the new order. Successful ICT reforms rely on politicians to outmaneuver, neutralize, and punish opponents of reform. The "right" technology is not enough. The "right" technology and the wrong politics leaves the revolution stranded high and dry on the sands of the past. The information revolution takes the "right" politics to make the kinds of institutional and structural changes required to bring the full benefit of technology to society.

The Balances Are Neither Absolute nor Identical
These four categories (private-public, monopoly-competition, domestic-foreign ownership, and centralized-distributed distribution) represent balances, not absolutes. The strategic restructuring framework is designed to be analytic and comparative, not normative. SRS is not concerned with judging these categories against an absolute international (or American) ideal. Experience and analysis teach that there is no one best way for achieving the benefits of the information revolution. Each country's accommodations and resistances to ICTs are unique. Each finds

its own balances. As figure 2.2 shows, developing countries can follow multiple paths to competition (from monopoly to open market) and ownership (from state to private).

These four categories of strategic and policy options for organizing the ICT sectors are conceptually distinct. Very few would confuse the public or private dimension with the foreign or domestic dimension. Although these distinctions hold up in theory, in actuality, the distinctions overlap. In many developing countries, especially the least developed ones, the tiny size and weakness of the local private sector means that almost any medium-to-large private enterprise is likely to be foreign. The private-public split in the ICT sectors of poorer countries quickly becomes a foreign-domestic split as well. And where the only significant domestic ICT service provided is the state-owned telephone monopoly, then the competition-monopoly dimension also merges into the state-private and domestic-foreign dimension.

Politics at the Heart of the Balances: Conflicts during the Shifts

The four shifting balances are not neutral in either their distributional impacts or their politics. These are massive global processes involving billions and billions of dollars, every nation, economic and political jostling, and perceptions of national security. The shifts are hotly contested, are bitterly fought, and have generated fiery passions of ideology and local interest. Producers versus consumers, rural versus urban, labor versus capital, civil servants versus private businessmen, high income versus low income, local versus foreign capital, fixed line versus wireless companies: the lines of potential conflict are all present and can be exacerbated by shifts of authority and resources. Because of the political centrality of ICTs, national elites everywhere have wisely decided that the information revolution is far too important to be left to engineers, economists, and computer geeks.

Which societal interests will get to control the richest and most politically sensitive sector in the modern world? Which domestic interests (and which nations) will gain the authority and power to make decisive decisions about the allocation of trillions of dollars of technological resources? Who gets all that power and all that money? To answer these and earlier questions about the relative importance of structural and nonstructural factors, we must review and compare material across more than one country. It is to these comparative issues that I now turn.

Some Methodological Issues

Why Comparative Cases?

The interactions among policies, politics, institutions, and structures are best understood by analyzing and comparing them in concrete historical circumstances across several countries. Working with comparative case materials at the country level complements and fleshes out the cross-national large "N" analyses with details from particular countries. It is only through these richly detailed historically specific cases that researchers can present an in-depth picture of the contexts of ICT diffusion. Comparative cases are the only means by which we can capture the nuanced interaction among variables that operate at different levels of analysis—structural, institutional, political. Large data sets can only take us so far; comparative cases complement them. Mauro F. Guillen and Sandra L. Suarez (2001) are among the handful of analysts who employ large-number data sets as well as paired-country comparisons to account for the diffusion of Internet service providers. They too are interested in both the comparative explanatory power of economic structures and the noneconomic variables like institutions. They have performed quantitative analyses of a 142-country sample concentrating on economic structure and then done paired comparisons between Argentina and Spain and between Ireland and Singapore, selected according to these countries' reliance on French (continental) or English legal systems. Guillen and Suarez find that structure does explain most of the variance between countries but that to more fully account for differences in Internet service provider diffusion rates across the paired countries, it is also useful to analyze the different incentives that legal systems provide.

Doing Comparisons: Most Similar, Most Different   There are several ways to select cases for disciplined, cross-national comparisons of policy outcomes. Typically, comparative politics employs either a "most similar" or a "most different" research strategy, and each strategy has plusses and minuses (Sartori 1997). The "most different" strategy can capture a wide range of empirical variations along independent variables to see what effect such variety might have on outcomes. The "most similar" strategy allows the analyst to hold more variables constant (such as size, level of economic growth, or region) and thus try to pinpoint the variable that seems to have the greatest impact on outcomes. According to Pennings, Keman, and Kleinnijenhuis (1999, 203), "A most similar approach implies that . . . the more circumstances the selected cases have in common, the easier it is to locate the variables that do differ and which may thus be considered as the first candidates for investigation as causal or explanatory variables. A most different approach involves . . . a comparison on the basis of dissimilarity in as many respects as possible in the hope that after all the differing circumstances have been discounted as explanations, there will remain one alone in which all the instances agree" (also Geddes 1990).

Because my research tries to capture the wide range of societal challenges and ICT responses found in very different kinds of developing countries and also seeks to explain the substantial differences in ICT performance outcomes that are found even in similar countries, I employ a "mixed" research strategy. This enables me to capture the strengths of each approach and to account for information and communication technology outcomes in many different kinds of countries.

Beyond suggesting cause-and-effect relations, this comparative approach also helps illustrate in a variety of settings the more general arguments about process that I make about the relations among structure, policy outcomes, and behavioral and institutional factors, especially strategic restructuring. That is, the structured comparisons permit a search for causation, an exploration of the constitutive picture of Internet diffusion in its own terms, and an examination of the ways that different actors interpret important developments and trends in their own subjective fashion.

In any comparative study, the researcher is obliged to make a choice—either to go "wide" by covering many countries in a superficial fashion or to go "deep" and try to capture the complex, often contradictory dynamics of a few countries. Each approach has strengths and weaknesses. For my purposes, going deep makes more sense than going wide and shallow.

To meet the "most similar" test, I concentrated on the principle independent variable (structure) and selected two developing countries with important structural similarities (China and Brazil). Both countries have comparable broad sectoral structures and are at similar levels of economic development.

Both countries are among the largest in the world in terms of physical size, and both have very large populations. Both countries dominate the economies of their regions. Furthermore, both are important markets for ICT services and goods. Both have large, influential subnational units with significant cross-unit variation. Domestically, both have substantial cross-regional differences in income. These are giant countries whose decisions will affect millions of their own people and millions in other countries.

Brazil and China have important differences as well, and some emerge in the cases studies, especially in terms of cultural context and the structures and dynamics of politics. Still, they provide a fruitful "most similar" comparison for exploring ICT diffusion.

To draw on a "most different" research strategy, I wanted to select a country example that contrasts sharply with the structural features just cited above. A companion contrasting developing country should be relatively small, have a very different level of economic development, and have a contrasting economic structure. Brazil and China have a substantial manufacturing sector, so I wanted to pick a country that hasn't. I looked at countries that had contrasting institutional structures, especially those from regions other than Asia and Latin America. The country I selected to fit the profile is Ghana. This small, mainly agricultural West African nation has sufficient structural differences to provide a robust contrast with Brazil and China and meet the requirements of a "most different" case.

Industry Selection: Why Focus on the Internet? With the countries selected, I then selected an industry. It was not my intention in this book to provide a complete case study of every ICT sector, industry, or application (although I did begin with that grand ambition). Instead, I chose to concentrate on only one industry—the Internet—that has become central to the emergence of modern knowledge societies. Tracking the growth of the Internet (relative to other ICT industries one could potentially analyze) provides a number of analytic benefits:

• Despite the importance of Internet diffusion, few comparative, empirical case studies are available anywhere, especially compared to the abundant research that is available on telecoms or even broadcasting.[2] Few sustained industry studies have been conducted in developing countries. Case studies of Internet diffusion are therefore especially valuable empirically.

• The Internet is so heavily dependent on upstream telecommunications infrastructures that studying the Internet also reveals a great deal about telecoms.

• At the same time, the Internet is increasingly linked to so many downstream activities in other information and communication industries, including radio and newspaper, that studying the Internet reveals much about a variety of other ICT applications. For example, the Internet is used increasingly by editors and publishers of conventional media to distribute their content downstream to their customers. The *Daily Graphic* in Ghana is published on a Web site, as is the *People's Daily* in China.

• The Internet is also fast becoming a platform for a wide number of other economic, social, and government sector applications, such as electronic commerce and education.

• Finally, because the Internet is a new, highly distributed resource, it lends itself to being utilized by grassroots groups in civil society, more so than big television or big telephone companies. The Internet offers us a look at what is reported to be a different kind of politics. Analyzing the politics of the Internet in each country—whether Brazil, Ghana, or China—reveals a great deal about what makes that country tick, from the ground up.

According to Milton Mueller and Zixiang Tan (1996, 82) in their study of China, "Two things have made the Internet a revolutionary innovation. Its decentralized, bottom up development gave users both more control and more investment responsibility. Also, it could tap into uses, technologies, and applications outside the control of telephone monopolies and established mass media interests. Both features made it an incubation site for new competitors, entrepreneurs and ideas." For all these reasons, I concentrate on the Internet in this study.

Conclusion

In this chapter, I have argued that broad structural features of national economies account for perhaps two-thirds of the differences between nations but that the remaining differences must be found by carefully analyzing the evolution of institutions, politics, and policies within a country (see table 2.1 and figure 2.3). I employ a modified structural framework to explain cross-national differences in ICT diffusion. My strategic restructuring framework seeks to fill in the analytic and conceptual gaps left by other models, by acknowledging the importance of economic structures but insisting that institutions and politics both contribute a great deal to explaining ICT outcomes in developing countries. Indeed, the *interactions* among structures, institutions, politics (including leadership), and outcomes should attract the attentions of engaged researchers and thoughtful practitioners. This modified structuralist approach is admittedly somewhat more expensive in terms of the time, resources, and knowledge that are required to apply it properly to illuminate ICT outcomes. It requires, for example, data on different kinds of variables at several different levels of analysis—such as macroeconomic data on sectoral structures and on gross domestic product per capita, institutional descriptions (of the type provided here), and evidence of institutional structure and performance. It also requires evidence of individual behaviors, especially of ICT leaders or information champions. All this requires extra work above and beyond other leading approaches, and obtaining consistent data on poor countries is rarely easy. Furthermore, the closer the researcher moves to the individual, micro level in any country but especially in poor countries, the more difficult it is to obtain specific knowledge. Still, this modified structuralist approach, while expensive, provides considerable intellectual payoffs by linking different levels together and showing the interactions among structural, institutional, and political variables in the three case studies—Brazil, Ghana, and China.

Appendix: ICT Institutions in Developing Countries

Ministries

At the top of the information and communication technology sector's formal hierarchy are the relevant technical ministries. Traditionally, they are the most authoritative state guides for the production and distribution of information in the modern sectors of developing countries. They have various names with overlapping responsibilities—ministries of telecommunications, of communication, or of information. Some countries have a ministry of communication that has telecom responsibilities and a separate ministry of information that controls broadcasting. Others combine telecom and broadcasting in a single agency. In many socialist and statist countries, the information agency is in effect a propaganda arm of the state. Computers rarely have their own ministry; different aspects are assigned to different ministries: hardware manufacturing may be lodged with the ministry of industry, while R&D and software may fall under science and technology. Other ministries have mixed responsibilities. Telecommunications is sometimes housed with other utility functions like transportation or electric power.

Many of these portfolios have been reshuffled in the face of the tumult in the technology and the commercial markets. Over the past decade, central governments have transferred responsibilities from ministries to special committees and then back to ministries again (as was done in the Fernando Collar administration in Brazil in 1990 to 1992).

Ministries under the old regime typically possessed similar formal responsibilities. These included policy making for the sector or subsector, policy monitoring, and issuing regulations for company operators in the sector, both public and private. Because these sectors were heavily statist, in most developing countries perhaps the biggest ministerial responsibility lay in close oversight of state-owned monopolies like television or telephone. The functions of the ministries in this regard might include ownership of the shares of the enterprises, appointment of their boards and senior executives, approval of their budgets, and financing of the enterprises' investment budgets (especially to serve areas that are not commercially viable).

In addition to these not inconsiderable formal responsibilities, ministries were the political eyes and ears (and occasional strong arm) of the central political authorities, able to impose politically connected staff and to insist on politically motivated investment priorities (such as wiring the communication minister's home village first).

The crashing waves of the information revolution's tsunami have greatly disturbed the settled complacencies of the ministries. The spread of new norms and expectations have subjected them to substantial new pressures, and the basis for their authority is shifting away from direct ownership and close control to a more arm's-length relationship through which they supply policy guidance and monitoring. Many agencies have been downsized, and workers retrenched. Their overall power has almost certainly diminished. There are notable exceptions, like China's superministry—the Ministry of Information Industry (MII)—which was created in 1998 out of the fusion of the powerful Ministry of Electrical Industries with the even more powerful Ministry of Post and Telegraph. MII is arguably more powerful today than in the past, though it too is feeling the competitive pressures of other bodies.

State Enterprises
The same forces buffeting the ministries have battered the state enterprises even more severely, as they have been subjected to commercialization, privatization, and, perhaps most seriously, real competition. For much of the post–World War II period, the commanding heights of the economy were entrusted to state-owned enterprises. Variously called *public enterprises*, *parastatals*, or *state-owned enterprises*, these bodies produced and broadcast the television and radio programs, invested in the land lines, connected the telephone calls (or not), and produced the heavy equipment that the other enterprises needed. In Brazil, these were enterprises like EMBRATEL, the state-owned long-distance telephone company, as well as Telebras, the publicly owned holding company for the twenty-odd separate companies that operated within each of Brazil's states. In Ghana, the Ghana National Broadcasting Corporation held a monopoly. In socialist or communist countries like China or India, state enterprises are extensive. In China, the local computer manufacturer Legend is state owned, as is most of the economy (but the largest share

of the country's gross domestic product produced in this sector comes disproportionately from the "private" or more independent company sector). Most of the biggest monopolies in the sector (television, radio, and telephone) were 100 percent state owned.

The organizational structures of these state enterprises matched their heft in the markets: they were weighty and top heavy. Relative to private enterprises, they were almost always overstaffed, sometimes by a factor of two or three. While the enterprises were formally under the technical ministries, very often they were the tail that wagged the dog and were far more powerful than the ministries themselves.

Since their monopoly positions guaranteed high incomes and high status, the enterprises had little incentive to perform well and so accumulated a very mixed performance record. Some did quite well along all dimensions—service quality, numbers of people served, financial returns. Many others performed poorly, especially in the mid- to late 1980s when developing countries were severely pressed by huge debt repayment obligations and by subpar international markets for many of the products they produced. Governments in every region then systematically starved their telephone companies of investment capital, simultaneously forbade them to raise their rates, all the while insisting on universal service or access for more and more people. This combination of lower revenues and higher service expectations guaranteed poor performance, which is exactly what happened. This period saw sky-rocketing telephone waiting lists, deteriorating call completion rates, shrinking TV audiences, and other signs of disaster. This collapse of so many systems led many local constituents to agree that drastic changes were needed in the structure and behaviors of state-owned enterprises. When the World Bank and other foreign advisors showed up at the doorstep with a new orthodoxy, exasperated consumers were ready for just about anything.

With so little competitive pressures on them, senior managers had few incentives to innovate or dramatically improve their services. State-owned television served up warmed-over programming with aging themes and formats. When new technologies came along, they were most often developed by more aggressive and innovative firms outside the state system.

By the early 1990s, the global trend toward commercialization and privatization began to reach the telecommunications sectors. Some countries, like Malaysia, moved early. Malaysia commercialized its telecom company in 1987 by transforming its legal status from a state company to one that now had to operate under commercial statutes just like private firms. It was partially privatized by the government in 1994, when it opened its shares to private Malaysian stockholders. Its technical and commercial performance improved, as often happens when privatization occurs, especially it if is accompanied by competition. In francophone West Africa, governments allowed new market entrants into radio and television, which pushed state enterprises to try to improve their own programming.

The essential role of the interplay among these institutions should not be underestimated. Not only are the intergovernmental relations among agencies critical, but so are the ties between government agencies and other actors, such as private-sector institutions and groups from civil society. In an efficient and balanced system of ICT governance, the separate institutions mesh smoothly so that knowledge flows from where it is produced to where it is needed, either through state or nonstate institutions. The most sophisticated analyses of economic development point precisely to these partnerships among institutions as the true catalysts for successful qualitative changes in productivity. My experience in the poorest developing countries is that the most difficult step for senior officials is to admit that private-sector interests have something useful to contribute to the national policy process. They too often view businesspeople as interlopers, if not the enemy.

Specialized Bodies

Given the innate conservatism of so many of these long-standing government bodies, it is not surprising that when government elites conclude that new technologies are important for the national economy, national security, and national welfare, they turn to bodies outside the regular ministerial system. Expertise in this quickly changing field of information and communication technology wasn't widespread in developing countries, so governments convened special task forces, commissions, and blue-ribbon panels to advise them on the new directions their countries should take. The number of nations who turned to task forces is itself notable, starting in 1992 with Singapore, followed in 1993 by the Clinton administration's National Information Infrastructure Task Force, and then eventually by similar bodies in Japan, France, China, and other nations. Later in the 1990s, countries as diverse as Ghana and Brazil became involved. To greater or less degrees, these government commissions absorbed representatives of diverse stakeholders into their memberships. Typically, they include scientists, government officials from supply-side ministries and enterprises, businesspeople, educators, and consumer advocates.

All these ad hoc bodies tended to take up very similar issues, including the need to build basic infrastructure, the importance of private investment, and the potential contributions to national development. Typically the bodies made their reports directly to the relevant minister or sometimes to the head of state. Sometimes these temporary bodies were transformed into more permanent institutions (as in China). Sometimes their leaders became ministers or were assigned other ICT duties. For most bodies, its exact organizational form was less important than its central message—that ICTs were important for the nation.

The purposes of these specialized bodies were technical as well as political. Leaders recognized that technical knowledge was low, understanding of the stakes involved was low, and the way forward was unclear. They also acknowledged problems in assigning bureaucratic rights and responsibilities and in juggling the roles of the private and public sectors.

Smart and secure leaders used these specialized commissions to reach out to key individuals and constituencies beyond the government. Some included labor and consumer groups; most included business and academic interests. Labor and business were especially important groups to include in these bodies, since both groups could in effect go on strike if they disapproved of the government's direction. Workers could literally strike when their employment security was undermined by ICT reform programs, few gains were visible, and other stakeholders were not expected to share the burden of privatization or downsizing. Business could also refuse to play along. If the rules and regulations were soft and uncertain or if what the government proposed was too risky or imposed too many burdens on private entrepreneurs and managers, then business would engage in a de facto capital strike.

One subset of specialized bodies is different than those with fixed or short mandates—the research and development agencies. Whether university based or free standing like the Chinese Academy of Sciences or Brazil's National Council for Scientific and Technological Development (CNPq), they made timely and important contributions to the early development of the ministries of information infrastructure in many developing countries. Work still needs to be done on these specialized institutions, including NECTEC in Thailand or the Council for Scientific and Industrial Research (CSIR) and other newly minted organizations in South Africa.

Regulatory Bodies

Regulatory agencies are the newest and the oddest institutions in the ICT sectors. Under the old regime, the need for a separate regulatory institution was not obvious: government owned, operated, and set the performance and evaluation criteria for the provision of telecommunications, broadcasting, and other ICT services. For each market, there was often only one company, which was controlled and monitored by one ministry. The monopoly model was administratively straightforward: government decided what it wanted and then told its company what to do.

By contrast, the competitive model is much more complex. No longer does only one company supply 100 percent of the market. Whether only two firms (a duopoly) or a dozen competitors, the monitoring and oversight are more difficult for government officials to do successfully.

As balances shift from one company to many, it also shifts from government to private ownership. Government officials can no longer simply call in enterprise managers and give them their marching orders. Private owners and investors can't be called in from time to time and instructed. Instead, they have to be convinced and provided with incentives to take action they might not take in the absence of regulatory incentives. Furthermore, the purposes of regulations have changed radically.

The old regime had regulations to guide production and supply ICT services, but the purposes of those regulations were to promote and sustain a dominant domestic public monopoly. This meant protecting and privileging the monopoly incumbent. But changing technology and accelerating globalization have brought greater pressures to permit new firms to compete head to head.

Government companies are no longer the only ones in the core ICT supply business. Countries open up to local competitors and to multinational companies. According to the new orthodoxy, governments are now supposed to shift from being the main or only supplier to being one supplier among several or to withdraw from the supply business entirely. They are expected to serve a new, high-minded, and disinterested role. No longer using every regulation to favor their company, they are now expected to keep an arm's length away from their own company and create a level playing field where no one company is given an advantage over the other. This can include equal access to operating and investment capital or to customers and particular niches in the market.

In effect, these changes have demanded actions that go against fifty years of practice: officials in fact are now to disadvantage and dismantle the incumbent and help the potential new entrants break into the market. From promoting monopoly to promoting competition, the new goals have been reluctantly and imperfectly embraced in developed and developing countries alike. The press for new pro-market regulatory structures has been quite galling to government officials in some developing nations. Even when supportive of the new goals in principle, developing country officials are still nationalist enough to view the new (usually expatriate) companies as foreign interlopers that are bent on cream skimming and cherry picking and that will not serve the public interest.

In institutional terms, this has meant the creation of independent or semi-independent agencies with their own staff and senior officials, all separate and distinct from the ministry. The new regime in South Africa created two bodies: the South African Telecommunications Regulatory Authority (SATRA) was the more traditional body, and the Universal Service Agency (USA) was designed to suggest innovative ways to distribute ICT services as broadly as possible across the society. Government later merged the telecom and broadcast bodies into a single regulator.

An institutional problem too little appreciated by enthusiasts of radical reform (especially those from the United States) is that countries outside of North America have had very little if any real experience with independent regulatory authorities. In some respects, these authorities are like American football, a complicated team activity that was invented in North America, which is being exported to a few other countries but is watched with some puzzlement and uncertainty by people of other cultures.

As the rebalancing proceeds, officials aiming to create the new institutions have found that moving from nonmarket to market conditions and reducing the role of government, ironically, had to be done, and done aggressively, by government itself. Only the state has the authority and the power to dismantle the monopoly and build up its competitors and a market. Officials also found that shifting the balances worked best with some kind of constituency behind it. Creating an autonomous agency free from heavy politicization required a politicized constituency in favor of depoliticization that would take aggressive political steps to create the new conditions.

Typically, the new regulatory institutions are designed to meet several tasks, which can include licensing new would-be market entrants, rulemaking (where regulators are given authority to establish specific rules necessary to implement broad government policies), enforcement and adjudication, management of scarce resources (like radio frequency spectra), and approving equipment and technical standards.

Here too the importance of interinstitutional relations is critical. A regulatory institution that is internally efficient but unable to make headway in disciplining other powerful institutions in its task environment will simply be unable to create a functioning competitive market for Internet, telephone, radios, or other applications.

Courts and Legislatures

The importance of institutional endowments and the allocation of legitimate authority across institutions within the ICT sector has been decisively argued by Brian Levy and Pablo Spiller (1996). In their cross-national study of the fit between newly designed regulatory agencies and the prevailing institutional patterns of a nation, they point to the inter-actions among legislatures, courts, and the executive. They show con-vincingly that as countries set out to create new regulatory structures, the designers must account for the overall authority patterns inherent within the general system of governance, including relations among the legislature, parties, courts, and other bodies. They draw a sharp distinc-tion between the more frequently analyzed regulatory incentives and the broader, often overlooked system of regulatory governance.

Joint Public- and Private-Sector Consultative Arrangements

I use the term *consultative arrangements* here rather than *consultative bodies* because private-public consultations still tend to be ad hoc and indirect in many countries. They may be intermittent, not well staffed (or have no independent staff of their own), and relatively nonformal. One of the most difficult institutions to create is the set of norms, expec-tations, material incentives, and practices that bring together all the relevant ICT stake holders, consistently, into a national dialogue. Yet the distributed, demand-driven nature of the information revolution requires many voices to be heard. This bold strategic step is neither easy nor automatic.

3

Strategic Restructuring in Brazil

Introduction

Brazil demonstrates vividly many of the puzzles of information communications technology (ICT) diffusion in developing countries. Here in the largest country in Latin America one confronts the disjuncture that can exist between the principal structural determinant of ICT diffusion (gross domestic product per capita) and the actual level of a country's ICT penetration, making Brazil an excellent candidate for the first case study in this volume.

Brazil's economic structure is relatively straightforward. The country accounts for about one-half of all the economic activity of the South American continent and is the eighth-largest economy in the world. Structuralist logic would suggest that it also would have the eighth-highest penetration of telecommunications and other media, including the Internet. But in important respects, Brazil is a distinct laggard. It may be the world's eighth-largest economy, but it ranks forty-second in telephone density. This puts it behind smaller Latin American neighbors like Argentina, Colombia, and Venezuela (McKnight and Botelho 1997). Only about a fifth of its people have telephones, and its per capita Internet hosts are 51.53 per 10,000 (ITU 2000).

Beyond accounting for anomalies between economic structures and ICT outcomes, I intend to explain the process through which these and other patterns have emerged. The strategic restructuring (SRS) argument I made in chapter 2 claims that distributional patterns will be driven largely by structures but mediated in important ways by institutions, policies, and politics. Brazil is a country where the state and multinational corporations have played decisive roles in the country's modern economic evolution (Evans 1995)—including the national distribution patterns of information and communications. The SRS framework acknowledges the potential importance of structure, institutions, and politics and explores how exactly these separate elements of the Brazilian information and communication sector interact with one another in a dynamic and complex social process.

Brazil presents a mixed picture of tremendous political conflicts in certain information technology industries and cooperation in others, of high aggregate telecommunications numbers in some areas and low per capita penetration in others. Brazil has one of the most sophisticated media industries in the world. Unlike many other developing countries, the print and electronic industries have long been privately owned and operated by a handful of powerful and wealthy families with the protection of the military or civilian governments in power. Besides a robust domestic market, Brazil also exports billions of dollars worth of TV telenovellas, feature movies, and software each year.

Unlike the country's poor telecommunications penetration, penetration for television and radio penetration rates are high, and the blue glow of TV sets is observable even in the poorest urban communities (favelas), where consumer electronic purchases have been growing at 50 percent annually. It is unclear at this point whether the new interactive digital information highways will repeat the more egalitarian pattern of the print and broadcast media or reproduce the enormous inequalities of the telecom sector.

The Structural Context

Brazil, the eighth largest economy in the world, has a per capita income of U.S. $3,060 and a sectoral structure that is 8 percent agriculture, 35.8 percent manufacturing, and 56.2 percent services (World Bank 2002). This structure can be contrasted with that of Ghana, for example, where agriculture produces 35.9 percent of the national GDP (but the largest workforce), industry 25.3 percent, and services 38.9 percent (World

Bank 2002). On the demand side, Brazil has a large middle class that lives the bourgeois life of western Europeans and that has a taste for modern appliances and services. On the supply side, the country has a well-developed indigenous manufacturing sector that includes industries that produce world-class ICT-intensive products like aircraft and also has one of the world's most successful television and movie content export businesses. This economic structure leads the observer to assume that Brazil is a country where ICTs play an important role in the modern domestic and the export economy.

A second critical element of structure is where the economy and social structure intersect—employment. In Brazil, 14 percent of the total population works in agriculture, 36 percent in manufacturing, and 50 percent in services. This demographic structure also shapes the demand for ICT products in distinct ways.

But these particular structural factors do not fully account for the national ICT distribution patterns. A key element of Brazilian societal structure is wealth and income distribution, which is one of the most unequal in the world. The wealthiest 20 percent in Brazil owns 71 percent of national income, which gives the wealthy an income level equivalent to that of Austria or the Netherlands, around U.S. $20,100. The poorest 30 percent, however, earn only $800, equivalent to per capita earnings in underdeveloped countries like Senegal or Indonesia (Brazilian Embassy 2000). This skewing of economic resources should be reflected in the design and content of ICT policies and the subsequent diffusion of technologies like the Internet throughout Brazilian society. Indeed, only about 2 percent of the population has access to the Internet.

Brazilian society is complex in many other respects, from its regional development to its racial mix. Its huge size alone is a major structural feature shaping Internet and other ICT diffusion, with 168 million people (1995) living in an area just slightly smaller than the United States (3,286,488 square miles). Across this national space, the vast majority of economic activity occurs in the south, which has 18 percent of the territory but 60 percent of the national income. São Paulo is the economic heartland of the economy, while cities of the north are far less developed. Fully 75 percent of the population resides in urban areas. Since the spatial distribution of economic activity is so skewed, Internet use would be expected to reflect these regional patterns. In fact, we find that 60 percent of Internet use is in São Paulo, 30 percent in Rio de Janeiro, and only 10 percent in the rest of the country: "Although Brazil has the most extensive Internet infrastructure in Latin America, it is also one of the most unevenly distributed. The nearly 1,300 Internet . . . [service providers] are concentrated in larger cities, and less than one in 10 urban areas . . . has local dial-up access to the Internet. The current total of 3.3 million individual users means less than 3 percent of the population have access to the Internet" (RITS 1999, 5).

The effects of geographic and spatial structuring on a country's ICT performance should not be underestimated. Singapore's tiny size is one important factor in that country's success in the modern ICT sector. By contrast, Brazil's vast geographic space imposes tremendous costs for ICT distribution and creates opportunities for media to develop in different geographic niches. Brazil has a heterogeneous ethnic structure as well, with people of African or mixed descent probably comprising at least half the country (the official figures on ethnic background are almost certainly skewed since being white equates with higher social status). The official figures are European 55 percent, mulatto 38 percent, African 6 percent, and 1 percent other. Afro-Brazilians are among the poorest and most politically disenfranchised (CIA 2002). We can expect that data on the ethnic or racial diffusion of ICT will closely reflect income levels.

Finally, the Brazilian political culture structures political and economic outcomes in particular ways. According to authors like Peter McDonough (1981) and others who have extensively studied Brazilian attitudes and values, Brazil's political values have a strong streak of authoritarianism backed by a high degree of political acquiescence among Brazil's poorer strata. These values are said to reflect the country's Portuguese past, the hierarchical nature of the Catholic church (90 percent of the people are Catholic), and the traditions of paternalism associated with the early plantation economies of the region. These long-standing values were reinforced between 1964 and 1985 by two decades of authoritarian military rule, yielding an elite-oriented political culture with selective repression, disenfranchisement, and only tenuous democratic checks on elite autonomy (Johnson 1998).

A strict structuralist perspective would predict that the Internet (and other media) will reflect these deep-seated social, political, and economic conditions. The strategic restructuring model predicts that structural features are mediated by institutions and politics. Structure shapes likely outcomes but does not determine each and every outcome; institutions and politics also play their part. One astute observer of Brazilian political economy concluded from his analysis of the country's computer industry that "a causal analysis based only on structural opportunities and or constraints is insufficient because it does not account for the interaction of process and structure and for the fact that cognitive as well as bargaining factors must be brought into play" (Adler 1987, 684). He too found that institutions, and groups of actors, were also important to understand the country's ICT industries.

The Role of Institutions

A country's institutions are the second big determinant of ICT diffusion. Institutions typically reflect aspects of national social structure but also maintain some relative autonomy (Evans 1995). There is no hard and fast point where structures stops and institutions begin, and they elide with one another at a variety of points. Based on the experiences of other countries, the most likely institutional agents of diffusion in Brazil and other developing countries could be expected to be multinational corporations and state agents (Haggard 1990). As Evans (1995) and others have shown, multinationals have played critical roles in the spread of technological advances. Indeed, the economic development of peripheral capitalism in the twentieth century was partly brought about by Japanese, European, and American corporations seeking factor and product markets and by state agents seeking to provide goods and services that the private sector would not or could not provide. Since the Internet is a foreign-born, relatively high-technology business, we might expect multinational corporations and the state to take the lead.

General Institutions

Among Brazil's most important general institutional patterns are federalism, the military, and institutionalized patterns of elite interactions. As with many large, diverse countries, Brazilian elites have tried to create some institutions that reflect societal and regional differences and others that bridge these differences. Thus, the country has a federal territory as well as twenty-six states that represent and channel local interests. Brazilian federalism and regional diversity have created unique incentives for the emergence of distinct information and communication markets around the country, as seen by the institutions responsible for the production and distribution of telecommunications services. Telebras, the holding company for telephone service, for example, consisted of a separate state-owned enterprise in each of the twenty-six states and Brasilia. Brazil's federal character is also reflected in the diversity of its broadcast media, where different regional capitals are home to different media houses, often family owned. In the economic capital of São Paulo, for example, media conglomerates Fohlio and Estado hold sway, while in Rio de Janeiro, the O Globo group owned by the Marinho family dominates.

The diversity among these institutions is also expressed in the evolution of the Internet. As companies in different regions pursue different diffusion strategies and institutions vie for influence within and across state boundaries, these differences become manifest, as we see below.

A second general institutional factor of importance has been the power of the military in Brazilian society. Throughout the 1960s, 1970s, and 1980s, Brazilian politics was dominated by the military, which affected the distribution of ICT resources in several ways. Top officers in the 1970s and 1980s recognized the military importance of information and other technologies, often giving ICT programs ample resources and special political protection. In one Brazilian institutional pattern, a specialized governmental agency or bureau—such as the Special Secretariat for Informatics (SEI), which influenced the computer reserve policy of the late 1970s through the early 1990s—receives considerable military support and is well insulated from populist appeals and economic interests. Another effect of military intervention was to suppress civil society.

Local initiatives, worker movements, and other independent initiatives were quashed. Some anti-authoritarian activists had to flee the country for a while, though some, like Carlos Aphonso, did return and became grassroots information champions.

At the same time, Brazil has long had a pattern of circulation and links among institutions (Evans 1995; McDonough 1981). Peter Evans (1979) conceptualized specialized links among "tecnicos" (technocrats), the military, and foreign enterprises as the "three-legged stool or "tri-pé"). Peter R. Kingstone (1999) describes how other Brazilian leadership patterns have affected economic reform. As in France, these institutionalized patterns of communication among leadership groups compensate somewhat for high degrees of administrative centralization in the leading institutions. Until recently, the interinstitutional patterns of the Brazilian ICT sector reflected the traditional orientations of the "old regime." These elite institutions acted as iron triangles and were largely impervious to populist inputs. The challenges of the democratizers and their liberal reforms have resulted in some institutional changes.

Institutions in the ICT Sector

This general societywide institutional pattern of military-enforced centralization, elitism, and federalism is also reflected within the contours of the information and communication sector. The diffusion of the Internet in Brazil has been decisively shaped by several leading institutions, including ministries, state enterprises, specialized bodies, research agencies, regulatory bodies, and joint private-public consultative institutions (state-level bodies have also been important). These bodies are described in detail in the appendix to this chapter.

Industrial Policies in the ICT Sector

Government actions intended to influence the evolution of an industry are called *industrial policies* (Diebold 1980). Whether in steel, shipbuilding, or broadband services, industrial policies are consciously designed to shape the structure, location, capital and labor intensiveness, ownership, and other features of an industry (Diebold 1980). The

Internet industry evolved under government-influenced pricing decisions, government-determined access to telephone leased lines, and government-led controls over ownership. Like all governments, the Brazilian government has used many instruments to shape the telecommunications, broadcast, publishing, and computer industries.

Unlike the telecommunications industry, which was almost entirely state-owned, the computer industry was mainly private and therefore required a more nuanced policy of incentives and persuasion. The underlying role of politics and strategic restructuring in the ICT sector is particularly visible and important here. Dozens of books, monographs, and articles have been written on the decades-long policy of the computer "reserve," and I do not reproduce them here.[1] But since the legacy of these policies have direct and indirect relevance to Internet diffusion, it is worth describing briefly.

Like many developing countries in the final quarter of the twentieth century, Brazil pursued an import-substitution industrialization (ISI) strategy that was highly skeptical of liberal assumptions of free trade and limited government (Haggard 1990). From the earliest days of the computer industry, the Brazilian government engaged in a kind of strategic restructuring for ISI, using positive and negative incentives to protect local markets from foreign computer companies, mainly those that were marketing portable computers. Beginning around 1977 by administrative fiat and later by legislation (1984) and continuing through its repeal in October 1992, these Brazilian markets were slowly closed to imports and foreign investment. The ideas and political support actually started in the early 1970s with a domestic coalition including nationalist and protectionist policy intellectuals, military leaders, and domestic hardware producers. As the ideas in this approach ripened through the 1970s and into the 1980s, some legislators began to embrace the ideas of creating a strong indigenous base for ICT development. The coalition held for years until a countercoalition came together that was formed of computer users and consumers who were frustrated with inferior domestic and more expensive gray-market imported machines. The Ronald Reagan administration in the United States also pushed hard on the Brazilian government to open what it saw as a lucrative global market. By the early 1990s, the domestic economic costs, the external pressures, and the general shift toward greater market liberalization merged to kill the reserve policy. The law protected the market for only eight years.

This potent legacy of nationalist and protectionist policies that were driven by an import-substitution strategy was the context within which Brazilian ICT entrepreneurs and policy strategists of the 1990s worked to promote the Internet industry and to learn the lessons of the economic costs of self-sufficiency and nationalist autonomy. Also, the political turmoil and acrimony surrounding the design, implementation, and ultimately the rescinding of these protectionist policies demonstrate conclusively that the evolution of information and communication markets is not automatic but is the result of negotiated interactions—competition, conflict, and cooperation—among a variety of market and government actors. To this day there is considerable debate over the reserve policy's costs and benefits to the country. Proponents insist it created a strong base of human capital, knowledge, and institutional sophistication about the way that information markets operate over the medium term. Opponents counter that the policies imposed costly burdens on corporate and individual consumers and stunted the industry itself by making it less competitive internationally. Studies by Antonio José Junqueira Botelho, Jason Dedrick, Kenneth Kraemer, and Paulo Bustos Tigre (1999) buttress the ICT liberalization argument, though they find that the new policies have hurt the hardware and components industry while lowering prices for consumers and helping the local software industry.

The Role of Individuals and Groups

Politics, Leadership, and Public Policy

One of the purposes of this national case study approach using strategic restructuring is to demonstrate the intricate, organic links among different independent variables that through their interactions yield particular ICT outcomes. The strategic restructuring approach claims that the Internet is the object of political tugging and pulling over particular outcomes and general rules and that these conflicts shape the Internet's spread. In the preceding sections, I defined *structure* and *institution* and indicated earlier dynamics in the information processing industries. In this section, I explore the fluid interactions among politics, leadership, and public policy that helped shape the evolution of the Brazilian Internet market.

The Origins of the Internet in Brazil: The Pre-Commercial Phase

New Internet-like information and communication services in Brazil started with bulletin board services (BBSs) in the mid- to late 1980s. BBSs are open dial-up systems used mainly for message exchange and chat rooms. They were cheap to maintain and often were operated on a shoestring budget by committed young people. These sites proved popular with community groups. The BBSs, maintained by several groups in Brazil, including the Brazilian Institute of Social and Economic Analyses (IBASE), began with only about forty-eight to fifty users, relying on the backbone of the Rio research network, RENPAC (C. Aphonso, personal communication 1999).

Through the mid- to late 1980s, interest in electronic messaging grew in the research community, especially among scientists and engineers. They wanted to use interlinked community networks to share data and research findings across universities. Starting in São Paulo and then Rio de Janeiro, they began to connect researchers together throughout Brazil and then in San Diego, California, and throughout the rest of the United States. The funds to feed this growing interest were provided by officials at the National Council for Scientific and Technological Development (CNPq). According to Professor Carlos Jose Pereira e Lucena, "We used Bitnet a lot, especially the physicists. I remember we used to subscribe to more than 100 journals and working paper series from the developed world, but it was so expensive. Then we discovered we could subscribe online, and it made a big difference to us because we wanted to stay up with the rest of the world" (personal communication 1998). Eventually the National Research Network (RNP) built a national scientific network to service this community.

These research and knowledge advances did not occur automatically. Rather, they were actively promoted by individual Brazilians who relentlessly pursued what was then a farfetched vision of bringing widespread Internet connectivity to their country. Yet diffusion did not flow from vision alone. These advocates lived in an environment of difficult negotiation. Just as there were information advocates, a much larger group of people didn't really care much about the Internet, and still another group actively opposed the decentralized, distributed, and populist vision advanced by the advocates. They had a more centralized, top-down vision that they too pursued aggressively. The core activists in their centralized vision were the power brokers in the state telecom monopolies.

The Emergence of the Information Advocates: The "Gang of Four"

Like the small cadre of Brazilians (called "the Group") who in the 1980s conceived, fought for, and implemented the computer market reserve policies described by Emanuel Adler (1987) and others, a parallel collection of like-minded individuals came together in the 1980s and 1990s to press for another common vision—wider ICT diffusion in Brazil. Like the Group, this cadre of colleagues was convinced that the state had an important role to play in ICT diffusion, though not through the protectionist policies preferred by the Group. Instead, they pursued far more liberal policies. They still used traditional political tactics, and their ultimate goals of nation building were similar to those of their predecessors. But Brazil's information revolutionaries sought a stronger, more ICT-savvy country where individual Brazilians played a major role in sector expansion.

Reading conventional histories of the Internet, especially outside the United States, reveals a lot about backbones and bandwidth but not much about human agency. Looked at more closely, however, we find real human beings behind the bandwidth and social networks underlying copper lines and fiber optics. These individuals pushed forward their own professional, institutional, and personal agendas to make the information revolution happen in Brazil.

In turn, these individuals worked within and through formal institutions, and these institutions shaped their expectations and the resources available to pursue those expectations. To understand the diffusion of these new technologies and the strategies and policies that enabled diffusion, we need to understand these individuals and the institutions in which they worked.

In all countries, many people pressed for rebalancing and restructuring leading institutions and policies. They operated across ministries and parastatals, in political parties, and in private firms. Identifying and interviewing dozens if not hundreds of people would be impractical for a large-scale comparative study like this one. At the same time, capturing the perspectives of a core group that is generally viewed as being important does help capture some of the dynamics of the restructuring process and helps examine the interactions among structure, institutions, and politics through an identifiable, if imperfectly representative, cadre of actors.

The Social Origins of the Gang of Four   The small group of men who found themselves at the forefront of Brazil's changing Internet policy in the late 1980s and 1990s were remarkably similar in their social backgrounds. Most of them were born into and raised in the middle ranks of Brazil's professional classes. They were for the most part the sons of lawyers, engineers, and doctors. They were educated in Brazil for their first degrees, and three went abroad for their advanced degrees, either to the United Kingdom or the United States, usually to earn their doctorates. By training and inclination, these men enjoyed working at the intersections where science, technology, and public policy came together, especially when in the service of their conception of the public good. This first generation of infonauts was uniformly public-minded. Their preferred terrain on which to pursue their personal and professional ambitions was the public sector, whether in universities, public research centers, or public administration.

Cementing these social structural and professional institutional commonalities were more direct ties. For example, two of the leading lights in the group attended high school together and also attended the same graduate school in the original heartland of cyberspace—California. Not only were Ivan Moura Campos and Carlos Jose Pereira de Lucena at UCLA graduate school together, but they both worked closely with one of the founding fathers of the Internet in the United States, Vinton Cerf.

Thus, most of the Internet enthusiast group who would come together in the 1990s met one another during the previous decade through their engagement with the institutional infrastructures of Brazilian science and technology. By the middle of the decade, they had risen to positions of authority in technical institutions of the policy world, where they could influence the design and conduct of ICT policies. This group of early innovators had a disproportionate share of influence over the incentives that shaped the subsequent evolution of the Brazilian Internet:

• Ivan Moura Campos, Ph.D., became secretary of the Ministry of Science and Technology (S&T) after serving as minister of S&T in the state government of Minas Gerais and as an influential senior official for much of the 1990s.

• Eduardo da Costa, Ph.D., became director of Softex, the federal program to promote the export of Brazilian-made software. This followed after serving as one of the three directors of the CNPq, the Brazilian national research authority.

• Carlos Jose Pereira de Lucena, Ph.D., chaired the subcommittee on informatics and development as a member of the presidential Advisory Council on Science and Technology. Lucena for many years taught at the Catholic University of Rio and was a long-time advocate of the research uses of the Internet.

• Tadao Takahashi is one of the main movers and shakers in the multiple networks that link research centers, government, and other bodies important to Internet diffusion. He has moved among several Brazilian technocratic institutions and long served as an ICT promoter and leader in the field. By the end of the 1990s, he was appointed by the government to serve as the head of the advisory committee on implementing Brazil's information society program.

The Gang actually consisted of more than four. Other colleagues were also important to the diffusion process in Brazil:

• Silvio Romero de Lemos Meira, Ph.D., a long-time academic, was also the president of the Brazilian Computer Society (Sociedade Brasileira de Computacao), which is affiliated with the informatics department of the Federal University of Pernambuco (UPFE) in Recife in the state of Pernambuco.

• Somewhat on the outside of this group but close to its members (especially Takahashi) was Carlos Afonso, who was the group member most involved in civil society and the nongovernmental organization sector. His organization, the Brazilian Institute of Social and Economic Analysis, (IBASE), launched the first open, commercial Internet service provider in the country in 1992, years before all other ISPs. Afonso is the one member of the group with deep roots in the NGO community and in populist politics: he traveled to Chile, Mexico, and other countries in support of progressive activities and was closely aligned with the left forces in Brazil.

This group was not just a one-time, coincidental collection of occasionally interacting individuals operating over long distances. Instead, the members remained in close contact over the years, trading professional positions, providing ideas and advice, doing political deals, and pushing forward the odd idea of something that came to be called the Internet. For them, self-consciousness was a strategic advantage. Indeed, they worked together so regularly in the early 1990s and so often in a mode of stealthy opposition to prevailing big bureaucracy policies that they began to refer to themselves as the "Gang of Four" after the small group of conspirators who struggled for control of China after the death of Mao Zedong in 1976. While the story of these half dozen IT conspirators intertwines over the decade, several key episodes capture some of the central dynamics of interelite relations and illustrate the ways that strategic restructuring was conducted in this policy arena during the 1990s.

The First Restructuring

In all countries where the Internet spreads rapidly, there comes a moment when the potential importance of the technology is recognized by experts in different institutions. This can be considered the Big Bang moment when like an exploding universe the perception spreads quickly and widely across the universe of (mostly governmental) institutions. We see this in Brazil and China, though less so in Ghana. This moment occurred in Brazil in the early 1990s, and the Gang of Four was directly involved.

The general macroeconomic and overall political climate always affects Internet diffusion. These realities can facilitate or hinder diffusion, though they rarely block it entirely. In Brazil, the early 1990s were a time when the Internet was on the cusp of spreading, but the country was caught in tremendous political turmoil. Brazil was returning to civilian rule and trying to learn civilian ways again. Economically, inflation was still high, and the growth rate was low. Between 1990 and 1992, President Fernando Collor presided over an awkward transition, beginning as a popular reformer and ending in disgrace as a corrupt and incompetent old-style politician. He was constitutionally succeeded by the vice president, but not until the next government of President Fernando Cardoso did the country experience greater economic stability. In the early 1990s, the inherited industrial policies of the past—heavily statist and monopolist with deleterious impacts on productivity—were discredited and unpopular, but the future was still uncertain.

According to one Brazilian informant, speaking of the Collor years: "This was a very difficult period to try to do something serious in the area of science and technology" (Eduardo da Costa, personal communication, April 6, 2000).

One tenacious individual was determined to make something happen with the new networking technologies that were starting to filter down to Brazil from North America. Tadao Takahashi, an engineer by training, was then working in the research division of Telecommunications Brazil (Telebras), where he encountered some of the Internet's new networking technologies as well as one of the other Gang members, Eduardo da Costa, who was also working in research at Telebras's facilities in Campenas ("sort of the Route 128 of Brazil"). Da Costa had worked at Telebras for eleven years starting in 1982, a few years after earning his Ph.D. in engineering in the United Kingdom. When one of the leading banks in the country decided it needed to expand networking capabilities, it invited Takahashi to launch an independent project (Eduardo da Costa, personal communication, April 4, 2000) to help develop these new networks. This period further whetted Takahashi's appetite for network knowledge and showed him what the technology could do. When he was asked to move over to help the government with the National Research Network, he agreed to do so in 1992.

The research community, supported by government funds from the Ministry of Science and Technology and CNPq, had built up the research backbone in the country starting in 1989. Anxious to press on,

Takahashi grew frustrated because the tumultuous national conditions of the period did not allow him to obtain the resources he needed to expand the infrastructure. He "couldn't get people to respond adequately because of the 'political musical chairs.'" Even after 1992, things were difficult because "there was a lot of movement and rotation among a relatively small group of people" (Eduardo da Costa, personal communication, April 4, 2000).

Takahashi and his colleagues found that creating an effective cross-institutional human network was proving to be impossible. They had ad hoc conversations with people in the state enterprises, the banks, and the universities, but these weren't structured or institutionalized. Few synergies existed. When links were created, the result was sometimes institutional jealousies and threatened egos combined with genuine policy differences, as occurred between researchers in Rio and researchers in São Paulo.

These individuals had to solve what economists and rational choice theorists call a "collective goods" problem—how to create a human, institutional network of relatively selfless people interested in the Internet who could figure out ways to build out infrastructure, promote applications, enhance human capacities, and pay for these ICT resources.

Enter Ivan Moura Campos. Campos is a dynamo of energy who seems always to be on the edge of his seat with a new idea or plan. He studied with Vinton Cerf at UCLA and was an early enthusiast of the Internet's potentials. In 1991, he left his university post in Minas Gerais to become one of the three deputy directors of the CNPq, the main institution responsible for financially supporting S&T in Brazil. Campos wanted to tackle the problem of creating a community of people across institutions.

Da Costa introduced Campos to Takahashi during a trip to Brasilia, having met Campos when both were lecturing at the university in Minas Gerais. Thus began a long period of intense cooperation that linked these three and several others into an Internet conspiracy. Contacts and enthusiasm, however, were no substitute for strategy and money.

After a series of formal and informal meetings, this group, in close consultation with colleagues around the country, devised a plan to move forward the country's commitment to Internet. They spent several weekends together writing a battle plan. This episode closely parallels an event in China where leaders in different institutions finally began to talk to one another and convince themselves of the Internet's critical importance and the need to persuade the powers that be of the urgency of their message.

In essence, the group sought to build up institutional capacities (and political constituencies) in three critical areas. One area was to further develop the basic backbone infrastructure, the requirement for modern national interconnection. This meant additional support for the National Research Network to build out interconnections to other state capitals. Second, they needed money for training and university-based research. And third, coming on the heels of the highly disputed computer reserve policy, Brazil needed to turn away from past inward-looking orientations and turn toward outward-looking export policies. Each component needed to fit together. The plan had a technical basis but was also designed to win political support, and there would be a prize for all the institutional players. The university to be selected, for example, would have to be in one of the less privileged areas of the country. The plan was good, but the country was still in turmoil.

Gradually, a political strategy emerged. The group presented its plan in early 1992 to Brazil's United Nations Development Program (UNDP) and was subsequently funded (initially with a pilot grant of $3 million). UNDP had already given a small amount of money (about $40,000) to initiate a project. A competition was organized for the university component, called PROTEM, with the award going to teams of research universities, one of which had to be from a less developed region. At this time, another close friend of the group, Professor Silvio Romero de Lemos Meira, was brought into the fold as an official member of the Gang of Four. The strategy was in place—Meira at the Federal University of Pernambuco, Takahashi at the National Research Network, Campos at the Ministry of Science and Technology, and da Costa at the export promotion office, SOFTEX, and at the funding agency, CNPq.

With these four in place and with a down payment available, the Gang of Four was now prepared to scale up its ambitions by a factor of ten. It argued the program to senior government officials, insisting that the country needed a new initiative to advance its high-tech sector, especially in information technology. Brazil needed more research and researchers and a new policy framework and fast, since the previous protectionist policies had just ended. A hardware promotion policy had been tried and failed, so perhaps now was the time to emphasize software (there was, however, general agreement among the Gang that while the reserve policy did not succeed in its immediate goal of building an independent computer hardware industry, it did produce a huge pool of trained people and effective institutions that would not otherwise have been created).

Much to the Gang's surprise, its request for $28 million was granted in the first half of 1993. Campos mused, "How did all this come together? I remember one incident that helps explain what was happening at the time. Remember, the Collor government was collapsing, and it was clear things were very shaky. So the various parties involved in the discussions of the package got together to confirm their mutual understanding of where things stood in these discussions, across the various bureaucracies. We were trying to find a way to insulate the process of reform we were pushing forward. That way, whatever might happen to the political guys, we would have some basis for moving forward to get all this stuff done. We said, 'Even if something bad happens, don't let big changes fall by the wayside if and when the government collapses.' Four days later, Collor fell. This was in September of 1992" (personal communication 2000).

According to da Costa's interpretation, another factor was at play. Some of the Gang's support came from an unlikely source beyond the usual suspects of the Ministry of Science and Technology, the universities, and so forth. The Ministry of Foreign Affairs was headed by one Fernando Henrique Cardoso, a very smart and committed economist who in just a few years would vault from foreign affairs into the presidency. Cardoso and a few other colleagues in foreign affairs and elsewhere recognized that globalization was becoming a powerful force. Brazil had to go beyond its comfortable and self-contained political economy and become more globally engaged and competitive. According to da Costa, "*Globalization* was a much stronger buzz word than *Internet* for Cardoso and his people." The government granted the money not because it was confronted by the challenges and opportunities of the Internet but because it had to confront the challenges of globalization, and the Internet project came along as one possible solution to what was looking like a bigger and bigger problem. In February 1993, the $28 million dollar deal was finally signed in an elaborate conference room at the Ministry of Foreign Affairs before an impressive collection of ministers. Also present, perhaps feeling a bit uncertain, was the president of the country's main telephone company, Telebras. (The Gang felt that times were so uncertain that any strategy had to have a hedge. Its hedge was to use the UNDP as a way to store their hard-gotten foreign exchange in an off-shore account so that it wouldn't lose value through Brazil's inflation.) After the $28 million deal was struck, there was another round of the oft-repeated musical chairs: Campos moved from CNPq over to the federal Ministry of S&T, and da Costa shifted from Softex to CNPq or more accurately held both portfolios simultaneously.

Beyond the Usual Commercial Players

Enter the Opposition   If in 1993 or 1994, one asked who would become the premier Internet player in the country, the answer would have been obvious—one or more of the state-owned telephone companies. After all, Embratel had a monopoly over all Brazilian interstate long distance, much like AT&T after the Bell break up in the United States. But then again, the state companies (like the Baby Bells) had a monopoly in their local markets and controlling access to consumers at home and work. Embratel was so sure of itself that in 1994 it invited hundreds of interested private- and public-sector bodies to a meeting where it impatiently explained that Embratel would henceforth be their audience's sole Internet provider (and all they had to do was sign up and, implicitly, get out of the way). Nearly everyone I interviewed who mentioned the 1994 Embratel meeting claimed that it spurred them to set up their own Internal service provider or support more competition. Embratel did launch its ISP in 1994 to stake out its claim in the exploding market and within two years offered a free home page, a chat room, access to newsgroups, and other services. The war was on.

By this time, there was growing recognition of the Internet's potential importance. One of the Gang of Four, Eduardo da Costa, remembered that "prior to [the mid-1990s] no one paid the Internet much attention. It was just a technical thing associated with research and universities.

Then later it became something associated with globalization and then later with privatization as well. Then it got more political and more visible" (personal communication 1998).

Carlos Afonso commented that "Embratel started to become very aggressive. They said, 'We will be the only supplier of ISP services in Brazil.' To prove this to us they cut off ALTERNEX for six months, saying that it was too large and poaching on their territory. I remember they would provide us contracts, of which nineteen pages would spell out clearly the obligations and requirements of the consumer and only one page on what they [Embratel] had to do. Their practical goal (or maybe just an unintended consequence) was to repress demand, since they wouldn't be able to meet it anyway" (personal communication December 2000).

Carlos Lucena noted, "We were furious because it cost us 75,000 per month for a leased line around, so it was millions a year for the universities and CNPq. I remember that Tadao [Takahashi] at RNP had to negotiate really tough to reduce the costs. The company didn't want to reduce our rates at all. Tadao was really furious and insisted on a 90 percent reduction. They finally agreed on 50 percent. We insisted that the schools especially needed these discounts" (personal communication 1998).

Embratel itself was getting nervous, because the nongovernmental organization IBASE had already entered the market by launching the very first Internet service provider that was open to everyone.

The Revenge of the Outsiders   Among the Gang of Four and others in the technocracy who knew the value of the Internet, concern was growing that Embratel might stifle the Internet or certainly dampen demand with high prices and gross inefficiencies. Some elements in the Ministry of Science and Technology, the research community, and other groups began to think about alternatives to a complete Embratel monopoly. In this context, Ivan Moura Campos wrote an opinion article for his boss, Getúlio Vargas, head of the S&T Ministry. In the article, he attacked the telcos monopoly and said that the National Research Network and perhaps others should be allowed to compete directly with Embratel. The article appeared in a prominent Brazilian news magazine and attracted considerable attention, especially since at that time rancorous political debates were raging over whether to privatize and open the economy up to competition.

Leading the privatization debates on behalf of Fernando Henrique Cardoso was his closest confidant and political advisor, Sergio Motta. A finely tuned political sense, tremendous loyalty, and years with Cardoso in the political wilderness made him one of the most powerful men in Brazil, and Cardoso appointed him Minister of Communications.

When a friend sent him a copy of Campos's article attacking the telcos' monopoly, Motta invited several people including Carlos Aphonso to dinner to discuss possible reforms. Soon afterward, he instructed his senior advisor to get together with his counterpart in S&T (who at this time was Ivan Moura Campos) to work out some options for government. Their biggest goal was to keep Embratel out of the Internet markets as a monopolist and make it compete with other companies. They recommended what they thought the government could bear politically—RNP competition, universal access to dial-up service, and most radical of all, the declaration of the Internet as a value-added service. This last would mean that, by statute, Embratel wouldn't be able to compete.

Positioning the powerful Embratel on one side against the S&T Ministry and a handful of researchers on the other did not seem like a well-balanced fight. But when Motta announced his final decision, he backed the anti-Embratel coalition unequivocally. Not only did he declare Internet a value-added service, but he decreed that state companies would be forbidden to compete in Internet markets. This left the arena open to private firms and to small and medium-sized companies. Campos and the others believe that while their advice carried some weight with Motta, the more important element was high politics: Cardoza had staked his administration's reputation on implementing an aggressive and effective privatization campaign. The state companies were furious and tried unsuccessfully to reverse the decree, but President Cardoza was apparently satisfied. Sadly, Motta died unexpectedly soon thereafter.

The ruling that declared the Internet a value-added service outside of state control reverberated throughout the country for years. Several Brazilian entrepreneurs in São Paulo pointed to it as perhaps the single most important ruling for their own business success. Without it, most Internet service provider business people confessed to me that they probably wouldn't be in business today.

Two Successful Episodes   These two developments—first, creating and institutionalizing a community of like-minded reformers within the main ICT sector with access to political and organizational resources and then successfully battling against big, monopolistic corporations—reveal the ways in which strategically placed individuals deliberately structured a reform process. This reform process led to the institutional conditions for a new competitive market in which Brazilian Internet services and goods emerged.

Strategic restructuring did not occur simply when *one* institution was reformed. Rather, restructuring was effective when a cadre of reformers was able to change procedures in an array of different institutions so that a progressive change in one was supported by complementary changes in another. Typically this requires a complementary strategy of "guerrilla attack" (Adler 1987) wherein some of the reforming information champions infiltrate existing institutions to alter their purposes and procedures, while others hammer on the doors from the outside. In the case of the restructuring of Brazil's Internet market, people like Carlos Afonso hammered hard from the outside, drawing on decades of left-wing grassroots politics with NGOs in Latin America. He and his colleagues succeeded in creating alternative institutions alongside inherited, if sclerotic, state institutions to serve their populist ideologies and constituencies. Others, like Ivan Moura Campos, scaled the walls and took over at the top. Both were engaged, in complementary ways, in strategic restructuring.

The Gang of Four did not disband after the antimonopoly decree. In May 1995, the government established a steering committee to oversee its implementation. Not surprisingly, the steering committee featured Ivan Moura Campos (representing the S&T Ministry), Silvio Meira (representing the consumers), Eduardo da Costa, Carlos Aphonso, Professor Carlos Lucena, Tadao Takahashi, and tech guru Gretsko Demi.

How did this group see itself? When pressed on the question, they deny that they were *tecnicos*, or technocrats. Lucena especially sees himself primarily as an academic, although one who is deeply committed to public life. He laughingly told me that the reports and studies he prepares do not go on his resume, since reports and public service carry little weight in the academy (personal communication 2000).

In his essay "Ideological 'Guerrillas' and the Quest for Technological Autonomy: Brazil's Domestic Computer Industry," Emanuel Adler (1987) points to some traits of an earlier similar group that pressed for the reserve policy in the 1980s. He reports that their numbers were small, so the coordination problems of larger groups were minimized. Initially, their issues were below the radar screen of senior policy makers, and hence they could build up political support and deploy infrastructures before the issue became politicized. In addition, their early political demands were modest.

Similar conditions existed for the Gang of Four. The problems identified in the rational-choice literature were overcome by group size and structure and by tactical and strategic steps, including selective incentives and a high degree of coherence around a common mission—the rapid diffusion of the Internet.

Still, in light of what followed, it is curious that these "first-wave" information champions did not interact more with their private-sector counterparts. There is little evidence of consultation with executives of small or large companies. With a few exceptions we discuss later—including Alexandre Mandic and Gretsko Demi—there was not much overlap between these first-wave public champions and the second-wave private-sector entrepreneurs (although later da Costa did open an e-business company and made the "up-and-over" transition from state to market).

Thus, by the early to mid-1990s, the information champions had produced something more than a technical network and less than a market. The system was still closed to most and was very expensive. The challenge of the next period was to open it to more people and push the research system toward a true commercial market.

The Commercial Period Gets Under Way

When Brazil's first Internet service provider offered service to anyone who could afford it, the initial period of a self-contained closed-architecture Internet community was eclipsed. When the first one or two such companies appear, then by my definition the country has taken a firm step toward structuring a real market for Internet goods and services. Such competition and openness have come to be the essence of the medium. Somewhat surprisingly, the first nonclosed Internet service provider was neither a research body, a state-owned corporation, nor a multinational corporation but a local Brazilian NGO—the Brazilian Institute of Social and Economic Analyses (IBASE).

The Green Information Revolution

Internet diffusion, like the spread of other scarce resources, can be accelerated by an external event heightening awareness, provoking political mobilization, and altering institutions. One event that accelerated diffusion was the world environmental summit held in Rio in 1992. These resultant changes were then managed and guided by individuals acting through a political network dedicated to substantive policy changes— and to networking in developing countries.

In the period preceding the 1992 summit, local Brazilian green groups and those based in the North developed close ties as they sought to coordinate joint efforts to get their issues on the government-dominated summit agenda. Preparing for the conference meant that Brazilian groups were in constant contact with external groups, and the Internet became the preferred way of communicating. Groups like the San Francisco–based Association for Progressive Communications (APC) and the Institute of Global Communications provided encouragement and technical support. APC, founded in 1990, was active globally in helping create a variety of listserve communities politically active in issues concerning the environment, social justice, and so forth, and IBASE was an early partner. Eventually, however, IBASE found that a variety of problems interposed. "We wanted to stay in touch with our international partners, but Telebras was so expensive and unreliable we got completely frustrated," said Carlos Afonso, one of the local organizers. "So we circumvented the PTT. We had separate links between São Paulo and the US, then Rio-US, but not São Paulo-Rio. So we decided to create a new network that would link them all" (personal communication 1998). Not surprisingly, Telebras was very uncooperative. Nonetheless, with determination and dedication, a new network was created. More and more Brazilians started to use the IBASE network, including those outside NGOs.

The Emergence of Competition

By 1994 and 1995, technically astute and thoughtful Brazilian entrepreneurs began to realize that this Internet thing had real potential to affect their own businesses. The community of people who cared about the Internet diversified. Technical gurus and policy wonks were joined by new actors who wanted to offer new services to new people—for money.

While the structure of the Brazilian political economy had not changed much, long-postponed social and political pressures had reached the boiling point. The new Cardoza government was prepared to channel those pressures toward institutional and policy reform. Cardoza used his political power to force changes in the organization and performance of the state agencies, in turn restructuring the incentives for private-sector market actors, leading them to innovate and modernize the economy. These changes were nowhere more important than in the telecommunications sector. Telecom privatization and reform were central to the presidential strategy. If Cardoza's strategic restructuring initially worked for telecoms, then the new incentives and regulations could produce changes in other markets, eventually spreading to the entire economy. The telecom privatization initiative was central to Cardoza's national economic strategy. The fundamental change in ownership would eventually go further than the May 1995 "value-added" policy altering access to Internet markets.

The Brazilian telecom privatization episode has been widely described elsewhere. To summarize, the industry went from having one monopolistic domestic owner (or two, if one counts Telebras and Embratel) to having multiple owners both foreign and domestic. To effect privatization, the Brazilian Congress took a highly controversial vote to alter the Constitution (August 15, 1995) and passed a new General Telecommunications Law in 1997. By the end of the first rounds of the sale, the state had realized about U.S. $19 billion through sales to private investors from Canada, Italy, Portugal, Spain, the United States, and

Brazil. An additional $128 million was realized through sales of concessions to private companies to operate fixed telephone "mirror companies" to go toe-to-toe with the established companies (Paschoalino 2000). Furthermore, the government created a set of new regulations and distributional targets that rewarded new telecom buyers that met stiff distributional targets and punished those that failed to meet the targets (Tavares 1998). Successful privatization of telecoms in Brazil was essential for vigorous and innovative Internet development. As one astute observer pointed out to me in São Paolo, the monopoly of Telebras meant a chronic undersupply of telephone lines, but because lots of new telephone lines are needed for the Internet to grow, undersupply of telephones meant undersupply of Internet: "No privatization, no lines; no lines, no Internet" (Margarita Polotnik, personal communication 2000).

As the new administration signaled its commitment to privatization, actors felt confident that the direction that change was taking was toward more liberal, competitive, and internationalized ICT markets. These actors in turn took steps to enter those newly liberal markets despite some remaining uncertainties.

The challenges for the Brazilian economic agents in this period were substantial, differing somewhat from earlier challenges. With some of the basic soft and hard infrastructure in place and telecom privatization underway, the new challenge was to search for business plans and material resources that allowed ICT entrepreneurs to be commercially viable. They would have to produce services and goods that customers were willing to pay for. They wanted to build and protect a viable Brazilian presence in a rapidly changing global industry. They also had to build and sustain a domestic political coalition to keep the liberalization process moving forward.

Key Economic Institutions

Institutions and the elites that run them are the critical players in information and communication technology restructuring. The key economic institutions in this turbulent period included the state-owned enterprises, the Brazilian entrepreneurs, the major Brazilian media houses, multinationals (northern and southern), the ICT business interest associations

(BIAs), and the nonprofits. For each category, I describe at least one example to illustrate it. The examples are meant to be illustrative, not exhaustive.

The State-Owned Enterprises (SoEs)

What role did the giants of the telecommunications industry play in Brazil's ICT restructuring? The state-owned enterprises (SOEs) like Embratel and Telebras were at the center of ICT industry reform as the main targets for purchase and as potentially important actors in the emerging Internet market. But according to respondents in the SOEs and outside, the staffs of the big state entities were so preoccupied with weathering their own privatization that they chose not to get much involved with the Internet. They were not yet players in the ISP markets. The government of Brazil did not plunge in to micromanage these markets through an interventionist industrial policy. While the sales of Telebras and Embratel reaped almost $19 billion for the government, they had little *direct* impact on Internet buying and selling; they did, however, restructure the medium-term incentives and opportunities.

The Brazilian Entrepreneurs

New market opportunities brought out new commercial entrepreneurs. The new entrepreneurs were similar in some respects to their "first-wave" counterparts. They often were from similar middle-class and pro-fessional family backgrounds and shared a vision of bringing the Internet to their people. These were early innovators, folding a fascination with technology into a far-reaching strategic vision of transformative Brazilian institutions. But if the first-wave champions were middle-aged rule writers and highly educated policy guerrillas, the second wave was younger, had fewer Ph.D.s, and were less likely to have spent as much time outside Brazil. Their vision was to advance commercial Internet opportunities. They were less interested in changing rules and more inter-ested in working within whatever rules were in place to achieve their commercial goals. They wanted big successful Brazilian companies, not big successful Brazilian research programs. They wanted to make money. But like wave one, they also knew they had to push colleagues and adver-saries to progress beyond their own organization. As one of them told me in São Paulo, "For us, it's a chance to make money and to make history at the same time" (C. T. Costa, personal communication 2000).The following discussion is not meant to represent all cyberentrepreneurs or necessarily typical ones. Rather, these are individual businesspeople who are frequently presented in the press and through interviews as leaders in their field. These are the *commercial* information champions—the private sector counterparts to the policy champions of the Gang of Four.

Marcelo Larcedo tops most "must see" lists in the Brazilian Internet business. He is admired for a number of accomplishments, including founding a successful ICT company and selling it twice for a great profit. Larcedo possesses an unusual combination of in-depth technological knowledge, commercial innovation, ingenuity, strategic insight, and modesty. His commercial coup was deciding early on that he could make money and help Brazilian diffusion by franchising his Internet service provider operations. "We became the McDonald's of the Internet industry in Brazil," he says half-joking" (personal communication 2000). He and his partner also designed a major technological innovation that at one point was purportedly used by more than half the banks in the country. Larcedo maneuvered through the mergers and acquisition fever at the end of the 1990s, emerging as a top executive in Terra, a leading IT corporation. His professional trajectory demonstrates that strategic restructuring occurs not only within and between public agencies but also within and between firms. The private restructurings can also change market structure and incentives and thereby reshape subsequent expectations and behaviors.

Larcedo recalls being a child and playing with the old perforated processing cards of the "ancient" computers and playing on an IBM laptop. He grew up in a southern Brazilian household in Porto Allegra, where his father was an engineer and test pilot. He began his studies as an electrical engineer but also took medical courses, surfed (at the beach) and practiced architecture before finally arriving at software development. To support his growing family (he had a son, who now works with his father in Terra), he worked for several Brazilian firms in the engineering and aircraft industries before he and a friend (also still with him at Terra) raised $300,000 from a venture capital fund to start a software and systems integration business they called NuTec. In 1991 to 1993, he lived in Silicon Valley to be close to his customers. In hindsight, he jokingly refers to NuTec as the "first Brazilian micro-multinational corporation." NuTec soon found that the Internet started as a tool for his business and then became his core business. (NuTec's experience parallels the experience of the Ghanaian entrepreneur Nii Quaynor, who also came to the Internet business because he found it essential for his own computer business.)

As their customers grew, NuTec gained about half of the local Brazilian niche market (companies like ACER still use software NuTec designed). Eventually, he and his partners began their own ISPs, and designed a unique marketing strategy by franchising their brand. Beginning in 1994 with revenues of 2 million reals, they built their system so that by 1996 they had about fifteen national operations—three owned and operated outright and the others franchised. In that year, one of the regional Telebras companies in the south, RBS, bought out a majority of NuTec shares, though Larcedo retained some holdings, and renamed the company ZAZ. Three years later, ZAZ was acquired by Telefonica of Spain and renamed Terra, and Larcedo was bought out again and named Terra's CEO (personal communication 2000).

Today, Terra is one of the leading Internet service providers in the country, with the ambition of becoming not only an Internet provider but a digital broadcaster with new talent and new studios designed for distributing content. "We see Terra as being a major Brazilian media company, not just an ISP," says Larcedo. But being a new firm with a start-up mentality, Larcedo is concerned about the future. "We are a new company. So we all must believe that we are dying tomorrow or the next day. We have to act like we're going out of business if we don't work as hard and as smart as we can" (personal communication 2000).

The new entrepreneurs share a continuing problem with many online businesses in Ghana, China, and other nations—very high access fees charged by the national and international backbones, which for Brazilian Internet service providers can run 80 percent of revenues. These high charges rarely reflect actual cost and keep the ISPs in a constant search for a new business model that avoids the monopolist position of these privileged sellers (Paschoalino 2000).

The Internet Strategies of the Major Media Houses

Brazil possesses several major media houses, each family-owned and each commercially engaged with digital content and delivery. Sometimes the major media houses are in partnership with each other, sometimes they are in direct competition. The four main houses are O Globo, owned by the Marinho family of Rio; Abril, owned by the Chivitas; Estado, based in São Paulo and owned by the Mesquita family; and Fohlio do SP, owned by the Freitas; Their influence on the political and cultural life of Brazil has been enormous and well documented. All have also developed strategies of carving out a commercial presence in cyberspace. How they determine and pursue their goals is a commercial form of strategic restructuring, since their actions shape market structures and, de facto, market rules. The strategies they pursue in the Internet markets are shaped by the strategies they pursue in traditional media. Their strategies are also the result of assumptions and calculations from key individuals in each family's management team. The powerful and long-standing role of private, family-owned companies in the media industry is a major point of difference between Brazil and other developing countries, including China and Ghana, where traditional media are state-owned.

Fohlio do SP and Universe On Line (UOL)   Fohlio do SP is a power house in São Paulo with highly diversified holdings. Its biggest venture in the online industry is as originating partner in Brazil's largest Internet service and content provider, Universe On Line (UOL). In business circles, it is viewed as somewhat curious that Fohlio has jumped into the big ISP business (and the Mesquita family has not, since it has somewhat more experience in this field), but Fohlio is felt to have benefited from not being a first mover and playing catch-up with its closest competitor by jumping into the business with both feet.

The family member who most took up the challenge was Roberto Freitas, who became fascinated with the commercial possibilities of the Internet in the early 1990s. His role increased when his father, the company's patriarch, curtailed his own executive power, leaving more room for Roberto and his brother Louis, who sought new market opportunities in the information technology industry and made the necessary internal reforms and external alliances to turn their vision into reality. According to Brazilian observers, Roberto and his brother possessed different gifts, with the older brother Roberto more interested in creative ideas and editorial content, and Louis more interested in the business's commercial side. Three years after IBASE launched the first "commercial" Internet, there were about 60,000 nationwide subscribers. Louis Freitas and some of his colleagues then began to review the performance of AOL in the United States. When compared, 60,000 "eyeballs" were seen to be insufficient for a Brazilian commercial venture.

By 1995, Roberto had convinced his father and other members of the management team that digital content and delivery was the way of the future. According to close observers, his challenge was, "Which way do we go to build a commercially viable presence in cyberspace?" (personal communication 2000). The company conducted an environmental scan to consider several options, including reviews of cellular, cable, and conventional TV. Ultimately, it chose to follow a strategy of developing local content and delivery that drew heavily on the AOL model. They called their new company Universe On Line (UOL).

Any such strategy required a strong management team and partners who could provide additional media outlets to complement Fohlio's customer reach. The management chose long-time Fohlio executive Caio Tulio Costa to run the new company. A highly respected journalist and media manager, in some ways he represents the manifestation on the commercial side of the Gang of Four. His experience also somewhat parallels that of Marcelo Larcedo of NuTec, but within the confines of one company, the Fohlio organization. When Louis Freitas invited him to help run UOL in 1996, Costa was responsible for both content and editorial functions for Fohlio magazines. An experienced journalist and journalism professor, Costa also helped computerize Fohlio's newsroom in the early 1980s. In the late 1980s, he served as Fohlio's European correspondent.

Abril To solve the problem of strategic alliances, Fohlio decided to pair with Abril (not Globo or Stado or a foreign company), which brought huge content reserves. It was an interesting pairing. The owners of Abril, the Chivitas family, had already pursued their own cable television strategy, a decision that almost brought the company to ruin because the expected cable revenues stumbled badly. They were perhaps ready for a new, arm-in-arm, low-cost entry into the digital world to acquire expertise and market access. When viewed from the outside, one could have argued that for Fohlio, the Stado organization would have been the logical partner because of its longer involvement with online services. But Fohlio allied with Abril instead, creating UOL, which quickly became the largest Internet service and content provider in Brazil. UOL claims to be the number one Internet company in the country, with 39 to 49 percent of the paying market and 85 percent of the market reach.

O Globo   Curiously, the largest family-owned business—O Globo—had holdings in TV, radio, and print but found itself out of the big UOL alliance and a step or two behind in its online initiatives. As the biggest, most secure media house, it perhaps did not feel the same sense of urgency as the others. Its initial steps were not impressive, and the company seems to have shifted its strategy several times with mixed effects.

The Revolution Comes to the Establishment: The Internet Strategy of the Mesquita Family   The Mesquita family offers an interesting case in private-sector restructuring. In contrast to the Freitas and Chivitas families, who allied together to create UOL, the Mesquitas took a gamble by holding back and *not* plunging into the information revolution as extensively as some of their competitors. Because of their delay, the Mesquitas have been sharply criticized by observers of the Internet and media industries. Their reasons for delaying seem driven partly by management style and structure, partly by the way their current assets are deployed, and partly by an evaluation of the future of the Internet market based on their understanding of other media markets.

Stepping into Rodriguez Mesquita's dark, wood-paneled corner suite is like stepping into a time machine. With dark rugs on the floor and framed family photos, including pictures of his great-grandfather Stados Mesquita, founder of the company, on the walls, this inner sanctum is not decorated in the typical high-tech minimalist style affected by other

ICT executives. The hazy glare and wall-to-wall cackling of computers in the reporters' newsroom seems miles away.

Mesquita seems to occupy the interesting and rather odd position in Brazil and in other countries of a very conservative revolutionary or a very revolutionary reactionary. He insists that he draws on the newspaper's traditional values and is committed to retaining the best values and qualities of an engaged media that deliberately aims to build citizenship and profits (personal communication 2000). In my interviews, he was one of the very few who was able to take a long-term view. The question is whether this sense of long-term civic commitment will translate into commercial success. His focus is narrow in its commercial targeting of financial and sector-specific clients but wide in his commitment to the values of responsible journalism.

Mesquita argued against the prevailing mindset in much of the industry, including some of his competitors: "You don't build a new world in two years. You need twenty-five years. . . . Think in terms of the next forty years, otherwise your view is too short term. I believe our markets are not yet ripe. That will take at least a little more than a decade." He points out that his company was founded by his great-grandfather in 1875 and reads me the paper's original motto about the obligation to serve the public. He updates the motto by saying, "Our success is not just a sheet of paper or a monitor screen" but rather "channels of relationships we have with our audience. . . . We have a responsibility to the whole person—not just as an economic agent but also a citizen, a person in a unique culture."

Mesquita has tried to marry his historically rooted vision to a contemporary strategy that appears on the surface to be a much more narrowly focused strategy than that of his competitors. Instead of using broadband to provide all kinds of content to all sorts of audiences, he develops and targets his content to selected audiences who need his product for business purposes. His company streams up-to-the-minute information and value-added analyses—data and reviews of Brazilian markets and foreign markets relevant to Brazil, especially financial, agricultural, and industrial industries—to his clients. In addition, Agencia Estado, the digital arm of Grupo Estado, has established partnerships with companies like FT.com, Economist Intelligence Unit, McGraw-Hill, and Dow Jones News.

Just a few steps from his old fashioned office is the nerve center of the enterprise—row after row of computer screens where reporters and writers sit elbow to elbow tracking the latest movements of dollars, reals, and deutschmarks.

This strategy is not without its critics. Others in the business find fault with Stado for missing the opportunity to be much more aggressive in the new information markets. Some tell of efforts they made to convince Grupo Estado to join other alliances. Others cannot understand why Mesquita didn't do more to leverage his company's assets. One interesting explanation attributes different corporate strategies to different family situations. The company that moved most boldly, Fohlio under Roberto Freitas, had at its helm a patriarch who was stepping back and two brothers who were stepping forward. At Abril, the Chivitas family had only a few people in their cousin generation. By contrast, the same generation in the Mesquita family had seventeen cousins. The future vision of ICT that Rodriguez Mesquita championed had to get the buy-in of a dozen or so other relatives, probably not an efficient decision-making structure. Some claim that Mesquita had difficulty selling the rest of the family on his new ideas. Another curious observation is that the individuals in the big media families who pushed most for a radical digital strategy were typically their parents' youngest child: less rigidity and greater vision.

In light of the current information industry shakeout, a cautious strategy is perhaps the most reliable. Time will tell whether the expansive or the targeted strategy will work best. Time will tell whether Mesquita's historical references are on target or merely post hoc justifications for strategic sluggishness.

Mullinationals: Northern and Southern
A phalanx of foreign enterprises entered the Brazilian Internet market with mixed degrees of success. These included North American giants like AOL and Microsoft, as well as wildly successful start-ups from other Latin American countries. From Argentina, for example, came Patagon.com, the brainchild of the brilliant twenty-something

Wenceslao Casoves. Patagon.com bought up existing online brokers and online-capable banks across Latin America to provide financial services. In 2000, 75 percent of the company was sold for $530 million, having performed well in Brazilian markets. StarMedia, another foreign firm, played a big role in the country during the early stages of ICT development but was unable to sustain itself and integrate Brazil into the rest of its Latin offerings.

Perhaps the biggest and most surprising foreign performance was AOL's clumsy attempt to enter into the Brazilian market. The first local president left soon after launching the local Brazilian company. Under his watch, a technical glitch was allowed to occur in the software sent out to customers, muddying AOL's reputation in the country. Some claimed other missteps reflected an overly U.S.-centric view of Brazilian ICT markets. Brazilians made a point of insisting to me that they were not just another Latin market or just another market like the United States. They were a unique culture (personal communication 2001; Romero 1999).[2]

AOL remains an aggressive player in the market, but its future seems more troubled than at their champagne launch in São Paulo. And while Microsoft, Yahoo!, Spain's Telefonica, and others are moving into Brazil's Internet market, these ISPs are certainly not dominating the market as one might have hypothesized earlier.

The ICT Business Interest Associations

Some private players are not firms but business associations of many firms. The Association of Brazilian Internet Providers (ABRANET) was founded soon after the Brazilian government's decision to declare the Internet a value-added service. It was founded as a classic business association to lobby government, share information, reduce transaction costs, and assimilate its members into a set of business norms. Its first president was early Internet service provider entrepreneur Antonio Tavares, founder of the start-up Dialdata. Launched toward the end of 1996, ABRANET members discussed such issues as how small and medium-sized enterprises can survive in a rapidly evolving market, as well as what regulations government should put in place for the various market players (personal communication 2001). As of early 2001, it claimed about 120 company members (ABRANET official, personal communication December 2000).

The Associacao do Media Interactive (AMI) is similar in purpose to ABRANET and represents some of the same firms (like UOL and NuTec). Led by a highly visible advertising executive, it is especially interested in content issues that concern suppliers and clients. In separate discussions with leaders of both organizations, there was not the acrimony one sometimes finds with competing bodies. "The market is growing fast enough for everybody," one of them concluded (personal communication 2000).

Other associations also promote Internet interests. An interesting U.S. transplant is the First Tuesday organization, which began hosting networking cocktail parties in the United States where investors, entrepreneurs, company executives, and others met and mingled over liquor and food. In the refurbished old train station of São Paulo, furious networking takes place, another of the universals of the emerging networked economy. Other more general bodies like the National Confederation of Industries and various chambers of commerce also try to advance Internet diffusion through regulatory reform and by informing their members of new developments. The American Brazilian Chamber (SP) even hosted its own successful ISP for several years before selling it to a private American company after some spirited internal debates (Chamber official personal communication 2000).

The evidence from Brazil shows a great deal of commercial activity and substantial restructuring of private Internet and telecom markets. The restructuring occurred both through new businesses formed de novo, as well as through strategic alliances and partnerships among major well-established national and international players. New business associations lobbied government and tried to reduce the transaction costs among members.

The Nonprofits

According to the umbrella organization for Internet promotion among nongovernmental organizations—the Information Network for the Third Sector (RITS)—"Among the nearly 250,000 Brazilian nonprofits, fewer than 1.5 percent have registered their own domain names and about the same number have some Web presence. . . . Most of the

Internet usage among third-sector organizations in Brazil is basically restricted to one or two institutional e-mail accounts (true even for some larger institutions that are heavy users of microcomputers)" (RITS 1999, 5). According to some sources, these low figures reflect both insufficient money and a lack of compelling interest and leadership within the nonprofits.

A final telling example of the imbalance between the private-sector and public-sector changes that demonstrates the absence of substantive, far-reaching, and serious ICT change in the Brazilian nonprofit sphere occurred in the early 1990s, when populist forces launched a sophisticated campaign to open the decision-making process of the Brazilian ICT sector. Like most countries, developing or otherwise, the administration of Brazil's telecommunications sector was a closed network of experts and vested interests. Virtually no formal political access was given to average citizens or consumer groups. This was a true iron triangle of ministerial, parastatal, and domestic economic interests. Even in broadcast, where assets were privately owned, tight collusion between government and the private media excluded widespread citizen input or consultation.

As the democratic forces in Brazil stirred again after decades of repression, the old closed model of centralized corporatist economic governance came under attack. A message of greater transparency and wider popular participation was echoed in calls for the decentralization, commercialization, and ultimately privatization of the telecommunications sector.

These trends came together in 1992 in a concerted political effort to open up decision making in the cable television industry. Indeed, the cable television act was the first piece of legislation that President Cardoza signed marking the first time that telecoms policy was actually negotiated with independent civic organizations (Aufderheide 1997, 574).

In the early 1990s, urban intellectuals, policy experts, labor groups, and other representatives from the private, noncommercial sector coalesced into several groups, including the National Forum for the Democratization of Communications. According to Patricia Aufderheide's (1997) excellent and detailed interpretation, the Forum became a stage for contention and cooperation and was pulled in different directions, with some group coalitions insisting on private investment and others countering with the more traditional statist argument that state-owned enterprises better protected the public interests. At the high point of the debates, a Social Communications Council was proposed as a permanent vehicle for public input and for the participation of NGOs, consumers, and others. Here was a chance for the nonprofit sector to expand its authority decisively in the emerging information society.

In the end, however, Brazil's richer and more powerful interests succeeded in neutralizing the progressive forces of the nonprofits. The Social Communications Council never saw the light of day. The Marinho family paper, *O Globo*, seized control of the emerging cable services market, and self-serving Ministry of Science and Technology officials retained their power. Aufderheide (1997) concludes that this stillborn effort to project nonprofit interests ultimately failed to achieve all its goals. But the politics around these gatherings brought about two somewhat contradictory trends. They "boldly demonstrate(d) the entrenched and stable elements of a centralized, presidentialist political system and a politically enmeshed business elite, even at a moment of wild instability in the global marketplace. . . . [Yet they also] demonstrate[d] the indubitable collapse of legitimacy of the simple equation of the public and the state, and a quest for social organization that can represent interests beyond those of governing and economic elites" (Aufderheide 1997, 593). These issues remain on the table today.

The subversion of civil society's role in ICTs also occurred in South Africa. There a similar initiative of broad-based consultations of grassroots and consumer groups had similarly modest outcomes as big corporate interests (in this case, the state telecoms) maneuvered to maintain their power. What is striking is that two different experts—Derrick Cogburn (1998) and Robert Horwitz (2001)—both reach conclusions similar to Aufeheide's: although the *process* of reform (or what I would call restructuring) was innovative and progressive, the final *outcomes* were not. In both Brazil and South Africa, the groups in civil society lacked the organizational wherewithal to sustain a long prodemocratic ICT campaign. Even when they might have won, the countervailing forces in the state and in private companies outmaneuvered them, and the grassroots groups were unable to restructure permanently the rules of the game to achieve the kinds of distributive outcomes they hoped for initially. These experiences do not auger well for opening up the old institutional patterns to greater access by popular forces. Without decisively breaking the iron triangle of technicos and opening it to other voices, the outcomes of policy processes are unlikely to alter distributional outcomes. If the popular forces and their allies fail to restructure access to the agencies that allocate scarce resources, old patterns and priorities will continue. The market alone is insufficient to remedy the entrenched patterns of very limited telecoms and value-added distribution. (Remember, only about 2 to 3 percent of Brazilians and only .5 percent of all Africans have access to the Internet. A full remedy requires opening political and institutional access more effectively.

The Digital Divide in Brazil

The problems that unconnected Brazilians face are not always problems of hard infrastructure access. As I argue in greater detail in chapter 6, poor Brazilians can't easily afford telephone charges, even if their villages were connected. Poor Brazilians lack the education and training to get benefits from the Internet that are comparable to those of the educated middle classes. Illiterate Brazilians may not find content that is entertaining or useful to them. Sometimes these groups yielded formal access but not "real" access. In chapter 6, I return to this distinction between formal and effective access.

Earlier I cited the privatization regulations that were designed to promote wider telephone diffusion. In addition, the General Telecommunications Law of 1997 created the Universal Service Fund (Fundo de Universalizacao dos Servicos de Telecommunicacoes, or FUST), which was written to address the social aspects of telephone services. However, with 1998 an election year, determining the source of funding for FUST, identifying the beneficiaries, allocating funds, and other issues were bogged down in the legislature.

In terms of Internet access, one proposed solution to the divide would be to provide Brazilians with very low-cost, locally made ICT boxes that would connect to the Internet and cost only $300. Each machine would have a modem, a mouse, a color monitor, speakers, simple browsing software, and not much else (it would not have a hard disk or floppies). The government's hope is that it would sell for about $300 and could be paid for on installments as low as U.S. $15 a month. To help reduce the divide and build demand, the government also wants to install these basic machines in public schools, which will give new Internet access to seven million children.

In yet another indication of continuity in the Brazilian ICT sector, according to SiliconValley.com, "the project's mastermind" is Ivan Moura Campos, one of the Gang of Four. Campos talks about creating incentives for the key actors, such as tax incentives included in a new information technology law.

The president of the Institute of Research in Applied Economics (IPEA) has pointed out that the level of poor Brazilians who benefit from public services varies substantially with the service: 2.6 percent of the poor lacked electricity in 1995, and 24.7, 25.4, and 92.3 percent, respectively, lacked sewers, trash collection, and telephone service. Telephone service is more skewed than many other services.

The problem facing Campos is similar to the one he and his colleagues faced in the early 1990s—how to put together a political coalition to push an idea forward. That coalition must design, produce, and distribute the new "volkscomputer." He points out that "this was not a First World problem—we were not going to find a Swedish or a Swiss company to solve this for us. We would have to do it ourselves" (personal communication, 2000).

Electronic Commerce in Brazil

Effective access is much less of a problem for businesses in Brazil. Today, according to a recent poll conducted by the Monitor consulting group, medium-sized Brazilian companies are as likely to invest in Internet applications as are large firms and invest about 10 percent of their revenues. Even as early as 1998, 13 percent of corporations had implemented extranets, and about 23 percent were projected to do so in that year. The main reasons that businesspeople gave for using Internet were to integrate more tightly with partners, to rapidly react to dynamic markets, and to improve supply chain management (personal communication, 2000). Beyond the Internet-focused firms I described above, traditional "bricks and mortar" companies, as well as service companies, have been active in the electronic space. Maria Ilca Lima and Ivan Alcoforado Jr. (1999, 134) describe how various Brazilian industries are managing to incorporate modern information services into their basic processes, including in automobiles, retail sector and transportation services. In the auto industry, for example, Fiat in Brazil "was the pioneer . . . offering on its site . . . all its models, optional items, price information and financing conditions . . . [transferring] to the Internet a significant part of the . . . work usually restricted to the . . . authorized dealers." Another report finds that in general e-commerce is more driven by traditional retailers than in other countries. For example, the supermarket Pao de Acucar launched Amelia.com, where its clients can order groceries, review products, and download recipes. Business analysts expected online commerce in Brazil to jump from $2.47 billion in 2000 to nearly $40 billion in 2003, especially when the telecom markets become fully deregulated.

In the service sector, firms like Grupo Catho have plunged into e-commerce with gusto. Grupo Catho is a wide-ranging professional services company based in São Paulo whose owner is committed to electronic commerce for one simple reason. With it, he can earn a lot of money by doing old things cheaper, faster, and better. He can now do some other things he used to do but had to stop because they got too expensive—like publish. And he can do some new things he had never done before. Grupo Catho represents a fascinating combination of old economy and new and the kind of contribution e-commerce can make in a developing country like Brazil.

In an interview in São Paulo the owner and president Thomas Case rattles off his company's statistics: the seventeenth-largest site in Brazil; 30,000 visitors a day; lists of 32,000 job openings (personal communication 2000). Grupo Catho sends out notices of job openings electronically to the customers in its database, according to their skills and preferences, using online questionnaires that he provides and they answer. Catho also does online interviews and skill testing for companies in Brazil and conducts regular compensation analyses online of respondents, who agree to participate in part because when the survey is completed Case sends a response showing how their own salary package stacks up to the competition. In addition, Case has decided to start publishing again; he had dropped out of that market because printing and mailing in the "real world" had become prohibitively expensive. Now he can be profitable in the virtual world of Brazil. He provides personnel placement, executive recruitment, outplacement services, and compensation analysis. Though he has been in business for years, he didn't become a "bricks and clicks" company until 1996. He says adding ICT to his business has been great.

Thomas Case is an American who has spent more than two decades in Brazil. Case is also vice chair of the Electronic Commerce Committee at the American Chamber of Commerce (AMCHAM). When asked what his committee does and whether it gets much involved in policy making, he answers bluntly, "We get together so we can make some more money. Our goals are pretty straightforward. We meet as a committee so we can share information on raising money, finding partnerships, get new customers, and so forth. That's our goal—getting a bunch of people in a room to do some business together" (personal communication 2000).

But Case and other businessmen also cite the low numbers of Brazilians who have bank accounts or credit cards (18 percent have credit cards), the low levels of trust in the reliability of the new technologies, the still underdeveloped traditional infrastructures like road deliveries, as well as the underdevelopment of the telecommunications infrastructures. But he claims that more and more business people in Brazil are willing to take the risks to seize the business opportunities that ICT provides.

Competition and Consolidation

By 2001, there were contradictory trends in the Brazilian markets for Internet services and goods. Awareness of the importance of the Internet was spreading, competition continued, and more interest was being shown in electronic commerce. But there was also ample evidence of market consolidation. The period after 2001 was marked by contradictory signals against the background of a sharp and unexpected technology market downturn across the developed and the developing world.

One indication of high uncertainty was the frenzy around the offers of free Internet services that occurred at the end of 1999 when one of the country's biggest banks, Bradesco, began to offer its customers "free Internet access." The idea was that customers who bank with Bradesco would receive free Internet access. Some careful observers in the Brazilian banking industry interpreted this strategy as mainly a public relations ploy to draw middle-class and upper middle-class clients to the bank as well as to reduce costs through electronic banking.

The decision to offer free Internet did attract the public's attention. Part of the marketing plan was to position the bank as a progressive and modern bank and thereby improve its image. Some report that the actual number of customers who responded to Bradesco's offer was tiny, since the small group likely to do so probably already had Internet providers, (business journalist, São Paulo personal communication 2001). New Internet clients were handed to other ISPs who actually provided the service. The ISPs had new clients, and for a while, the bank's shares increased in value.

The impact of free Internet on Brazil's national Internet service provider market was not without controversy. Some argued that Bradesco's ploy badly undercut other ISPs in the market. The bitter reaction of the Brazilian Association of Internet Providers suggests that it did. The president of the Association, Antonio Tavares, said, "We're witnessing an attempt to conquer the Brazilian Internet by institutions that have never given anyone anything free during their existence" (Romero 2000a, B2). This was certainly a signal that the old days when many small companies could easily enter and sustain themselves in markets were probably over. "The small providers will have to find other ways to survive or they will disappear," since "you have 10 large portals competing for advertising money and now you have the big banks," said the local head of Yahoo's Brazil operations (Romero 2000a, B2).

There was another wrinkle. Just before Bradesco launched, another group of Brazilians had contemplated the same idea and were preparing for a similar venture. The bank's announcement forced them to start up sooner, and IG (Internet Gratuit, or Free Internet) was launched by a group of Brazilian backers from the communication and public relations industries. According to one member of the team who was present at the restaurant table when the idea was first put forth, there was genuine excitement that this would be a way to get the Internet to many more Brazilians. However, by 2001, IG had switched its name to Internet Guaranteed because the management had discovered the same lesson that others painfully discovered in other countries: free Internet was a badly flawed business model. A senior executive at UOL took the position that the IG movement actually added a million more people to the market than would have otherwise entered. UOL did not seem too bothered by the free Internet assault (UOL executive, personal communication 2000).

These kinds of market disturbances will certainly continue, especially in light of the market collapse. Uncertainty is likely to be the principal certainty for the foreseeable future. And it is not at all clear whether these new dynamics will foster market consolidation or continued hypercompetition. More powerful institutions are entering the market. Foreign firms like AOL and Microsoft are becoming more aggressive. UOL and the other media houses seem committed to doing business in cyberspace, bring with them eyeballs by the millions. Furthermore, it is apparent that with privatization now a fact of life, telecom companies are now expanding into Internet services.

Conclusions

This chapter began with several questions. First, why was there an apparent structural disjuncture between Brazil's high gross domestic product per capita status and its relatively low telephone and Internet penetration? Second, what was the nature of the process through which structures, institutions, and individuals interacted to produce the policy and technical outcomes that emerged? Third, who were the main actors in this process? To answer these questions, I employed the strategic restructuring model developed in chapter 2.

The causes of the disjuncture between Brazil's high GDP per capita and modest telecom penetration lie in both structural and nonstructural factors. Structural factors extended beyond the traditional indicator of

GDP per capita to include wealth and income distribution—poor people lack the wherewithal to go online consistently. There is also an elitist political culture that seems to promote simultaneously popular demobilization and elite hypermobilization. No powerful pro-poor coalition emerged. As the model suggests, there were also institutional patterns and political dynamics that helped shape ICT outcomes.

In terms of institutional actors most responsible for growing the Internet market, I pointed out initially that I expected multinational corporations, the state, and international governmental organizations (IGOs) to play the largest roles in Internet diffusion. There were three surprises here. First, neither the multinations nor the IGOs played the anticipated critical role in initiating and sustaining Internet diffusion (though one could find examples of each's involvement, like the Association for Progressive Communications (APC) at the U.N. conference in 1992). But theories that posit the inevitable dominance of these two actors at the early stages of market development or technological change are mistaken in this case and probably others. Second, it was a local nongovernmental organization (IBASE) that was most critical in the early days of Internet diffusion and created the first open, nondiscriminatory, and commercial Internet service provider. Third, the role played by the state was so diverse and had so many contradictory impacts that it is almost misleading to speak of "the state's role," since it didn't have one single role. Different state institutions played different roles in the diffusion process at different times, in different sectors, in different places. On the one hand, "the state" helped to block computer diffusion through its "computer reserve" policies through the late 1980s and into the 1990s. On the other hand "the state"—through agencies like the national Research Network (RNP) and the National Council for Scientific and Technological Development (CNPq)—helped diffuse the Internet more widely by financing a national backbone across state lines. At one time, the local backbone operators in the states of Rio and São Paulo tried to restrict others from opening participation in the network more widely to nonresearchers. At another time, the CNPq and the Ministry of Science and Technology tried to expand Internet participation.

Another unambiguous conclusion is that different groups sought to define the course of Internet diffusion according to their own vision.

Throughout much of this period, the big, powerful, state-owned enterprises like the Brazilian Telecommunications Company (Embratel) tried to control the entire process, encouraging diffusion under its own control, and blocking diffusion under the control of others, whether the others were private, NGO, or even other state actors. The Brazil experience suggests that several distinct diffusion strategies are advanced in the process of Internet diffusion by different actors who are tied to particular institutional interests. In Brazil in the 1990s, there was a top-down monopolist diffusion pattern and a more liberal and distributed model.

Whether an institution promoted the top-down or bottom-up version hinged partly on that institution's prior position in the emerging ICT markets and partly by the influence of individuals within those institutions who steered them in one direction or another. The role of small groups of ICT experts proved decisive at critical moments in the history of the Internet in Brazil.

At the start of the Brazilian information revolution, when the initial key institutional and physical infrastructures were being constructed, the motive force for innovation was a small group of information activists based in and around government research units and ministries. These state-based influentials did not fight for the state to retain or enhance its power, as one might expect, but lobbied instead to extract and permanently exclude it from the production and distribution of Internet services (cf. Vogel 1996). This certainly reflected national and global shifts in attitudes toward state power but also reflected the individuals' conceptions of who they were. In interviews, they described themselves not as tecnicos, bureaucrats, or even civil servants but as engaged policy intellectuals who were not tied to a single institutional perspective. These individuals were also very mobile across institutions, shifting from research centers to state-owned enterprises to state administration to private or semi-private institutions and then back again. In effect, they created *social* networks that predated the *technical* networks and that have subsequently informed the constant evolution of the technical networks. To put it squarely: no social networks, no technical networks. The social interactions among friends and colleagues and their opposition to the top-down diffusionists in a context of advancing privatization shaped the hard infrastructure too. These findings parallel the work of Gerald M. Easter (1989) in Soviet Russia and others who use an elite network approach to demonstrate how such leaders can influence state formation and development, even while shaped by institutions.

The Brazil evidence also shows that Internet diffusion must be explained in dynamic as well as structural and institutional terms. The answers to particular research questions about the role of institutions and individuals emerged within a particular historical context and through a unique process of distinctive phases. Each stage differed according to the extent of technological commercialization, the composition of the leadership, and especially the institutional and political challenges faced by the relevant actors.

The opening phases of innovation occurred when several challenges emerged and were met. The initial challenge was to build the supporting technical infrastructures, to restructure institutions and regulations governing Internet diffusion, and to mobilize political and financial support. This process began when a small core group of technically skilled and politically savvy individuals coalesced around these Internet challenges and created a self-conscious group that shared a common vision of a distributed, liberal Internet market. Self-identifying themselves as the Gang of Four, they learned to work closely with one another in the late 1980s and early 1990s and ultimately created a successful public-spirited conspiracy that created both soft and hard infrastructures (wires and applications, as well as laws and institutions).

Based on that common vision, these individuals and their colleagues in other public institutions collaborated and worked hard to remove bureaucratic road blocks, restructure relevant existing state institutions like CNPq and the National Research Network, and rewrite existing ICT regulations. Critically important for the spread of a new culture of information and for institutional restructuring was the core group's demonstrated capacity to *persuade separate institutions to start communicating and cooperating and create new institutions in the process (*i.e., the Internet Steering Committee and the National Research Network). The Gang of Four also had to convince top political leaders that their liberal diffusion model was good for the country and that material resources and political protection should be mobilized in their support. This included neutralizing powerful institutional opponents who did not fully share their liberalizing vision and building up a core political coalition of support. The early creation of programs and institutions that brought together like-minded elites in universities, businesses, and governments cemented a base for subsequent liberal Internet expansion.

The opponents to liberal diffusion were not necessarily against "more information" as a matter of principle. The opponents were not against all new information; rather, they wanted to be the ones to distribute and control it under institutional arrangements of their own choosing. Eventually, they were neutralized through the political process. For example, if pro-reform Communications Minister Motta had not imposed a ban on state telecom monopolies entering the value-added services market, then the history of Brazilian Internet diffusion would be quite different.

The second phase of Internet diffusion saw a group like IBASE set up its own Internet Service Provider on commercial terms and try to become self-sustaining as well as supply a needed public service. The third phase from the mid-1990s onward saw a wave of private-sector entrepreneurs move into these quasi-markets with energy and resources, creating genuinely competitive conditions in which the number of ISPs blossomed from a handful to over three hundred. The current period of the early twenty-first century shares elements of continued competition but also trends toward consolidation as big local and international players enter the market.

Thus the Brazilian market passed through a precommercial stage, a commercial stage, a period of competition, and a fourth ambivalent period of both competition and consolidation.

Throughout all the periods, the attention given to distributional issues by high-level ICT experts and elites was surprisingly modest. I encountered few radical reformers pressing the issue. It seemed less an issue in Brazil than in Ghana, as I show in chapter 4. This may reflect the fact that the disparity in access to ICT resources parallels the disparity in access to other scarce resources even more central to the poor, such as education access, land access, political access, and wealth holdings. Is politics being changed by ICT, especially the polities of the poor? Democratization may be advanced through ICT. The 1998 presidential elections saw a huge percentage of people vote online, reported to be about 35 percent. But thus far the experiences of nonprofit groups do not suggest that interactivity has changed politics. Perhaps when more than 2 or 3 percent of the population has effective access to the Net some progressive changes will come; but so far, there is little evidence that ICTs act as an independent variable to influence significantly the balance of power between the powerful and the weak. Perhaps under the new administration of president "Lula" the attention will shift.

The role played by individual ICT leaders and innovators in Brazil was greater than I originally expected. Their influence may reflect the slice of Internet history I chose to analyze—the early initial innovations before major institutions were created anew and old institutions restructured. While it is difficult to argue counterfactually, it is probable that Brazil would not have followed the same path under different leadership. The innovators were drawn from a group that many theories would judge relatively unlikely to lead—a small cadre of local, technically trained policy intellectuals and policy entrepreneurs, followed by a second wave of local private-sector entrepreneurs. Brazil confirms the findings of Jon Guice (1998), whose analysis of the early years of the Internet industry in the United States reached similar conclusions. He too found that the evolution of Internet infrastructure was fluid and indeterminate, and he summarized his findings into four maxims: it could have been otherwise; innovation requires many; technologies have meanings; and all technologies are network technologies. Human agency, he implies, really matters. Let us now see how the modified structural framework can point us to particular differences and similarities between this large Latin country and the West African country of Ghana.

Appendix: ICT Institutions

The Ministry of Communications
Under the administration of President Fernando Cardoso, the Ministry of Communication became an important center of influence and power. As a new president, Cardoso appointed his closest political confidant, Sergio Motta, as Minister of Communication, and relied on them to apply pressure on other governmental agencies and their relevant political constituencies to accept the radical ICT sectoral reformation

Cardoso desired. Previously, the Ministry had operated like similar bodies in similar countries—as the protector of the old regime. Historically, the Ministry of Communication did the planning, coordinating, regulating, and supervising of the telecom sector and the postal service. Eventually, as the political winds changed, the main protector of the old regime became its chief dismantler, especially after a series of new legislative acts was passed by the parliament in 1996.

The Ministry of Science and Technology

This was the other critical ministry-level body in Brazil. Created in March 1985, the Ministry of Science and Technology assumed responsibilities formerly housed in autonomous secretariats and other bodies. Brazil's difficult economic condition meant that S&T's budget resources declined almost from its beginning. But by the early 1990s, it had become active in the informatics industry, in part reflecting the evolving thinking about the country's computer reserve policy. In 1992, it was given responsibilities for "formulation and executing development policies for the computer science sector." It also has responsibility for stimulating the transfer of technology among universities, research centers, and the private sector.

State-Owned Enterprises

The two largest state-owned enterprises in the sector were the Brazilian Telecommunications Company (Embratel), created in 1965 to handle interstate communications, and the Telebras system, created to handle intrastate communications and was based in each of the states starting in 1972. Prior to Telebras, municipalities, states, and the federal government could offer services, each with its own rates and services; Telebras absorbed more than a thousand small and medium-sized telephone companies to consolidate them into state-level organizations.

Astute observers of Brazil like Lee McKnight and Antonio J. J. Botelho (1997) have concluded that some of the gaps between Brazil's structural potentials and its lagging performance are caused by institutional failures of these parastatal bodies. For years, the Telebras system has been unable to manage itself well enough to deliver the kinds of services that its charter mandated and its customers expected. In the 1980s and the early to mid-1990s, it became a kind of laughing stock for its inability to deliver services and its failure to integrate investment, pricing, and maintenance. Line maintenance was poor, and investment was less than half of that required. The government and Telebras let investment fall from 3.28 percent of gross domestic product in 1975 to only 0.5 percent in 1994, clearly an unsustainable pathway: "High prices, nominally to help subsidize the poor, have depressed demand and put the service out of the reach of the poor. But in spite of notoriously poor service, Telebras' monopoly position enabled it to be enormously profitable. It was rated as the world's 22d most profitable service firm by *Forbes* magazine" (McKnight and Botehlo 1997, 264). While some of the performance anomalies were the result of poor management by Telebras and Embratel, some were caused by self-serving practices by other government institutions like the ministries. Some responsibility must be put at the feet of the government, which failed to reform the sector. Taken together, these political and institutional failures yielded a weak telecom industry that especially disadvantaged the already disadvantaged.

Earlier institutions were established to promote and protect the growth of the domestic computer industry and were important for the evolution of the Internet. These included bodies like the Commission for the Coordination of Electronic Processing Activities (CAPRE), created April 5, 1972, replaced by the Special Secretariat for Informatics (SIE). These were specialized bodies, well insulated from outside pressures, that served the protectionist purposes of one section of the Brazilian civilian and military elites (Bastos and Cooper 1996, 238–272).

Another important institution in the evolution of the Internet in Brazil over many years was the National Council for Scientific and Technological Development (CNPq). As the principal national research support body in Brazil, it is somewhat analogous to semiautonomous funding agencies like the National Science Foundation in the Untied States. CNPq is designed to stimulate production of useful knowledge for economic and social development as well as to affirm Brazil's cultural identity. Several of the information champions described previously were influential officials at CNPq.

An important related research body was the National Research Network (RNP). In the early days of the Internet—the late 1980s—this agency had the responsibility for building out the interconnected national backbone. They were the Internet service providers' Internet. In 1988, the Ministry of Science and Technology convened representatives from the CNPq, the FINEP (Financier of Studies and Design), and three other institutions from Brazil's most advanced states. This group was called to promote research and created a new body to concentrate on interstate network connections in the process. By 1991 to 1993, the National Research Network had a 64k line at 9.6 kbps and engaged in training and promotional activities. By May 2000, when the new RNP2 backbone was inaugurated by the S&T Ministry, the RNP had five international connections and was set to join the Internet 2 consortium with speeds up to 155 Mkbps.

The National Telecommunications Agency (ANATEL)

Latin America has more independent regulatory bodies than any other developing region, and Brazil is an excellent example. Created in 1997 as part of the path-breaking liberalizing legislation of the late 1990s, the National Telecommunications Agency (ANATEL) is an independent federal agency that was assigned some of the responsibilities formerly held by the Communications Ministry. ANATEL's main tasks are to implement the telecommunications national policies, propose a plan for universal communication services, resolve conflicts of interest among telecom providers, act in defense of consumer rights; issue licenses to private-sector companies, foster competition and prevent market concentration, and establish rates and tariffs (ITU 2001).

The Internet Steering Committee (ISC)

A joint creature of the Ministries of Communication and of Science and Technology, the Internet Steering Committee (ISC) was appointed to accelerate Internet expansion through technical activities like domain name registration, promotional operations, and technical procedures. The government created this specialized body to help implement the momentous May 31, 1995, decision that declared the Internet a value-added service and barred big national telecom companies from controlling the market. Many of the members of the first wave of Brazil's Internet pioneers were appointed as members (personal communication, 1999).

Other Groups   More recently several other specialized bodies were created. The Electronic Commerce Committee is a joint private-public group whose mission is to help advance e-commerce in the country. Among its duties are to share information and studies on e-commerce, to explore ways of enhancing private-public partnerships, and to promote e-commerce for small and medium-sized enterprises. Government agencies represented include the Ministry of Science and Technology, the Ministry of Commerce, and the communication regulatory agency ANATEL. Private institutions include the Internet company trade association ABRANET and others.

To provide guidance for Brazil's shift toward a more information-rich, sophisticated knowledge society, the government created an IT task force headed by Tadao Takahash. [Personal communication, 2002] Other relevant bodies have been Brazil's universities, such as those in Minas Gerais and Bahia, which hosted several Internet research bodies, as well as some of the state governments that aggressively pursued state Internet developments.

Nongovernmental Organizations

Two nongovernmental organizations that have been especially active in ICT matters are the Brazilian Institute for Social and Economic Analyses (IBASE) and the Information Network for the Third Sector (RITS). IBASE was created in 1981 to democratize economic and social information during the military dictatorship and promoted a variety of technical and organizational solutions to the lack of ICT information, including information on the new ICT innovations, among activists in Brazil (Afonso 1996, 62). It played a critical role in the diffusion of the Internet in Brazil. RITS was created in 1997 to provide the nonprofit sector with useful information through the Internet and to offer the sector access to the most modern communication technology and knowledge management resources (RITS 1999, 1). It works in turn with the more than 250,000 formally registered nonprofits. The long-term effectiveness of these activities in changing power balances is problematic, of course. They seem to expand the access of nonprofits to ICT resources, but the evidence does not show conclusively that the addition of new technology resources has altered other fundamental political or economic relationships. Evidence suggests that power relations do not change.[3]

4

Strategic Restructuring in Ghana

Introduction

In this period of global transition and the information revolution, Ghana exemplifies the constraints and opportunities that confront the political leadership of a poor nation trying to navigate turbulent economic waters. Political and economic leaders are waking up to the realities of a new world that increasingly is playing by rules shaped by globalization. Some Ghanaian leaders recognize that if they restructure their political economy and displace their less strategic-thinking neighbors who are more passive on information and communication technology (ICT) matters, then they can possibly become an information "gateway to West Africa." Already, new data processing centers are springing up. Nonetheless, knowledgeable Ghanaians also recognize that other African countries, as well as countries on other continents, are dramatically accelerating even faster into the digital future. Concurrently, non-governmental organizations (NGOs) and private-sector elites are deeply concerned that recent Ghanaian governments did not fully "get it" and that short-sighted politicians will manage to thwart the plans for restructuring the ICT industries toward greater openness and opportunity.

There is not universal accord over the path ahead in Ghana. One faction of Ghana's elite is struggling to make a difficult transition from a strictly export-oriented, protected, nearly monocrop agricultural economy to one marked by mixed agriculture, industry, and services. They are aware that in all three sectors, ICT will play an increasingly important role in their national life. However, an even larger faction of Ghana's leaders seems less disposed to restructure the old ways of doing the nation's business and more reluctant to try to seize change and direct it purposively. This conservative group believes in and benefits directly from the distortions that government creates through its close control of national markets, including information and communication markets. In light of the active political opposition to greater liberal reforms, merely recognizing opportunities is not enough to successfully restructure the sector and to accelerate diffusion. Any pro-ICT reform program must win over, neutralize, or ignore antireform coalitions and campaigns.

Beyond the political friction, Ghana possesses huge structural barriers to becoming a knowledge society that include poverty, low levels of education, and poor ICT connections. At the same time, however, Ghana is also a country with a long history of commitment to human capital development, vigorous entrepreneurialism, and far-sighted vision by charismatic leaders, such as the country's controversial and popular first president, Kwame Nkrumah. The proreform forces might win, and the momentum seems to be with them for the moment.

Which tendency will predominate? Will conservative politicians and age-old structural constraints maintain their authority and overwhelm the new digital directions that some parties would like to pursue? Or will progressive and visionary leaders mobilize supporters to overcome the more rigid and constraining structural features of the country and to outflank the conservative backward-looking elements of the elite? It is hardly surprising but still telling that ICT issues or transformation toward a knowledge society were nowhere near the top of the agenda during the historic Ghanaian election that replaced Jerry Rawlings with John Kufour, although the new government claims to want to do more to take up the challenges of ICT. Time will tell.

Aside from the national-level challenge of bringing the latest ICT services to the country as a whole, Ghana also faces the inherent internal distributional challenges posed by the global information revolution that are discussed in chapter 3. My research has identified a well developed sense of the distributional risks of the ICT revolution among its indigenous digerati. This awareness of opportunity and risk is evident in the ICT sector among many entrepreneurs and leading government officials. Ghanaians of many walks of life and political persuasions recognize the twin elements of the external gap and the internal gap—getting ICT into the country and then getting ICT to all the people in the country. Interviews conducted in Accra in March 1999 revealed tremendous sophistication regarding these twin challenges, which were well captured with nuance and clarity by the president of the Accra Lion's Club, Gifty Reynolds Annan-Mensah.

Annan-Mensah runs a boutique in Accra that sells a variety of everyday objects, including iced drinks. To enter a new market, she recently installed a telecommunications center, in part to serve clients in the Atomic Estates area of Accra, much of which was not yet connected by telephone. Her boutique possesses a Pentium processor (with Windows 98), several telephones, a fax machine, and a scanner, and she sells telephone calls, access to the computer, and e-mail services. She is still learning about the Internet and is convinced the demand for Internet services will grow. Regarding distribution, she feels that the current situation of the economy will exacerbate divisions between the haves and the have-nots: "Already there is a big gap between these groups. The coming of ICT will add to the gap between the rich and poor. They have started teaching computer in some schools, even the primary schools, but mostly private schools. The public schools are so far behind, and most do not have access to computers" (personal communication 1999). Like most we interviewed, she believes this gap can be corrected by government and private interventions. But government must act quickly. In fact, village schools typically have no electricity and few, if any books or maps.

The Structural Context

Ghana is one of the poorest countries in the world (see table 4.1). Its annual per capita income of $390 ranks it number 106 among all nations (CIA 1999). Its literacy rate is 64.5 percent, life expectancy at birth is 57.14 years, and it has 11,653 kilometers of paved road for a country of 238,540 square kilometers. Yet for much of its long history, Ghana was renowned for its wealth of natural resources and their export. The area today called Ghana (named after an ancient kingdom) was known for centuries as the Gold Coast and was the source of much of Europe's gold in the Middle Ages. In the nineteenth and early twentieth centuries, the country gained considerable agricultural wealth through its export

Table 4.1
Structural Context for the Development of Information Technology in Ghana

GDP position	GDP real growth rate: 3% (2000 est.)
	GDP per capita (purchasing power parity): $1,900 (2000 est.)
	GDP composition by sector: Agriculture 36%, industry 25%, services 39% (2000 est.)
Demography	Population: 18,887,626 (July 1999 estimate)
	Labor force: Agriculture 60%, industry 15%, services 25% (1999 est.)
Geography	238,540 sq. km., 10 regions (Ashanti, Brong-Ahafo, Central, Eastern, Greater Accra, Northern, Upper East, Upper West, Volta, Western)
Political structure	Constitutional democracy with a unicameral Parliament. Ruling party is the New Patriotic Party. Other political parties include the National Democratic Congress, People's Heritage Party, National Convention Party, People's Convention Party, Every Ghanaian Living Everywhere, and People's National Convention.
Other factors	Rule of law
	English language
	Geographic position
	Literacy rate (64.5%)

Source: CIA *World Factbook 2001* (2002).

of cocoa. Ghana has also exported people, first as slaves but more recently as a major part of the African brain drain.

Ghana has maintained an extraordinary international reputation due to its highly educated and well-trained professionals, who can be encountered everywhere around the world—in the most senior positions of international organizations like the World Bank and the United Nations, as well as in private companies and banks. Thus, the challenge will be to repatriate that wealth in human capital to help the country create a knowledge society. An interesting and unsuspected side effect of the information revolution is that it permits overseas expatriates to stay in close contact with their homeland, and a veritable digital diaspora of Ghanaians has sprouted around the world. Some are tempted by the new opportunities to return home and do so. The sinews of Ghana's information society are being made by returned "sons of the soil."

For the past three decades, however, the country has undergone wrenching economic collapses and political chaos that thwart the ambitions of many entrepreneurial individuals. In 1960, Ghana and South Korea had about the same level of gross domestic product (GDP) per capita. Now forty years later, South Korea's GDP is way up, and Ghana's GDP is way down. Under its selfish and shortsighted postcolonial governments, Ghana had neither democratized fully nor achieved economic development. But pressed by the World Bank and its own implosion starting in the early 1980s, Ghana began a gutsy if fragile recovery effort that has helped restore hope and regular economic growth, as GDP grew at an average annual rate of 4.3 percent between 1988 and 1999 (CIA World Factbook 1999).

Still, what kind of information and communication diffusion would we expect of a very poor country where per capita annual earnings are about one-half the cost of a new computer, where 61 percent of the population are farmers, where the combined primary, secondary, and tertiary school gross enrollment ratio is only 43 percent (U.N.D.P Human Development Report 2000), and where there is 0.81 telephones per 100 inhabitants (ITU 2000). The bottom line is that low literacy and low GDP per capita suggest that the demand for ICT and the availability of supply will be low. As a rule, poor countries like Ghana lack the financial, institutional, and managerial wherewithal to sustain ICT manufacturing industries.

Recent Policy Context: Background
Since ICTs are deeply embedded in society, we are obliged to analyze and understand a country's underlying societal structure—the dimension of the problem that both neoclassical economics and technodeterministic paradigms overlook. The structure and performance of the ICT sector are mediated through the society's political authority structures. An essential component of the societal context in Africa in general and Ghana in particular is its patrimonial political systems. According to Max Weber's tripartite distinction among charismatic, patrimonial, and legal rational bases of political authority, patrimonial systems derive their

authority and power from the position of a supreme leader who exercises material and political influence, partly through reference to honored tradition and partly through leadership skills. Patron-client networks figure prominently in such systems.

It is widely acknowledged that patrimonialism—or more precisely neopatrimonialism—is found in all developing regions. There is also consensus among scholars that this system is central to the conduct of political life in Africa. As a set of values, patrimonialism is generally adhered to by people throughout society from bottom to top—heads of state and supreme rulers, chief executive officers (CEOs) of state corporations, managers in telephone offices, workers, and peasants. The ICT sector is not exempt, and the allocation of scarce resources in broadcasting, telecommunications, and computers reflects those values and behaviors.

The political life of Ghana certainly fits the African patrimonial patterns. From the first president, Kwame Nkrumah, who renamed himself Osagyefo ("the redeemer") and surrounded himself with all the trappings of traditional authority, to the last president, Jerry Rawlings, who jealously guarded his chiefly and presidential prerogatives, this pattern prevails. The political opposition in Ghana complained for years of what they called the Rawlings regime's high-handed and undemocratic practices of political intimidation and manipulation. These have attenuated somewhat since the move to more open political rules after 1993 and with the democratic election of President Kufour in 2000. Given these prevailing political patterns, we would predict neopatrimonial influences in the politically motivated allocation of licenses, preferred access to state sales of privatized assets, and promotions to senior positions in state companies.

As Michael Bratton and Nicholas Van de Walle (1997, 64) point out, neopatrimonialism and its pervasive patron-client ties have profound and usually disastrous consequences for economic efficiency and productivity: "As a consequence of clientelism and the use of state resources, neopatrimonial regimes demonstrated very little developmental capacity. Lacking political legitimacy, rulers survived through coercion and clientelism. The large state apparatus they had created as much for patronage as anything else was costly as well as inept, undisciplined and unresponsive. . . . Public investment was inadequate because a disproportionate share of public monies went to pay a bloated salary bill for the large number of offices reserved for the political class. Typically, public infrastructure was poorly maintained and state agents lacked operating funds." The other major consequence of neopatrimonial and corrupt behavior is that it creates a climate of risk and uncertainty that is inimical to attracting investors, whether local or foreign (Bratton and Van de Walle 1997). This lack of investment further undercuts the prospects for growth, and actually strengthens the hand of those who control scarce resources of all kinds.

Structural Reform: Background
During the 1980s, the Ghanaian national economy plummeted. The country seemed to hit rock bottom in the early 1980s, and the international financial institutions (IFIs), especially the International Monetary Fund (IMF) and the World Bank, stepped in and forced market-oriented reforms on Ghana as they did in other poor countries. Beginning in the early 1980s, the World Bank insisted that the government drastically reform its macroeconomic policies and institutional structures as a condition for any new Bank lending and most of the world's other public and private banks would not lend without the imprimatur of the World Bank. Ghana submitted to its first structural adjustment program (SAP) in 1983, received an initial structural adjustment credit of $126 million, and obtained a total of $1 billion in adjustment lending between 1985 and 1999.

The Washington-mandated structural adjustment programs typically included currency devaluations, reductions in budget deficits, institutional changes such as the commercialization of state-owned enterprises (SOEs), and staff retrenchment in the civil service and SOEs. Currency devaluations and budget-balancing initiatives were prominent components of the programs as well. Indeed, the four core policy balances that we have described for the ICT sector—more competition, more foreign investment, more private-sector power, and fewer centralized controls—were also targets for World Bank adjustment programs across the board.

The economic collapse and performance pathologies of the 1970 to 1980 period resulted from the way all the negative policy pieces of the regime fit together and reinforced one another. State ownership and

Table 4.2
Ghanian Tertiary School Graduates

Year	Total	Country Population	Tertiary School Graduates (% of population)
1970	1,344	8,788,945	0.00015
1980	2,821	10,998,495	0.0003
1982	2,212	11,358,979	0.0002
1985	2,277	13,182,900	0.0002
1986	439	13,731,421	0.00003
1987	1,240	14,122,715	0.00009
1989	2,238	14,933,048	0.0001
1990	2,627	15,360,394	0.0002
1991	2,739	15,804,813	0.0002

Source: UNESCO; U.S. Bureau of Census International Database.
Note: More recent figures are not available.

centralized controls tied to monopolies yielded the worst of all worlds for ICT sectors and others—little access to basic service for most and substandard unreliable services at high rates for those connected. The longer the telephone system limped along under these balances, the more severe these pathologies became. Ghanaian monopolies found it more and more difficult to maintain the fictions of meeting their public service obligations along ICT equity or efficiency grounds and of budgetary responsibility. It is insufficiently appreciated how much the popular support for substantial telecom and other reforms that came in the 1990s resulted from the abysmal and worsening performance of the ICT sectors. Thus, Ghana entered the decade of the 1990s with a badly deteriorated hard ICT infrastructure and a short supply of local expertise in all ICT sectors. The "softer" infrastructures of education and training so essential for a successful transformation toward a knowledge society were also substandard. Notice that for a total population of 18.9 million, the numbers are low; that they collapsed after 1985 reveals how badly conditions deteriorated in areas that provide the base for a knowledge society (see tables 4.2 and 4.3).

Caught between a rock and a hard place, at the tender mercies of international capital and disaffected, disgusted would-be consumers, the

Table 4.3
Adult Literacy Rates, Ghana

Year	Both Sexes (%)	Population
1980	44	10,998,495
1985	51	13,182,900
1990	58	15,360,394
1995	65	17,632,692

Source: U.S. Bureau of Census International Database.

Rawlings government initially combined populist, nationalistic political rhetoric with conventional liberal reforms. This bombastic language continued even when it was clear that for the most part Ghanaian leaders' hearts were not in it. Yet Ghana slowly became a kind of showcase for relatively successful African economic reforms, and as a consequence foreign aid (but not much private foreign capital) flowed in.

Whatever the motivations for economic reform and however piecemeal or lukewarm the reforms sometimes were by the early to mid-1990s, a common view and vision for the economy in general and for the ICT sector as well began to emerge among the senior members of the government around President Rawlings. One of the most prominent in articulating and enforcing this view of economic reform was Rawlings's senior economic advisor, P. V. Obeng, who rose to become a de facto prime minister of the country. Extensive interviews with Obeng confirmed this view of the shared vision at the top: Ghana had to get back on track, and this included, however reluctantly, the orthodox structural adjustment program, including promoting private investment both foreign and (more begrudgingly, for political reasons) local. There was a sense too that Ghana had to become competitive with its neighbors (like Ivory Coast, Senegal, or Gambia) by becoming a gateway to West African markets. And an important part of that strategy was the telecommunications sector.

At the beginning of the 1990s, Ghana possessed the standard ICT balances described in chapter 2. The main sectors—communication and content—were fully dominated by government, with the Ghanaian private or NGO sectors playing small roles in the design and implementation of public policies, which were thought to be the special responsibility and preserve of the politically powerful, of top civil servants, and of the military. These basic patterns of the distribution of economic and human resources are long term in nature. They cannot be changed quickly, and they also impose their own constraints on the resources that institutions have available to them and the prioritization of the tasks that confront any society at a given point in time. These features of social, economic, and policy structures in turn operate largely through their imprint on institutions, and it is to them that we turn now.

The Role of Institutions

The Internet did not emerge in a vacuum but within the context of an institutional space loosely divided into several different sectors, especially computers and telecommunications. At various times, conflict, cooperation, and competition emerged among the institutions within these sectors as each struggled for influence over the emerging services of the Internet. After considerable jockeying for position, Ghana obtained full Internet connectivity in 1995 as a result of cooperation among several organizations, including Ghana Telecom (UNECA, 2002). Leading institutions are described in the appendix. The key institutions that played a role in Internet diffusion in Ghana and the individuals who run them were linked together in a variety of formal and informal ways that changed over time. Institutional monopolies and weaknesses were the backdrop for individual initiatives.

The Contribution of Individuals to Internet Diffusion

We saw information champions in Brazil. Who are their counterparts in Ghana who reach across sectors? The tripartite interactions among individuals in the private, public, and NGO sectors also launched the information revolution in Ghana. As in other developing countries, the local evolution of sectoral reform was guided and propelled by a handful of proreform individuals mostly in private firms and nonprofit organizations. The government revolutionaries were uncommon in

Ghana. By contrast, in China and Brazil, we find more government-driven restructuring.

But in many, if not most, developing country settings, government is literally the bastion of the status quo being attacked from the outside by the NGOs and by private-sector local and foreign entities and from the inside by a handful of change agents who were sympathetic to global shifts and to local pressures. The senior civil servants and the executives in the state-owned enterprises were often the staunchest defenders of the status quo because they felt that they had the most to lose. But there were important exceptions.

The Role of Individuals

An Information Revolutionary in the Public Sector

Finding an information revolutionary within government's ranks is unexpected, but within the constraints of office and constituency, Edward Salia, head of Ghana's Ministry of Communications, was a government ICT revolutionary. In the context of a political environment that in the early 1990s was still highly statist, xenophobic, anticompetitive, and patrimonial, especially when contrasted to East Asian or Latin countries, Salia was a true believer. As Minister for Transport and Communications, (later "communications" became its own Ministry) he was the point person in the fight with the conservative forces in Ghana, including many in his own ministry, who believed the proposed liberal reforms would sell out the country to foreigners, would gut any real meaning of national autonomy, and would condemn the rural areas to permanent exclusion (even though under the current system they were excluded en masse). According to one Ghanaian active in the opposition to these liberal reforms, "These changes, they are all the doing of the World Bank. Salia is just their errand boy" (personal communication 1997).

Salia early on was convinced that the transition toward a competitive, digitalized, distributed, low-cost digital world was inevitable and that his ministry and indeed his country as a whole needed to move to take advantage of these changes. In essence, he believed that conserving the old policy balances would not help his country but condemn it to backwardness. In an interview, Salia stated, "I felt I had no choice if Ghana was to move ahead." Over and over, he called for a full program of strategic restructuring that was marked by greater privatization, more foreign involvement, greater competition, and substantial reduction in the controlling role of the state in the economy. The results would be substantially less authority and control over scarce resources by the government civil servants that he nominally represented.

In conferences and public meetings, Salia often had to battle with his own staff and also with the senior executives of the state telephone parastatal. The establishment had few incentives to support alien reforms. He argued for privatization, greater market initiative, foreign investment, and other liberal reforms. The public exchanges between the minister and the state telephone CEO were often sarcastic and sharp. Salia used public meetings as a bully pulpit to move his own colleagues farther down the road toward reform. At the time, the outcomes of these public disputes and bureaucratic battles were unclear. The state telephone executives sought to blunt the slide toward privatization and competition through delaying tactics, and the conservatives looked like they might win in Ghana as they did in other countries like Nigeria or Thailand—by opposing rate reforms, by worker resistance, and by other actions, often with the backing of the trade unions, which feared unemployment if the parastatals were forced to restructure.

Despite the resistance, Minister Salia was backed by the Rawlings government and was able, step-by-step, to restructure the policy regime and the structure of the markets for telecommunications, cellular telephony, and even broadcasting. Salia, and his successors Ekow Spio-Garbah and John Mahama, succeeded for several reasons: Ghana Telecoms was running out of money, telecom service could not be much worse and had few remaining defenders, the World Bank was pushing hard from outside, and the government went along and even provided some leadership.

In Latin America, the typical sequence for these restructurings tends to begin first with privatization and later competition. In Asia, there are closer controls on ownership but a greater willingness to permit competition (Petrazzini 1995). Across Africa, with its small bourgeoisie, small markets, and large state sector, the picture is far more mixed. Most countries start with the modest administrative step of splitting the post office from the telephone company (the old PTTs). Telecommunications is then commercialized or put under commercial law and expected to cover its own expenses. Privatization and foreign ownership typically come in hand when African governments permit multinationals to move into local markets.

Salia and the Rawlings government took on several of these restructuring battles simultaneously across the board, including foreign investment and privatization. Privatization, the most politically difficult of all reforms in Africa, went surprisingly far and surprisingly fast in Ghana. Beyond the more widely accepted practice of opening the new cellular markets, Salia developed two unusual and politically risky strategies that challenged the monopoly of Ghana Telecom head on. The first restructuring strategy was to seek out a private partner for Ghana Telecom. He privatized part of the national telecommunications company by selling some of its shares to a more experienced firm with deeper pockets. Given the capital and expertise required, this would inevitably be a foreign private partner.

Ultimately, Malaysian Telecom (MT) successfully bid on the privatized shares of Ghana Telecom. MT is based in another developing country and has an interesting history of investing in Africa, including a massive billion-dollar plus investment for one-third of South Africa Telecom in 1997. The Ghanaians, like the South Africans, apparently reasoned that another developing country might be more responsive to Ghana's economic and political challenges and also might be more palatable to local nationalist elements. Also, MT had already experienced its own successful privatization campaign in the 1980s. The results, however, achieved less than the Ghanaians desired.

Despite the need for foreign expertise and money, Ghana, like most other developing countries, encouraged foreign firms to seek out partnerships with local people, and well-connected insiders eagerly sought partnerships with the foreigners. Sometimes the local partners were actually familiar with the ICT business. Others were simply well-connected locals who had good friends in high places. In poor countries like Ghana, which have a small skill base in absolute and relative terms, the local partner is more likely to be a small-business entrepreneur who helps organize the local market for foreign interests rather than an experienced ICT businessperson.

The second strategy the government pursued, especially risky for poor countries with small markets, was to restructure the telephone market by creating an entirely new second telephone service supplier. Salia sought out a direct competitor who could go toe-to-toe with the incumbent Ghana Telecom to drive down prices and drive up consumer access. This strategy of pursuing a second telephone company speaks to three of our balances—private ownership and management, foreign ownership and management, and the shift toward greater competition. By 1992, about forty private telephone-related companies were in operation, including a local cellular phone and a paging company. Other companies went into installation and maintenance of terminal equipment.

Salia and his team were very aware of the distributional issues discussed in chapters 2 and 3, issues that have distinct political reverberations. They were certainly worried about appearing to sell out their countrymen to foreign capitalists. As a consequence, they took pains to build in some distributional requirements into the criteria for awarding contracts.

The distribution of scarce resources, like access to a telephone, is not the only difficult and politically charged distributional issue in the sector. There is also the complex question of the distribution of company ownership. Just as the Ghanaian government sets the parameters of the foreign interests that could invest, they also determine the local private interests that could participate in telecommunications reform. Will all citizens able to raise the requisite financial and technical resources be permitted to compete equally for shares of the slowly opening lucrative ICT markets?

In most political economies, the answer is usually no. Political and social factors weigh as much as money or expertise to shape who gets what and for how much when telecommunications and broadcast licenses are put up for sale. They are so scarce and valuable that the demand is usually far greater than the supply. Scarcity, high value, and high uncertainty drive eager would-be buyers to engage high-paid lobbyists and well-connected cronies. In the United States, former congressmen or senior government officials often smooth the way for would-be buyers. Africa is no different in this respect.

But in patrimonial political economies, patronage and political support from the top down is very nearly a "make it or break it" requirement for doing substantial telecommunications (and other) business. In the absence of other norms and institutions, patronage is often extreme and marked. Anyone seeking a state license or loan in such political economies can expect to have his or her application closely vetted by the political authorities. An applicant from the "wrong" political party, the "wrong" region, or the "wrong" ethnic group operates from a severe disadvantage. Corruption results.

A very visible and highly politicized case occurred in Zimbabwe, where President Robert Mugabe opposed awarding a cellular license to a political opponent, and the case bounced up and around to the highest authorities of the country, including the Supreme Court and the legislature. In the early 1990s, Strive Masiyiwa, a U.K.-trained electrical engineer who also owned a power switchboard factory, sought to operate Zimbabwe's first mobile telephone service and had actually signed up approximately 6,000 subscribers (Econet Wireless 1996). In addition, Masiyiwa had asked Zimbabwe's state-owned Postal and Telecommunications Corporation (PTC) to be his partner in this venture. However, despite the regime's rhetoric of privatization and black empowerment, Masiyiwa's efforts were frustrated by the Mugabe regime. According to observers, the refusal to grant this entrepreneur a license was primarily driven by the fact that the patrimonial ruling group around Mugabe saw Masiyiwa and others like him as a threat. As a result of the intransigence of PTC and other public officials, Masiyiwa selected a Connecticut-based company, Telecell International, to be his partner and took the PTC to court. After a somewhat prolonged battle, the Zimbabwean Supreme Court broke the government monopoly on telecommunications and stipulated that private companies should be granted licenses to offer communication services.

I interviewed people in Ghana who reported the same discrimination in awarding licenses on the basis of political loyalties. One informant complained bitterly of having all the requisite permissions, expertise, overseas partners, and cash and then being denied an opportunity to compete for the licenses he sought because, he claimed, he was a prominent member of the political opposition to the National Democratic Congress government. Others in the opposition believe that the allocation of frequencies has been transparent and above board.

Whatever the patrimonial outcome, it was apparent by the mid- to late 1990s that some members of the Ghanaian elite were trying to hitch their own stars to restructuring the old ICT regime. A new coalition formed around the opportunities for commercial success that these changes provided. Henceforth the telecommunications market would no longer be a strictly Ghana government-owned, monopoly supplier with an anti-service attitude. Instead, the country now had a mixed private and public duopoly that was beginning to exert pressures for lower prices and better service; it had foreign investment paired with local investors; and it had, as we see below, the beginnings of a regulatory structure to promote competition. The public component was still dominant, but a critical shift toward private ownership had begun. What it still lacked was an effective regulatory body to help keep the old Ghana Telecom power-house in check so it would not unfairly squeeze the newer market entrants. These were the background changes in which the Internet industry evolved. The impetus for change came not only from these champions for change within government but also from radical champions in the private sector.

An Information Revolutionary in the Private Sector

At first glance, the second individual who has contributed immensely to Internet diffusion and sectoral restructuring in Ghana, Nii Quaynor, lacks the bearing of a born revolutionary. Tall and soft-spoken, he is a reserved and modest man. Born in Ghana, he spent about two decades in the United States, where he led a classic knowledge society career. After earning a B.A. at Dartmouth College, he earned a Ph.D. in computer science from the State University of New York at Stony Brook and then spent years in the private sector with Digital Equipment Corporation as a senior software engineering manager. Yet Quaynor's ambitions, tightly focused plans, and accomplishments of building an ICT industry in Ghana from the ground up have been nothing short of revolutionary. Quaynor has built not only his own new firm, Network Computer Systems (NCS), from scratch under conditions that were hardly propitious, but he has almost singlehandedly built a national ICT industry from the ground up, providing a model of entrepreneurial success for Ghana and indeed for the entire region. Recognizing these talents, the

authoritative publication of the global Internet society, *On the Internet,*
wrote as early as 1996 (Sadowski 1996) that "NCS has provided a won-
derful model for countries everywhere, showing how the information
needs of business can drive Internet working in a country. It has accomplished connectivity with no outside funding, relying only on in-country
expertise as an entrepreneurial effort paid for by business customers.
NCS should serve as a model for us all."

Like many change agents of cyberspace who operate mainly inside
developing countries, Quaynor was driven by an intense hunger to help
ensure that his country and his people weren't left behind as the rest of
the world rocketed ahead. And he knew he had the knowledge and training to help. He was the classic modernizer as described by Alexander
Gershenkron (1962) in *Economic Backwardness in Historical Perspective.* After many years abroad, Quaynor was asked to return to Ghana
as a consultant to work on providing information services to the national
oil company. Back in Accra, he had recognized great opportunities to
offer computer services to companies and individual consumers that
were not being provided for adequately or economically at that time. He
turned this insight into a flourishing information and communication
business. From the beginning, his strategy was to pursue the business
customer and not to concentrate on NGOs or the government. How did
he do it?

Quaynor recognized that the rebounding economy had a developmental need and a potential commercial niche for someone to supply
information processing services, including hardware, software, network
management, system design, and troubleshooting for private companies.
In 1993, he found he needed Internet interconnectivity to conduct
his own business, so working with a dial-up MCI account, he started
his account. Like his counterparts throughout the developing world,
Quaynor began by selling computer hardware and software and then
branched out into the Internet as one of several business lines. Hardly
anyone in Ghana knew what the Internet was at that time, and as is true
in many other developing countries it was and still is not much of a
money maker but helps a company keep a hand in what could become
a lucrative business.[1] Recognizing that others could possibly use his services too, he began his Internet business with a base of about 200

customers, and on August 21, 1995, began an Internet service provider with a dedicated leased line with a speed of 14.4 kps (Osiakwan n.d.). Prior to this, he had discovered that his expense for a dial-up was approaching the cost of leasing directly a line from Ghana Telecom, and he wondered how to further extend his business.

At this point, Quaynor made a major breakthrough in his strategy. Partly through luck, partly through novelty, and partly through the connections that are so necessary in patrimonial systems, he was able to bypass the telephone company. With his old telephone line costing him $7,500 per month to Ghana Telecom and $5,000 a month to British Telecom and rapidly running out of bandwidth, he had to come up with another solution to the problem of bandwidth so that he could service his current and anticipated customers (see table 4.6). His solution was to propose bypassing Ghana Telecom altogether and use his own direct international satellite link. When he made appointments at the Ministry of Communications and asked the staff there to install a link for him to connect directly with his customers, the staff said they were unable to do so. They had never been asked before, this was a new technology, and they apparently had no official guidelines. They responded that since they couldn't do it, why didn't he set up such a link? Quaynor interpreted that as permission, and on Ghana Telecom's authorization he set up his link.

Quaynor purchased a class C earth station satellite dish, arranged for a very small aperture terminal (VSAT), and set up his own Internet gateway. In addition to owning two satellite dishes, NCS recently launched a 2 mbps satellite (expandable to 45 mbps) connection to the Internet backbone via Teleglobe (Osiakwan n.d.). NCS has also established points of presence in Kumasi and Takoradi and increased its customer base to approximately 10,000 dial-up subscribers and thirty corporate clients employing 500 dial-in lines operating on more than twenty servers. As a result of these improvements, the price of NCS's Internet connection dropped dramatically from a high of $100 to $25 for unlimited single dial-up accounts (excluding the fixed $50 registration fee).

For many developing governments, this is sheer heresy: these governments, especially those of the authoritarian kind, don't take kindly to private citizens who run their own private satellite services that link them to foreign companies and countries and could perhaps compromise national security. This kind of behavior represents a major restructuring of the rules of the game of the telecommunications sector. When Ghana government officials were interviewed years later, they said they "regret the decision to this day" (personal communication 1997).

In later interviews, I asked Quaynor how he managed to be so successful within the context of Ghana's sometimes tumultuous political climates with its powerful patron-client structures and the regimes' fears about political threats from new or unknown quarters (like the Internet). Quaynor casually mentioned that he had actually attended the same secondary school with President Rawlings and some of this closest advisors and confidants, and they knew him well as one who took development seriously and was unlikely to embarrass the establishment with his plans for this new Internet "thing." Even though something of an outsider— literally as a long-time expatriate abroad and politically as one outside the core ruling political circles—Quaynor could be trusted. This long-term social networking confirms a broader sociological point: *technical expertise and organizational sophistication are imperative to lead successful ICT change, but so is entry into the indigenous patron-client political system*, itself a manifestation of the broader political cultures in which the ICT systems are themselves embedded.

I have argued that the different market and political positions held by different actors lead them to take different strategic positions on market restructuring, which in turn affects outcomes in different information and communication industries. Yet finding hard evidence of how market or structural positions affect negotiating positions and outcomes is difficult, since these are typically politically sensitive issues.

For example, it is apparent that under the Rawlings regime Quaynor's Network Computer Systems (NCS) company occupied a privileged position in the Ghanaian ICT market and in the councils of government. There are several bits of evidence: NCS had the only VSAT in the country until one year later, when Africa On Line also acquired a VSAT. NCS today is one of three private companies in Ghana that holds shares in the state-owned Ghana Telecom (it is said to be around 5 percent of GCom, the 30 percent shareholder of Ghana Telecom). Nii Quaynor by all accounts is a trusted advisor to the highest levels of government and is frequently invited to attend senior meetings by top government leaders. Do these conditions affect his policy positions?

Some Ghanaian businessmen and -women who lack such privileged commercial and political positions suggest that NCS and Quaynor benefit commercially from their advisory positions. They complain that NCS has grown too comfortable and does not feel the pinch of government policies the way that other companies do. Some say that if its president collaborated more closely in alliance with the other commercial actors in Ghana and were more aggressive, then the private sector would be able to push government more toward progressive, proprivate-sector, and competitive policies. One of Quaynor's critics' biggest complaints, for example, is that private companies that bypass the inefficiencies of Ghana Telecom by building and operating their own international lines are still contractually obliged to pay GT what they would have paid if they had actually used its so-called services.

As more companies enter the Ghanaian market, we will expect to see even more jockeying for favor and advantage and perhaps new forms of commercial and political alliances. It is not yet perfectly clear what impact the regime change is having on NCS' business performance, and whether the new government that replaced Rawlings will reward its own ICT entrepreneurs and punish NCS or other current industry leaders. It appears that there have been some repurcussions for NCS.

I have tried to demonstrate that individuals like Nii Quaynor and Minister Edward Salia really do make a difference in the timing and extent of institutional and policy reforms. They provide, among other resources, the critical element of leadership. In the terms used in chapter 2, for example, Salia exercised several kinds of leadership, especially political and structural leadership. Quaynor, too, showed multidimensional leadership (issue leadership, for example) by forcing the ICT issue onto the public agenda and serving as a de facto spokesman for the emerging Internet industry. He became Mr. Internet in Ghana. Indeed, through his aggressive championing of African causes in international meetings, he is often one of the few—sometimes the only—African at international Internet meetings, becoming a kind of Mr. Internet for Africa, not just for Ghana. He is now a member of the board of the Internet Corporation for Assigned Names and Numbers (ICANN), for example. Despite his mild demeanor, he can be outspoken about what he sees as the de facto exclusionary practices of the North but also critical of the failure of other Africans to seize the moment and help press their own case more consistently and effectively.

Information Revolutionaries among the Nonprofit Sector

Christine Kisiedu is one of those dedicated professionals that the library science profession seems to attract the world over. She is struggling with years of neglect and wants to leave a digital, wired legacy for the future. But it isn't easy. Another teacher, Mumuni Dakubu, described the conditions at his university in the late 1990s and his efforts (personal communication 1997):

We're still working at a very primitive level. The students at Legon don't have their own independent or separate access to computers. Instead, they must go to the library to send and receive e-mail. The university has e-mail through the library on a fidonet bulletin board. Access to this cyberworld is distributed in name only; the portals are real doors, and there are only two of them in the library. Currently, students queue up at the consoles, and someone types in the outgoing e-mail messages for them and then prints out the incoming e-mails for everyone. They eventually pick them up here, or we try to carry them to their rooms by hand. This is closer to old-style telegraphs than new-style cyber-messages. Also, because we don't have our own internal telephone system at the university, every time we make a call within the university, we have to go through Ghana Telecommunications, and that's expensive.

He and Kisiedu worry that the high cost alone will drive away their students. One minute of e-mail costs 200 cedis. So for 100 people to use the system for one hour per week costs 6 million cedis or U.S. $3,000. This is an excessively large telephone bill. Kwasi Ansu-Kyeremeh, senior lecturer at the School of Communications Studies, also at Legon, captures the dualism inherent in these modern technologies. On the one hand, he reports, "The impact of ICT has been massive in Ghana. We're undergoing our own communications revolution. Until 1995, there was only one state-owned TV and radio station. Now there are many independent stations, including the university one. These stations broadcast interactive programs, so it is no longer just the state propaganda that is available to the general public. People are encouraged to set up new stations" (personal communication 2001).

Ansu-Kyeremeh also sees what he calls a chain reaction with the Internet: "Information trickles down from the elites using the Internet to the general public. The press uses it quite frequently and then broadcasts or prints the information gained over the Internet to reach a mass audience." Previously, information was heavily controlled by the government. Still, he worries that "in the form it exists now in Ghana, ICT will likely exacerbate problems." "The big challenge," he says, "is whether Ghanaians are going to integrate selectively these new tools into the cultural conditions of Ghanaian society." He wonders aloud, "Why can't we adopt the technology to our culture even as we adapt our culture to the technology"? (personal communication 2001).

In Ghana, the Internet incubated in the safe confines of the Accra campus of the University of Legon before being tested in the competitive rigors of the private market. In brief, the African Association of Universities wanted to start a type of e-mail service called UUCR (University to University Copy Protocol) for universities in the region and selected Legon as a kind of hub for its activities in the West African region. It was used mainly by researchers and especially by Ghanaians who had lived overseas and become familiar with electronic mail. So for many years, it was the only Internet service provider for itself and others in Accra.

A major problem is that the national "leadership does not show as much interest as it should in any of the institutions," says Kisiedu. "When we do this work, we feel sometimes we are getting the runaround. There really isn't as much interaction between the public-sector people and the private as we would like or as we need. We go into the ministers and brief them, but . . ." (personal communication 1997).

Still, in between the part-time work and teaching in overcrowded classrooms, these scholar-activists have found the time to press their own institutions to adjust to the knowledge revolution, to teach their students, and often to act as informal advisors, counselors, and trouble shooters to other revolutionaries in the private sector and in government. So Dakubu and Kisiedu try as best they can to get support: "Part of the problem is that no one seems to be in charge. The university says it can't get money for computers from the government; when we go to the government, they say it's our responsibility, and they show hardly any interest in Internet and information issues." But UNESCO has given some money to support a study on Internet use and impact. They are hoping to get money from Denmark for a fiber-optic backbone for the campus. Meanwhile, the Americans may support a wireless system that would allow Internet use on the campus while bypassing the old telephone system. They have prepared a proposal to the World Bank's Information for Development (*info*DEV) program, and the U.N. Development Program has promised equipment and training for forty people. Bringing the knowledge revolution to a poor university in a poor country seems to be a full-time job for a team of a dozen.

But there are benefits: "We no longer feel so isolated. We can contact someone out there, and sometimes they will respond with a solution, a proposal, an idea" (Christine Kisiedu, speech delivered in Addis Ababa, at the Economic Commission for Africa Addis, 1996). Still, the number of people being trained in computers is inadequate. Commercial operators like Africa On Line complain that they can't hire or keep good staff. According to one AfOL executive, "Those students at Legon just don't get enough hands-on experience in school. They may have ten to fifteen computers for 700 students. This doesn't prepare them for real jobs" (personal communication 1997). The executive complains that this problem also means that his sales force cannot adequately explain what his goods and services can do, especially tough when computer companies are, as much as anything else, trying to explain into existence a market demand that isn't there yet or is growing very slowly. Leadership is needed in the market to explain these new products and their capabilities to business leaders, NGO leaders, government officials, and personal users. And as a professor observed at Cheikh Anta Diop in Dakar, "Too many students can only work on old computers like 386s and other systems no longer used in the market today" (personal communication 1997).

In this first phase within Legon University, a handful of innovators pressed to reallocate scarce institutional resources to attract the attention of senior officials and to alter the rules of the institution to make them more conducive for Internet diffusion. Despite their considerable (individual and collective) commitments, these information champions proved unable to make much headway in restructuring this particular institution. Energy and imagination weren't enough. They lacked the leadership support at the top ranks of their institution to break open standard operating procedures and put ICT issues more centrally on the institution's own agenda.

Furthermore, there were so few financial or human resources in the institution, so little organizational slack, that they found few places that could meet their needs. Finally, the information champions seemed unable to reach out and create effective alliances with other champions in other institutions like NGOs, firms, or government. This suggests that some notion of social capital may be a useful way to conceptualize the mechanism for Internet diffusion, since it seems to involve individuals and groups establishing enough trust to be able to create the social networks that are the precursors to technical networks.

In chapter 2, I discussed a series of common stages or phases—precommercial, commercial, competitive, and consolidation—that developing countries pass through. Ghana, like Brazil, also experienced a phased emergence of these new technological services in the institutional context of the mid-1990s.

Precommerical Phase: How the Internet Came to Ghana

Internet connectivity in Ghana began in 1989 as a pilot project initiated by the Pan African Development Information System (PADIS) and the International Development Research Center (IDRC) of Canada, the only institutions in the country initially connected to the Internet (Osiakawan n.d.). The project sought to connect African countries to the Internet cheaply under the Capacity Building for Electronic Communication in Africa (CABECA) initiative. Specifically, the system employed FidoNet to connect the Ghana National Scientific and Technological Information Network (GHASTINET), the Association of African Universities (AAU), and the Technology Transfer Center (TTC) to GreenNet in London via dial-up. However, due to the financial, infrastructural, and other problems plaguing the network, the AAU opted to establish AAUnet to link unconnected African universities to the Internet. By 1997, the AAU network had approximately twenty-three subscribers, and several subscribers had more than one user. The health sector also established HealthNet, which is located at the KorleBu Medical school and connected forty subscribers to the Internet via a low earth-orbiting satellite, including the Ghana medical school and the United Nations International Children's Educational Fund (UNICEF).

Internet Leadership in Universities

Ghana experienced a dramatic expansion of its ICT services in the 1990s, triggered by the deregulation of the telecommunications sector and a five-year SAP plan entitled the Accelerated Development Program (ADP) supervised by the Ministry of Transport and Communications. This expansion was characterized by the introduction of mobile phones, pagers, FM radio, cable television, and finally the Internet. According to the World Bank (1999),

In less than four years Ghana had implemented one of the world's most ambitious telecommunications reform programs. In 1997 Ghana became the first developing country to introduce privatization and competition in all areas of service [cellular, Internet, etc.] in all parts of the country. Ghana Telecom was partly privatized, and a second supplier licensed a consortium of two U.S. firms and the Ghanaian National Petroleum Corporation.

The final results have been impressive for the consumer. From an average ten-year wait for telephones, a density of one telephone per 400 and a PTO with huge losses, the situation has brightened. For the first time in its existence, GT now earns a profit; in 1997 alone, the number of connected fixed lines increased from 90,000 to 120,000, and Ghana Telecom's revenues jumped from 55 to 75 million cedis. Moreover, the company plans to meet its rollout obligation of 225,000 lines in three years, which will be two years ahead of the five allowed under the license.

Most of the precommercial Internet development occurred in non-market institutional contexts—universities, research centers, and NGOs. In Ghana, as in so many other countries, a small handful of courageous people led the charge within the groves of the academy. They share professional profiles with their counterparts in other countries. Some were in library sciences, like Christine Kisiedu, and others in computer sciences. Some, like Olivier Sanga, formerly of the University Cheikh Anta Diop, started in history and the humanities and then became infoactivists.

An accurate picture of these particular academic groves does not resemble Stanford, the Sorbonne, or Cambridge (England or Massachusetts). In all too many developing countries from South Asia to Africa south of the Sahara, years of military misrule and anti-intellectualism have produced weak and dilapidated educational institutions cowed by the state and inadequate budgets. Buildings are run down, lawns are uncut, walkways are cracked, offices contain little more than a battered desk and a broken overhead fan, library shelves are understocked and empty of recent journals, and professors are so underpaid that most drive taxis, run corner stores, or consult to pay their bills. Compared to my first visit to Legon in 1975, my visit twenty-two years later was sobering and sad. The difficulties faced by students, professors, and researchers at the oldest and most prestigious school in the country were indeed demoralizing. It is difficult to imagine that any information revolution or knowledge society can be sustained unless and until these conditions are substantially improved.

The ICT infrastructure at Legon has improved markedly in recent years. The university currently has a large fiber network intranet. Moreover, the Balme Library, one of the main ICT centers in Ghana, possesses a well-equipped computer laboratory and competent technical staff and was the hub of the Interlibrary-Lending and Document Delivery in Developing Countries project (IFLA/DANIDA), which involved the libraries of the University of Development Studies at Tamale and the University of Cape Coast. Although Balme Library only had one 286-processor personal computer in 1990, it now has over twenty-five personal computers, three Windows NT servers, and one Linux box. Currently, approximately 70 percent of the library is linked to a local area network (LAN), and all the computers have Internet access. Lastly, the library provides Internet access to five Ghanaian university libraries, the Institute for Science and Technological Information (INSTI), and e-mail access to other individuals and organizations.

A Transition Period toward the Commercialization Phase

Selling commercial Internet services in the mid-1990s was a challenge to everyone who tried. In developing countries like Ghana, it was doubly tough. Potential clients are poorer and are less familiar with the service and how it can help them. In developing countries, the initial work of the seller of Internet services is in large measure one of making a market by explaining to potential customers why they need something that they have never had before, even though it is expensive to use and relatively difficult to operate. Much of the selling involves a lot of hand holding, as it does everywhere. This is more true in poor countries, where knowledge of the uses of the Internet is not widespread and where the institutional supports (network managers, help lines, and so forth) are not available. One must be an evangelist as well as a salesman and hardware supplier. And one must be a revolutionary, willing to break down antiliberal, anti-Internet government restrictions on the spread of the services.

By 1996, as described above, Nii Quaynor had moved from a customer base that began with his own Network Computer Services (NCS) operation (1988), expanded to include other computer clients, spread outward to international organizations (such as embassies and international bodies) and NGOs, and then finally attracted a business clientele that remains his bread and butter and half his customer base. In 1997, when I first interviewed Quaynor, the Internet accounted for only 20 percent of his revenues, and of his staff of sixty people, about ten worked on the Internet at his office. After a long business day and a long conversation late one evening about Internet in Accra, he sighed and said, "It's still a losing business."

In some other countries, the transition from precommercial to commercial is built on close collaboration between the nonprofit university and research communities and the emerging entrepreneur sector. In Senegal, for example, the local experts at the Cheikh Anta Diop University were consulted frequently by start-up companies in Dakar. Some of the start-ups were owned by businessmen who had computer sales and servicing companies and who were anxious to branch into this new thing called the Internet in 1996 and 1997. Eventually, university professors in Senegal started a publication, *Informatique*, that helped bind the budding community together. Today another electronic journal, *OSIRIS*, links Senegal's researchers, policy makers, NGOs, and others into a common community. In Senegal, the initiatives of France's innovative foreign research agency (then called ORSTOM), a strong and collegial local university research community, almost a dozen start-up Internet service providers, as well as continual expressions of interest among senior government officials created an architecture of interest that was quite different from the Ghanaian architecture.

In Ghana in the early years, I found little evidence of interelite collaboration and cooperation. There were fewer businessmen, researchers, community activists, and government officials interested in Internet diffusion. Therefore, in Ghana, the jump from precommercial to commercial was more discontinuous than elsewhere. It began with a single reverse brain-drain expert—Quaynor—who was brought back as a teacher and consultant and who then saw commercial opportunities in computer sales and services and in providing Internet access to the broader Accra community. The university continued on its own modest path of internal development, and the government did virtually nothing to promote the medium directly. NGOs were slow in moving, and it took a while for other entrepreneurs to enter the Internet service provider market.

The willingness of the top political leadership to go along with a reform program was one of the key factors contributing to ICT success during the early phases of Internet diffusion in Ghana. Nii Quaynor by himself could not have succeeded as a lone entrepreneur. He needed a social network that he could mobilize into a political support network. This process of marketization or commercialization (the structuring of an initial market) can be conceptualized as an upwardly sweeping chain of influence. First was Quaynor as the startup entrepreneur. As the opportunities for his company expanded, he needed higher protection. Edward Salia of the Ministry of Communications backed Quaynor because he believed it was the right thing to do for the sector and the country and because President Jerry Rawlings had clearly indicated that economic liberalization should be encouraged.

But Minister Salia's support alone was not sufficient for the big push needed in the ICT sectors in the 1990s. A higher political authority was needed, and that authority was Rawlings's senior economic advisor, P. V. Obeng. So Obeng backed the minister, and President Rawlings backed Obeng. Authority to operate as a commercial firm relatively unhindered passed from President Rawlings, to Obeng, to Salia, and eventually to

NCS and other firms. All of this was made more palatable and possible because of the political reliability of the players up and down the line.

The Competitive Period

Private Internet Service Providers
Despite being a highly uncertain business, by 1998 the Ghanaian market for Internet services had one additional local Internet service provider called Internet Ghana and one continentwide company called Africa On Line (AfOL). AfOL was started by three Kenyan graduate students studying at MIT in Cambridge, Massachusetts, in the United States, who returned home to begin this service. After Kenya, they expanded to five other African countries (Ivory Coast, Ghana, Zimbabwe, Tanzania, and South Africa). After several years of operation, the company was bought out by the U.S. owners of the early online content provider Prodigy, who launched additional services in several African countries. In March 1996, AfOL approached Ghana and moved into a market that had been, up until that time, the monopoly preserve of NCS.

Africa On Line commenced its services in November 1996 with a 64 kbps leased line connected from Ghana Telecom to its hub in Boston, which eventually was expanded to 128 kbps. The company also possesses a VSAT network that operates on an internal bandwidth of 2 mbps and links most of the regional capitals to the Internet, including far-flung regions such as Tamale and Bolgatanga. Because AfOL is part of the GRIC Communications, Inc. roaming consortium, its subscribers can access their e-mail and Internet accounts in approximately 172 countries. By 1998, there were 179 communication centers active in four Ghanaian cities with 22,000 subscribers nationwide.

Like their major competitor (NCS), AfOL is more concerned about being one of the first entrants to make a market and to gain advantage. It was worried about an inability to obtain a VSAT like NCS. AfOL was, however, one of the first companies to have a fully digital leased line. Its start-up was tough, especially between November 1996 to February 1997, and unlike NCS it lacked the cash generator of also making repairs and sales. Among Ghana's population of 20 million, there are only 500,000 active computers and 100,000 local e-mail addresses (Quaynor

2001). AfOL managers also complained that the government was so new to these kinds of activities that it sometimes almost suffocated the market through obstructive interventions, by ignoring its development potentials, and by making virtually no serious attempts to promote the Internet. Still, by 2000, the market was thriving and becoming more competitive.

Another Internet service provider, the locally owned Internet Ghana, established its first point of presence (pop) in Kumasi and sought to provide affordable and efficient Internet connectivity to individual and corporate users. It commenced operations with a bandwidth of 64 kbps that has since been expanded to 2 mbps. Some claim that Internet Ghana was the first Ghanaian ISP to "install and operate a full digital link to the Internet in West Africa," though that claim is open to some dispute. The company also introduced cybercafes to Ghana and provided free e-mail addresses. The company currently has approximately sixty corporate and 2,500 individual subscribers.

In 1996, a new content provider, Ghana Classifieds Ltd., was established. According to its chief executive officer, Ashim Morton, Ghana Classifieds focused on content and Web site development to "promote access to the Internet and all its value-added resources." The company describes itself as a full multimedia entity that offers news, business, and other related information on Ghana via its Web site, which is hosted abroad at <http://www.ghanaclassifieds.com>. In keeping with its mission, Ghana Classifieds has developed Internet Web sites for approximately thirty Ghanaian corporate organizations. It also provides a listing of several organizations on its Web site, including banks, hotels, NGOs, and other entities.

Other content providers have emerged in the Ghanaian market. Webstar Internet (35 percent owned by NCS) commenced operations in Ghana in 1997 to "deliver high-quality Web sites that are organically designed to visually communicate our clients' message and ensure their satisfaction" at <http://www.webstar.com.gh/design.html>. The company has been at the forefront of Web development and advertising in Ghana, and it introduced Ghana to Web-based advertising. The company now serves approximately thirty clients and has designed several Web sites including two—<http://www.gcaa.com.gh> and <http://www.carnival

.com.gh>—that were voted by online service "Woyaa" as two of Africa's top sites (Osiakwan n.d.).

In 1999, four new Internet service providers—AfricaExpress Communications Network, InterCom Data Network (IDN), Information Technology Services (ITS), and Ghana Telecom—(Osiakwan n.d.) obtained licenses to provide various Internet-related services to the Ghanaian market, but only the first company is fully operational at the present time. AfricaExpress—at <http://www.africaexpress.com/Company.htm> —was incorporated in March 1998 as "an Internet Access and Internet Content Provider with specialization in Web site design, Maintenance and Hosting." Its services include e-commerce, electronic mail, Internet access, sale of virtual servers (Web space), and Web site design and domain name registration. AfricaExpress is linked to a server in the United States via a DS3 fiber optic Internet connection, which runs at a speed of 45 mbps.

InterCom Data Network (IDN), which was fully operational until recently, is a joint venture between IDN Inc. and Transit Networks, which are both U.S.-based Internet service providers. IDN, which started providing Internet services in 1999, was shut down by Ghana's National Communications Authority for operating a commercial voice-over-Internet protocol (VOIP) (see <http://www.itweb.co.za/sections/telecoms/200>). Prior to the closure of IDN on July 11, 2000, and the brief detention of its chief operating officer, Francis Quartey, the company "deploy[ed] the most extensive Internet wireless network in Accra and Tema [and] route[d] a 2 mbps link to the Internet through Transit Networks via Ghana Telecom's earth satellite station at Nkuntunese" (Osiakawan n.d.). In addition to offering twenty-four-hour technical support, IDN charged $25 per month, one of the lowest Internet rates in Ghana.

Another company, NetAfrique (available at <http://www.netafrique.net>) has recently emerged to provide audio and video streaming, custom training and implementation, domain registration, Web hosting, e-commerce, intranet and extranet, and Web development services. Other entities that may evolve into full-fledged Internet service providers in the coming years include Ghana Telecom and Westel, the country's two national telephone companies. As a result of the introduction of the ISPs, by the end of 1999, the Internet subscription rate in Ghana had increased to 18,000, while the user domain was approximately 300,000 (Osiak-wan n.d.).

NGO Access in the Competitive Phase

Between 1979 and the writing of the new constitution in 1992, an authoritarian military government controlled every aspect of Ghanaian group initiative. The government was distrustful of any independent social group, whether business, labor, or NGO, and took steps to ensure that they did not challenge the regime. When I asked one observer in the NGO sector why NGOs had not been more aggressive in promoting Internet in the early period, she responded (personal communication 1997),

You have missed an important point. From 1979, when the military took over, up to the writing of the new constitution in 1992, NGOs in Ghana were very weak because we were under a military regime that was worried about NGOs' political motives. So after they cracked down on a bunch of them early on, people got extremely nervous about being a member of an NGO. The military boys always were worried that an NGO would be antigovernment and would orga-nize people against them. It's really only after the new constitution, when people saw that the government was serious about not cracking down so much anymore on NGOs, that Ghanaians began to get organized again into NGOs. After the 1992 constitution was ratified, people waited a few years to see if government was serious. Then after about 1995, they started getting active again. So there is a real flowering of NGOs after 1995.

She points out that after 1995 the press also began to be more critical and forthright.

Access, Equity, and the Internet

In Ghana, there have been few studies of the Internet, and virtually no studies have been made of its distributional impacts. Yet we can gain a glimmer of the distributional implications seen through the eyes of knowledgeable Ghanaians themselves. Access, of course, always begins with institutions and organizations.

Research I conducted in Ghana and other countries found that when computers are introduced into an organization in a developing country, they are used by the senior staff almost entirely, frequently in offices kept locked inside the directors' suite. As the NGOs' computers are networked and gain Internet access, the first communications are most likely with other NGOs abroad, especially if the NGO (as often occurs) is affiliated with an international body in London, Paris, or New York. Alfred Osei, of the Hunger Project in Accra, said his office uses the Internet, telephones, and fax to communicate with its headquarters in New York and with other projects in Africa (personal communication March 29, 1999). Eventually, the more advanced use the system to gain cheaper two-way communications with their own affiliates or field offices in the countryside. Very few organizations in the poorer developing countries have intranets or local area networks internal to the entire organization. Osei also mused about the distributional impacts of the new tools: "If the spread of information is done mainly through computers, this will be to the disadvantage of rural people, and the gaps between rich and poor will increase. The rural areas will be left behind because, unfortunately, they still have no access and no training."

Some NGOs, acting as agents of change, have also been adept at using ICTs to promote community development and empowerment. Specifically, the Kumasi-based Center for the Development of People (CEDEP) recently provided courses in computer literacy, Internet use, and typing to approximately seventy clients (Fontaine and Foote 1999). These clients included forty-five males and twenty-five females, fifty-three of whom were students, teachers, administrators, and technicians. In recent years, other NGOs have offered general and focused seminars in Kumasi on topics as diverse as "Y2K: Origin, Myths, Realities, and Solutions," "The Internet and Its Benefits to Society," and "The Computer as a Tool in Medicine."

Most of the NGO leaders interviewed in Ghana conveyed the sense that the new technologies bring exciting rewards as well as worrisome risks like those cited by Osei. On the positive side, most of those interviewed in NGOs believe, with the editor of the *Weekly Insight* newspaper, that because of the Internet, "it is possible to disseminate information quite easily. . . . This is much better than before when there was a lack of information available. It is no longer possible for governments or particular interest groups in Ghana to control information. This acts as a check on government. . . . The impact of technology has been very big for the press in Ghana" (personal communication 1999).

The majority of the Ghanaians interviewed felt that the most effective use of the Internet is in combination with other media like the traditional press and the radio: "The media use [the Internet] a lot, which in turn gives access to information to many more people", (personal communication 1999). Radio is the most powerful medium, and information can be broadcast that educates people all over the country very quickly. These technologies are expanding people's world view, although slowly. NGOs use them to get out their message. According to the head of the Ghana Social Marketing Foundation, which educates the public about birth control issues, radio and TV are definitely the biggest and most effective means of reaching so many people for so little.

C. Okoroafor, the head of the Ghanaian Association of Women Entrepreneurs (GAWE), concluded that computers are "having a big impact amongst a small sector of society" (personal communication 1999). Enthusiastic about its business possibilities, she said, "It will be huge in communication, and this can only help. The African Federation of Women Entrepreneurs (AFWE) is encouraging all African associations to become computer literate because it will really help their work. This is one area they feel really should be improved. It just costs us too much time and money to try to do business over the phone and mail within AFWE."

Yet she admits the risks: "IT will widen the gap between rich and poor if there is not widespread access. Right now, it is rather cost prohibitive." And according to the former vice president of the Ghana Journalists Association, technologies in themselves do not create disparities, but the inequality gap will widen "if we do not promote the technology equally in all segments of society. Access to technology and training on how to use it are key. The policies the government pursues are more important than the technology itself."

At the Center for Policy Analysis, one senior analyst pointed back to the intersection where the technologies confront society: "If used properly, IT should improve inequalities. This is why we feel civil society has to be empowered." He noted that broadcasting radio shows in the listeners' local language is an example of media being used to empower people. Several respondents in the nonprofit sector pointed again and again to the tremendous change wrought by open radio, after years of government propaganda and very limited and biased reporting. Especially exciting were the call-in radio shows, some broadcast in local languages, where callers ask questions and make comments in the language of their choice. "Essentially," said the senior analyst, "information is power for people, and the potential for bridging the inequality gaps is great" (personal communication 2000).

In conclusion, the NGO officers interviewed were very sensitive to the double-edged sword that ICT represents. They believe it is good for the country as a whole and especially for those who are well educated and well-to-do, and they are anxious to get it. Most recognize that it may also exacerbate the existing inequalities. Curiously, the only two non-Ghanaians we interviewed from NGO organizations differed from the Ghanaian consensus. When asked about the potential (re)distributional aspects of ICT, each answered that they did not think ICT has had or will have much of an effect on class differences. "They already exist," said one," and are very stark, and the gap won't be widened or narrowed by access to the Internet" (personal communication 2000). Another emphasized the promotional aspects of ICT. She pointed out that "Ghana has promoted itself as the gateway to West Africa, and the Western world has accepted that status. The Internet has brought more attention to Ghana, and that is going to be a key in promoting development, especially through tourism."

The beginning of the Kufuor administration prompted new life in the ICT consultative process, which had become desultory at the end of Rawlings's rule. In personnel terms, new ministers came in, new personalities were seconded to the "Castle" (the executive office of the president), and new workshops and consultations began. As with most new governments, there was pressure to start with a clean slate and come up with a new ICT plan. There appeared to be some political jockeying by the three Ministries of Communication, Information, and Science and Technology. External players got into the act as well, with UNDP, the Economic Commission for Africa, and various consultants offering solutions to challenges of e-readiness. Eventually, a new national policy panel was oppointed, chaired by university don Clement K. Dzidonu, which during 2002 and 2003 met with representatives of government, civil society, the private sector and universities. They produced "An Integrated

ICT-Led Socio-Economic Development Policy and Plan Development Framework for Ghana," a good analysis of ICT issues and examples, but not a document that set sharp priorities. The government has a new plan in the works but has not yet issued it.

Conclusion: Politics, Vision, Leadership, and Institutional Change in Ghana

We began our discussion of Ghana by posing several political economy questions: What do the political leaders and technocrats of a very small, very poor country do when pressed on all sides to restructure one of the country's core infrastructure regimes? How do they accede to or resist local and external demands while meeting any patrimonial elite's paramount goal—holding on to its own power and influence in the face of substantial challenges to reform? How much room to maneuver do the information champions really possess? Which social actors have pressed for change and which have opposed?

Several conclusions flow from this analysis of competing elites' efforts to restructure ICT industries in a very poor African country. First, strategic restructuring, as we defined it in chapter 2, is definitely occurring in Ghana. Privileged groups do struggle to impose their definitions of the four policy balances and to preserve their own high status positions in society. In the Ghanaian context, the precise details and dynamics of strategic restructuring were shaped by patrimonial politics in a weak state and weak economy. Yet in spite of the weaknesses of state and economy, a robust Internet industry did emerge after the mid-1990s. At the end of the day, advanced technological industries emerged in this economically backward society, despite poverty and inexperience with advanced technologies.

I believe that the interplay of structure and agency is the critical element of Internet diffusion in Ghana. Poverty, a weak middle class, poor schools that produce far too few engineers, bad roads, and low political transparency really do reduce the societal demand for the Internet, reduce the supply of people needed to manage and maintain the new knowledge networks, and reduce the means at their disposal to do so. Structure is unforgiving.

The weakened national structures inherited from the 1980s imposed serious constraints on the financial and human resources available to rehabilitate the old and create the new ICT markets in Ghana in the 1990s, including the Internet. They also shaped the types of ICT problems that needed to be addressed. In poor countries that are at low levels of economic development ($390 per capita per year), dominated by agriculture, that have few skilled scientists and technologists, and that have a weak democratic tradition, new technologies like the Internet do not spread easily. There is not enough disposable income to sustain Internet growth that is fast and widespread. A weak resource base virtually guarantees weak and unreliable institutions in poor countries. Dominant institutions on the whole buttressed the old ways of producing, transmitting, and using information, and pushing Internet-friendly reforms was more likely to get one fired than promoted. But we also saw in Ghana that structure and institutions always leave human beings with considerable leeway to select the priorities they prefer and to pursue particular strategies, employing different combinations of resources and using various means at their disposal.

Ghana's class structure did not give precise instructions to each individual about how to behave toward ICTs. It didn't dictate the contours and details of industrial policies toward the constituent ICT industries. Different individuals responded differently to these incentives. So within the cramped structural and institutional constraints, a small group of information champions did emerge who aggressively pressed for change in private markets and public institutions. These local champions were complemented by external pressures from bilateral and multilateral institutions.

Individuals emerged in public, private, and NGO institutions who partly overcame these difficult structural conditions. They fought every day, agitated, cajoled, wheedled, begged, and borrowed to create knowledge networks. They played tough defense and offense to keep politicians and government bureaucrats from killing the knowledge networks. They did this for selfless and selfish reasons, as one might expect. In spite of difficult conditions there was a cadre of information champions who agitated to spread the Internet, even when it meant forcing changes in other ancillary institutions like government ministries or state-owned enterprises. Information revolutionaries did emerge in Ghana to a surprising extent, in both the public and private sectors.

I saw less NGO leadership, however, than I originally expected. Some leaders had appeared in the separate NGO organizations, but no fully committed, unambiguously enthusiastic national leadership cadre emerged to unite the sector or to seize the reins of promotional or issue leadership for the country as a whole. Certainly, president Rawlings failed to do so. In Ghana, the cross-institutional networks were weaker than in some other African (Senegal) and non-African countries. The leadership was thin (it had only a few people at the top), narrow, institutionally insular, and not particularly consistent. Much of the burden of leadership fell to a private-sector entrepreneur and information revolutionary—Nii Quaynor—to advance the cause nationally. There was not a lot of collective action. It may be that the trust, reciprocity, and shared expectations we associate with social capital had been badly eroded after a decade of military rule. NGOs were repressed, and entrepreneurial initiatives repeatedly slapped down. Without the social networks of human ties built up carefully among individuals and institutions over many years, the necessary technical networks cannot easily emerge. Authoritarianism may erode the needed social networks that are the real backbones of Internet expansion.

I found that the relationships among societal networks and technical networks were complex, mutually dependent, and much more diverse that I originally expected. Technical, hard Internet networks rode on the back of societal networks. Quaynor's social network—the social capital he had invested over the years between high school and the present—helped pave the way for the diffusion of the wired networks. In the vernacular, you have to be wired to get wired. The technical networks are deeply intertwined with the societal. The two grow together like twisted strands of DNA, deeply connected and mutually penetrated, each giving shape to the other.

The societal networks affected the technical networks in subtle ways. Preexisting societal networks were brought into play by some individual entrepreneurs to gain access to ICT resources like VSATs. Both commercial power and political power were exercised through networks. As one Ghanaian businesswoman told me when asked about entrepreneurs in the political opposition: "That's an oxymoron. There's no such thing as an opposition entrepreneur" because if you go into the opposition, you get no contracts or loans. In patrimonial countries like Ghana, successful businesspeople cannot afford to strongly back the political opposition. The literature on the entrepreneurial and business classes in developing countries shows unambiguously that their political autonomy and influence are always narrower by far than their economic weight would suggest.

Still, as important as these patrimonial and other networks are, it is curious that patrimonial calculations did not entirely dominate the allocation of scarce resources in the Ghanaian ICT sector. The patrimonial power network was not the sole factor shaping the evolution of the Internet in Ghana. Political power played its part there as it does elsewhere, but it did not entirely dominate the allocation of this scarce resource. Room remained for entrepreneurial and service imperatives as well.

In countries like Ghana, the Internet has spread far beyond its initial narrow boundaries. However, it is probably certain that with more politically open conditions and less patrimonial politics, much more could be done. If the national leadership were truly enthusiastic and promotional rather than simply permissive, then average Ghanaians might have even more and better access to networked knowledge than they have today. (ECA, 2002 p. 3).

In conclusion, the strategic restructuring of the Internet and other ICT markets in Ghana occurred fitfully in stops and starts, more in some sectors and institutions than in others. The linkages among individuals and groups within and across institutions occurred through a dynamic process that was far more political than technological or financial and required substantial leadership, especially to get the process moving.

Appendix

Institutions

Ministries

The Ministry of Communications   The Ministry of Communications was established in 1997 when the Ministry of Transport and Communication was split, to "facilitate the strategic development and application of the best practices and uses of the various communications resources—human, material, and technological—for effective communications throughout the country" ("Ghana at a Glance" 2000). Policy was set within the narrow confines of the senior levels of the ministries and the companies, without much consultation beyond. In telecommunications markets, policies like tariffs, standards, priorities for building lines, and so forth were largely intragovernmental affairs. Very few private actors were available for consultation in the national telecom system since most outfits were state owned. Consumer complaints about poor electricity supply or water services went mainly unaddressed, as did complaints about the telephone company. After all, in 1999, the waiting list for a telephone line in Ghana was 2.9 years ("Ghana at a Glance" 2000). There were no regulatory hearings or other channels for addressing public-service concerns.

The Ministry of Information   A Ministry of Information served as the central locus of public information and propaganda and had oversight responsibility for radio and television. Its minister was close to former President Rawlings, and this highly politicized ministry was eliminated in the 1990s. Some of its functions were transferred to the new Ministry of Communications formed in 1997.

State-Owned Enterprises (SOEs): Ghana Telecom (GT)
Ghana Telecom, which was incorporated in 1995, replaced the telecommunications division of Ghana Posts and Telecommunications Corporation (GPTC) as a result of the accelerated development program (ADP) reform initiative described in depth below ("Overview of Ghana Telecom" n.d.). According to the Ministry of Communications, GT's business strategy is comprised of the following elements: enhanced marketing and customer services, improved management and organizational structure, introduction of new technologies, mobile services, and new value-added products.

GT is one of Ghana's largest companies, with assets recently estimated at U.S. $222 million, and has been at the forefront of telecommunication

Table 4.4
Features of Ghana's Telecommunications Network

Switching network	90% digital
Transmission network	33% digital and radio
Backlog of lines	300,000 lines
Customer access	6% wireless local loop
	Copper based (paper, jelly)
Gateway	2 International Exchanges
	Satellite access via standard A, AOR earth station
	Terrestrial radio microwave access to ECOWAS subregion
Data	Leased lines, 9.6 kbps
	Switched, X.25, 5 nodes (Datatel)

reforms in the country. In line with the accelerated development program's call for privatization, GT "privatized its mainline operations by awarding a Malaysian-led consortium (Telekom Malaysia) a 30 percent share in the company for $38 million with full management control." These and other related reforms resulted in a marked increase in the country's telephone line capacity in general and connected lines in particular. Specifically, 100,000 lines were connected in 1997, and as of March 1998, the number of connected lines had increased to 112,000 ("National Information and Communication Infrastructure Country Proposal: Ghana" 2001). Additional information regarding GT's network is provided in table 4.4.

Regulatory Bodies: The National Communications Authority (NCA)
The accelerated development program created a new body, the National Communications Authority (NCA), which was established in October 1996 by an act of Parliament and charged with "creat[ing] transparent mechanisms for the regulation of the telecommunications sector and promot[ing] a stable operating environment for all participants, while promoting fair competition and efficiency" ("National Information and Communication Infrastructure Country Proposal: Ghana" 2001). The NCA's specific areas of responsibility include the following:

• Advise the Minister of Information on policy formulation and development strategies for the telecommunications industry.

• Ensure strict compliance with the act and the regulations made under it.

• Grant licenses for the operation of telecommunications systems (as defined in section 44 of the act).

• Assign, allocate, and regulate the use of frequencies in conformity with international requirements pursuant to any relevant treaties, protocols, or conventions to which Ghana is signatory.

• Prepare and review the National Frequency Allocation Plan.

• Establish the national numbering plan, and assign numbers accordingly.

• Act internationally as the national body representing Ghana in the area of telecommunications.

• Designate standards of telecommunications equipment.

• Determine a code of practice relating to dealings by operators with international telecommunications operators, and regulate international accounting rates.

• Provide guidelines on tariffs chargeable for the provision of telecommunications services.

• Establish training standards for telecommunications operators, and monitor the implementation of the training standards.

• Provide, where reasonably practicable, advice and assistance to operators in the telecommunications industry in Ghana for a fee.

• Maintain a register of operators.

• Establish regulations for protecting the storage and transmission of electronic data and their transmission.

Research Institutions

Council for Scientific and Industrial Research (CSIR)   The Council for Scientific and Industrial Research (CSIR) was established in 1968 and reconstituted in 1996 (<www.csir.org.gh>). CSIR's main vision is to "become a centre of excellence in Research and Development (R&D) by generating technologies that are responsive to demands of the private sector and socio-economic development."

The CSIR was the first agency to establish electronic mail service in Ghana. Furthermore, its research center INSTI created GHASTINET, an electronic mail host designed to link Ghanaian research institutions with each other, and since 1989 has managed the network, including the "preparation of policy proposals and plans, procedures and uniform standards for adoption by GHASTINET participants, and the coordination of these activities to minimize duplication and foster resource sharing" (Institute for Scientific and Technological Information 1999).

Ghana Internet Connectivity Committee The Rawlings government created a special commission—the Ghana Internet Connectivity Committee—to follow the African Information Society Initiative (AISI) initiative of the Economic Commission for Africa. The Ministry of Finance made a commitment to increase telecommunications resources for the universities, but it is not clear whether this body really achieved much or even met regularly. One member who was appointed to the body complained to me that of forty people appointed, only one was a woman.

Nongovernmental Organizations (NGOs)

Public Outreach After the mid-1990s, not only were NGOs gaining greater acceptance by the regime and some greater political leverage, but the new parliament provided, in principle, other channels for popular influence over infrastructure resources. The Minister of Communications Ekwow Spio-Garbah organized several public outreach efforts. The first was a telecommunications stakeholders' retreat held in January 1998 that brought together over seventy-five participants from a variety of backgrounds, including public-sector members such as legislators, policy makers, and heads of communication agencies, as well as some from the private sector. The meeting sought to develop new ideas for telecommunications policies and to create a small network of people in the field who could work cooperatively. This was in part an initiative to put on the table the public monopoly and iron triangle structures of ICT policy making in Ghana. Out of the meeting came a call for a strategic unit that could plan and act proactively and the following formal declaration:

The Ministry of Communications will convene a National Communications Conference during 1998, which will bring together Stakeholders both within and outside the communications' sector, so that suppliers, consumers, policy makers, and legislators can develop ideas further and deliberate on a draft communications document, and establish a . . . programme of implementation.

A second, more widely consultative meeting was held in early October 1998 and brought together stakeholders to propose tangible policies. Specifically, the conference addressed both technical matters like the Postal and Meteorological Services, as well as "governance, partnerships, and collaboration with NGOs, women, and the informal sector." The October meeting on Ghana's national telecommunications policies certainly was broadly consultative. But as with many such ICT efforts in Ghana and other countries, follow-through was lacking. A one-time consultation, however well meaning, does not a transformation make. The government failed to create new channels to provide continuous input into policy making, and the policy process was not made more transparent. This pattern follows the experiences of Brazil, South Africa, and other countries. It remains to be seen, therefore, whether dynamic policy changes are sustainable without profound organizational reforms internal to government and reforms in the channels of access that the public has to ICT policy-making and implementing bodies.

Ghana National Information and Communications Committee (GNICC)
The Ghana National Information and Communication Committee (GNICC), an initiative coordinated by Balme Library of the University of Ghana, Legon, is composed of individuals from the academic, government, research, and private sectors (AISI-Connect National ICT Profile). The GNICC developed a draft national telecommunications policy and has received support from domestic and international agencies, including the Ministry of Information, Science, and Technology and the Ministry of Communications. In addition, the United Nations Educational, Scientific, and Cultural Organization (UNESCO) has provided U.S. $250,000 for a proposed project that will link Ghanaian universities and research centers.

Privately Owned Media

There were marked institutional and policy changes in the broadcast sector as well. Following commitments made by the Rawlings regime starting in the mid-1980s to reduce government's role in the economy and in the face of growing popular demand, the Ghanaian government slowly began to allow some private control of TV and radio. Strict controls began to erode and fall away rapidly in the early to mid-1990s. In broadcasting, for example, the new 1992 to 1993 constitution permitted freedom of the press and forbade licensing of any medium of mass communication. Soon after but not without some major delays, for the first time, privately owned radio stations sprouted in Ghana.

The World Bank has referred to the explosion of privately owned and diverse media in Africa as the "second liberalization" of the continent. By 2000, for example, Ghana had fifty-eight authorized FM stations (forty-nine on air and nine GBC stations) and seventeen authorized television stations (twelve operational, with three on the air and the rest cable or the wireless system called MMDS). At the beginning of 1994, by contrast, there were only one-third the number of broadcasters and half as many television broadcasters. At the same time, and probably sparked by economic growth and public policy, TV set ownership accelerated from 265,000 to 800,000 between 1993 and 1996. Some of this is probably due to the rise in disposable income as economic growth spread throughout the country, sparked by new capital inflows (mostly aid) and the initial effects of the structural adjustment program, but some is probably also related to the liberalization of ownership as well.

It is impossible to measure precisely the extent of public participation in the ICT debate in Ghana or to calculate the impact that such discussions are having on public behavior and policy; however, the consensus among those I spoke with is that the culture of silence that characterized much of the 1980s has been broken. Perhaps because of the relative anonymity afforded by radio, Ghanaians are now talking about all manner of topical issues. According to one observer, "Open phone lines, assurances that you may speak in your own language, and well-publicized accounts of actions taken to look into and resolve citizens problems have, it seems, led many to believe for the first time that their voices, their needs, and their concerns do matter. They have become more confident in themselves and thus empowered to become active citizens" (personal communication 1999). If the meaning of competition is captured in the number of players in a market, then it appears that Ghana has become competitive in broadcasting.

JoyFM was the first Ghanaian and West African radio station to stream live real-time audio via its Internet Web site, <www.myjoyonline.com>. It was implemented by Ghana's leading Internet company, Network Computer Systems (NCS), as are some of the other FM stations in the country. The Web site features news, features, a discussion and chat section, and an audio feature and records approximately 5,000 hits daily, according to Cyril Heyman, its general manager. As testimony to the station's global reach, a U.K.-based magazine recently included it as one of the best 100 Web sites in the world. In addition to JoyFM, other Ghanaian media outlets maintain a presence on the Web site. One such outlet, VibeFM, an Accra-based radio station, has its own Web site, <www.vibefm.com.gh>, which provides daily news from Ghana in text format as well as other features. Prominent Web sites with general information on Ghana are listed in table 4.5.

Cellular and Other Services

Other value-added telecommunications, like paging or cellular telephony, were similar to the Internet and quite distinct from traditional plain old telephone service (POTS). These new technology services emerged into a policy hollow space, since no competing firms, institutions, political coalitions, or interest groups occupied the terrain. For cellular telephones, paging, call forwarding, call waiting, and other services, these empty spaces made it possible for entrepreneurs to create and structure an entirely new market, a new dynamic of demand and supply that simply did not exist before. These were new technologies, new businesses, new consumers.

Unlike POTS in Ghana, no huge, single, powerful, and jealous actor was poised to crush anything that encroached on its once-privileged domain. Cellular services were new, limited, and unfamiliar. Ghanaians found these new niches quickly took on a very different political and commercial cast. There were no workers to fire or downsize; there were

Table 4.5
Prominent Ghana Web Sites

Information Outlet	Web Site
All About Ghana	www.allaboutghana.com
Daily Graphic newspaper	www.graphic.com.gh
E-Broadcast	www.ebroadcast.com.gh
Ghana Broadcasting Corporation	www.gbc.com.gh
Ghana Chat	www.ghanachat.com
Ghana.com	www.ghana.com
Ghana Elections	www.ghanaelections.com
Ghana Forum	www.ghanaforum.com
Ghana Media Gateway	www.ghanamedia.com
Ghana News Agency	www.gna.com.gh
Ghana Review	www.ghanareview.com
Ghana Web	www.ghanaweb.com
Ghanaian Chronicle	www.ghanaian-chronicle.com
Ghanaian Times	www.gtimes.com.gh
JoyFM	www.myjoyonline.com
NewsinGhana	www.newsinghana.com
VibeFM	www.vibefm.com.gh

Table 4.6
Cost of Leased Lines

Country	Cost of Leased Lines (U.S.$ per month)
United States	$300
Ghana	2,500
Argentina	4,800
Nigeria	6,000
Armenia	9,000
Kenya	11,000

Source: ITU (1998).

only workers to hire. There were no licenses to take away from some and give to others; there were only new ones for the state to allocate. And as a new and unfamiliar technology, it seemed more plausible to permit foreign private participation since only they controlled the new supplies. In other words, in these new industries there was very little to be dismantled, destroyed, or restructured. What I call strategic restructuring could proceed without much opposition because it did not involve redistributing scarce resources from one party to another.

Public-Private Partnerships

Several Ghanaian business interest associations have made steps toward involvement with the Internet. The Ghana National Chamber of Commerce (GNCC) is perhaps the most visible business association in the country. Its purpose (and the purpose of similar bodies, to which I return in chapter 7) is to lobby government for probusiness policies, to reduce transaction costs between businesses, and to socialize new members into showing behavior that is appropriate for commerce.

Like other African business associations, the GNCC was slow to take up the Internet as a tool for doing business (Wilson 2000). Interviews that I conducted in the third quarter of 1997 in Accra disclosed that GNCC had only recently arranged for an Internet system for the Chamber. As with all organizations, it found that its biggest challenges were to build capacity and awareness among staff and to build awareness among their corporate members. The executive director of the Chamber found that progress was slow because many members were small and medium-sized firms that lacked the financial resources of the large foreign firms to wire their companies: "The $33 per month is just too much for them. The big banks, mines, and insurance companies can afford the fees, and they are already connected" (personal communication 1997).

But in spite of the costs, the director felt the new Internet had begun to make a difference in his operations. He found it most useful as a facilitator of more regular contacts with Chambers in other countries. This included not only individual companies but also groups and associations like the European Chambers, which have joined together in Brussels to follow developments in Africa, especially the commercial opportunities under the Lome Treaty. His GNCC was also linked to the business associations from developing countries gathered together through the Group of seventy-seven (G77) nations. Their own network, called IBNet ("the electronic Silk Road" in their literature), helps connect the Ghana Chamber and those of other African nations to the growing global network of electronic commerce. At the time I visited, the GNCC lacked a Web page of its own. It did have an e-mail address, and the G77 hosted a site for them, which can be accessed at <http://www.g77tin.org/gncchp.html>.

5

Strategic Restructuring in China

Introduction

If ever there was a case to be made for the societal and institutional embeddedness of information and communications technology, it is the People's Republic of China. The broad features of this highly centralized, socialist command economy, with its top-down institutional dynamics and political monopoly have greatly affected the design, development, and diffusion of the Internet. The relationships between social power and the diffusion of information and communication technologies (ICTs) are also much sharper than they are in countries where political elites are less determined to control the Internet's spread.[1]

At the same time, the situation in China is not simply a protean struggle between sharply drawn opposites—freedom and control, Internet and no Internet, communism and capitalism. The realities of China's political economy—and the Internet industry embedded within that political economy—are subtle and nuanced. As is true elsewhere, the new technologies have influenced social behavior, accelerated entrepreneurism, enhanced transparency, and promoted new ideas of democratic participation. Yet China's Internet market is substantially driven by competitive jockeying among powerful groups in agencies, ministries, government-owned companies, and private bodies, including Internet service providers (ISPs) and Internet content providers (ICPs). In Brazil, we saw stiff competition among individuals and institutions that sought to impose their vision of Internet diffusion. We see the same pattern of top-down authoritarian visions competing with bottom-up liberal visions in China.

All these actors try to protect their turf under the existing rules of the game and to better position themselves to benefit (as individuals and institutions) from further anticipated restructurings. In this process of strategic restructuring, they create mutual dependencies and alliances among existing and would-be decision makers across a wide variety of institutions and sectors. When these and other forces determined to create a market for Internet services, some want to buy services, others to provide services, and still others to prevent services. Through this interaction of potential buyers and sellers, mediated through the state, a new market was created in China and continuously restructured between 1990 and 2000. To this extent, competition to control scarce ICT resources in China is comparable to the effort to control all scarce resources in China. As Kenneth Lieberthal (Lieberthal 1995; Lieberthal and Oksenberg 1998) and others have shown, this is always a bargaining process. But more than bargaining simply over outcomes, potential players also bargain intensely over how to restructure the rules of the game. Like institutional power brokers the world over, Chinese leaders are being pressed by changing technologies, domestic demands for openness, and international pressures for liberalization (under World Trade Organization accession). The realities of greater and greater Internet penetration is already reshaping the aspirations and behavior of young Chinese urban sophisticates, a politically salient group. This is a revolution that the current generation of Communist leaders wants to win. Mao Zedong led the Communist revolution in China in the 1940s, and Deng Xiaoping brought revolutionary changes by restructuring China's national economy to be more efficient and market-oriented—each while operating within the ultimate authority of the Communist Party. The challenge for the current leaders in China is to nurture and sustain the information revolution while maintaining the Communist Party's monopoly on ultimate power. That is a full order.

The Structural Context

Karl Marx once wrote that men make their own history but not under conditions of their choice. Economic and social structural conditions shape a great deal of the emerging information economy, and Internet diffusion is a critical starting point. One structural factor in China is the country's vast size and huge population. More than a billion people live on almost 10 million square kilometers, which offers unusual opportunities. It also imposes unusual constraints on China's information infrastructure. Huge distances impose huge infrastructure costs. Huge population density makes physical access less problematic.

The total area of China covers 9,596,960 square kilometers. It has twenty-two provinces, four municipalities directly under central control (Beijing, Shanghai, Tianjin, and Chongqing), five autonomous regions (Tibet, Xinjiang, Ningxia, Inner Mongolia, and Guangxi), and two special administrative zones (Hong Kong and Macau). Its estimated total population is 1.273 billion with fifty-four minorities (CIA July 2001). The gross domestic product (GDP) per capita (purchasing power parity) was $3,600 in 2000, and GDP composition by sector is agriculture 19 percent, industry 49 percent, and services 32 percent (1997). An estimated 50 percent of the labor force is in industry, 15 percent in agriculture, and 35 percent in services, while the annual growth rate is an impressive 8 percent (CIA 2000). China's population distribution and economic structure have several possible implications for ICTs. The economic structure means that China has a potential for commercial demand, and supply responses to meet that demand. But countrywide diffusion—at least for individual household demand—will probably be limited by low levels of income, especially in the poorer western and central regions. During the last years of the 1990s, rural per capita income rose only about .5 percent, to the equivalent of U.S. $365. At the same time, urban income rose 27 percent, to about U.S. $659, and it appears the disparities have gotten worse. Small farmers will become more and more dispossessed through privatization and government efforts to consolidate agriculture sector holdings. This is forcing millions of Chinese to migrate to the cities to look for work. Experts estimate that China's permanent floating population is between 130 and 200 million. These pose major structural challenges to the government.

Yet as important as these economic structural features are, they are not fully determinative. A few contrasts with India are telling. India is a country roughly the same size as China. It has a population of .9 billion, with twenty-five states and seven union territories spread across

3.3 million square kilometers). It also has similar economic structures: its GDP composition is 25 percent agriculture, 30 percent industry, and 45 percent services (CIA 2000). Yet in spite of these similarities, the two countries have sharp differences in ICT diffusion. For every one thousand people, China has 110 telephone lines to India's thirty, China has fifty-four mobile phone subscribers to India's three, ten personal computers to India's five, and sixteen Internet users to India's four (Pyramid Research 2000; Nua Internet Surveys 2000). Since their size and economic structures are similar, do these differences reflect political factors, such as China's authoritarianism and socialism versus India's democracy and pluralism? Or are these differences cultural?

Political culture is an important structural variable for any country, and China is no exception. Its long tradition of Confucian teachings shapes attitudes toward authority and individual and collective responsibilities. Millennia of strong top-down leadership at the local and, at times, national levels has reinforced the population's tolerance for strong governmental controls (Walder 1986). These aspects of political culture are important for understanding diffusion's pace and pattern in China.

Institutional Context

As noted in chapter 2, economic and social structures shape many of the outcomes we observe in the information economy, but they do not do so automatically or entirely. Structures operate through institutions, and institutions carry their own independent weight in shaping outcomes. As in Brazil and Ghana, a nation's general non-ICT institutions are important and shape the ICT sector in fundamental ways through the supreme authority of a simple national political party; the hierarchy and interactions of central, provincial, and municipal institutions; and the hybrid forms of state and private communal property. China, like Brazil and Ghana, also possesses a wide panoply of institutions in the ICT sector— from the extremely powerful Ministry of Information Industries (MII), an even more powerful specialized governing body under the state council, and state-owned enterprises like China Telecom. These institutions are described in this chapter's appendix and are mentioned frequently throughout the chapter.

The Policy Context

As in all countries, China's enthusiasm for the Internet has been shaped by the country's historical and policy background.

Support for Science and Technology

In almost every interview I conducted in greater China (mainland China, Hong Kong, and Taiwan), interviewees answered general background questions about the years leading up to the current ICT period by making it clear that the Communist government has been deeply committed for decades to the advance of science and technology. In fact, they felt that the explosion from 1,600 Internet users in 1994, 16.9 million in early 2000, and 22.5 million by early 2001 was in substantial part a harvest of these earlier commitments at the highest levels to science and technology (CNNIC 2001a, 64).

One early demonstration of the government's commitment to science and technology was the policy decision by Chinese leader Deng Xiaoping to begin sending thousands of Chinese students abroad to be educated in the West, especially in the sciences. Beginning in 1978, this program sent a total of 340,000 students overseas, and in 1998 17,622 students were studying abroad (CERNET 1999). The party remained committed to this policy even though by some estimates 90 percent of the students sent to the United States remained there. My research suggests that the Internet is being built by some of these same students who are returning to China in growing numbers.

Another sign of early government commitment to science and technology was the creation of several high-level science and technology national commissions, particularly a number of high-level advisory groups on electronic industry and "informatization" as it came to be called in China in 1996 (Foster and Goodman 2000, 15). Based on interviews and documentary history, the Chinese leadership saw early on that the electronics industry would be key to its domestic welfare and also to its international status and power. According to one Minister of Electronics, who went on to become premier, China "must develop electronics as eagerly as we developed atomic bombs" (Mueller and Tan 1996, 56). Whether called *electronics industry*, *digitalization*, or *informatization* the new technologies were viewed by those at the highest levels as resources to enhance China's advancement and maintain the Party's hold on power. The government committed billions of dollars to adding 73 million telephone lines during the five years from 1992 to 1996, more lines than the rest of the developing world combined.

These trends had at least three consequences for Internet diffusion. First, because individuals in China's most senior policy-making positions were sensitized to science and technology, they were predisposed to recognize the broad national importance of these innovations and hence supported their rapid diffusion, even when the political implications were ambiguous or potentially threatening. Second, the trends of the 1980s and early 1990s created an expanding institutional infrastructure of skilled people who were able to promote and manage technological innovations. This result also occurred in Brazil because of its computer market reservations policy. Third, these trends put in place a rapidly expanding physical infrastructure that accelerated Internet diffusion. When new ICT applications arose, a strong basic infrastructure was in place to carry them. These three trends meant that there were institutional, physical, and other incentives in place to spark interest in China's ICT industry. And more so than in any other developing country, there was intense competition over who would control the infrastructure and the services.

A Continuing Contradiction

Even today, however, much of what happens to the Internet in China is driven by the fears of the current political leadership. These concerns about restructuring are often quite explicit and are something of an open secret. At one briefing in Washington, D.C., a senior official of the Ministry of Information Industry explained China's position in plain terms. The government faces a deeply felt dilemma, he said. On the one hand, Chinese leaders are profoundly aware that their predecessors made decisions that caused the country to miss the early years of the industrial revolution. The current leaders do not want to be known as the ones who missed the many benefits of the next great epochal revolution, the information revolution. At the same time, many elements of Internet diffusion (and ICT diffusion in general)—"if permitted to unfold in an uncontrolled manner"—might threaten the "peace and stability" provided by the current Communist leadership. He contrasted the controlled, slower liberalization being conducted by the Chinese leaders with the chaos engendered by their Russian counterparts (personal communication January 2000). Still, President Hu Jintas, like his predecessors Jiang Zemin and Premier Li Peng face a historical choice. If they open too fast to the ICTs, then they risk being swept away by groundswells of popular demands for greater political and economic liberalization. If they open too slowly, then they risk being swept away by popular anger over China's economic backwardness and by the shame of repeating their predecessors' errors. They fear that the West and close Asian neighbors will pull ahead in the game of geostrategic competition. It is unsurprising, then, that Beijing is carefully feeling its way among contradictory imperatives. Mao Zedong wrote in his little red book that a revolution is not a dinner party. This seems as true for the digital revolution today as it was for the Communist revolution over fifty years ago.

The Four Phases of Market Structuring

The Precommercial Phase   As in Brazil and Ghana, the structuring and restructuring of Internet markets in China occurred over several distinct periods. The precommercial phase of Chinese Internet diffusion began in September 1987 when Qian Tianbai sent an e-mail from China "across the Great Wall and communicated with the world" (CNNIC Web site). At that time, Qian was head of the Chinese Academic Network, a project based at the Beijing Computer Appliance Institute in cooperation with Karlsruhe University in Germany. The CANET was China's first computer network, and Qian, almost universally viewed as the "father of the Internet" in China, is widely respected for his technical and political skills in bringing together people around a common goal of greater communication within the research community.

Perhaps the single most important project in the precommercial phase of China's Internet development was a multiinstitutional initiative to build a triangular network in the capital city that linked the country's two top universities (Tsinghua University and Beijing University) with its top scientific body, the Chinese Academy of Sciences. Designed as an interinstitutional network for supercomputing, the National Computer Networking Facility of China (NCFC) would also promote cooperation among scientists at these three leading institutions. The supercomputing network was funded through a World Bank loan for "key disciplinary development projects." The advisory committee assembled to manage the project was an institutional "who's who" of the Chinese science establishment, including the State Planning Commission, the State Science Commission, the Chinese Academy of Sciences, the National Natural Science Foundation, the State Education Commission, as well as the three main partners.

According to members of the group, including its cochair Hu Qiheng, an interesting conflict developed between Chinese scientists and World Bank project advisory officials. The loan was explicitly designed to link the three domestic institutions—Tsinghua, Beijing, and the Academy of Sciences. Yet by 1989, more and more Chinese were learning about the global Internet, and they too wanted access. Therefore, they lobbied the advisory committee to expand the project so that it would have a capacity for international as well as local connections. The World Bank advisor, however, objected to the expansion as beyond the scope of the loan.

The upshot of the project (and perhaps of the dispute as well) was to expand the number of leaders in the science and technology community who were excited about the potential benefits of interactive, two-way, networked scientific communication. Especially interesting is that the advisory board members of the NCFC project included representatives of government agencies like the Ministry of Science and the Ministry of Education. This newly created institution seems to have provided a critical forum of common experience and learning, a network bridge between senior government people and the research community. The interpersonal bonds and learning proved to be important to the subsequent path of Internet diffusion. This was the point where the infectious enthusiasm for the Net leapt from the academy to government—an essential incubator that facilitated the forward movement of the Internet.

Over the next several years, ICT enthusiasm spread from researchers into government circles. The network initiatives took two channels—one to continue building domestic capacity and the second to search for links outside China. China's researchers found political and institutional challenges in both, as international connections were not easily obtained. On the external side, there were political as well as technical problems for getting fully connected. Politically, the dominant world power in the Internet—the United States—viewed China's motives with suspicion. Senior administration officials were not anxious to have Communist China gain the new, networked technology. Nonetheless, Chinese delegations raised the issue in a variety of bilateral and international forums. For example, some experts from the NCFC consortium raised the issue of China's full interconnection at the annual meeting of the Internet Society (INET) in 1992 and again in 1993. According to a document prepared by the China Internet Network Information Center (CNNIC) of the Chinese Academy of Sciences, "In June 1992 at the annual INET'92 (annual meeting of the world Internet Society) held in Japan, Professor Qian Hualin met the person in charge of the International Internet Department of the National Science Foundation of the U.S. He discussed the issues on the formal interconnection into the Internet. However, he was told that there were political barriers for Internet interconnection because there were many American governmental organizations on the Internet" (CNNIC Web site).

Qian Hulin raised the same issue in the 1993 meeting and then attended the Coordinating Committee for Intercontinental Research Networking (CCIRN) meeting after the international INET meetings "and raised the protocol to discuss the issues for China's interconnection into the Internet. He wrapped up support from much of the audience. This conference played an important role for China's interconnection with the Internet" (CNNIC 2000).

According to another Beijing scientist, discussions continued with the U.S. National Science Foundation (NSF). One senior NSF official of Chinese ancestry said he saw no reason why China shouldn't be connected to the Internet. Finally, "In January 1994 the NSF of the U.S. agreed to the request for NCFC's interconnection into Internet. In March

1994, a 64 kbs special line was opened and tested." Eventually, Sprint, a U.S. company, was brought in to help construct the Internet backbone: "On June 28, 1994, the Tokyo Science University assisted Beijing Chemistry University in its interconnection with Internet and trial operation. In September 1994, China Telecom and U.S. Secretary of Commerce [Ron] Brown executed the agreement on the Internet. The agreement provided that China would establish two 64K special lines through Sprint (one in Beijing, the other in Shanghai). The construction of the ChinaNET started" (CNNIC Web site).

The inherent political logic of Internet architecture as designed by independent-minded Americans was openness, but this design was countermanded by political and institutional imperatives of the Chinese leadership that wanted a closed and controlled Internet architecture. Despite a big push for external links, only four international links were actually established. Two were based at research centers—China Education and Research Network (CERNET) and China Science and Technology Network (CASNET). Two were state-run "commercial" lines—China Telecom's ChinaNET and the country's recently sanctioned telecom supplier Ji Tong Communications Corporation's China Golden Bridge Network (ChinaGBN). In this way, the government sought to gain international access but only through a narrow checkpoint (or four narrow ones) to protect against unsuitable content. This infrastructure architecture would help the government block Chinese from visiting certain sites.

Thus, by the closing years of the precommercial phase, a pattern was established in which competing elites across different state entities cooperated when it suited them, while pursuing their own initiatives and priorities. Programs and initiatives proliferated, and Internet use multiplied. Then at a certain moment, central government and Party leaders stepped forward to "rationalize" this confusing profusion of activities and technologies across various and diverse ministries by imposing strict national ICT regulations. The year 1996 was the "crackdown period" (Mueller and Tan 1996).

A Transition Period toward the Commercial   Somewhat curious if not contradictory signals were being sent to Internet users, however. At the same time that the central government was enacting restrictive rules regarding the Internet, they simultaneously were encouraging continued Internet expansion but always under the control of the central Communist Party. After all, despite restrictions, Internet users rose from 620,000 in 1996 to 8.9 million by the end of 1999. The number of Internet hosts jumped from 1,003 in January 1997, 18,396 in December 1998, 16.9 million in early 2000, and 22.5 million in early 2001 (CNNIC 2001a, 64). Internet content providers proliferated. As Peter Lovelock (1996) and others argue, the central political elite saw Internet diffusion as compatible with maintaining their own influence and power. The Internet, they seemed to believe, could be made to advance centralized control and Chinese Communism. The pattern of diffusion and Chinese Communism itself might have to bend, but they wanted both their Internet and their Communism. As a result, by the end of 1997, state ministries, committees, and offices had established 114 information centers, provincial governmental organs had established 32 information centers, and 1,000 state-owned enterprises had set up their own network system (*China Computerworld* 1997).

The years from 1993 through 1995 can be viewed as a transition between the precommercial and commercial periods. In September 1994, the Ministry of Post and Telecommunications began Internet service with only 1,600 Internet users. Two portals were established—in Beijing and in Shanghai. At the end of March 1995, the Ministry began trial operations. On June 20, 1995, Internet service began its full operation (*China Computerworld* 1997, A21). The opening salvo in this transition was the 1993 special committee on commercialization, and it ended with the approval of the first Internet service providers in 1996. By 1996, the first fully private commercial ISP, Beijing Information Super Highway, was founded, and others soon followed. Internet services broke out of their strictly academic research boundaries. Between these critical events, separate government agencies from the Xinghua News Agency to the country's highest governmental decision-making body, the State Council (similar to a cabinet), began pursuing self-directed Internet initiatives in a characteristic effort to protect existing turf and stake out the new cyberturf. The big question would be how the dominant state elites would structure the rules of the game of this new industry. Despite powerful structural and institutional probabilities, actual outcomes of the four balances were products of negotiation. During this transition period, the existing activities in the research and development cluster continued apace. What differed is that private individuals began to persuade authorities to let them create new Internet projects on their own.

During the first half of 1993, the Communist Party leaderships debated internally how best to handle Internet expansion in light of several concerns. One concern was fueled by the cluster of educational elites in the Beijing and Tsinghua universities and research centers—the dawning recognition that the new networks had direct relevance for national economic development. A second concern was that these networks and their users were expanding rapidly outside Party and government control and that initial evidence of what were considered "abuses" was beginning to appear (Mueller and Tan 1996). A third concern was that China's regional and global competitors were starting to take the Internet's economic and political aspects seriously. And a fourth concern was the new American administration that came to power in 1992 and that took as an early theme the importance the Internet and the information revolution. After the creation of a National Information Infrastructure Commission in Washington, D.C., in 1993, government elites around the world created a spate of "copy cat" commissions (reinforced by Vice President Al Gore's speech to the International Telecommunication Union (ITU) in Buenos Aires).

Thus, the R&D cluster remained quite active at the same time that a flurry of government-centered initiatives revealed that political leaders realized the potential importance of these markets. They then had to decide how best to restructure ICT governance to capture the Internet's benefits. As in Brazil, early "Netizens" in China employed a number of bulletin board systems (BBSs).

In the second quarter of 1993, several important ICT initiatives restructured the sector toward greater competitiveness and wider access. The first initiative was the pet project of Hu Qili, who was a major force for greater competition in China's "markets." He also worked behind the scenes, probably in alliance with a group that included then Vice Premier Zhu Rongji, to build up the basic backbones over which information flowed and to aggressively promote the applications that individuals and organizations needed to modernize China. This project was known formally as the National Public Economic Information Network and popularly as the Golden Bridges project. It was presented for discussion at a conference held on March 12, 1993, and presided over by Zhu Rongji. By the end of August, the Premier Li Peng approved U.S. $3 million to fund the project's preliminary components. The Golden Bridges project was to be the backbone infrastructure that would "informatize" and "nationalize" the domestic economy around which other ICT services could run. This information highway would roll out wide-bandwidth multimedia networks that other networks could use to transmit data. In June 1994, the State Council announced new regulatory notices—No. 18 [1994] Notice from the State Council Office—to guide the Golden Bridges project (CNNIC 2001d). The project demanded billions of dollars and thousands of hours from government and state-owned entities. In the end, it helped lay the hard infrastructure and policy infrastructure for Internet "commercialization," including electronic commerce.

The next initiative began at the end of 1993, when the government announced the creation of one of its high-level "interministerial" bodies to press the ICT issue across various government groups. The Joint Committee of National Economic Informatization was chaired by Vice Premier Zhou Jiahua. Hu Qili was also a prominent member and used this committee as a platform for pushing the ICT/Internet agenda. The committee, a senior body, had to revisit the four balances, and by the end of this transition period, it had come down on the side of more competition—but mainly among governmental bodies. This was a direct challenge to the Ministry of Post and Telecommunication' monopoly creation, China Telecom. Liantong, or Unicom, the first officially approved competitor to China Telecom, was established in 1994 by three powerful bodies—the Ministry of Electronic Industries (MEI), the Ministry of Electric Power, and the Ministry of Railways (under MEI Minister Hu Qili). This was an important step toward liberalized competition balances but left untouched the other critical balances between public and private issues and domestic and foreign issues still bedeviling the market.

The Commercialization Phase: 1996 to 1997 Conventional commercialization suggests the establishment of a private legal entity managed by private individuals within a system of mostly fixed laws protecting, among other things, property rights. In socialist and other highly statist countries, however, commercialization refers to the transformation of the juridical status of a state-owned company into one that operates under commercial law (Kornai 1995). In these contexts, commercialization is advanced by public officials in public ministries. In China, firms are so subject to arbitrary, after-the-fact decisions by government that we must employ the term *commercial* guardedly. Furthermore, given China's overall political economy, no private company can survive without intimate ties with leading government officials.

Determining the first, second, or third Internet service provider is problematic in any country, especially in China.[2] The MPT defined Internet service as "value-added suppliers," so in principal anyone could get into the market and not worry about a ministry threat.

Nonetheless, among the industry leaders and experts I interviewed in Beijing and Hong Kong, it was generally agreed that the first "commercial" Internet service provider was opened by Jasmine Zhang in 1995. The years 1995 and 1996 were therefore the opening of the competitive period. A very savvy and energetic woman, Zhang's new venture was called Beijing Information Highway Technology Co., and it opened the door for "ordinary" people to begin accessing the new networks. Prior to her venture, only those in government or the research and teaching cluster had access, although some researchers used their institutional accounts to resell Internet access to those who could not get it otherwise (Mueller and Tan 1996, 88). Another private commercial entrant around the same time was ChinaNet Info Tech Co., founded by Michael Wan, which opened its doors for service in April 1996.

Because of all these changes, by 1996 the average Chinese could, with adequate financial and cognitive resources, gain access to a national network for e-mail and other services on the global Internet. Commercial ICT firms with various mixes of ownership, capital structures, and strategies proliferated and have continued to do so. But 1996 was also the year when the central government stepped in to sharply impose its own political and economic logic. After 1996, government controls would become a fluctuating mix of top-down and bottom-up initiatives.

While some competition did flourish initially, fledgling entrepreneurs came up against an unavoidable roadblock: access to leased domestic and international lines was still monopolized by China Telecom. As a monopoly, it could charge exorbitant rates, provide poor service, and generally behave arbitrarily in the growing market with almost no sanctions. It put other competitors in an almost untenable position: it was a service wholesale supplier, a government regulator, and a retail competitor all in one. The other state supplier, Unicom (and then CNC, the third competitor), had not proven strong enough to make much of a dent in ChinaNet's and China Telecom market power. They were protected by the MPT (and its institutional successor MII), which was quite strategic in positioning itself with a combination of organizational effectiveness, strong strategic interests, and flexibility. Under the long-term leadership of Minister Wu, who is traditionalist in his skepticism about competition and his enthusiasm for enlarging the power of MPT and later MII, the Ministry has nonetheless been effective in ICT modernization. Wu's agenda of rapid and widespread telephone network build-out, foreign competition exclusion, and domestic political aggressiveness has been quite successful. Indeed, the MII has been stunningly successful in building out the equivalent of a Bell-Atlantic telephone system in each of the past several years, which is more lines than all the rest of the developing world combined.

The Competitive Period: 1998 to 2000   After the first handful of Internet service providers were established by Jasmine Zhang and others and consumers spread beyond the academy and government, the growth curves that we see globally took hold in China. No longer were bulletin board systems adequate. In 1997, the China Internet Network Information Center (CNNIC) began to publish regular statistics on the Internet. Up to October 1997, CNNIC reported 620,000 individual Internet users, connected through 299,000 computers, 150 ISPs, and 1,500 World Wide Web sites by November 1997. By 1998, there were 542,000 computers connected to the Internet, and users surpassed 1 million. Going into the year 2000, there were 8.9 million users. Fueling this explosion were the new Internet service and content entrepreneurs (described in detail below). The number of ISPs rose to 500 by the end of 1999 (Foster and Goodman 2000, 59). By the end of 1999, hundreds of licenses had been allocated, although not all were operating. Here is how the party described its progress (*People's Daily* September 25, 2000):

During the Ninth Five-Year Plan period, China's information industry has emerged prominently as a new growth point of China's national economic development, becoming the principal part of high-tech industry and the representative of new productivity. The information industry not only has exerted significant influence on Chinese people's daily life; more important, it has become an important indication of China's comprehensive national strength as well. It is acknowledged as the strategic industry for China's economic and social development in the next century. During the Ninth Five-Year Plan period, the annual increase rate of China's information equipment manufacturing and service industries has stayed at over three times as much as that of the GNP. . . . The gross value of communication services ballooned from 98.9 billion yuan in 1995 to 211.3 billion yuan in 1999. This remarkable development speed has laid a foundation for China to become a large information technological product manufacturer. . . . The country, which used to produce mainly low-grade consumer goods, has now comprehensively effected a shift to the manufacture of investment-related high-tech products. . . . China has carried out a comprehensive rearrangement for the development of information industry so as to promote the formation of several enterprise groups, which are internationally competitive, and set up an information industry system which may grow up independently. . . . China's information industry has . . . also become a strategic industry boosting the readjustment of China's economic structure.

As the markets in Beijing, Shanghai, Guangzhou, and other cities grew more competitive and structurally sophisticated and the Internet's versatility became more obvious to ordinary consumers, the information revolution became increasingly problematic for government and party officials. As Internet diffusion exploded, the Beijing government imposed some of the harshest restrictions in the world on the four core policy balances. Rapid technological growth was simultaneously combined with harsh policy restrictions. These restrictions and uncertainties imposed severe constraints on ambitious, would-be entrepreneurs from China and beyond.

Nevertheless, the institutional entrepreneurialism and bargaining exhibited earlier among Chinese agencies and ministries continued apace and even accelerated. As agencies and ministries tried to carve out bigger pieces of the rapidly expanding Internet action for themselves, the national market grew chaotically on both the supply and the demand sides. There was the continued proliferation of "golden" projects, joint ventures with foreign and domestic investors, ministerial grabs on regulatory authority, and efforts to establish state-run Internet service providers at the municipal and provincial levels. The growth and maturation of the Chinese Internet market exhibited some of the same trends we see everywhere, as entrepreneurs and managers seek a strategic formula that works in an unfamiliar and tumultuous market. Beijing in the first half of 2000 was awash in talk of changing "business models" as each relevant ICT company tried to remain afloat, leading Chinese businessmen in Beijing and Hong Kong to refer to 1999 as the year of the ISP and 2000 as the year of the ICP.

In China's ICT sectors, as in other sectors, state officials kept their fingers in the pie, and it continued to be difficult to discern where "public" elements ended and "private" elements began. One cause for the changing business models and the difficulties of entering the market was the stranglehold exercised over Internet service and content entrepreneurs by the Chinese government. ICT entrepreneurs in China confront a Kafkaesque sequence of seemingly unachievable requirements:

1. First, the would-be businessperson must get a license. If he or she intends to operate in only one state, then the local office of China Telecom issues the license. If he or she intends to operate across provincial borders, then MII headquarters issues the license. One interviewee referred to this as only a "paper license." "I call it that," he said, "because it doesn't mean anything. It's just on paper, not in reality. It doesn't entitle you to anything more than to go to the next step. But even here, you can never get even the 'paper license' on the first try. You need to go again and again. And this doesn't guarantee that you will get the next things that you need."

2. The next step is for an applicant to get a telephone line. Installation costs $2,000, and the monthly charge for ISPs is $300. (The regular commercial monthly cost is about $150, and residential is much less.)

3. Then the would-be Internet entrepreneur applies for a leased line. In the United States, a leased line costs about $1,200 per month. In China four years ago, it was $80,000 per month.

4. Then the businessperson must register with the Ministry of Public Security.

5. Internet service and content providers must also submit to content regulations, so managers must do a great deal of self-policing.

And in return, I asked my respondent, what does the customer in China get? "The customer?" responded my interviewee. "Oh, he gets bad service, slow speed, no content, and very high prices." This entrepreneur found especially galling another requirement of the digital gauntlet. One's company must also submit its business plan to MII/China Telecom: "This is ridiculous, since China Telecom is also in the same business as we are (as an ISP retailer). This is like giving your competitors your whole business plan! What they try to do is to force you to team up with them. Then they either absorb you or run you out of business. They can undercut your every price, and then when you're finished, they raise their prices again" (personal communication 2000).

This same respondent, quite knowledgeable about China's Internet market, reported that such onerous requirements are the main reason that while more than 500 ISP licenses have been issued, perhaps only ten to twelve Internet service providers were operational by the end of 1999. Most were waiting until conditions change, especially (they hoped fervently) when the World Trade Organization deal finally gets implemented.

From Internet Service Providers to Internet Content Providers

Most companies initially entering the Chinese market concentrated on supplying Internet services as their first commercial objective (though some, like BIHTC, tried to sell hardware as well from the beginning). By 1999, this business strategy was under tremendous pressure because of high charges for leased lines and other predatory costs imposed by China Telecom. Some Internet service providers then began to diversify from access supply into content supply as Internet content providers (ICPs). Reportedly more than 1,000 ICPs were operating in China as of 2000.

Other firms, like ChinaByte, made a different strategic gamble and supplied specialized content from the start. They believed more money was to be made with more value-added services. ChinaByte's CEO said that his company chose to concentrate on a specific niche—information about the hardware and software products of the digital age. Backed by media mogul Rupert Murdoch, this focus also steered ChinaByte away from more controversial news reporting.

Toward Market Consolidation?

In the thin Chinese Internet services market (reaching only 1.78 percent of the population by 2001), where the potential market cap is nothing short of astronomical, it is not at all clear what will happen next (CECA 2001, 33). But under the circumstances, any "consolidation" we see over the next couple of years will likely be as short-lived and dynamic as most other market trends. We must assume that the market will remain thin and expanding, with change and uncertainty the constant.

Consolidation may occur after competition takes off and market shares become more concentrated. It does not require that the market move decisively to oligopoly or monopoly, only that the top four or five firms substantially increase their market share. Once this status is reached, the market is assumed to have fully developed and is expected to experience subsequent shifts that follow those typical of mature markets.

One can identify the likely winning candidates and their current positions. Certainly the three or four big telecom players want to maintain and extend their power. Media players like Xinghua News Agency would certainly like to move into these new markets. Smart banks (riding the interest in e-commerce) and smart bricks-and-mortar companies will move more and more into the information space. Of course, the extant big players in the market are also aggressively moving to consolidate their power.

In the last quarter of 2000, the *New York Times* ran a story in its business section whose headline claimed unequivocally that "Web Sites' Merger Signals Consolidation of China's Internet Industry." It reported that Charles Zhang's Sohu.com would buy ChinaRen.com in a $30 million deal and that "it is the first of several such mergers now under discussion in China where the Internet is jammed with thousands of under-financed, money-losing Web sites that have been surviving largely on foreign investment capital since they began appearing two years ago" (Smith 2000, C-13). The merger gives Sohu more users than its nearest two competitors, Netease.com and Sina.com. Like Sohu.com, which went public in July 2000, both are also listed on the Nasdaq. All three sites go head to head in competition for Chinese users. But in an example of the social networking that characterizes even the competitive and consolidation periods, Sohu.com's Charles Zhang met one of the founders of his rival company ChinaRen.com when both were students in the United States—Zhang at MIT and Chen at Stanford.

The uncertainties that shook the U.S. and other ICT markets also shook Chinese markets. However, market turbulence did not prevent foreign firms from moving in. The top five sites in China remain Chinese-operated, as are five of the top seven (Netease.com with 3.41 million users, Sina.com with 2.90, Sohu.com with 2.84, Yeah.net with 1.83, ChinaRen.com with 1.69, Yahoo.com (U.S.) with 1.59, 263.net with 1.40, and Microsoft.com (U.S.) with 1.22 (Smith 2000).

One difficulty in predicting consolidation in China is the simultaneous entry of new market players at each end of the corporate range, from tiny start-ups to corporate giants. Another difficulty is what some might consider odd combinations of public agencies and private groups that are thrown into an increasingly competitive market where rules are murky. Several of these elements of potential Internet consolidation can be glimpsed in the founding in 1999 of China Netcom Corporation Ltd., or CNC (Edward Tian, CEO). Netcom demonstrates political and commercial elements at least as interesting as its technical elements. Its founding shareholders include the Chinese Academy of Sciences, the Ministry of Railways, the State Administration of Radio, Film, and Television, and the Shanghai municipal government. Netcom describes how it has taken advantage of the easing of market rules to compete with telecom powerhouses: "As a new-generation operator in China, CNC will seize the opportunities presented by telecommunications deregulation and the development of a broadband IP network to meet the challenges of international competition and promote China's information industry" (Company brochure n.d., 5).

Regardless of institutional actions and market structure, China's Internet demand is likely to grow rapidly in the future. By 2001, Internet penetration had reached about 7 percent of the population of China (34 percent in Hong Kong and 31 percent in Taiwan) and had grown by more than 400 percent between 1999 and 2000 (*Asia Cyber Atlas* 2001). The exact pace and direction of diffusion in the next expansion phase of the Chinese Internet market will hinge on the strategies pursued by national elites and their effectiveness in building political coalitions for selective change and continuity. This will be a major challenge to government and party leaders as they maneuver to restructure the country's political economy.

The Information Champions in China

Background

China's social networks reflect historical and Confucian traditions, and by linking elites across various institutions and vertically within them, they provide the specific settings within which Chinese negotiate with one another to promote or block economic restructuring. The more fluid networks intersect with the more long-standing institutions in a variety of formalized and informal ways.

The interactions among social networks, institutions, and policy outcomes are well documented in the scholarly literature on China. Writers like Kenneth Lieberthal (1995), Margaret Pearson (1997), Lucien Pye and Mary W. Pye (1985), and others have written extensively on the role that informal private networks play in Chinese governance and the ways that networks intersect with, subvert, and support formal institutions. According to Pye and Pye (1985, 292), "In China a wide divide has always existed between formal government, emanating from the imperial or national capital, and the private governance that rules the daily lives of people." Arguably, the modern Chinese Internet exists in the space between the formal agencies of government and the informal agents of private society.

Other scholars have contrasted China's formal and informal networks with Western models of rule-based behaviors and with other Asian models in countries like Japan and Korea, where intersections occur in different ways with different outcomes. Pearson points out that parallel networks are not necessarily bad and have been used with good effect in Japan and other nations where clientist networks have created competence. However, "the same does not appear to be true of China's informal business-government ties" (Pearson 1997, 155). These informal ties can be useful advantages for individuals who successfully manipulate them. But this "is a connectedness that fails to increase competence" (155–156) and fails to "increase the collaboration between business as a whole and economic bureaucracies" (156). She cites Peter Evans's (1995) work on the links between clientism, connectedness, and competence (156 n. 41) in Latin America and Asia. In China, a slow and contradictory series of collaborations and conflicts over Internet policy is shaping today's outcomes.

Lieberthal (1995, 192) refers to the way that the Chinese leadership institutionalizes its power through social networks: "The actual configurations of political power are best understood by leaving behind the organization charts and instead thinking in the terms Chinese officials use when they talk among themselves about their system. In their vocabulary, the key concepts concerning the organization of power are the *kous* [and] the *xitongs*. These organizational arrangements and tensions encompass both the party and government sides of the system."

Other authors refer to the Chinese concept of *guanxi*, or connections. Writing about the state and social networks in China, Wang (2000) points out that the interplay between formal institutions and informal networks is a critical determinant of state policy and economic outcomes. In his interviews in China, he found that while "many of the interviewees complain about the gross inadequacies of China's legal system in protecting their property and contractual rights, they find that *guanxi*, or informal personal relationships based on trust and reciprocity, provides a viable alternative." He continues in a reference to business investment and start-ups: "Since Chinese laws and policies tend to be ambiguous and even contradictory, and since important regulations and information may not be available to the public, to rely on documents and announcements alone is far from sufficient. Well-connected individuals serve as an important source of dependable information" (Wang 2000, 19).

Wang's observations exactly capture the dynamics that I observed inside China's information and communication industries. They underline the critical role that privileged access to information plays in the Chinese political economy. Under circumstances in which information is a privileged resource that must be extracted from formal and informal sources, strategic restructuring is a tricky business. Too much emphasis on individuals obscures structure's impact. The breathless accounts of journalists like Sheff [Sheff] obscures the real dynamics between structure and agency. Adam Seqal [Seqal, 2002] provides better balance, and individuals do play important roles. In China, as in other countries from Ghana to Brazil, understanding the social networks through which individuals exercise power is a prerequisite for understanding the technical networks that power creates.

The following individuals illustrate some of the trends found among many ICT champions in China, especially among the entrepreneurs.

The Private Pioneers

Jasmine Zhang (Zhang Shuxin)   When knowledgeable Chinese speak of Jasmine Zhang, a kind of respectful hush creeps into their voice as they implicitly pay homage to the first person to have the vision and courage to start China's commercial information revolution. Unlike in many other developing countries I visited, women hold a number of influential positions in the ICT sector in China.

In May 1995, Zhang created the Beijing Information Highway Technology Company (BIHTC). It was the first nonstate, private Internet service provider in China. By 2001, the company had about 100 employees and a capitalization of U.S. $2 million. Prior to BIHTC, Zhang had organized bulletin board systems, but most of these were not connected to the Internet. Her purpose was to provide a range of services to her customers, including basic ISP services such as e-mail, file transfer protocol, telnet, and Web access. She also provided online services through her Information Highway Space, which included news, talk forums, financial quotations, education, and entertainment—

in other words, a nearly full-service Internet service and content provider.

Early on, however, Zhang was realistic enough to realize that her tiny subscriber base of 3,000 was nowhere near what she needed to earn a profit (she estimated that she needed ten times that): "China's user base is simply too small right now to support a profit-making enterprise" (Wang 2000). In the meantime, she, like many other early Internet entrepreneurs, tried to stay afloat by selling other services and goods.

In addition to her hardware sales, Zhang sold her flagship product, a Chinese-language software package that gave her customers access to a variety of online information, including news and even the latest train schedules. It was provided free to customers who registered for her services for about U.S. $38.50 annually—low by U.S. standards but not cheap in China. The charges were RMB .05 per minute, or less than U.S. $1 per minute. The good news was that since her company was created before the State Council issued regulations requiring all Internet service providers to link through the Ministry of Post and Telecommunications' ChinaNet, she was able to send her Internet traffic through the international gateway of the China Academic Science Network (CASNET).

Despite Zhang's energy and early entry, BIHTC was unable to hold on through the twists and turns of the changing Chinese laws. In 1996 (as is described above), the draconian rules set forth by the government included the requirement that only government channels could be used for news. Zhang closed her Beijing operations, moved to Hong Kong, and started with a new company.

Edward Zeng (Zeng Qiang)   If anyone personifies the hustle and bustle, the flash and dash face of Chinese Internet entrepreneurial energy it is Edward Zeng. At the turn of the century, he seemed to be e-everywhere, in e-everything, all the time. He was intent on staying at the cutting edge (or the "bleeding edge" as it is sometimes called) of the Internet industry in China as it twists and turns and seemingly reinvents itself every half year. Although he is not one of the largest ICT entrepreneurs, Zeng's experiences capture important elements of the industry's dynamics.

The first time I met Zeng, his self-confidence and self-assuredness were evident. At a meeting of senior executives in Silicon Valley, he gave a sales pitch about his company to e-leaders from around the world and criticized the Chinese government, especially the very powerful Ministry of Information Industry (MII), for trying to do too little too late in the ICT sector. Zeng claimed that MII administrators spent too much of their time trying to block positive initiatives and too little time helping the people who are trying to do good.

"But that's all right," he declared, since "as soon as MII puts up one restriction, all of us find a way to get around it ten different ways." This might not be a surprising declaration in some settings, but it was made in the presence of one of the powerful vice-ministers of MII, who was also sitting in the conference hall taking careful notes. It was evident that Zeng's political ties were strong and that his allies could probably protect him from any political fallout that resulted from his criticisms of the MII minister. But political ties and political skills, however, must be supplemented by vision, knowledge, and strong social networks.

When I interviewed him and some of his staff in Beijing in May 1999, his company SparkIce had just gone through another round of self-transformation as it tried to stay ahead of the quickly changing times. As 2000 drew to a close, SparkIce, which began with China's first network of cybercafes in 1995, described itself as a "China-based interactive import/export marketplace and market-maker for products manufactured in China" (China online 2000). Zeng's ambition at the end of 2000 was to provide the megaportal for businesses seeking to buy Chinese-produced goods and services. At a subsequent meeting two years later the company was selling similar services.

In the process of moving this company from mainly serving individual Chinese customers in retail outlets (cybercafes) to current trend of providing services to businesses, Zeng has had to construct a complicated series of alliances with new and existing social networks within ministries, state-owned enterprises, and transnational corporations.

According to one authoritative source, "In an attempt to help Chinese enterprises contribute to China's foreign trade by means of the Internet, Zeng decided to allow 700 Chinese businesses to set up virtual stores on the SparkIce Web site free of charge. . . . Thanks in part to government support, SparkIce was able to greatly expand its e-commerce business volume in the first half of 2000, and it expects to grab one-third of China's estimated $150 million in online transactions in 2000" (China Online 2000). The company was active in several different activities, including

• Cybercafes (then thirteen, with ambitions to buy, refurbish, and franchise 100 for retail and business customer),

• Internet telephony,

• business-to-business data services,

• Internet service provider,

• Web design and hosting (through ChinaRep),

• Debit payment, and

• Alliances with China Central Television (CCT) to have SparkIce the exclusive provider of CCT's online video broadcasts.

New Zeng initiatives abounded. In May 2000, the Ministry of Information Industry selected the company to be a state e-commerce pilot enterprise. He also reportedly had a deal with Germany's Metro to sell Asian-made products. The core of the latest vision seemed to be to create an international-quality trading platform for Chinese companies that want to sell abroad and for foreign companies that want to buy Chinese products (personal communications).

To the foreign untrained eye, SparkIce appears to be a regular private company, but in China the boundary line between a private company and a state firm is quite porous. According to Zeng and independent observers, no company like SparkIce could survive in China without substantial and active government protection and some direct state investment. Zeng seems to have been able to negotiate all of the above.

Zeng has parlayed his early knowledge of Internet matters into much appreciated advice to the middle and upper levels of the national governmental hierarchy and those charged with setting national ICT policies. This apparently strengthened his human capital with the people who make the Internet rules. According to ChinaNet, "Zeng has connections with the State Development Planning Commission and the National

Bureau of Statistics and even enjoys the support of Premier Zhu Rongji and President Jiang Zemin. He claims to spend one third of his time courting official favor by serving as a policy advisor, teaching at state-run business schools, publishing articles in state media, and cementing deals with state-owned enterprises." In interviews with Zeng, it is apparent that his teaching activities, especially at a business school in Beijing, expose him to the up-and-coming "netpreneurs" and e-managers who will be his future customers, a standard outcome in U.S. business schools as well.

By the late 1990s, Zeng had become an outspoken advocate in Beijing at the highest levels for new initiatives like e-commerce. He pressed hard for technical improvements, modernization, and to a certain extent for policy and institutional changes but not for major political reforms that would threaten elites. This position allowed him to gain the licenses, the regulatory permissions, the contracts, and the money he needed to survive in the semistate, semiprivate environment.

In interviews, Zeng, like many of his colleagues in China, came back again and again to a classic dilemma in emerging markets: how do you structure a new market when potential consumers don't have a clue what they should be buying from you? The first challenge is to educate potential consumers and convince them you have something valuable. According to Zeng, this has been one of the principal successes of his cybercafes and one reason that he retains them (although he says they are profitable, something not always claimed by cybercafe entrepreneurs in other countries). As Nii Quaynor in Ghana also points out, a great deal of "hand-holding" is required to increase consumer sophistication in developing countries, but these proactive behaviors are not necessarily captured in the price of an ICT service.

Not surprisingly, in such a competitive and ambivalent environment, Zeng has critics. Some are doubtful as to whether Internet cafes will generate enough revenue to sustain themselves. Some believe Zeng's only real skill is self-promotion that has produced few tangible results. Still others say establishing Internet cafes as e-commerce service centers is a premature step, given China's many obstacles to e-commerce. Moreover, they argue, his business-to-business model closely resembles that of his competitors Alibaba.com and MeetChina.com.

Zeng's first big ambition and first ICT initiative was to bring the Internet to a wider cross-section of Chinese: "I wanted to bring as much Internet connection as possible to as many people as possible as quick as possible" (personal communication 2000). Cybercafes were his way to doing so. Our first conversation in China took place in his first cybercafe. Chinese young people and a few foreigners moved around the airy room filled with tables and computers, playing cybergames or just surfing. In between they ordered Coca-Colas or green tea. With delight still in his voice, he proudly waved his arm toward the room and said: "This was my dream. Building a place where many Chinese people would come to use the Internet." In November 1996, the first cybercafe came into being, and the cost per hour online currently is RMB 30 (about U.S. $4).

In the mid- to late 1990s, at the peak of the cybercafe boom, Zeng was widely covered in the Chinese and foreign press. *Business Week* called him one of China's most controversial entrepreneurs. *Time* magazine recognized him as one of the country's outstanding Net entrepreneurs, and he was named a Future Leader for Tomorrow by the 1998 World Economic Forum. President Clinton visited one of Zeng's cybercafes during a trip to China, and one of Zeng's companies (Dragon Pulse, a company database) was referred to in the signing ceremony between President Clinton and President Jiang.

Part of Zeng's good fortune was to be born into a professional family; his father is a doctor and his mother an architect. He grew up in Beijing and attended the prestigious Tsinghua University, where he earned a bachelor's degree in applied mathematics in 1985 and a business administration degree in 1987. Like many young people, Zeng joined a government ministry, in this case the strategically important State Planning Commission. He served as a policy advisor, and one of his responsibilities was to help establish a national macroeconomic database: "That's when I first really saw the real possibilities for using information" (personal communication 2000).

His next move was to Canada to study at the University of Toronto (he had also visited Japan, where he was when the May 1989 Tiananmen Square student massacre occurred). After gaining a master's degree in finance in 1990 and then working briefly for the Canadian government as a statistician, he felt prepared to create his own company. Like his countryman and fellow cyberstar Charles Zhang, he too linked up with North Americans who were interested in developing business connections with China: In 1991, he began to establish a computer and international trading company. In 1993, he founded SparkIce Asian Company. The company includes an undisclosed level of Canadian investment. Zeng says the purpose of the company was to raise financing for takeovers on North American stock exchanges. When he returned to China in 1995, the SparkIce name came with him, and he set up SparkIce Information System Engineering. He returned home in this field to make money but also to help introduce China to the new information and communication services he had seen in North America.

Zeng's big moment came in 1996. Drawing on his connections, he was able to enter a partnership with China Unicom, a powerful partner that led him to immediately open up his first Internet cafe. According to ChinaNet, by 1997 his company was the second largest Internet company in China.

Building on his commercial initiatives (in partnership with a huge state company) and his salesmanship, he rapidly built out a number of new initiatives. In our interviews, he repeatedly described how he came to realize that all the key actors, government and business, needed better statistics on all aspects of the Chinese economy. Soon after he returned to China, he used his old ties at the Planning Commission and the National Statistics Bureau to obtain the exclusive rights to one of their biggest databases, which contained key economic and financial information on 750,000 Chinese companies. This was his first foray into the precursors of electronic commerce. By 1997, this five-year database (CNet) became Dragon Pulse, which Zeng claims was the country's first comprehensive online business directory and database. He found good markets in foreign firms and has been pursuing the B2B route ever since.[5] But since the dot-com crash, his companies are feeling much more pressure, and the future seems less bright.

Edward Tian (Tian Shuoning)   Nearly everyone I spoke with in China seemed to agree that Edward Tian was one of the original information revolutionaries and that I had to meet with him. When I did, I could see that in addition to being a man of impeccable practical understanding, he also carries a compelling vision of China's future as a knowledge society. He has had an extraordinary national impact on the important middle period of Internet market expansion in China and continues to have major influence on its further growth and consolidation.

An example of his breadth and vision emerged early in our conversation. From his new offices atop a modern Beijing office building, where he is CEO of China's third-largest telecommunications company, China Network Communications (CNC), he told me he had bought a little place in the country, about 40 miles from downtown Beijing. "You know," he began, "many young people here in this city are as good as they are in Silicon Valley. They are well educated and sophisticated. But only 40 miles from here, people are living like they did two centuries ago. Or if not living like that, their mindset is like it has been for centuries." Concerned about the possible digital divide within China, he asks, "So what do the young kids in the village look forward to? Will they have the same ICT opportunities as the kids in the city? They too need to have hopes and dreams. The city kids see great hope in the future. We need to make sure all China's children do" (personal communication 1999).

Like several of the other information champions, Tian came from solid middle-class stock:

My parents were educated. In fact, they were educated in forestry in the Soviet Union in the 1960s. But then when relations deteriorated with the USSR, people educated there were mistrusted, and we had to move. We moved way out to Lanzhou, which is very isolated. My parents were worried about my education, and I was educated largely by my grandmother, a school principal. Then when the cultural revolution hit, things got very bad. We were forced to the countryside for "reeducation." I never will forget that when I was five, the Red Guards came to my grandmother's house. We always had a lot of books in the house, but she had hid them under the bed. The Red Guards searched the house and found them and then dragged them all to the front yard and put them in a big pile. Then they set them on fire. I never will forget that sight of burning books. The memory of that is still very much with me today. Now, with broadband [networks], nobody will ever be able to burn up the network. These changes will make that impossible, I hope. . . .

I left China in 1987. It was then a pretty depressing place, and like most Chinese students going abroad, when I left, I had no intention of returning. After Tiananmen Square, I thought I should do something more practical than pure science. I started studying environmental science, things like wildlife management. [He already had a master's degree in biology from the Chinese Academy of Sciences Graduate School in Beijing.] Then a little later I started getting interested in the Internet.

In an interview with *Wired*, he claimed that he was quite influenced by a speech that U.S. Vice President Al Gore gave in 1993, which alerted him to the potentials of the Internet:

I finally graduated from Texas Tech with a Ph.D. in environment management. While in school, I started to meet some people who eventually became my partners. There was Jim Ding from the University of Texas in Arlington. How did I meet him? Actually, we met through the Internet. For broke and lonely Chinese students in faraway Texas, the Net was a good way to meet others like you. The Internet was cheap, and it was a great network to meet people. Then by the time I finished, I guess I was getting a little older, and I was starting to feel more responsible toward China. I didn't feel that way originally, but I did then. I thought maybe I should go back and contribute. And frankly I missed the country. James Ding and I talked on the Internet and about the Internet. We decided to return and do something together. So we set out to look for people we could convince to come work with us in China.

The result was AsiaInfo, a company they founded in 1993 as a systems integration and Internet software company. Tian was the first president and a board member. By 1995, Tian and Ding were ready to return to China. Even though he had a degree in environmental studies, he was hooked on the Net. Looking about for markets, AsiaInfo targeted the big giants in telecommunications. And as they say, the rest is history.

In brief, Tian constructed the backbone for the modern networks of China, both for national-level companies and provincial governments. He built them well, and he built them quickly. In all, Tian and his team built more than 100 major network projects in the country. He recognized the importance of attracting good talent, other information champions with good skills and education, and he recruited students who had studied abroad to come work for his company. His national customers included ChinaNet, Shanghai Online, and China Financial Data Network. In the process, Tian and his colleagues also created a social network that paralleled (and perhaps surpassed) their technical network. All this good work won AsiaInfo a lot of contracts and a number of awards from groups like Fidelity Investment Co. and the World Economic Forum, which selected Tian as a "world-class entrepreneur."

Not one to rest on his laurels, Tian said yes when some institutions in the country banded together to create a large new telecommunications company—China Net Com or CNC—and asked him to head it. The shareholders included the Chinese Academy of Sciences, the State Administration for Radio, Film, and Television, the Ministry of Railways, and the Shanghai municipal government. The new company became a broadband Internet provider network and built a 6,000 mile IP-based, 20-gigabyte fiber optic backbone that covers fifteen Chinese cities, one of the world's fastest. When China Telecom was later split in two, one part for northern and another for southern China, China Net Com and China Telecom South CNC was absorbed and Tien became a senior executive of the merged company.

Several elements in Tian's story are especially relevant to this chapter's themes. The first is that Tian, a very successful private-sector entrepreneur CEO, was invited by the top leadership of several state entities to head up a new public enterprise, the first time a nonstate CEO has been recruited to lead one in China. Second, he was given full authority to hire the best people possible, and he has already recruited colleagues from Motorola, Microsoft, and Marconi with competitive salaries and even stock options. Furthermore, the corporate governance of the CNC is more like a Silicon Valley company than a traditional state-owned enterprise. It is poised to become a new kind of Chinese company.

Tian is aware of the challenges but claims that this will be a rare opportunity to make a big difference for China's information and communication industries. Small wonder he has been called the chief Internet architect in China. He has been at the center of the strategic restructuring process, shifting the balances between private and public and competition and monopoly. His latest position in the merged CNC and Netcom continues this trajectory.

Charles Zhang (Zhang Chaoyang) In some ways Charles Zhang is another classic example of the information revolutionaries. To many Chinese, he has become a role model for young Chinese who wish to study overseas, return home, and accomplish big things in China's tumultuous e-world: "I am not from Beijing. I was born in the interior of the middle west—Xi'an. It is an old city, not too much developed but with a long history" (personal communication). He is the elder child of two physicians, and all his siblings are also college educated. After finishing secondary school, he left China in 1986 to study in Cambridge, Massachusetts, at MIT. By 1994, Zhang was finishing his dissertation in materials sciences in MIT's Physics Department and won a postdoctoral fellowship. Since the early 1990s, his teachers had pushed computer use for physics experiments, and as he did some programming, wrote software, and became familiar with computers, he gradually developed an interest in ICT, though it was not his primary scholarly focus at graduate school.

When he finished his doctorate, Zhang decided he wouldn't be content just to go into traditional materials research. In a refrain heard over and over again among the Chinese ICT returnees I interviewed in Beijing, he said, "I wanted to do something that was relevant to China" (and added, "something that was not relevant to physics"). At around the same time, MIT was getting more interested in expanding its activities in China and searching out opportunities abroad for the university and offered him a position as associate liaison officer in the development office.

Zhang worked closely with Provost Mark Wrighton for a year and a half in Cambridge, during which time he traveled back and forth to China, including one trip with the provost and MIT president Charles Vest:

After so many trips to China, I realized that there were many opportunities in the PRC. But I needed some kind of vehicle to get me back there. I talked to many companies around Boston and throughout Massachusetts, but not so many were interested in China at that time.

In fact, many of my Chinese friends thought I was crazy for trying to return, since at that time so few of them wanted to go back since things were so difficult. But I did have some friends who were going into business then, including some in the Internet business. One was George Miller in Boston. He was one of the first to realize that the Internet could be used for business purposes (remember, these were the early days). George set up Internet Securities, whose purpose was to service financial and investment companies interested in emerging markets. He was providing online information to them and wanted to open offices in Latin America and Asia, including China. So we discussed the possibility of my opening his Beijing office, which I did. This was just the vehicle I was looking for. Again, my friends thought I was crazy for going back to China in the first place, especially to go back and work for a thing called an Internet company for such low wages. They laughed at me at the time.

When I got to Beijing, I had to learn the dial-up technology, which I had never really used. When I tried to get a dial-up account, I was probably one of the first people to do so, absolutely one of the first. I remember there were only about 3,000 users then. By April 1996, I launched Internet Securities in Beijing and built up the office there. Our business was aggregating information from the various state research bureaus and statistical offices that collected data for central planning purposes.

Was there a group of people in the city who met and discussed the Internet? I'm not so sure, but I wasn't much involved. Maybe the people around Jiang's Beijing InfoHighway. But not being in such a group was not a barrier for me. [When I asked him if he was hindered by not being born in Beijing, he answered no.] *Guanxi* may be required if you're in the real estate business, but remember this is a brand new industry with no history, so no one official in Beijing really cared about it, and you didn't need connections.

After some time, I went back to Cambridge and talked to Miller and to some of my professors and told them that I was getting interested in starting my own company. They were very supportive. One of my academic advisors even said he would put some money into it. So did Nicholas Negroponte (a leading ICT guru). That was very encouraging to me at the time. And George Miller was supportive also, even though it meant I would be leaving his company. He understood, and said, "Look, just build my office in Beijing and then go off to do your own thing." So between April and November of 1997, I raised about $220,000 to start up an Internet business. I knew I wanted to do Internet, but I still wasn't perfectly clear yet exactly what I did want to do.

In the beginning, we had several different ideas. We did some Web development in November and December of 1997. Maybe we wanted to do ISP, maybe system integration. We said, "Let's start helping companies build their Web sites." We spent a month looking for contracts at companies, for customers who wanted to develop this new thing called Web sites. But we were getting only a few customers. I wanted to set up a server to do this, but this was not a familiar thing yet in China. Eventually I was able to convince someone in the government (the deputy director of the Beijing Ministry of Post and Telecommunications) to open up their infrastructure to one of our servers: "Just let us put a server on your backbone." I think this was the first server on the Chinese backbone.

I thought this agreement was really historic, and I bought a bottle of champagne to celebrate. My Chinese colleagues at the P&T said "No, that's not necessary." Today of course we have 300 megabyte, but then, it seemed like a big deal. I'm not sure they appreciated that it was a big milestone.

But the question remained in Beijing as it did in all cities around the world at the same time: what was the right strategy to stay in e-business? In the mid-1990s, all the companies in town were also struggling to define a strategy. Back in the United States, AOL was reinventing itself as an Internet content provider, not just an ISP. Said Zhang,

We focused on developing people's Web sites for them. We slowly built up our customers. We got 100, then 300. I remember how we celebrated when we finally reached 500 customers. We also experimented with different content. We regularly read *Wired* magazine and the Hotwired Web site to follow the trends in the new industry. We were always looking at other business models. We read that Web sites should be free, for example.

But remember that China was still an underdeveloped country, and it had very underdeveloped markets, all kinds of markets—transportation, retailing, and others as well as Internet markets. Faced with not much knowledge about our services, we really had to educate our market. This was a business expense, but we had to do it. Every two weeks, we would hold training sessions here in this office. They would be mostly our customers who would come. To get more people interested, the sales team would go through the Beijing telephone book and just call up potential customers.

But things started to get tough. When Information Highway, the first real commercial ISP, started to decline in the market, people said that if a big company like that could decline and fail, how could an even smaller one succeed? As time went on, we had thirty sites, then 100, then lots. In fact, it was hard to keep up with them. All our staff was spending all their time designing sites. But we wondered if this was really cost effective. So I wondered whether we could index and track all these new Chinese sites, and I assigned someone to do that. Soon I began to see this was more cost effective for the company than just designing the Web sites, since that took a lot of manpower and effort, two or three people working hard on it to build up one site. With indexing I could assign just one person at first. In May 1997, I met Jerry Wang, the cofounder of Yahoo, and told him about what I was doing. I was aware of his business strategy too. But he wasn't too impressed with the market in China at that point. But we decided to go ahead with the strategy anyway, and that became the main Sohu.com idea—that is, a search engine and portal—and we shifted our staff from Web design to indexing.

The lesson that Zhang had to learn was the lesson of other information revolutionaries. When market structures are changing almost on a monthly basis, the leader has to learn to experiment and be open to signals coming in from the business environment. The leader has to be able to turn around and reshape a strategy that simultaneously follows and anticipates big changes. With a strategy identified, the company leadership has to design an operating structure that flows from and advances that strategy. In the private sector as in the public, imagining the right strategy, leading the organization to change, mobilizing the resources, and protecting the company from the public and private predations was more than a full-time job. In this odd new business, a businessman like Zhang had to follow the market and provide people with what they wanted and were willing to pay for and also had to educate them in the process.

The 1996 to 1998 period was a period of widespread experimentation, learning how to learn, and hanging on to the right business strategy. By February 1998, Zhang had settled on a strategy, a business plan, and an organizational structure that seemed to match the technology and services that people in China wanted then. Based on the new business plan, the business took off, and Sohu.com became one of the largest Internet companies in China. However, the market continued to churn. Facing a difficult period of consolidation and contraction, Charles Zhang rethought his corporate strategy for Sohu, prompted by millions of dollars of losses per quarter ($4.3 million in the third quarter of 2000). By the second quarter of 2003 the *Wall Street Journal* (Kahn 2003, R4) reported that Sohu's net income rose to $7.53 million, with revenues tripling over the previous year to $19.3 million. Rather than continuing to follow the original advertising-based Internet strategy, he radically shifted into the short messaging service (SMS) market. The growth of cell phones (which has a 75 percent market penetration for cities like Beijing) provided a powerful lure and opportunity to service this young market—so much so that his competitors, NetEase and eventually China Mobile, also entered the burgeoning market.

Observations about Social Networks in China

Structural, institutional, political, and other factors intersected in China in a variety of ways with the fluid and heterogeneous group I call the information champions or information revolutionaries. First, the Internet spread so fast and far in China simply because some people in the early 1990s wanted to rapidly promote and diffuse it and because they were allowed to do so by institutional authorities. Beginning within the scientific communities and then continuing among the returnees from study abroad, a relatively small but high-energy group of e-enthusiasts emerged who eagerly took up the mission to accelerate China's Internet diffusion. Some did so to advance their research, and others to create commercially successful businesses. Many were personally committed to helping their country advance. The accelerating interests of this heterogeneous group of technocrats, bureaucrats, and returnees coincided in the early 1990s, when they all pushed to expand the new technologies.

These champions created Internet service providers, sold services and products, promoted ICT use, and trained customers. In case after case, they lobbied the guardians of the telecommunications sectors so they could operate on their own terms.

Second, Chinese officials were initially tolerant and then ambivalent about Internet diffusion. Somewhat surprisingly, state and private-sector entrepreneurs and policy advocates were able to operate successfully within the confines of the Chinese Communist political system. Authorities allowed the Internet to spread in part because in the early days they did not know much about its societal implications. Officials in state institutions were initially slow and ill informed and allowed the champions to spread the Internet. This follows the pattern seen in Ghana and Brazil.

Later, when the initial build-out occurred in the opening commercial phase of the mid- to late 1990s, senior officials decided that the Internet was too worrisome to ignore but too important for them to repress entirely. It was at this point in the mid-1990s that the strategic restructuring of rules, regulations, and institutions began.

Third, the champions' campaign occurred at a particularly felicitous time. The government was in the midst of an aggressive economywide liberalizing program of ICT production, distribution, and expansion. This great telecom push forward was unparalleled around the globe: the Ministry of Post and Telecommunications and then the Ministry of Information Industry built the equivalent of a Bell Atlantic telephone system every year for many years. This was achieved in part through the centralized efforts of China Telecom and the MII and later through the commercialization and demonopolization of the sector, also the pattern observed in Brazil and Ghana.

Fourth, the rapidly changing social structure of China in this period provided the broader societal context within which the champions operated—a growing Chinese middle class with the education, income, urban access, and intellectual curiosity to pursue new technological innovations. It is probably this slowly changing structural reality—the expanding bourgeoisie—that more than anything else will drive sustainable Internet diffusion (as well as the taste for democracy). China's social structure provided the growing professional class whose sons and daughters would become the first generation of young nerds, techies, and information revolutionaries. As this happens, Internet champions are being drawn less and less from those Chinese who have studied and worked abroad. Curiously, I did not find as much evidence as I anticipated that *guanxi* has driven the evolution of the Internet, although the highly ambiguous space between public and the private and between formal and informal rules was filled by interinstitutional networks, as Kenneth Lieberthal (Lieberthal 1995; Lieberthal and Oksenberg 1981) and others argue. Furthermore, I know that I lacked the time to fully analyze the lines of family and personal influence. Still, the dynamics of diffusion did not seem entirely driven by social network logic (any more than they were driven entirely by the logic of economic efficiency). Rather, intersecting rationalities determined outcomes, dominated at various times by one party or the other.

Fifth, technology mattered. The new ICTs were falling in price, accelerating in power, and able to bring real value to Chinese users, giving new resources and capabilities to different groups.

The dominant player once again was the Ministry of Information Industry, under Minister Wu's leadership. The Ministry sent out a number of teams to visit government officials, think tanks, and businesses to ascertain what this thing called e-commerce was and what the Ministry should do about it. One effort involved prepaing endless drafts of potential e-commerce regulations and incentives, which were shuttled back and forth between several offices in the MII and their counterparts in the State Council.

The financial sector also had interests in expanding e-commerce. Not surprisingly, state banks sought to capture the emerging policy space. The People's Bank of China partnered with several overseas think tanks to launch the International Information Industry Congress (IIIC), whose annual meetings brought together people across the institutional spectrum but especially in financial services to discuss standards, confidentiality, payments procedures, and so forth.

Also involved, not surprisingly, were various groups under the State Council's commercial offices. Senior official He Jia Chang spent months in the United States at the Kennedy School of Government in Cambridge to help prepare a report on the commercial implications of e-commerce.

In spite of, or perhaps because of, the intense jockeying for position and competition to define new rules, the long-awaited electronic commerce framework had not yet emerged by mid-2001. There was some expectation that new laws would emerge from the National People's Congress meeting in March 2001, but apparently none was forthcoming. One proposal backed by several dozen delegates stated that "The law should take into consideration the security of e-commerce, prevention of hackers, taxation, and telecommunication market access. It should also cover the protection of data, intellectual property rights, trade marks and domains, as well as the responsibility of Internet providers." The bill also may call on government to create a secure electronic payment system (William Foster, personal communication April 13, 2001).

One substantial area of concern was the high uncertainty in partnerships between local entrepreneurs and foreign investors. MII had taken a firm stance against majority shareholding by foreigners. However, some of the leading dot-com firms had substantial foreign participation. Uncertainty over foreign participation once again allowed government officials to exercise their own political and economic discretion.

This is only a small sample of the many overlapping and competing activities that grew up around the issue of electronic commerce. Out of this messy process, some new rules and accepted practices emerged. Like everything else in China, these new norms resulted from various Chinese elites negotiating with one another to restructure digital policy domains.

Current Problems and Barriers to E-Commerce

Businesses conducting e-commerce in China and with China face several obstacles, whether extending and improving their current commercial bricks and mortar activities or first entering e-commerce market services. As in other developing countries, barriers to e-commerce in China include transaction security, sophistication of the online banking system, cyberspace laws governing liability, the quality and quantity of auxiliary infrastructures like roads and airports, customs clearing efficiency, and the development of trust: "The Chinese are used to doing business on the basis of personal relationships. Given the complexities of working under the state, individuals have had to depend on *guanxi* (connections) to get things done. In addition, neither the legal nor the physical infrastructures have existed nationwide to support settlements, delivery, and material acquisition" (Foster and Goodman 2000, 44). Finally, China faces severe e-commerce awareness problems. The trust problem still exists: "It is not clear to many Chinese whether you are getting what you want. It is not surprising that cash on delivery is the preferred way of paying for goods purchased over the Web" (Foster and Goodman 2000, 44).

The important frontline organizations in e-commerce are firms, whether foreign, domestic, private, state-owned, or mixed. Surveys indicate that the Chinese state-owned enterprises are more likely than private ones to invest in ICTs, probably indicating the formers' access to state financing: "SOEs are much more likely to invest in ICTs. The situation, however, has developed where many SOEs have multiple information systems that do not talk to each other. . . . The private or 'cooperative' companies, in contrast, are much less likely to invest in costly information technology. However, they are keenly aware of all the hype about e-commerce, and many are looking at ways to develop solutions based on standards and freely available software" (Foster and Goodman 2000, 45).

Rule setting in electronic commerce took on a particular Chinese twist. Institutional rules were once again left largely undefined, reflecting the historical legacy of Chinese bureaucracy and the cultural preference to keep important policy domains undefined so that senior decision makers can exercise discretion. Strategic restructuring in China repeats the pattern of leaving strategic gaps or empty spaces that are then filled by the mandarins.

Restrictions on Direct Foreign Investment in China

The political elite is deeply worried that direct foreign investment (DFI) will subvert Chinese national autonomy in ways that will be detrimental for the Communist Party. As a consequence, the government has severely restricted where DFI can go and placed ceilings on how much DFI is permitted. Much of this has been the source of heated negotiations between Chinese and foreign parties and within China itself. As a result, there is a huge grey area of policy open to varying interpretations and subject to being honored in the breach. This is very much a contested terrain today.

As William Foster and Seymour E. Goodman (2000) point out in their excellent study of the Internet in China, the strong cultural preference for face-to-face negotiations in commerce and for personal ties and *guanxi* will intersect with the impersonal rigidities of the Internet in unknown ways. Chinese traditionalism is unlikely to overcome the Internet, and Internet modernism is unlikely to overcome Chinese values. Along these lines, Ming-Jer Chen, of the Wharton Business School, wonders about the future interaction of strong Chinese values expressed in family-owned enterprises and Internet networking.

As electronic commerce in China skyrocketed after 2000, several interesting institutional innovations took root. Some senior officials at the MII began to recognize the leading global and local trends in e-commerce, especially the dominant role that private-sector actors played in designing and implementing e-commerce solutions, rewriting policy rules and forging national strategies (personal communication 2000). The MII reached a point where its huge size, bureaucracy, and slow speed were blocking its capacities to learn fast enough. Much of the energy for a new strategy came from the State Informatization Promotion group, which was charged with encouraging more ICT use. At the same time, other institutions in other sectors recognized similar dilemmas and pressed for changes. And as Tony Saich (2000) and others have described, activists in civil society were also seeking ways to mobilize support, becoming more aggressive as e-commerce interest grew.

The outcome of these top-down and bottom-up dynamics was the formation of several new associations. Registering a fully autonomous nongovernmental organization like a chamber of commerce or an independent union is virtually impossible in China, and would-be institutional entrepreneurs must find a sponsoring state body (such as a ministry or state-owned enterprise) and register with the Ministry of Civil Administration (MCA). When competition among sponsors leads to stalemates, the contending groups can appeal to the State Council.

In the case of electronic commerce, several groups have been vying for MII's attention and authority. The winning coalition created a body called the China Electronic Commerce Association (CECA), set up in June 2000. There is also an active China Information Industries Association. According to its literature (CECA 2001, 1), CECA "provides a link between the government and enterprises and institutions . . . [and] aims to promote the development of e-commerce, encourage technology innovation, and improve . . . management methods." More specifically, the Association will "publicize relevant policies, laws, and regulations;

put forward suggestions or advise on the development of e-commerce to relevant departments of the government; assist the government to make or revise" these new directives. It would also "carry out academic study and training courses," develop educational and training materials, get involved in quality control and certification, and "develop the domestic and overseas market and organize exhibitions of e-commerce products for enterprises to enhance international cooperation."

It is not yet clear whether CECA will successfully meet its broad mandate or whether it is just a flash in the pan with no staying power. As with other new quasi-NGOs in China, its work is conducted substantially over the Internet and is thereby engaging both the politics of information technology and the technology of politics. If national and international conferences are any indicator of leaders' interest in a topic, then electronic commerce seems to be at the top. In April 2001 alone, China's senior-level conferences included the Fifth Annual China International Electronic Commerce Summit; the conference on Globalized E-Commerce: Infrastructure, Capital Investment, Models of Success; and the International Symposium on Network Economy and Economic Governance (cosponsored by the United Nations Development Program and China's State Development Planning Commission, Ministry of Finance, MII, People's Bank of China, State Statistics Bureau, and Beijing Municipal People's Government). These many venues indicate in part the competition that is taking place among contending institutions to define the topic.

The Current Status of E-Commerce in China

Despite these efforts to mobilize support, Chinese e-commerce revenues are low. A recent report by Iamasia (a Hong Kong–based research company) found that only 10 percent of Internet users on the mainland and about 7 percent of the total population used it to buy or sell (as compared to 13 percent in Hong Kong and 10 percent in Taiwan). The survey found that two-thirds of Internet users are uncomfortable with making Web purchases, and three-fourths of those in Hong Kong said they would not try e-commerce in the next twelve months: "In Internet-related investments, American investors in leading Chinese ICP portals may be the most prominent new trend. Sohu.com attracted Intel,

Dow Jones & Co., International Data Group (IDG), and the Massachusetts Institute of Technology (MIT), while China InfoHighway has formed an alliance with Microsoft. Sina.com and China.com count Dell Computer and America Online, Inc. (AOL), respectively, among their backers. These investments and partnerships are only a few of the vast number of relationships between American-based firms and the Chinese entrepreneurs engaged in the Internet business" (Anderson 2000, 22).

Investment and Sales The MII estimated that in 1999 China's e-commerce Web sites had combined revenues of 200 million RMB, (U.S. $24.2 million), more than double that of 1998 (Anderson 2000, 22). Online shopping has also reached U.S. $62.9 (CECA 2001, 61). By the end of 2000, over 600 online stores had sites, a huge increase in the groups, institutions, and individuals who wanted to get involved in electronic commerce. There were over 500 Internet service providers in China by the end of 1999 (Foster and Goodman 2000, 59). Of these ISPs, 100 are part of China Telecom. Many ISPs are also owned by local Post and Telecommunications Administrations (PTAs), such as Capital Online in Beijing, Guangzhou Vision, and Shanghai Online. These ISPs diversify into developing and hosting content as well as providing system integration services. ISPs must be licensed by the MII and gain global access through one of eight interconnecting networks. They are forbidden from directly connecting with a foreign ISP (Foster and Goodman 2000, 59): "If the Internet allows Chinese businesses to increase their exports while increasing the amount of value they provide, the Internet could have a phenomenal effect on the country" (Foster and Goodman 2000, 44).

Current Users Most businesses use the new ICTs for e-mail. Some are starting to build Web pages, and others approach other businesses to host their Web sites. They are also starting to participate in global business-to-business exchanges like Chemconnect.com. *Virtual China* reported that from 200 to 400 of the buyers and sellers on Chemconnect.com are from China (Landreth 2000): "Not only will these firms be able to integrated into supply management chains and automatically provide data on production and logistics. Chinese businesses have been quick to be listed on Web intermediaries such as Chinamarket.com, MeetChina.com, and Alibaba.com" (Foster and Goodman 2000, 62).

The most important piece of e-commerce is management's willingness to restructure internal organizations to use new technologies. But it is difficult to get data on these intrafirm restructurings.

The Internet and Democracy

If the potential for a substantial restructuring of commercial relations in China has accelerated, so too has the potential for a more political restructuring of Chinese authority relations. But the operative word is *potential*. Among the ICT literature's early guiding assumptions was that the new media promote democracy. As William J. Drake, Shanthi Kalathil, and Taylor C. Boas (2000) write, China is often pointed to by senior U.S. policy makers, starting with President Bill Clinton and Vice President Al Gore, as a country where the Internet will prove "an irresistible force of democracy." Yet "in none of the democratic transitions that have occurred around the world over the past two decades could one plausibly argue that the Internet played an important—much less crucial—causal role. . . . As the Internet spreads through China, then, it leaves a multifaceted imprint, one which cannot be easily characterized as either wholly conducive to democracy or as wholly reinforcing the institutions of authoritarianism" (Drake, Kalathil, and Boas 2000, 1; see also Kalathil and Boas, 2003).

Some Chinese activists and dissidents have certainly used the Internet to try to open more civil society space for health care associations and religious groups like Falun Gong, for example. At the same time, the Chinese government has also tried to use the Internet for its own political purposes to strengthen central-state capacities. I have been unable to find any definitive evidence that these new technologies have been decisive in contentious, high-stakes political outcomes. There is little evidence that the new information technologies are more important than other basic tools of politics and power—money, authority, and institutional position—or that the Internet is more important than other applications, like radio and television.

The question of whether the Internet strengthens grassroots organizations or central government leadership in my view is a false dichotomy. The Internet is probably doing both simultaneously. The Internet appears to be simultaneously expanding better communications among progressive Chinese citizens seeking to carve out civil society space and improving the administrative and financial controls of the central government in Beijing.

My comparative work in Ghana, China, and Brazil suggests that while these new technologies seem to advance global trends like "openness" over the medium to long terms, the extent, speed, and details of the way ICTs accomplish these outcomes are in no way predetermined. They exist as social potentials, not as inevitabilities. All parties develop Internet strategies to advance, block, and shape the market to serve their own purposes. As the global middle class grows and (if it) remains true to the progressive politics of its past, it may eventually take up the congenial weapons of ICTs to carve more space from authoritarian controls over society.

Chinese Intellectuals Join the Fray

In China, public-sector leaders dominate ICT diffusion, though private-sector entrepreneurs have played a small but growing role in sector restructuring. Unlike NGOs in countries like Brazil and even Ghana, local NGOs in China seem to be largely absent from the communication and information revolution. By the late 1990s, one began to see more intellectuals from universities and research centers getting engaged with cyberissues. They developed forums and social sites for more open discussions about the digital revolution. But they were not decisive.

One example is a small group of intellectuals and writers who meet from time to time to discuss a topic of common interest in the ICT field (personal communication 2001). This small group calls itself a digital forum, where friends active in the ICT sector meet. Most of the members are writers, academics, and intellectuals who do not work in the ICT industry but are deeply interested in its possibilities. Several write ICT-related columns for China publications. The forum is loosely organized, as befits the Chinese model. It seems to work as follows. One member initiates a meeting to discuss a topic that one of the group is working on. Members of the group have produced a book series on different aspects of ICT. While recognizing the importance of analysis about the information revolution from around the globe, they felt strongly that there was not enough writing that looked at critical ICT issues from a Chinese perspective. For example, one of their members wrote a scathing and widely read piece on Microsoft in China. Another, Guo Liang, has written his own book on the history of the Internet. This dynamic and far sighted professor at the Chinese Academy of Social Science also helped edit a series on ICT in China funded by Beijing Information Highway, which according to some sources has sold over 100,000 copies. Guo, an academic who has studied the works of Scottish philosopher David Hume, is one of the information revolutionaries struggling to transform China into a twenty-first-century knowledge society.

Government Control of Content

Transforming China will not be easy. Chinese society lacks the Western tradition of free and independent citizen gatherings. Nor are freedom and individual autonomy encouraged and protected by the Communist Party regime. These features are extended to the regime's treatment of cyberspace content. Not only does the regime control the available content of outside Web sites, restrict content allowed on Chinese Web sites, and selectively block sites interpreted as "harmful to state security and public morals" (such as the *New York Times* and *Washington Post*), but China also creates competing content. In the information revolution, the current elites are simply extending the norms of control they exercised for fifty years in the real-world media. Since the Communist Party's takeover in 1949, the party and government have owned and controlled print and electronic media of all types (the *People's Daily* is the organ of the Communist Party, for example). The following news report is indicative (Benton Foundation 2000):

China strengthened its censorship over the Internet Tuesday, clamping restrictions on web sites offering news reports and requiring chat rooms to use only officially approved topics. The new regulations would likely create more headaches for Chinese web sites, already reeling from tough competition and a shortage of investment funds. But it could boost government-controlled media struggling to enter the Internet age. The rules require general portal sites to use news from state-controlled media, seek special permission to offer news from foreign media, and meet strict editorial conditions to generate their own news. Only state media would be allowed to set up news sites and even then only with government approval, the rules said.

In my conversations with senior media representatives in China, I was struck at how eager they are to make a digital transition and to do so on their own terms. The more they venture into cyberworld, the more they realize they must compete for "eyeballs" just like commercial companies (yet within the strictures of the Communist Party). For while on the mainland there is not much real competition for viewers, across the border in cyberspace the Chinese surfer has a surfeit of viewing and listening options.

The *People's Daily* has a massive Web site and in the late 2000 renamed it People Net. One of the earliest sites was launched by the government's own central news agency, Xinghua News Agency, at the dawn of the Web age in 1994. The new company was able to capture the catchy URL China.com, and its offices in Hong Kong looked like any other hustling and bustling online business. Though it has attracted major investment and a stock market listing, it has not been able to capture as large an audience as its more private competitors, like Sohu.com or Netease.com.

Xinghua and the *People's Daily* are not the only state bodies to put up Web sites. The major news media within China, such as *Guangming Daily*, CCTV (China Central Television), and several key regional papers and broadcasts went online long ago. Official estimates put the number of news sites as high as 700 (Hartford 2000, 258). According to one observer, "The five most important state media websites will receive funding directly from the central government. These are the Xinghua News Agency (www.xinhua.org), the *China Daily* (www. chinadaily.com.cn), the *People's Daily* (www.peopledaily.com.cn), the State Council News Office (china.org.cn), and the China International Broadcast Station (cnradio.com). Reports in the Hong Kong press suggest that "funding these sites will receive could total RMB 1 billion (U.S. \$120 million), an amount that would roughly equal foreign investment in China's Internet sector to date. . . . The government is attempting to level the playing field for state media by effectively hobbling free-market competition" (Economist Intelligence Unit 2000).

The restrictions on imported foreign content and foreign Web site access are in part designed to protect national and local interests. This does not exclude foreign alliances. On the morning that I interviewed executives at ChinaByte.com's Beijing offices, they were preparing for a meeting that afternoon with their foreign partner, Rupert Murdoch (their local partner is the extremely well connected *People's Daily*).

As a hotbed of media development and sophistication, Shanghai is typically at the forefront of trends that migrate into China proper. It is reported to have a potential ICT user base of 1 million. Sites include <www.shanghai.gov>, a major portal for this sophisticated city with site sections in English, Japanese, and Chinese. Details on local social services and neighborhood networks, with limits to local and national laws and regulations, are found on <www.sq.sh.cn>, the Shanghai community service network. Even the local legislature has its own site for releases on matters pending before the Shanghai People's Congress, <www.spcsc.sh.cn>.

Interviews I conducted with senior nonicpal leaders in Shanghai in April 2002 demonstrated their aggressive commitment to becoming the preeminent cyber city in the region.

Antidemocratic Efforts by Government

Astute observers of China (Lovelock 1996) have pointed out that current political elites have their own particular reasons to promote Internet expansion. To advance those political, economic, and social interests, they seek to restructure access to these new resources in ways that meet their needs and "national interests." Intranets and Internets are the leverage tools for greater central coordination and control over a sprawling and sometimes recalcitrant bureaucracy. The Internet is helping the top Communist leadership reform the bureaucracy (by cutting personnel and reducing the number of ministries) and keep track of the latest departmental developments. The central government also sees it as a way to track and control fractious provincial and local officials. Keeping a close watch on the Internet and creating in-house versions of service providers also permits the dominant state hierarchy to hedge its bets and keep a foot in the local commercial markets.

To retain the Internet's positive benefits while avoiding its negative repercussions, Chinese government officials engage in the following antidemocratic strategies, some aimed at the final consumer, others aimed at Internet service providers and other companies:

- Monitoring Internet use by consumers,
- Requiring users to register with local security agencies,
- Limiting links or gateways between the national and the international networks (to keep China as one big intranet),
- Closing down local Web sites, including personal sites,
- Blocking access to "undesirable" international sites,
- Intimidating potential and actual users,
- Denying ISPs the right to own international gateways,
- Forcing ISPs to divulge their business plans to government,
- Keeping ISP prices high by charging them monopoly rates for backbone access,
- Requiring all content providers to get their news and information only from government approved sources, and
- Intimidating ISP and ICP owners with threats of jail sentences.[4]

China's first cyberdissident, Lin Hai, was sentenced in January 1999 to a two-year prison sentence for "inciting the overthrow of state power" because he shared 30,000 Chinese e-mail addresses with *VIP Reference*, a pro-democracy Internet journal based in the United States. At the time, Lin was running a company that offered Web design and other services, and his family argued that he was just sharing user addresses to promote his business. Lin's case highlighted the fear of the Internet among Chinese authorities, who like the medium's economic promise but not its potential for aiding political challenges to the regime. "They realized once they had him in detention that he's not your hard-core dissident," said one diplomat (Chang n.d.).

One authoritative source wrote in 1999 that China Telecom's position on Internet service providers is almost strangling them to death. *China Economic Quarterly* confirmed what my research found—that the monopolists have "no compunction to date in squeezing as much money from these businesses (ISPs) as possible, with the result that whereas in the United States line rental only accounts for 5% of an ISP's costs, in China the average is nearly 80%" ("Big Brains Limited" 1999, 27). It goes on to note that "given a playing field so tilted against them, most independent ISPs have not only found it impossible to compete with

ChinaNet; they have found it impossible to stay in business without receiving some degree of assistance or lenience from China Telecom" (27). One result is that many entrepreneurs with licenses don't offer ISP services. Others have been completely coopted by China Telecom. These strategies are not unique to telecoms, of course, but occur across the political economy (Saich 2000; Lieberthal and Oksenberg 1988 on the energy sector).

Anti-antidemocratic Strategies by Consumers

Chinese citizens also employ their own tactics to gain and sustain freer access to the Internet, such as

• Seeking access to Web sites that shield a user's digital trail and guarantee anonymity (experts have concluded that any Chinese who really wants to get access to international sites can do so without too much effort),

• Tapping directly into one of the China-based, government-controlled Internet service providers with international links,

• Failing to register properly with authorities, and

• Striking alliances with extant organizations that offer technical connections and political protections from state regulations.

Tony Saich (2000), in his insightful article "Negotiating the State: The Development of Social Organizations in China," reaches similar conclusions about interest groups beyond the ICT communities. According to Saich, most analysts of China have underestimated the capacities of non-state groups "to influence the policy-making process or to pursue the interests of their members" (Saich 2000, 125). Social organizations "have devised strategies to negotiate with the state a relationship that maximizes their members' interests or that circumvents or deflects state intrusion. . . . the interrelationships are symbiotic rather than unidirectional (Saich 2000, 125). But as I develop further below, the ICT populists also mobilize to pressure the state elites more directly to change their policies. They work through a mix of public appeals through the press, calls for greater openness at professional meetings and seminars, and personal social networks and contacts.

The Digital Divide in China

The digital divide that is most worrisome to Chinese leaders seems to be the regional split between the economic backwardness of China's western region and the burgeoning wealth of the south and east. They worry about whether the new ICTs will worsen or reduce an already politically troublesome division. In conversations with policy analysts and intellectuals, this was the main theme that arose when the issue of a digital divide was mentioned. For China, the western problem is worrisome because the region's poverty challenges government doctrine and because the region abuts politically unstable Central Asian countries like Afghanistan and Pakistan. Some officials in the ICT sectors are anxious to find ways for the new technologies to address national inequalities.

There is less discussion in China than one might anticipate about the digital divide and ICT access. After all, social and economic equity has been a central theme since Mao marched with his Communist Party comrades to take over the mainland. But compared to the discussion of the digital divide in other developing countries, the issue has been relatively unexplored in official Chinese discourse. This is in part a research problem: it is difficult to find Chinese engaged with the issue. Nor is there much in the published literature on the topic. But a glance at comparative growth statistics indicates the causes of concern. The wrenching collapse of Mao's economic initiatives and Deng's return to greater market rationality exacerbated regional disparities and the urban-rural split more generally.

In a speech to the Global Information Infrastructure Commission's 2001 annual meeting, entitled "Active Participation in Narrowing Digital Divide," the Vice Minister of MII, Lu Xinkui (2001, 2) emphasized the international dimensions of the divide. In his analysis, the divide is a North-South problem, and the solution is technical assistance. But he also insisted that "the voice of the developing countries can be better heard and their legitimate rights and interests can be concretely protected."

When he turned specifically to China, he pointed to the tremendous growth the sector has seen over the past decade (25 percent growth in the industry according to Lu, or three times national GDP growth rates). Lu (1998, 5) acknowledged that more attention must be devoted to the domestic divide and that the government plans to concentrate its "informatization" efforts on several areas—sector, regional, enterprise, and social informatization. At the end of his six-page speech, he mentioned that the government would "make more efforts to narrow down the digital divides between the eastern and western parts of China, and between the poor and rich areas" (Lu 1998, 6). The divide is very real. In 2000 the China Internet Network Information Center reported that the coastal areas and Beijing are rich in Internet resources, while others are poor (Anderson, 2000, p 24) Beijing has about one fifth of China's Internet subscribers, followed by Guandong (12.9%), Shanghai (11.2%) and Jiangsu (5.9%) and Shandong (5.2%).

In the first half of 2001, the United Nations Development Program was working with the government of China on a new initiative to reduce the digital divide. The U.N. agency provided $2.5 million for a pilot project to show how ICTs can be used for development. Working with China's Ministry of Science and Technology (MOST), the initiative will concentrate on agriculture.

I believe that the absence of digital divide fervor in China reflects several trends, the most important being that along many dimensions many Chinese have in fact seen substantial improvements. Applications have expanded. Modern Internet backbones and telecommunications infrastructures have been built. Like most developing nations, the beep, ring, and chime of cell phones is inescapable, and China will soon have the largest cell phone population in the world. In 1999, the total number of mobile phone users was 41.97 million; in 2000, it was 85.26 million; and in 2001, it was 120.6 million, the highest in the world (CECA 2001, 56). Other appliances have also grown rapidly: over 10 million televison sets were in use in 2000 (CECA 2001, 56).

The spread of these appliances and the networks that support them reflect a second access dimension—financial access. With economic growth at 9 to 11 percent a year for most of the 1990s, people have more money to buy more things, which includes information and communication goods and services. GDP had an average annual increase of 7.5 percent in the 1990s (CECA 2001, 62). Similarly, Chinese authorities have pushed to provide training in science and technology. The numbers are nowhere near adequate for the country's current condition and soaring ambitions, but educational advances have important implications for political perceptions of access and equity. Content availability is also a key element of access, and we have seen dramatic growth of Chinese content on local and international Web sites. The number of Chinese-language pages is expected to surpass the number of English-language pages by 2010.

The equity figures along gender lines reflect a growing percentage of women using the Internet. In 1999, the ratio between male and female using the Internet was 86 percent to 14 percent, and in 2000, it was 70 percent to 30 percent (CECA 2001, appendix). As noted elsewhere in this chapter, the anecdotal evidence suggests that women are in visible and powerful positions in the Internet-related scientific, commercial, and policy institutions of China, a potentially important dimension of gender access (see <http://asia.internet.com/cyberatlas/2001/0116-iamasia.html>).

The chasm between slow growth in China's west and the fast growth in the east is China's important divide, digital and otherwise. In fact, the problem is so big that it is not politically correct in China to discuss it in depth. It carries more than a hint of being an issue of state security and hence is a delicate subject for domestic intellectuals and policy makers. Regrettably, there is not much accessible information about the institutional mechanisms for delivering ICT services to urban and rural populations. To recall, the United States has about 459 PCs per 1,000 people; China has 9. The United States has 661 telephone lines per 1,000 people; China has 70. U.S. productivity has soared in recent years due largely to enhanced information processing; China's productivity is much lower. These differences hold great implications for China's strategic and economic position in a rapidly evolving world supermarket.

The interactions among these international and domestic factors—political, economic, commercial, social, and technological—will determine whether the new technologies exacerbate or reduce the digital divide inside and outside China. The risk is that the nearly celebratory attitude toward the rise of the Chinese technocracy and middle class will push the progressive distributional dimensions, especially the unequal regional growth, back into the shadows.

The risk is real because of the sky-high popularity and elevated status of the new dot-com entrepreneurs and information champions among today's youth, even with the global downturns. They have become the new role model for modern China's rising generation. They also provide an ideological focus for the country's rising middle classes. It remains to be seen whether the values of Chinese e-elites prove any more progressive than their Western counterparts. China may reach the point where the massive infrastructure build-out of the 1990s and rising incomes are not enough to reduce the gap between the Chinese have and have-nots.

The Bottom Line

At the macro level, it is difficult to track a strong causal relationship between Internet diffusion and democracy. Internet use in China is regularly doubling, but by most formal aggregate indices democracy is not doubling every six months. The process is far more nuanced and ambivalent than a one-to-one relationship would suggest. But little evidence can be found that the Internet has brought major changes to the macro political economy of China.

At the micro level, more individual Chinese believe themselves to be more informed, more aware of their human rights and political possibilities, and more empowered by their engagement with the global Internet. Prodemocracy impacts are likely to be greater among the intelligentsia, where diffusion and effective access is greatest.

At the meso level of institutions and organizations, reports of improved interorganizational and intraorganizational communications via the Internet are difficult to substantiate; evidence is thin and ambiguous (Drake 1995). As Tony Saich (2000) and others point out, the critical questions for the future of ICT and democracy will be at the intersections of top-down conservative restructuring pressures as they meet with the bottom-up pressures and perspectives of e-entrepreneurs, e-activists, and others who are less concerned with ICTs as such and more interested in their applications to the substantive social and political problems of the day. These relationships are likely to be reciprocal, negotiated, and symbiotic.

Let me turn now to the way these intersecting logics expressed themselves in key areas of electronic commerce and political democracy.

The Possibilities of Electronic Commerce Raise the Stakes in China

One of the new elements in the recent period of Internet consolidation and competition in China has been was the emergence of electronic commerce as a serious concern. In China, as in Brazil and other developing countries, business executives and senior government officials have recognized the revolutionary potential of e-commerce to upset commercial and even political hierarchies.

What Is Electronic Commerce?

As we saw in the case of Brazil, there is no easy single definition for electronic commerce, any more than there is a single definition for conventional nonelectronic commerce. But because the top PRC leadership remains committed to a form of communism, then structuring new e-commerce rules is problematic, raising basic issues of property and efficiency. Recall that electronic commerce is first of all the use of electronic means to conduct part or all the activities associated with market functioning—including product research, order placement, payment transfer, payment verification, receipt of services or goods, product consumption, and postsale customer service. E-commerce can consist of one or all these activities.

Second, these electronic commerce activities are typically conducted through appliances like personal computers or cell phones, and they ride on top of underlying institutional and physical infrastructures. Effective banking institutions and laws governing consumer protection are critical institutional infrastructures, and e-commerce also needs efficient customs agencies at the ports, well-maintained roads for product delivery, and other key physical infrastructures.

Third, and more metaphorically, electronic commerce can be considered a newly discovered territory or continent with potentially great wealth, where interest among contending parties is great but where maps and roadways are lacking. Unless rules and roads are put in place, conflict will ensue.

For developing countries like China, the opportunities for electronic commerce are great. But so are the barriers. Survey after survey from China and other parts of Asia, the Middle East, and Latin America find several major barriers to electronic commerce:

• Low levels of public awareness among corporate and government executives and among the rank and file,

• Small market size (especially low personal computer penetration),

• Weak institutions (especially in banking, such as low levels of credit card use) and rudimentary regulatory framework (such as laws governing contractual obligations and responsibilities, privacy, taxation, and standards),

• Unreliable or absent parallel physical infrastructures,

• High levels of uncertainty about e-commerce's technological and commercial directions, and

• Lack of human resources, such as trained managers.

As more and more government leaders realize electronic commerce's potential and its implications for China's global status, competition increases. China's long-term economic and geostrategic interests are tied in part to the resolution of who gets to shape and define e-commerce political struggles. This places more responsibility on the shoulders of those who are designing an e-commerce code and raises the stakes for competing ministries to push harder for a piece of the cyberaction.

Thus, the Internet attracted even more senior-level attention with the explosion of electronic commerce. More so than other ICTs, electronic commerce arrived on the back of a long-term rise in direct foreign investment and substantial increases in economic growth (in contrast to other Asian nations hit by the 1997 financial crisis). For example, China has attracted more direct foreign investment than any other developing country, averaging an annual increase of 15 percent over the decade of the 1990s. Over the first half of the decade, 1990 to 1996, the number of multinational companies operating in China soared from 300 to 16,000. By the end of the decade, fully half of the Fortune 500 companies were operating in China. Within this longer-term trend, electronic commerce emerged.[3]

Like other countries around the world, China has relied on a variety of techniques to move information in a timely manner from one location to another. Prior to the spread of packet switching and Internet content provides protocols, companies and government agencies in China and elsewhere used electronic data interchange (EDI) to move information electronically. The Ministry of Electronic Industries, prior to its merger with the newly created Ministry of Information Industry (MII), had a specialized unit that regulated EDI.

Compared to today's Internet, EDI was slower and more expensive (by a factor of ten), but it was effective for its time. EDI has been defined as "The electronic exchange of trading documents that precludes the need for traditional paper documentation" (Petrazinni 1996, 94). But unlike the Internet, which has open, nonproprietary protocols, EDI was closed, proprietary, and less interactive than the Internet. For the Chinese regime, its secure and closed nature made it less politically problematic than the Internet. The challenge for China, therefore, was to effect a transition from the old information system to the new information system.

China already has various pieces in place for electronic commerce. In some respects, the electronic economy is already well launched. The country is already MasterCard's second biggest market in the world ("Big Brains Limited" 1999, 29). And it is one of the world's three biggest markets for what may be the next big thing in e-commerce—cellular telephony. The State Council has granted eight licenses to interconnecting and access networks—two to academic and research networks (CERNET and CSTNet) and six to the commercial networks (ChinaNet, ChinaGBN, Uninet, China Netcom, China Mobile, and CIETNET) (Foster and Goodman 2000, 58).

Perhaps the most ambitious initiative in this area is the Golden Projects initiative, an integrated program inspired and launched by Minister of Electronic Industries Hu Qili in the early 1990s as part of an effort to modernize the sector (see table 5.1). Originally conceived around three principal axes, it has since expanded to encompass eleven. Each is targeted toward a particular infrastructure or application, and each has a select set of implementing partners. Golden Bridge (Jing Qiao) was is designed to create a public network backbone for e-commerce. Golden Bridge Network (Ji Tong) provides connectivity to governments, state-owned enterprises, business organizations, and Internet service providers. It competes with China Telecom and by 1999 had more than 100,000 dial-up users (Foster and Goodman 2000, 59). Golden Card (Jing Ka) aims to build a modern and secure credit card clearing system across the country. This is a kind of electronic money project. Finally, Golden Customs (Jing Guan) the leading foreign trade information project, would improve export-import trade management.

Current E-Commerce Players in China

Government Institutions   As in all countries, the responsibilities for e-commerce in China are not well defined. The less certain they are, the less extensive e-commerce will be in any country, China included. E-commerce involves a variety of activities, including ordering services and goods, delivery, and payment settlements. These activities require physical and institutional infrastructure support. In China, the responsibility for the physical infrastructure includes the seven local backbone providers, the value-added private telephone system, and the Internet service providers. The main policy players seem to be ICT bodies like MII and the operating companies that implement policies. The companies themselves have also become de facto policy authorities. Other bodies beyond the ministries include the State Planning Commission, the State Economic and Trade Commission, and the China Council for the Promotion of International Trade. By the end of 2000, there were more than 1,500 e-commerce companies (CECA 2001, 76).

For several years now, the Chinese authorities have been sorting through various e-commerce elements to design their own legal and regulatory framework. Initially drafted by a number of MII technocrats, the current version worked its way up through MII and then to the State Council, which returned it to MII for further work. Concomitantly, the Chinese government prohibited transmission of "state secrets" over the Internet, mandated that news material be sourced from an official press, required foreign companies to register encryption software used by their employees, and banned Chinese companies from buying products protected by foreign encryption software. According to State Council regulations (Article 6 and 11) in December 1997 (Lapres 2000, 26), Internet users had to:

• Obtain proper approval (from the Ministry of Public Security) before using computer networks or network resources,

• Complete and return to their Internet service provider a form designed by the local public security office, and

• Refrain from entering computer information networks or using the resources of the network without permission.

The existing laws and regulations are spotty and uncertain in their applications (see table 5.2): "The definition of state secrets remains vague, and even information that has already been published in the foreign press may be designated a state secret." Prohibiting Web sites from employing their own journalists or from publishing information without official approval seems to contravene the International Covenant on Civil and Political Rights, which China has signed but not yet ratified. Article 19 of the Covenant protects a person's "right to seek, receive, and impart information and ideas of all kinds, regardless of frontiers, either orally, in writing, or in print, in the form of art, or through any other media of his choice" (Lapres 2000, 64).

The Commercial Sector In the commercial sector, companies like SparkIce were challenged to perform in China's new competitive environment. By the late 1990s, it was apparent that a consumer-based business model in China would be difficult to support. Internet service providers couldn't create enough revenue to justify the investment expense. More Chinese firms followed counterparts elsewhere and experimented instead with business-to-business strategies (companies I interviewed sought to launch integrated export platforms, create databanks for Chinese firms, and build portals in cyberspace for a variety of Chinese-made products, among other ideas).

The upshot of these trends was that by 2001 Chinese e-commerce Web sites were increasing their revenues dramatically. But the estimates are virtually impossible to verify, and they are wide ranging. MII concluded that e-commerce sites amounted to $24.2 million in 1999, double their estimate for 1998. But other sources have estimated that business-to-business (B2B) and business-to-consumer (B2C) revenues were together closer to $40 million. A later estimate found B2B generating $9.27 billion in 2000, and B2C $47.1 million. At the same time, the number of online stores dropped from about 600 in 1999 to about 250 by mid-2001

Table 5.1
China's Golden Projects

Name	Main Participants	Purpose
Golden Bridge (Jin Qiao)	Ministry of Information Industry, State Information Center, Ji Tong Co.	To build a public network backbone and international network interface capable of transmitting data, voice, image, and multimedia information
Golden Customs (Jin Guan)	Ministry of Foreign Trade, Customs Department, Ji Tong Co.	To establish networks capable of handling foreign-trade taxes, foreign currency settlements, domestic returns, quota management systems, an electronic data interchange (EDI), and an import-export statistical database
Golden Card (Jin Ka)	People's Bank of China, Ministry of Information Industry, Ministry of Internal Trade, Great Wall Computer Co.	To establish an electronic-based financial transaction system and information service; to have 200 million credit cards in use in 400 cities by early in the twenty-first century
Golden Sea (Jin Hai)	State Statistical Bureau, People's Bank of China, State Information Center	To build a data network linking top government leaders with other institutions, organizations, and offices under the direct jurisdiction of the Communist Party Central Committee

Golden Macro (Jin Hong)	China Export-Import Bank, Ministry of Finance, State Information Center	To develop a state economic and policy support system by setting up a database unifying industrial, tax, price, investment, resource, capital, energy, transport, and communication information
Golden Tax (Jin Shui)	Ministry of Finance, Ministry of Information Industry, State Taxation Bureau, Great Wall Computer Co.	To make use of computerized work unit tax receipts and direct bank connections to aid the flow and use of funds across China
Golden Intelligence (CERNET, Jin Zhi)	State Education Commission	To enable teachers and research professionals to have timely and precise information and to enable international and local communication and cooperation
Golden Enterprise (Jin Qi)	State Economic and Trade Commission	To design and build an integrated enterprise target (quota) and distribution system; to build a countrywide enterprise and product database

Table 5.1
(continued)

Name	Main Participants	Purpose
Golden Agriculture (Jin Nong)	Ministry of Agriculture	To develop an agricultural supervisory, calculation, and forecasting system
Golden Health (Jin Wei)	Ministry of Health	To develop and apply computer technology and scientific information distribution to the medical sector
Golden Info (Jin Xin)	State Statistical Bureau	To develop real-time information flows
Golden Cellular (Jin Feng)	Ministry of Information Industry	To provide the basis for a coordinated mobile communications strategy; to develop national roaming standards and systems
Golden Switch (Jin Kai)	Ministry of Information Industry	To build China's domestic digital switch manufacturing industry
Golden Housing (Jin Jia)		To create a property information network

Source: "Big Brains Limited" (1999).

Table 5.2
China's Internet-Related Regulations

Regulation	Issuing Body	Date
Regulations for Protection of Computer Software	State Council	June 1991
Interim Provisions on the Approval and Regulations of Businesses Engaging in Opened Telecommunications Services	Ministry of Post and Telecommunications	September 1993
Measures on the Regulation of Public Computer Networks and the Internet	Ministry of Information Industry	April 1996
Computer Information Network and Internet Security, Protection, and Management Regulations	Ministry of Public Security	December 1997
Revised Provisional Regulations Governing the Management of Chinese Computer Information Networks Connected to International Networks	State Council	May 1997
Commercial Use Encription Management Regulations	State Council	October 1999
International Computer Information System Network Security Regulation	State Bureau of Secrecy	January 2000

(figures from William Foster, personal communication April 2001; Foster and Goodman 2000, 34).

The ambitions of Chinese entrepreneurs increased along with company profits. Dozens and then hundreds of private, semiprivate, and public commercial companies began countless experiments with electronic commerce.

At the same time, government officials tried to figure out how their agencies should handle e-commerce, there was a great deal of jockeying for position, and outcomes reflected the interests of those who positioned themselves best. Political networks shaped technical ones.

These findings are not unique to China. Janet Abbate's (1999) book on the history of the Internet in the United States demonstrates unequivocally the degree to which physical infrastructure and its protocols reflect the values, priorities, and current practices of those who design them (Abbate 1999).

The social and political character of these new Internet entrepreneurs remains to be seen. We do not know if they will be fully coopted by the current hierarchy, creating a conservative social amalgamation. Or will the information revolutionaries and their fellow political travelers constitute an emerging counterelite? Certainly, the history of incipient business groups in emerging markets of Asia and Latin America should not lead us to assume that they will demonstrate great political or social autonomy (Pearson 1997). They are unlikely to have anything approaching decisive economic or political power in the Chinese emerging order.

Over the long term, ICT in its several forms will almost certainly create greater openness, transparency, and participation in China. Communications one-to-one, one-to-many, and many-to-many will foster procapitalist and prodemocracy conditions. Over the long term, so will the structural impacts of embedded ICTs as they reshape investment patterns, productivity, and the structure and location of the workforce, making it more service and white-collar oriented. Knowledge workers require more education than agriculture or industry workers, and with education comes the thirst for greater personal autonomy and freedom (Inglehart 1990).

Conclusion

Why the Internet Spread as It Did in China

I have argued that the diffusion of the Internet in China is best understood as the interplay among structural, institutional, and political factors as they interacted with one another and evolved over the decade of the 1990s. Part of the Internet diffusion puzzle in China is that the country's top leadership is simultaneously among the most aggressive and repressive in the world in its control of the spread of the Internet and yet has allowed China to attain one of the highest rates of Internet expansion in the world, doubling every 720 days.

As I suggested at the start of this chapter, the main reasons behind the puzzle are not technological or strictly economic. Rather, China's leaders are seeking multiple outcomes—diffusion and control, access and denial, innovation and obedience. So far, they appear willing to sacrifice a unit or two of potential innovation to gain a unit or two of control. I would characterize this approach as carefully controlled Communist diffusion.

China's precise balances were negotiated by fiercely contending elites at the top of governmental, private, and mixed organizations. Over the course of the decade, the constantly shifting ICT rules reflected in part the constant renegotiation among these parties as their power ebbed and flowed. Each year saw slightly different rules governing the demand and supply of the new services. But if the precise evolution of the Chinese ICT market was unique, it also followed the general trajectory of similar markets in other countries. At the end of the 1990s, Chinese Internet markets were more private, international, and competitive than they had been at the start.

In China, the concept of strategic restructuring once again permits us to capture the background features of structure and the behaviors of individuals struggling to make their way amidst new and confusing social conditions. And between structures and individuals, through their positive and negative incentives, Chinese institutions played an important role in shaping diffusion. Leading experts in the communist party and bodies like the State Council are more and more interpreting ICT diffusion in the broader context of "informatization". In my conversations with them they repeatedly press the contribution ICT diffusion must make to industrialization, investment competitiveness and job creation. "Informatization" is the current dominant strategy to build a world class Knowledge Society. (Personal communication 2002; Hu 2002; Dahlman and Aubert 2001)

Future Trends
As structural, institutional, and especially political factors interact over the coming five years, they will continue to be dramatically shaped by political negotiations and resulting policy dynamics. With a new president, this will be a time of considerable transition and uncertainty. This political transition occurs at a time when China's World

Trade Organization openings are bringing far-reaching economic dislocations.

We have already seen at least two waves of reformers in China's Internet diffusion—the first wave of technocrats in research centers and universities and a second wave of highly educated technical people with commercial interests, many recently back from abroad. There seems now an overlapping third wave of even younger, more China-educated cyberentrepreneurs who are interested less in policy issues and more in making money. This group has not traveled abroad nearly as much.

I would predict a new fourth wave that blends new with old. We will see an "up and over" phenomenon as more technocrats, bureaucrats, and politicians working within the state move over to the private sector (Wilson 1990). There is already anecdotal evidence of this as some public officials have entered private ICT industries. When this happens—or accelerates—I would expect to see more entrepreneurs mobilizing social and political connections to get what they want through "privatization."

With the opening of the country's economy to the opportunities and threats of globalization under the WTO accords, China's Internet strategy of controlled diffusion will be harder for government leaders to maintain. Without more corporate fluidity, more flexible labor markets, and more managerial autonomy, China might not be able to achieve the next level of economic efficiencies required by manufacturing companies like Legend (computers) or other exporters seeking foreign markets. The kinds of economic efficiencies needed for structural transformation will be difficult to achieve with suboptimal information and tight controls over innovation and corporate behavior.

A recent study by the Institute for the Future looked into the future of the Internet in China (China Foresight Project 2000) and concluded that the core drivers of change between now and 2005 will be the availability of capital for Internet development, the availability of managerial talent, and an evolving regulatory environment. Under a scenario of available talent and "go-fast regs," the study's authors anticipate wide diffusion of networks and applications, with 15 to 20 percent of the country covered by wireless and 75 to 100 million people using the Internet. Online revenues for B2B would hit $20 billion to $40 billion a year and for B2C almost $5 billion. The most negative of their six scenarios—tight capital, scarce managers, and go-slow regs—yields only 30 million users via e-mail and government approved sites, a tiny percentage of users with access to the World Wide Web, and B2B revenues of only $.5 billion. In this scenario, political disintegration leads the government to shut down the Internet. However, the experts estimate that the most optimistic scenarios are the most likely. (The titles of their six scenarios are suggestive: "Stars Align for Fast Internet Growth," "Internet for Economic Growth, Not Social Opening," "Tycoons Drive the Internet," "The Internet as a Tool of Social Control," "Government-Directed Internet," and the "The Flame Is Turned Off.")

While the scenario builders pull their punches, the main driving force is decidedly political. In the future as in the past, the Chinese experience demonstrates the importance of politics and policy as Internet diffusion's driving forces. Structural factors matter, but countries can go beyond or fall below apparent structural limits. Leadership matters too. But despite all of this competition and jockeying for position among sectors, China has achieved what few other developing countries have. Even without democratic India's huge English-speaking population and technically trained middle classes, authoritarian China has exceeded democratic Indian Internet diffusion. The Internet may eventually bolster democracy, although it doesn't bring it today or tomorrow. As in the pre-Internet past, democracy and development are a long-term affair. Every country must pursue its unique national vision toward a knowledge society.

Appendix: Institutions and ICT Infrastructures in China

Ministries

The Ministry of Information Industries (MII) is China's major ICT decision maker and regulator, a superagency that oversees telecommunications, multimedia, broadcasting, satellites, and the Internet. MII is the central authority for planning and overseeing the development of China's electronics, telecommunications, and electronic information industries. It is responsible for setting up laws and regulations for each sector and for coordinating what the Chinese call the "informatization" of the country. The MII is the sole organization ultimately in charge of all networks. There was considerable debate within China and by outside observers alike before the Ministry was created out of the merger of two other ministries—the Ministry of Post and Telecommunications (MPT) and the Ministry of Electronic Industries (MEI). There was worry that a superministry would stifle initiative and strengthen central bureaucrats from one of China's most powerful—and conservative—bodies, the MPT, headed by Minister Wu Jichuan. The MPT won this restructuring battle, and Wu became head of the new ministry. Some of the current confusion and slowness in the ICT sector reflects this forced merger, as two separate entities have joined, however unhappily. MII was given specific control over Internet domain names and provider addresses, officially supervises China Telecom, and plans, constructs, and administers private networks for the Communist Party and other government ministries. One of its biggest policy challenges is balancing the four core policy issues, particularly foreign participation. On China's WTO entry in July 1999, the MII announced that the value-added telecom services related to the Internet (e-commerce, intelligent networks, and paging services) would open to foreign investment and competition and that foreign capital would be permitted to own 49 percent of shares in 1999 and 50 percent two years later. The new rules should level the playing field. Other rule changes may help the competition between public and private entities (now skewed heavily toward the former) by giving domestic firms more chances to develop and by granting local Chinese investors majority ownership over Internet businesses.

The State Information Office is the State Council's public relations and news office. It is currently drafting rules governing news coverage of the ICP sector. The Propaganda Department of the Chinese Communist Party governs rules concerning news content. The State Administration of Radio, Film, and Television supervises China's cable networks and online broadcasting. The China Securities Regulatory Commission approves online trading and public offerings.

The Ministry of Public Security and the Ministry of State Security deal with encryption and try to ensure that the Internet is not used to leak state secrets, conduct political subversion, or spread pornography or violence, as defined by the government. Another body—the State Administration for Industry and Commerce (SAIC)—standardizes the registration of Web site names and protects the legitimate rights of Chinese site owners. According to the Provisional Regulations on the

Registration of Web Site Names that went into force on September 1, 2000, each Web site is allowed to register no more than three names, and the owner of a Web site enjoys the exclusive right to the site's registered names.

State-Owned Enterprises

As a socialist country, China's economy has historically been controlled by state-owned enterprises. While their share of the local economy has dwindled in recent years, part of the challenge in understanding China is to find the blurry boundary between public corporations and private ones.

In a 1999 move to spur greater flexibility, competition, and efficiency, the MII launched major restructuring efforts dividing the basic telecom service industry into four state-owned companies specializing in different types of service: China Telecom (the landline telephone business of the former China Telecom), China Mobile, China Satellite, and China Unicom (which absorbed the paging business). China Netcom was recently added to build a broadband Internet provider network.

China Telecom   China Telecom is the biggest player. It started as the former Chinese telephone behemoth, the Telecommunications Bureau, which was established in 1994. In May 2000, the China Telecom Group was established. It mainly deals with networks and equipment of fixed-line telecommunications. It also deals with information services based on fixed telephone lines such as voice, data processing, and multimedia. Its total registered capital is RMB 222 billion (U.S. $30 billion). China has the second-largest fixed-line network in the world. On July 20, 1999, the number of telephone lines exceeded 100 million. In 1999, 23.19 million new users got telephone lines. Up to 1999, the total asset is RMB 433 billion (U.S. $50 billion). Later it began its narrowband integrated services digital network (N-ISDN) service for the Internet and had a total of 168,000 users. It has connected twenty-five major cities in China and ten countries worldwide. On April 28, 2000, it began its Internet service to twenty-five major provincial capital cities. It adopted an integrated network on ChinaNet to provide voice and fax services. In 1999, a total of 2.16 million people were using China's public computer networks.

China Unicom   By spring 1998, the State Council approved Unicom, the second national telecommunication network (Foster and Goodman 2000, 18). This new telecommunication network is a national Internet provider backbone with the ability to connect with the global Internet. This was a radical step at the time, the result of much behind-the-scene wrangling between procompetition and anticompetition forces. Unicom has 163 branches and six subsidiary companies. It provides paging service, CDMA (code division multiple access) mobile networks, and wireless networks in China.

MII invigorated Unicom by appointing powerful and well-connected leaders to its board and allowing it to roll out Internet telephony services to 100 cities. Unicom is building on its telephony backbone and is planning to offer other value-added services such as secure networks. According to MII, "China Telecom and China Unicom, the two telecom enterprises, will compete with each other according to new market regulations and rules of the game" (Foster and Goodman 2000, 19), but Unicom is definitely under MII's control, and in the Chinese lexicon it is like a privileged and a trusted son. In that capacity, it has been allowed to build "a national IP network with global connectivity and can also be counted on to help control the volatile Internet" (Foster and Goodman 2000, 19). On June 16, 2000, China Unicom, sold 245.9 million shares at U.S. $19.99 per share, raising $4.91 billion in the largest-ever public sale of shares of a Chinese state-owned company. Users have exceeded 10 million. It has invested 23.8 billion RMB (U.S. $3 billion) to set up a data network covering 250 cities in China to provide ISP services and wide and narrowband ISDN services.

China Netcom (CNC)   As the need for policy rebalancing began to be acknowledged by the upper levels of government, the demand for competition and efficiency grew. The latest fruit of the need for more competition and efficiency is China Netcom (CNC), a curious coalition of new stakeholders anxious to get into the rapidly expanding telecom markets. CNC started out as the IP Network Model Project and was sponsored by the Chinese Academy of Science, the Ministry of Railways, and the State Bureau of Radio, Film, and Television (SBRFT). Each invested 300 million RMB in the project, linking fifteen cities on the east coast, including Beijing, Shanghai, and Guangzhou.

China Netcom takes a different technological strategy than China Telecom. By running the Internet protocol directly on fiber (IP/DWDM, or dense wavelength division multiplexing) the costs associated with running ATM equipment are eliminated. Though IP/DWDM cannot provide the quality of service guarantees associated with ATM, its advocates argue that they can provide enough bandwidth to make quality of service less relevant. The fifteen-city backbone being built by China Netcom operated at 40 gigabytes per second when completed in July 2000. Its business includes VoIP (voice over Internet protocol), bandwidth allocation, Web hosting, video on demand (VOD), and telecommunication education. In the spring of 1999, Netcom received approval from the State Council through the State Development Planning Commission to build the network and connect it to the global Internet. It was also authorized to participate in the voice over IP trials. Now it is developing a fast-speed CncNet—IP over DWDM throughout China.

Edward Tian, one of the leading information champions in the country and founder of AsiaInfo, became CEO of China Netcom. A visionary and pragmatist, his role as an information champion is described in this chapter above. Another power behind China Netcom is board member Jiang Mianheng. In addition to being the former Chinese president's son, he is one of the information industry czars in Shanghai. After Netcom was founded, he moved to a leadership position in the Chinese Academy of Science—a move, some speculated, that was motivated by his father's desire to remove him from the commercial limelight. However, he remains on the board of China Netcom.

Established on June 2, 1999, China Mobile provides basic voice service and various types of value-added services such as fax, data transmission, mobile secretary, voice mail, short message, calling number display, call transfer, call waiting, IP telephony, information ordering, mobile phone bank, and wireless applications.

In addition to these three state-owned enterprises, China now has seven other companies allowed to link directly to the international Internet networks.

Specialized Government Bodies

In 1996, faced with a confusion of important issues that cut across bureaucratic lines, the State Council set up a Steering Committee on

National Information Infrastructure (NII) to coordinate Internet policies. This was a classic move by the Chinese government leaders to facilitate greater communication among the vertically isolated, "stovepipe" ministries (Lieberthal 1995). To avoid a view of policy and especially policy innovation that is strictly bureaucratic and narrow, the Steering Committee was assigned full responsibility for every major issue relevant to informatization in China, including the following:

- Formulating policies, regulations, and laws,
- Developing strategic plans and monitoring the implementation of NII,
- Coordinating cross-ministry projects,
- Coordinating and supervising major issues regarding China's Internet,
- Coordinating the technology R&D and developing standards related to China's NII, and
- Performing other functions assigned by the State Council.

An earlier committee was established in 1993. The second Steering Committee was chaired by Vice Premier Zou Jiahua. Then in early 2000, the Steering Committee for National Informatization was established by the State Council. Wu Bangguo, the vice premier, assumed the director's position, and Wu Jichuan, Minister of the Ministry of Information Industry, became the vice director (China Computer World 2000), demonstrating the continued power of Minister Wu.

Research Institutions

The two major research institutes on the Internet are the Chinese Academy of Sciences (CAS) and Tsinghua University. The early leader was the CAS, which conducts scientific research on a wide variety of topics, including technology transfer and Internet-oriented research and development. It also operates infrastructures. The CAS is also in charge of CSTNet, one of China's four largest networks. It provides Internet service to research communities, governmental organs, high-tech organizations, and enterprises. It has more than 100 optical fibers, over forty satellite stations, more than ten digital data network (DDN) lines, and a 4 mbps international channel connected with the United States. It has

108 databases, totaling 483 gb. Its major research is high-speed computation, network application, and database establishment and maintenance. It is also responsible for the .cn domain name registration.

A sign of the times today is the breakdown of some interinstitutional borders. For example, the CAS's partner in many Internet-related activities is Tsinghua University, the premier research university in China with over 20,000 students and 7,100 staff teaching computer science, telecom, electronic engineering, and other fields. The Hong Kong tycoon Li Ka-shing donated U.S. $10 million to Tsinghua University recently to support the establishment of a research center for the Internet technology of the future. And this project will be headed by the China Education and Research Network (CERNET), developed by Ministry of Education in 1993 as the first nationwide education and research computer network in China (Tan, Foster, and Goodman 1999, 49). The center will focus on developing the next generation of Internet technology, commonly known as Internet 2. The Ministry of Education will also invest U.S. $5 million in research into Internet 2 technology across the country. After the construction of the research center is completed, it will become an important base for Chinese information technology research.

One of the premier institutions today is the China Internet Network Information Center (CNNIC), established under the Computer Network Information Center of the Chinese Academy of Science. It was created in June 1997, commissioned by the former State Council's Informatization Office. The CNNIC, probably the premier Internet-related research institution in China, has several functions, including research and development, technical consulting services, and international cooperation. Its most important activities are to create and maintain a detailed, authoritative, and twice-yearly survey of Internet diffusion and usage demographics. Its reports are widely cited within China and beyond. CNNIC also acts as the national domain name registrar and maintains the national directory database on users, addresses, and domain names (CNNIC 2001b).

China's Major Internet Networks
Thus six major networks: ChinaNET (China Telecom), ChinaGBN (China Golden Bridge Networks, operated by Ji Tong Communications

Table 5.3
China' Major Internet Service Providers

Chinanet www.chinanet.cn.net	Operated by China Telecom, the country's dominant Internet provider and offering services in all major Chinese cities. At the end of 1999, Chinanet had a total bandwidth of 291 Mbps, or 83 percent of Chinese connections to the global Internet backbone. Though China Telecom itself is the dominant Internet service provider for Chinanet, a few small ISPs operate by leasing Chinanet resources from China Telecom. But China Telecom's high leasing fees have effectively prevented these small ISPs from becoming significant players in the ISP business.
Chinagbn www.gb.com.cn	Operated by Jitong Communication Co., Ltd. In January 1994, the state-owned Jitong was founded to operate the network but did not launch its Chinagbn services until September 1996 (nine months after Chinanet). Jitong is also the main ISP for Chinagbn and offers IP telephony and other Internet services.
UNINET www.uninet.com.cn	Run by China Unicom, China's second telephone operator. Has developed extensive cellular and paging services. In southern China, Unicom is using its IP network UNINET for IP applications such as voice over IP and fax on IP but plans to offer Internet-access services on UNINET in 100 cities in 2000.
CNCNET	Run by China Netcom Corp. Netcom is largely in the planning stages, but this new telecom operator will base its network on connections to existing broadcasting and railway networks, and it will offer wholesale broadband access as well as local Internet service in major Chinese cities.
CERNET www.cernet.edu.cn	The Ministry of Education's campus network, linking China's major education and research institutes. CERNET provides mainly scientific research and educational information.
CSTNet www.csnet.net.cn	The China Science and Technology Network offers its services to the public, but the majority of its users are provincial and local government agencies and state-owned enterprises. Though some of these enterprises have Internet access, CSTNet is not primarily a business-related network.

Corp.), UNINET (China Unicom), CNCNET (China Netcom), CERNET (China Education and Research Network, operated by the Ministry of Education, now the State Education Commission), and CSTNet (China Science and Technology Network, operated by the Chinese Academy of Sciences (see table 5.3). According to CNNIC, China had a combined international bandwidth of 351 mbps (million bits per second) by the end of the 1990s.

6

The Information Revolution and the Global Digital Divide

One of the most puzzling aspects of the information revolution is its differential impact on the rich and the poor. While it is generally agreed that the revolution will not affect everyone equally, there is less agreement on its precise distributional impacts. Are they positive or negative? Large or small? Widely spread or regionally limited? Are they occurring throughout the economy or only in a few sectors? Are the distributional impacts the same everywhere, or are they driven by each society's peculiarities? Will equality rise or fall over the short, medium, and long terms? These questions fall under the rubric of digital divide or information gap. To answer these questions as broadly as possible, I draw insights from chapters 3–5 and now shift from the single-nation studies presented in those chapters to large cross-national samples. With the empirical base established I return to the SRS model in chapter 7.

The Meanings of the Digital Divide

Trying to define *digital divide* is not a recent problem. In the 1970s, a heated debate raged over the information and communication technology (ICT) asymmetries between North and South and what to do about them, captured in the phrase "New International Information Order" (Frederick 1993). A 1984 study warned of a split between information have and have nots (ITU 1985) and analyzed distributional issues in great detail. More recently, the United Nations Educational, Scientific, and Cultural Organization (UNESCO) (1997) promulgated its "Right to Communication" document, addressing implications of the information have and have-not gap.

There is a long tradition within the telecommunications sector of striving for universal service and universal access. Governments have traditionally pushed public utilities to distribute their services more widely. *Universal service*, within the confines of advanced world economies, has meant nearly universal telephone availability in the home. Governments under old monopoly systems used internal cross-subsidies to ensure that poorer populations could afford telecommunications services (Hudson 1997). By contrast, *universal access* refers to ensuring some kind of ICT services within a "reasonable" distance of most citizens, whether in the home or in public institutions like schools, community centers, and government agencies.

The definitions of *universal service* and *universal access* have changed with technology, material circumstances, and social expectations. Being connected in 1900 or in 1950 involves something quite different than being connected in 2002.

Today *digital divide* refers to an inequality in access, distribution, and use of information and communication technologies between two or more populations. This access definition can be applied to different populations within a single country (the intranational digital divide) and in two or more countries or regions (international digital divide). When people refer to the global digital divide, they typically lump these two different aspects together; they are closely related but distinct.

Not every difference is a divide. Where one population or region has 95 percent penetration of a given technology, and another has a 92 percent penetration, we cannot logically speak of a divide. Digital divides are large structural impediments to equal access. A ten-to-one differential between digital haves and have-nots in India may not be as politically significant for the poor as other key government services. In the United States, a racial or gender gap of two-to-one might be more politically charged than a ten-to-one gap in another country. Because access is so central for properly conceptualizing the digital divide, let me unpack and redefine the concept.

The Global Digital Divide
Drawing from the country experiences of Brazil, Ghana, and China, I conclude that access to information and communication technology

requires a number of distinct elements to be present to ensure effective as distinct from formal access.

Physical Access   Physical access is the most frequently discussed aspect of access and refers typically to the proximity that the potential user has to physical infrastructures and applications in a well-defined geographic space. It is usually measured through the distribution of ICT devices per capita or the density of their enabling infrastructures, such as land lines per thousand.

Financial Access   Financial access refers to the capacity of individuals and communities to sustain their payments for commercial or subsidized services. A useful measure of financial access is the cost of the ICT services relative to annual income. Financial access reflects the costs charged to users in a market, with the income per capita of the people served by the market. The higher the disposable income of a population, the more likely it will be able to afford information and communication services.

Cognitive Access   Cognitive access is the potential consumer's intellectual capacity to find the information she needs, to process that information, and to evaluate and employ it to meet her needs. A thoughtful report refers to fluency in information technology (FIT), which describes the rich assortment of ICT skills for everyday ICT use; the fundamental concepts of the basic principles of networking, knowledge management, and so forth; and the intellectual capabilities to see the broader picture of where ICTs belong in modern society. The precise mix of cognitive skills required differs from country to country and individual to individual (National Academy of Science 1999).

Design Access   Design access refers to human-machine interface. Design access encompasses the hardware and software that are appropriate to the potential users in a given population. It is especially relevant for people who are hearing or visually impaired but also for illiterates for whom icons and voice recognition could bring the benefits of the information revolution. Radios powered by a hand crank, translation software programs, and solar-powered telephones are other instances of specialized design access.

Content Access   The potential user in a developing country will find all these other forms of access quite hollow if when she goes to the Web, the Internet, or the television, she finds nothing available in her language or no content relevant to her daily needs. Content access—access to relevant programming, stories, and reports—is critical for the information society. Especially critical here is access to materials in the user's own language, whether Swahili or Tamil. One senior official in the government of Mozambique told me, "I feel very sad about the Internet because there is not a single page on the whole worldwide Web with anything in my maternal language." In most developing countries, the poor and less educated speak only a local language or dialect, and access to local content in local language leads back to the need for trained and sophisticated individuals with the ICT fluency to be able to produce much of that content.

Production Access   For developing countries, especially, content access cannot be divorced from production access. To be truly sophisticated and fluent in the emerging broadband, interactive environment, users need the confidence and capacity to be able to produce their own content for their own local consumption. The reality is that so much of the vaunted information superhighway runs in one direction only—from North to South. There is much less content produced by the South for the South, and much less that flows from South to North.

Institutional Access   The next two forms of access also take us out of the realm of technology and into the heart of the information revolution—institutions and politics. Institutional access refers to the variety of organizational forms and regulations that have emerged around the world as contending groups struggle to structure access to digital content in particular ways. We saw in chapter 2 that telecenters in Asia, Africa, and Latin America have been designed with a wide variety of institutional forms—public and private, widely distributed and geographically limited, linked to post offices and public kiosks and tucked away in difficult-to-reach institutions. The numbers of users are greatly affected by whether access is offered only through individual homes or whether it is offered through schools, community centers, religious institutions, cyber-cafes, or post offices, especially in poor countries where computer access at work and home is highly limited. Institutional innovation is needed in developing countries to get access beyond the confines of the upper and upper middle classes. Even with nearby technical connections, money in hand, and good training, if you are a poor Haitian, Peruvian, or Cambodian, your access will be restricted to the ways that information is channeled through NGOs, private firms, and public institutions.

Political Access   Finally, we come to political access. It is a truism in the development literature that the most successful development projects are those where the affected populations participate actively in the design of projects, which ostensibly serve their interests. White elephants litter villages in the developing world, failed monuments to well-meaning foreign aid donors who design projects, parachute them into local communities, only to see them wither away. Agriculture projects, employment schemes, and factories lie unused because they failed to conform to the needs of the local people. ICTs projects are not immune to this syndrome. Villagers have a greater chance of getting sustained reliable access to ICTs if they gain political access to the decision making for design and distribution. This is not a technical matter; it is a contentious political issue involving authority and power over who gets to participate: "It is important to develop means of ensuring public input as new policy-making bodies are formed, whether they are self-regulatory or governmental, domestic or international" (Baird 1999, 7).

Political access means that the consumer has access to the institutions where the rules of the game are written, rules that govern the subsequent allocation of scarce ICT resources. As we saw in the previous chapter, when consumers have meaningful and legitimate access to regulatory agencies, government advisory bodies, joint private-public boards, and other institutions, then suppliers are more likely to be responsive to their needs and concerns. When consumers can influence the rules of ICT access, they are better able to ensure sustainable access. When consumers have democratic political access, they are more likely to play by the rules they helped design. Effective institutional access is a key global issue, too, as distributional concerns are raised in the Internet Corporation for Assigned Names and Numbers (ICANN), the World Trade Organization (WTO), and other international rule-making bodies.

The problem, as we see in Brazil, Ghana, and China, is that politics is typically seen as a zero-sum game: if group X gains more power to shape outcomes, then group Y feels its power diminished. If NGOs gain greater decision-making access to set distributional priorities for telephones, then civil servants and managers of state-owned enterprises correctly perceive they have less power.

It is also politics that in the final analysis bundles all these forms of access together. In the real world, these various dimensions of access do not occur naturally. They are typically supplied by different institutions, in different locations, at different times. Bringing them all together so that the potential consumer can have physical, financial, cognitive, design, content, and other forms of access is the work of politics and institutions.

Beyond Access   With these multiple forms of access in mind, we can distinguish between formal and effective access. Putting a computer in a school is formal access. Stringing a telephone wire to a village is formal access. Ensuring that people in the village can pay for the services, can find relevant content, know how to use the technologies, and are engaged and represented in the policy process is effective access.

The concept of access is fine as far as it goes. However, it does not capture the entire range of relationships that citizens and consumers have (or should have) with ICT services as they move into an unexplored and unfamiliar broadband environment. Arguably, access has a somewhat passive connotation and is insufficient in periods of radical change. The average user must be proactive in his or her engagement with unfamiliar technologies. *Participation* and *engagement* are more appropriate concepts to capture today's new possibilities and challenges. Full citizenship and full access in a knowledge society requires full engagement with all these components. The differences between the average citizen and the information champions illustrate the point; the latter are the most engaged with the social, economic, and political possibilities of ICT. The more active ICT innovators there are in a society, the more likely it will become a knowledge society. We can capture some of this spirit of participation and engagement if we consider the practical ways that potential users actually pursue the information and communication services that they want. Figure 6.1, a kind of heuristic decision tree, points to the dynamics in play as technology is distributed throughout society. These are certainly not the only sequences of diffusion, but they are likely ones. Further research is needed to uncover exactly how these sequences unfold under different settings in developing and other countries. Since the vast majority of the world's population remains unconnected to modern communication networks, searching for patterns of people's first-time access and engagement will remain an important research question for a long, long time.

Table 6.1 provides a snapshot of some key aspects of the Digital Divide. Depicted are two categories—households with telephones and households without. Of households without telephones, around 50 million are on official waiting lists, roughly 250 million can potentially afford services, and nearly 700 million do not have telephones and cannot afford them. Evidently the 250 million people who are financially able to support access remain undersupplied because financial access is not matched with physical and other forms of access. For manifold reasons, substantial underinvestment has stunted access. In India, for

Table 6.1
The Phoned and the Unphoned, World Households, 1996

	Millions of Households
Households with telephone service	500
Households without telephone service:	
Waiting list	50
Can afford	250
Cannot afford	680

Source: ITU (1998).

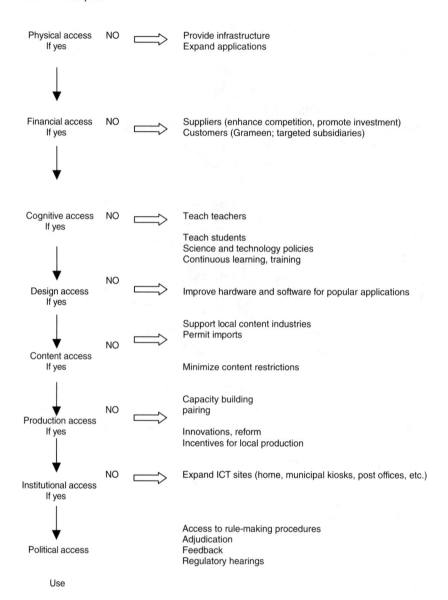

Figure 6.1
Negotiating the Digital Divide

Figure 6.2
The Critical Domain of Action

example, the income gap between rural and urban areas is nearly four to one, and yet the telecom gap is sixty to one.

Figure 6.2 was developed while working with Canadian and South African authorities to garner support for universal access (Global Access to Information and Communication Technology, or GAIT) and with the Global Information Infrastructure Commission (GIIC). The short horizontal line to the left indicates the currently serviced commercially viable population. The long horizontal line to the right symbolizes the unserviced, commercially nonviable population. In the middle lies a gap of 250 million to 300 million households. The challenge to public policy and corporate strategy is to extend the left line to the right. Serving the left-side population is relatively low risk; serving the right-side population is relatively high risk.

Determinants of Differential Diffusion: Demographic Causes
Demographic features of consumers are also important in shaping access to ICT. The most determinative features are income, education, age, gender, and a rural or urban location. Greater access is most associated with greater income and education. It is also positively associated with urban residence. ICT services are most used by young, urban, affluent, well-educated urban males. These factors consistently arise cross-nationally. Evidence suggests that certain applications are more sensitive to demographic differences. Access to radio and television is more widely distributed across income, education, and age differences than access to the Internet.

Table 6.2 suggests one way to think about how demographic features intersect with access dimensions. In policy and analytic terms, we want to know how gender, geography, income, education, occupation, and ethnicity intersect with physical, financial, cognitive, design, content, production, institutional, and political access.

Table 6.2
Demographics and Access

	Demographics					
Access	Gender	Geographic	Income	Education	Occupation	Ethnicity
Physical						
Financial						
Cognitive						
Design						
Content						
Production						
Institutional						
Political						

Demographic factors demonstrate the real world's impact on the virtual world. If the real world is unequal, the virtual world will be unequal. Argentina's technology minister Dante Caputo commented, "We cannot make the same mistake twice, allowing the new economy to become just as unequal and unjust as the old economy in Latin America. We have to do everything in our power to make sure that the poor have access to the Internet. It is our best chance to begin to achieve some kind of social and economic justice here (Faiola 2000, A25). The permanence or impermanence of demographic differences is at the heart of policy debates.

Total Costs
Experts from the North tend to underestimate the institutional and structural challenges confronting developing country leaders. For example, power supply is external to most calculations for computer users in developed nations. But computer enthusiasts in poor countries often mention the unreliability of their electricity supply. (The Nigerian National Electric Power Authority, or NEPA, has for years been called Never Expect Power Always.) The deeper we look, the more issues of structure become important. In developed countries with abundant human, institutional, and material infrastructures, potential consumers

have the collateral support required to run a computer. As technology increases in developed countries, support services become invisible.

When we apply the modified structural approach, it reveals that technological systems are deeply embedded within a network of institutions, values, and behaviors. Ignoring or overlooking ICT's systemic and embedded nature risks compromising technical performance and distributional impact, as I demonstrated in the case studies on Brazil, Ghana, and China. Embeddedness profoundly affects costs and effective access. While some costs are embedded within a single institution, others are entwined in networks of collateral institutions that put sustained access at risk. Consumers and commentators are often unaware of the invisible and unfamiliar ICT architecture that effects costs. These costs and institutional commitments are represented in figure 6.3.

At the peak of the pyramid sits applications—the hardware that constitutes the most visible elements of the ICT system. Typically this is a computer, telephone, or other device. When analysts speak of access and costs, they are typically discussing this level. The second level represents software components. Analysts may mention software's importance to

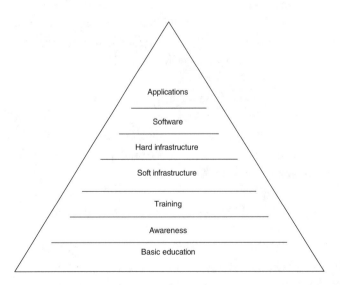

Figure 6.3
The Cost of ICT Applications

developing countries but often neglect to study how software must be made locally appropriate.

At the third level is the hard infrastructure required to link appliances to distributed ICT systems and create operational systems. At the fourth level is the soft infrastructure—the engineers, secretaries, systems managers, software buyers, trainers, purchasing agents, installers, help-line operators, systems integrators, and other essential human elements.

The fifth level of support is training. Effective and sustainable ICT systems provide user-targeted training. Training is often viewed as a way to get employees working adequately, but it also is an investment in creating more empowered knowledge workers. One of the features of wealthy societies is that training becomes a full-time activity. Training is an important feature to sustain rapidly changing information and knowledge systems.

The sixth structural level is awareness of ICT potentials. Awareness refers to the supply of simple, clear messages about the uses of technical systems. Quite distinct from training, awareness of ICT capabilities (crop prices or stock quotes) is an especially important ingredient when first introducing sophisticated information systems into developing nations. Potential users must be convinced they want and need ICT services. This function is partly served by private organizations through advertising, but social institutions like schools and NGOs also play important roles.

Basic education is the final and fundamental layer on which the entire pyramid rests. Countries with advanced knowledge systems must have good education systems. Basic education provides the raw material needed for knowledge production, and is as essential as steel was for the industrial age or fertile ground for the agricultural age.

The Puzzle of ICT Diffusion: Optimists, Pessimists, and Structuralists

Once the concept of ICT diffusion is defined, the next step is to understand its dynamics and explore its effects on other aspects of society. Will the divide between rich and poor converge, or will it diverge? A variety of competing claims have been made about the future of the digital divide and convergence, and they hinge on hypothesized cause-effect relationships.

Those who are optimistic about convergence between rich and poor have high expectations that the requisite institutions, private groups, and governments will work together to minimize the biases, frictions, and transaction costs that are likely to arise. Such scholars are also optimistic about individuals' capacities to process data and information effectively (Alstyne and Brynjolfsson 1996). Pessimists are unsure that such conditions will unfold. They are more likely to believe that individuals and institutions resist change and that change is costly. Optimistic, pessimistic, and neutral approaches predict quite different societywide, macro-level outcomes in large part because each has a different view of meso- and micro-levels processes (Rodriguez and Wilson 2000). They differ over whether institutions are sticky and rigid or flexible and innovative.

The Optimists, the Pessimists, and the Structuralists

Optimists hypothesize that developing countries' relative ICT status will converge with rich countries'. ICT use in both poor and rich countries will grow, but optimists believe that the poor will grow faster and close the gap. They don't assume that Botswana and Belgium will soon enjoy the exact same level of ICT use overnight but predict that Botswana's growth rates will be higher than Belgium rates and that they will meet at an undefined future date. Optimists focus on empirical observations of current rapid expansion of technologies like the Internet and extrapolate them into the future.

By contrast, the pessimists believe that the digital divide is a gaping hole and will grow worse, no matter what is done. Some economists, such as Francisco Ferreira (1999), argue that competitive advantages for first movers is so great that late adopters will not catch up. Others argue that the institutional, cultural, or economic impediments to informatization are so great that poorer countries and communities will be permanently blocked from catching up with advanced countries. Some believe Western interests will do their best to block the diffusion of the new technologies in order to maintain their own global advantage.

Structuralists believe that ICT outcomes are more contingent. They claim that when ICTs are introduced into a social system, the resulting diffusion patterns will follow already prevalent patterns of power, education, and wealth. In their view, ICT will not transform a society; the relationship is likely to be more reciprocal, but first society transforms ICT, not the other way around. Once in place, ICTs become available to be used as a tool or resource by any group that can seize them. The exact distributional outcomes depend on the material and social conditions, and the balances of power and influence, within the system in question, whether national or global. Whether convergence or divergence occurs within a particular society depends on several factors, including the society's structural nature, its public policies in place, the dynamism of its private sector, the particular technology in question, and other factors. Divergence or convergence will depend on how these factors interact. Which of these three scenarios—pessimists, optimists, structuralists—best fits the evidence?

Empirical Findings

Since the relevant data are so sparse and uneven for developing countries, it is difficult to resolve these distributional controversies unambiguously. There is enough evidence, however, to reach some preliminary conclusions about ICT trends in various countries. This section draws heavily on work done jointly by Francisco Rodriguez and this author (Rodriguez and Wilson 2000) concerning the gaps between Organization for Economic Cooperation and Development (OECD) and non-OECD nations. Commissioned by the Information for Development program (*info*DEV) at the World Bank, the study sought to analyze the digital divide in a rigorous and empirical way. We drew on the OECD's language to define ICTs inclusively as the set of applications that electronically facilitate the processing, transmission and display of information. ICTs were not restricted to one technology.

Methodology
We examined two distinct dimensions of the digital divide problem to compare the information gap internationally to capture as many multidimensional complexities as possible. We understood the importance of

physical access and infrastructure but wanted to avoid relying only on traditional physical infrastructure indicators. Therefore, we first examined the current distribution of actual ICT applications, including fax machines, Internet hosts, and others. To explore some of the softer access issues shaping ICT diffusion, we also looked at what we call *ICT inputs*. These are factors like capital investment, training, cognitive skills, and other inputs that greatly influence ICT development.

When we first reviewed information technology use or output patterns across several different applications, we noticed unusual findings. Some single indicators of technological advance were quite mixed. For example, Japan had fewer Internet hosts per capita than Slovenia, and Qatar had more television sets per capita than Sweden. Yet no one would claim that Qatar or Slovenia is more technologically advanced *in general* than Japan or Sweden. Similarly, many poor countries have much higher rates of mobile phone penetration than developed ones—not because they are more technologically sophisticated but because their land lines are so dysfunctional that mobile phones are seen as necessities. We were hard-pressed to say that one country had made more technological progress in ICT than another. We also did not want the selection of one indicator over another to bias our findings. We needed to design a sensitive approach for multiple dimensions.

Our solution was to create an index of technological progress (ITP). In designing this index, we made a number of methodological choices. The final choices were driven by restrictions imposed by the available data and the research question at hand: Is the ICT gap growing between North and South?

To determine whether convergence or divergence was occurring, we had to make four major choices:

- Select the most relevant information and communication technologies,
- Select the countries,
- Select the time period, and
- Design the analytic model.

Selecting the Technologies   In making our choices, we were guided by the existing literature and by conversations with colleagues at the World Bank and other institutions. We usually found several different positions on each choice. This was especially true for selecting appropriate technology indicators meant to capture the essential meaning and extent of the global digital divide.

There was general agreement that one should capture the newest, cutting-edge, and fastest-growing technologies that provide the base for the future e-society. Computers and the Internet therefore should be central to our effort.

Others who have worked for many years on telephone penetration, like Heather Hudson (1997), insist that telephones should be viewed as important ICT outputs, given their centrality to both commercial, government, and residential activities. Some observers insisted that we should also recognize the central importance of traditional print media like newspapers and broadcast media like radio (the latter being the most widely distributed by far among electronic media).

Because we were most interested in the newer technologies but wanted to provide some realistic balance in our index, we selected a broader representation than either pole alone urged. Our solution was to construct an aggregate indicator of five applications—Internet hosts, personal computers (newer ICTs), broadcast television, mobile telephones, and fax machines. We believe that telephone lines can be viewed as enablers and underlying infrastructures as much as applications and therefore included it in our input category. Recent studies suggest that a good predictor of Internet diffusion is, in fact, telecommunications availability.

However, sensitive to the charges of others that we might bias our findings through our selection of the variables, we constructed several alternative indices using other applications to go beyond our use of Internet hosts, PCs, televisions, cell phones, and fax machines:

• Our core ITP index consists of only two indicators—Internet hosts and personal computers (PCs).

• Our broadest index consists of a basket of seven applications, including the core five (Internet hosts, PCs, televisions, mobile phones, and fax machines) plus newspapers and radios.

• We also constructed a forward-looking index that is based on widespread predictions that future broadband communications are most likely to flow through some combination of televisions and telephone lines. The forward index consists of Internet hosts, PCs, telephone lines, and televisions.

Selecting the Countries   Our preference was to include every developed and undeveloped country in the world in our sample. Regrettably, there was no single ICT database that includes the needed indicators. At the World Bank, we were able to obtain contemporaneous data for 110 countries, but this coverage is biased by more heavily representing the richest countries. We had to exclude nearly one hundred countries as a result, especially among the poorest. This skewed distribution regrettably introduces an upward bias in developing country performance on ICT.

Selecting the Time Period   The temporal coverage proved to be the most problematic and the greatest constraint on cross-national comparisons. Time-series data on the Internet were limited since many developing countries did not get connected to the Internet until the late 1990s. Yet information about Internet hosts and PCs was central to our research. We were able to get full coverage of all our indicators in the 1992 to 1997 period for only twenty-four countries out of a possible 200 but felt that twenty-four relatively developed economies was too biased a sample. The next best data set was for the period 1994 to 1996, which provided almost twice the number of comparable observations, forty countries in all (Rodriguez and Wilson 2000, 17). We chose to use the larger number of observations over a shorter period of time, which imposed substantial limitations on our interpretations. These are the best data that could be obtained from either public bodies (World Bank) or private ones (trade associations also provided data).

Selecting the Analytic Model   Developed mainly by Francisco Rodriguez (Rodriguez and Wilson 2000, 14), the principal components analysis model aims to capture the common sources of variation in the main variables we were measuring. In other words, this statistical technique identifies the underlying factors that make all the five ICT variables move together.

The Model's Findings

This section answers the questions posed by the optimist, pessimist, and structuralist frameworks about the following issues:

- The state of the current ICT gap (the digital divide),
- The longitudinal trend in ICT inequality globally,
- The trends of global economic inequality,
- The relationship between patterns of ICT inequality and economic inequality,
- The effect that ICTs seem to have on economic growth,
- Domestic shifts in equality in developing countries brought about by ICT diffusion, and
- The reason for successful diffusion of ICTs in developing countries.

Access Gaps: Physical, Financial, Content, and Cognitive Before reporting on the findings generated by the index of technological progress, it is worth pointing out that other methodologies used to calculate the digital divide found very sharp access gaps. Our first review of the most straightforward evidence from the International Telecommunication Union and other bodies found a staggering structural divide for ICT outputs—physical infrastructure (Rodriguez and Wilson 2000, 10). Our evidence found that "although the average OECD country has roughly eleven times the per capita income of a South Asian country" (already a substantial financial gap), "it has 40 times as many computers, 146 times as many mobile phones, and 1036 times as many Internet hosts. The differences are less marked with respect to forms of technology that have been around longer—particularly television sets—but they are still there" (10).

Pippa Norris (2000) has analyzed long-term trends in North-South gaps in the use of traditional and new forms of communication. She found that the gap between the rich and the poor for traditional media like television and radio had not changed substantially over many decades. Poor countries had lower per capita consumption of communication services in the past and still do today. The old ICT gaps have not closed, and now a new ICT gap has joined the old.

A similarly distorted picture emerged from our analysis of the ICT inputs—the cognitive basis for effective ICT diffusion. (Although I initially thought the input gaps in developing countries would be greater than the output gaps, the reverse proved to be true.) For several critical input measures, the developed nations are far ahead of the underdeveloped: "OECD economies invest nine times as much of their income in Research and Development—that is in creative, systematic activities intended to increase the stock of knowledge and on this basis to devise new applications—and have roughly seventeen times as many technicians and eight times as many scientists per capita as the economies of sub-Saharan Africa" (Rodriguez and Wilson 2000, 10). These numbers indicate a yawning gap between North and South in precisely the basic physical infrastructures and cognitive capacities that countries need to build toward future ICT use. For example, rich countries account for 97 percent of the world's patents. Content access is at least as skewed as infrastructure access. For the United States alone, content by itself is the single largest national export—$60 billion from overseas sales in software, movies, books, and so forth. The disparities in languages available on the Internet are also a telling indicator of content inequality. Multilingual output is growing toward greater diversity, but it begins from a very low base.

Applications and physical infrastructure are very uneven in the new media as in the old. Developed counties have 312 Internet hosts per 10,000 people while developing countries have only six hosts per 10,000 (see table 6.3): Physical, financial, cognitive, and content inequalities are stark at the international and domestic levels. ITU data report that the ratio between infrastructure in urban and nonurban areas is far greater in poor countries than rich ones. Disparities are also far greater for rich households than poor ones (see tables 6.4 and 6.5).

Returning to the Rodriguez/Wilson **Index of Technological Progress**, we found that the diffusion of the five technologies in the ITP was highly correlated with per capita gross domestic product (GDP). This confirms the discussions in chapters 1 and 2 of the relationship between structure and diffusion. The top ten ITP performers are members of the Organization for Economic Cooperation and Development (OECD); the bottom ten performers are Laos and nine African nations. Some strong

Table 6.3
Cross-Country Inequalities in Internet Hosts

Country	Hosts per 10,000 People (2001)
Australia	1,183.40
Brazil	95.31
Canada	931.90
China	0.69
Germany	294.58
Ghana	0.11
India	0.81
Japan	559.03
United States	3,714.01

Source: ITU (2001).

Table 6.4
Cross-Country Inequalities in Internet Users: Urban/Rural Disparities

Household Income Level	Teledensity	Urban	Rest of the Country
High income	49.5	60.2	47.8
Upper middle income	15.4	24.3	13.8
Low middle income	8.0	23.3	6.6
Low income	1.4	5.7	1.0
World average	10.3	25.0	9.1

Source: ITU (1998).

performers among the developing countries include Hong Kong, Singapore, and Mauritius. The lowest-ranking OECD country was Greece at 44; the highest-ranking developing country was Mauritius at 48. Other interesting points emerged. While ICT use is generally correlated with GDP per capita, a position at the upper end of the economic scale is no guarantee of being a top performer on the information index. Belgium, for example, has a higher GDP per capita than Finland but lags behind in technological development. As we observed in our case studies, other factors are at work, including government policies and institutions.

The gap between the information haves and have-nots is substantial and worrisome, well beyond other disparities. In some instances, cross-

Table 6.5
Within-Country ICT Inequality

	Personal Computer Use (percent)	Internet Use (percent)
Population by education (Australia):		
University degree or tertiary qualification		34
Secondary school education		12
Population by race (United States):		
Whites	47	27
Blacks	23	9
Hispanics	26	9
Women:		
Latin America	20	7
United States	68	54

Source: Wall Street Journal of the Americas; CABECA study 1998; U.S. Current Population Survey 1998.

national ICT differences are more than a thousand to one, while the economic disparities may only be ten to one. These gaps exist for ICT inputs as well as outputs and products.

If we observe links between low income and low use of ICTs and between high income and high ICT use, does the same pattern obtain for other resources as well? Logically, we might expect poverty in ICTs to parallel poverty in other services like education or health. But my preliminary research suggests there is not much cross-issue continuity between ICT and other inequalities.

Dynamic Trends in ICT Inequality   We know that the static digital divide is substantial between North and South. But another critical question is whether the ICT gap is growing, shrinking, or remaining the same. Are the pessimists, optimists, or structuralists right about trends in inequality? Table 6.6 indicates growth patterns in cross-regional differences in infrastructure expansion. Latin America shows its dominance in teledensity growth. In 1999, the growth of Internet hosts showed considerable divergence but also a mixed picture across regions.

Table 6.6
Regional Patterns of Convergence and Divergence: Growth in Internet Hosts, 1999

Region	Rate of growth
Africa	18%
Asia	61%
Europe	30%
Latin America	136%
South America	74%

The ITP index helps smooth out of these mixed patterns. The answer to whether optimists, pessimists, or structuralists are correct hinges on the outcome of ITP comparisons. If the index is higher for developing than developed countries, we know that poor countries are narrowing the digital gap and may at some point catch up with rich countries. If the developed countries index is higher, the gap is growing.

We calculated ITP indices at two points in time—1994 and 1996 (we found no reliable and complete data on Internet hosts before 1994). Our results show that in 1994 the average developed country ITP was 34.7 percent and that by 1996 the average had risen to 56 percent. Among developing countries over the same period, the index rose only from 10.3 to 15.3 percent. Only one developing region, East Asia, seems to be keeping up with the richest. China, Hong Kong, Malaysia, Singapore, Thailand, and Vietnam averaged 23.8 percent. Even at this pace, these ICT changes were barely adequate to keep pace with the developed nations. East Asia would pull even with the developed nations only by the year 2055.

The poorest region, Africa, had the lowest index score. Its ICT access grew from only 3.1 to 4.3 percent. At this rate, it will never catch up with OECD countries. The Middle East, despite its elevated levels of oil-generated wealth, did not perform as well as its wealth might suggest, rising by only 13.6 percent. Latin America (17.1 percent annual growth) and Eastern Europe (20.1 percent) performed better but well below what is necessary to keep up with developed countries' performance.

Once again we find interesting anomalies. The Slovak Republic, Tunisia, and Vietnam improved their standing at rates that parallel developed economies. On the other hand, Algeria, Morocco, Egypt, the Russian Federation, and Oman performed badly.

The Bottom Line Our evidence suggests that the developing world is not catching up with the developed world. According to our index of technological performance, the average growth rate is 23 percent in the rich countries and only 18 percent rate in the poor countries. The ICT gap is bad and getting worse. The current digital divide, a substantial five-point split, is likely to grow as the developed countries continue their accelerated growth. Across the board, information and communication technologies are becoming more unequally distributed.

Three years is too short a period of observation to allow us to reach definitive conclusions. This trend could be a short-term aberration from more egalitarian future outcomes. However, the extent and direction of the gap seem consistent with other recent studies that have analyzed the issue (World Bank 1999).

To prove that these trends were not just an artifact of our statistical techniques, we recalculated some of the relationships using different technology baskets. We found that the common source variation method worked well and that a high correlation existed between our basic index and the auxiliary indices. Our forward-looking index (core Internet and PCs plus television and telephone) had an impressive .97 correlation with the basic index. The core index of only PCs and Internet hosts had a correlation of .94 with the basic aggregate indicator. When we measure the basic index with the broad index (which measures the five core applications plus the traditional and widely distributed media of newspapers and radio), the fit is even higher—.99. These correlations suggest that these are basic and fundamental trends in ICT industries.

Other outcomes are possible for future ICT diffusion patterns. Diffusion may become more random and stochastic, losing its regular pattern. A second possibility is one put forward by economists such as Paul Krugman, who believes that earlier old media have passed through a bell-shaped trajectory—from less inequality of use to more and then back to less inequality. This dynamic is driven by the falling costs and declining technological complexity of the applications.

While good data on domestic diffusion patterns by income do not exist, the raw numbers on domestic diffusion of radios and TVs in developing countries and other ICTs support their hypotheses. Jeremy Greenwood (1997) makes a similar argument. Looking at earlier trends, he too argues that as new skills spread, disparities will be reduced. The historical and comparative evidence suggests that these relationships hold when new technologies are introduced.

The picture is different internationally. Looking at the period between 1970 and 2000, Pippa Norris (2000, 15) finds that even for old media, "the gap between postindustrial and developing societies has not diminished in the last thirty years, if anything, the reverse." Norris reports that "the inequalities of access between rich and poor are slightly greater today than three decades ago. . . . If we can extrapolate from this pattern to newer forms of info-tech, this suggests that the relative disparities between developing and postindustrial nations we have observed in the 1990s will not necessarily close as more and more people go online. The prognostication is that early adopter countries seem likely to maintain their relative lead, leading in new forms of info-tech, even while laggard societies attempt to catch up" (Norris 2000, 15). One might add an even greater note of pessimism. The new media are more cognitively and organizationally difficult than the old.

On the basis of the available (if imperfect) evidence, one must conclude that, for the short to medium terms, the optimists are clearly wrong. While it is still too early to declare a decisive finding, the evidence points to a short to medium trend toward greater inequality. The ICT gap is not shrinking as they insist but growing. The pessimist scenario seems to fit the facts well. The structuralist hypotheses can also be supported by the observations but require a review of the structural context and trends in the global political economy to see whether they correlate with ICT diffusion patterns. (Recall that the structuralist argument predicts that the diffusion of ICTs in a system will closely follow the patterns of income and wealth distribution in that system.)

Patterns of Global Wealth and Income Distribution

The global economic structure in which ICTs diffuse is far from egalitarian. In some countries, citizens earn an average of $30,000 a year, and in other countries, citizens earn $365 a year. That fact alone is sufficient for structuralists to conclude that ICT diffusion will also be unequal and, like other scarce resources, will flow to the most privileged individuals. The most educated and wealthy possess the means to obtain ICT applications first, have the skills to use them most effectively, and are the most likely to transform their first mover or innovator status into economic, political, and social advantages.

An extensive review of long-term global trends in income distribution over time by World Bank economist Lant Pritchett (1996) found that global inequality is not declining. He attacks the conventional wisdom that economic convergence is occurring between rich and poor countries and concludes that the global income gap is diverging. Pritchett estimates that between 1870 and 1985 the income ratio between the richest and poorest countries increased sixfold. The work of Robert Barro and Xavien Sala-i-Martin (1995) reaches similar conclusions. As with ICTs, there is substantial interregional variation, with East Asia outperforming the rest and attaining growth rates that outstrip the developed economies' average.

Examining similar data, Mitchell Seligson (1984) finds that the poor are becoming less poor, but the rich are becoming richer, faster. Poor countries' gross national product fell from 4.3 percent of industrialized countries' in 1950 to only 2.5 percent in 1980. By the mid-1990s, it had fallen to only 1.7 percent. Thus, between 1950 and 1995, the relative gap between rich and poor countries widened by 60 percent.

The figures for domestic economic inequality also point to conclusions relevant for a structural argument. There is substantial cross-national and cross-regional divergence. In general, domestic inequality appears to be up sharply over the past decade in formerly socialist countries such as China, Russia, and Hungary. There are also important regional disparities (Seligson 1984): "In the ten years from 1988 to 1997, East Asia's headcount poverty rate (share of the population living on less than one dollar a day) declined at 12 percent per year, while Eastern Europe and Central Asia's poverty rate increased at nearly 4 percent per year. South Asia has also done relatively well on this measure, while poverty reduction in Africa, the Middle East, and Latin America has been modest at best."

Does ICT Contribute to Inequality?

Over the past decade, global ICTs and global inequality by some measures have increased dramatically. Still, the relationship between these two trends has yet to be demonstrated conclusively. Scholars have devoted only limited empirical and theoretical attention to this question, especially in developing countries. The studies we do have are not encouraging (Rodriguez and Wilson 2000, 25). Research in the United States and other developed countries has concluded that ICTs have contributed to substantial inequality increases over the past decade. An earlier furious debate among experts on whether foreign trade or information technology contributes most to inequality trends has for now been decisively resolved: ICT has been the main culprit. The effects flow through the substitution of capital (such as computers) for labor and through better preparation of well-educated and trained workers. As Francisco Ferreira (1999) points out, even if we assume that access to computers and other ICTs was perfectly equal, users with greater education, training, and cognitive skills will use them more effectively, giving them an advantage in today's labor and product markets. Following this logic, underlying economic inequality leads to greater ICT inequality, which tends to further reinforce economic inequality.

The counterlogic marshaled in favor of the case that ICTs reduce inequality is not unpersuasive. As we saw in chapters 1 and 2, some evidence suggests that ICT diffusion contributes to reducing organizational hierarchy, informational asymmetries, and barriers to market entry. Still, based on the compelling structuralist logic and the available empirical evidence, prospects for ICT reducing inequality in developing countries are dim for the short to medium term. The greater risk is that ICT will worsen the gap between the haves and have-nots in poor countries. The number of skilled and highly educated people in typical developing country workforces is quite small, so the benefits may be even more concentrated. Evidence from a major cross-national study headquartered at the University of California in Los Angeles shows that Internet connections for upper-income populations are substantial in many developing countries, while connections for lower-income populations remain quite minimal. All other things being equal, a small techno-elite is likely to garner a greater share of economic and social benefits in a developing country than in a developed country, where larger middle and upper classes gain greater access to ICT benefits.

In Rodriguez and Wilson (2000, 35), my coauthor and I conclude that "analysts and policy makers need to be careful about simple claims regarding the putative relationships between information and communications technologies, on the one hand, and other societal outcomes like productivity, investment, and inequality, on the other." The data don't support any clear-cut and consistent conclusions about these relationships; they are much more complicated than they first appear. ICT inequality and ICT access have both increased in China and Hungary. Yet in Sweden and Finland, ICT has increased dramatically while inequality has been stable. This suggests to me that beyond structure, institutions and politics may play a big role in relative inequality and further suggests the explanatory power of the structuralist model.

Technological Progress and Economic Growth
There is also a surprising degree of ambiguity in the relationships between ICT diffusion and economic growth. This is curious and counterintuitive in light of the amount of attention devoted to the subject. Development agencies and independent experts sometimes claim that more is better: if you provide more capital investment in ICT and wider ICT diffusion, then you gain more economic growth. However, the relationships are actually ambiguous. Productivity growth rates in the United States were lower in the 1973 to 1990 period than in the years between 1948 to 1973, though ICT was being rapidly diffused in the second half of this later period. More recently, Robert E. Litan and Alice M. Rivlin (2001) have found that productivity accelerated sharply in the United States in 1999 and 2000, some of which was contributed by ICTs, so there may be a threshold effect operating. But in developing countries, the evidence relating productivity growth and ICTs is scarce and unreliable, and there is not much comparable work on other developed countries.

When we analyzed the relationships between the index of technological progress and economic growth, I expected to find a positive correlation. We found the opposite. *There is no apparent link between the level of ICT usage and the level of economic growth.* High-growth

economies like China, Thailand, Chile, and Lebanon have been star performers on the economic side; unexpectedly, they fall in the lower half
of the distribution on our index. We produced similar results when we
used ICT core variables. Some colleagues at the World Bank and elsewhere have pointed out that we might obtain different results if instead
of relating the rate of economic growth to the level of ICT, we analyzed
the rate of change in technological progress as the explanatory variable.
We redid the analyses and found that the new association was actually
slightly negative, although not significantly so. We obtained similar
results when we changed the time periods for both the dependent and
independent variables (Rodriguez and Wilson 2000, 36–37).

We did not conclude that ICT investments are irrelevant to economic
growth; we believe they are essential to long-term growth and international competitiveness. Indeed, the evidence trickling in from the developed economies suggests that the lead time required to build up technical
infrastructures like Internet backbones and to create the necessary "soft"
infrastructures of institutions and policies is substantial (Litan and Rivlin
2001). This has been true for all networked technologies, including
broadcasting and electricity. We saw in chapter 2 how difficult it is to
foster the institutional changes required to use new technologies effectively. The concept of integrated technical and societal institutions is critical to poor countries' ability to effectively diffuse new technologies and
to advance a knowledge society. The bottom line seems to be that ICTs
may contribute substantially to growth but that the contribution is by
no means inevitable. Some countries find that a dollar invested in ICT
may yield more than one dollar of economic growth. For other countries, ICT does not have such positive yields. The outcome most likely
depends on a country's specific policies, institutions, and politics and on
the kinds of intense jockeying for position we saw in chapters 3 to 5.

Economic growth, in turn, is important for economic equity. The
cross-national evidence suggests that stagnant or declining economies are
unlikely to engender greater equality. On the other hand, economies that
are growing are more likely to produce greater equality. Here again,
however, the most desirable social outcomes (greater growth and greater
equality) are not automatic. Gaining both of these good things requires
as much art as science.[1]

How Can Developing Countries Accelerate Access?

If the short- to medium-term impacts of ICT on economic growth are ambiguous, the short- to medium-term policies required to promote effective access to and use of ICT resources are clearer. What factors are most associated with ICT expansion? Based on a statistical analysis of several different variables and a careful reading of the scholarly and policy literature, we found that developing countries that are able to achieve and sustain high scores on our index of technological progress

- Encourage investment in human capital,
- Have low levels of government distortions (that is, have market-determined interest rates, exchange rates, and so on),
- Have governments that respect the rule of law and protect property rights, and
- Sustain an "enabling environment" of democratic rights and civil liberties.

When countries have environments that promote stability and respect for the law and democratic rights, outcomes such as rapid ICT diffusion are more likely. This suggests that there is no quick fix in promoting diffusion. A market-determined economic structure and a positive domestic enabling environment account for most of a country's ICT successes or failures. But even at the same level of gross domestic product and with similar enabling environments, different countries can achieve higher or lower ICT performances by manipulating policies, institutions, and politics. There are important policy interventions that can and should be done. But sector-specific remedies are insufficient by themselves to create the culture of communications so essential for innovation to spread and be sustained.

From Access to Networks

Earlier in this chapter, I made a distinction between formal and effective access. Effective access recognizes that access is composed of multiple constituent elements that must be available to potential users in the right place and the right sequence to gain access to the information they need, at the moment they need it, and in the form they need it. In this section,

I extend the concept of effective access further by linking it explicitly with the idea of societal networks.

Metcalfe's Law

A good starting point for combining the concept of effective access and the concept of knowledge networks is Metcalfe's law, named after Robert Metcalfe, the 3Com Corporation founder who also created the Ethernet protocol. According to Metcalfe's law, "The power of the network increases exponentially by the number of computers connected to it. Therefore, every computer added to the network both uses it as a resource while adding resources in a spiral of increasing value and choice" (Metcalfe 1999). Metcalfe's law describes the distribution of modern communications network benefits. It helps us resituate the digital divide discussion from the context of an individual's access to a single technology or application to the broader dynamics of the networked economy as a whole. Like Moore's law (the Intel founder's observation that processing power doubles every eighteen months while costs remain constant), Metcalfe's law has been used in several ways—as a signpost of conventional wisdom about the benefits of the Internet, as a justification for official action or inaction, and as a scholarly research hypothesis defining what is most important. The law was popularized and reformulated by techno guru George Gilder (1993) in an article in *Forbes* magazine, where Gilder argued that the value of a network grows as the square of the number of its users increases.

Metcalfe's law has been subjected to valid criticism by economists like Hal Varian of the University of California at Berkeley, who question the linear assumption that each additional network member will be just as valuable to those already connected as were earlier members (Shapiro and Varian 1998). Surely there are some diminishing returns, both organizationally and in terms of individual processing abilities, as more and more members are added to a network. The last ten members added to one's network may not be as valuable to an individual as the first ten. As useful as it is, this prominent digital formulation is decidedly mute on the subject of the costs of exclusion from information and communication networks.

Wilson's Law

A more profound critique of Metcalfe's law, especially relevant for developing countries, is to flip its principal puzzle on its head and ask, "What is the *cost* of excluding individuals from a rapidly growing information and communications network? And who bears those costs?" One could also ask whether there are substantial institutional and other impediments to achieving the full benefits of ICT networks?

To critique Metcalfe's law, let me draw several key empirical findings about the experiences of information champions depicted in chapters 3 through 5. Progressive Brazilian, Ghanaian, and Chinese innovators encountered many multidimensional challenges to combatting entrenched bureaucratic interests and bringing about liberal ICT diffusion. The information champions in those countries found serious institutional and political impediments standing in the way of the liberal ICT distributional reforms they desired. In Brazil, competing groups across different institutions and different urban areas encountered repeated disputes and roadblocks in building out the architecture of the Brazilian Internet backbone and defining the rules of access to it. In Ghana, Nii Quaynor found it difficult to elaborate his Internet services in Accra for reasons of interest, income, and infrastructure. Despite the centrality of such dynamics, these important real-world complexities are excluded from what has come to be called Metcalfe's law. Those who employ that law frequently overlook the many frictions that characterize networked interactions and minimize the relationship of the network to the nonconnected.

This is especially problematic in a broadband, digital interactive environment as these new technologies become the multimedia delivery platforms on which are carried more and more public and private services. Exclusion from having a television or a telephone in the industrial age was costly. Exclusion from interactive broadband global knowledge networks in the digital age carries even greater penalties. The digital divide is not simply between the information haves and have-nots; it is also between the networked and the nonnetworked.

Let me offer an alternative way of framing the issues, a counterpoint to Metcalfe's law. Call it Wilson's law of networked inequality: The actual and opportunity costs of exclusion from an interactive communication network are multidimensional (economic, political, and social), increase over time, and are borne by both the excluded and society.

The starting point of Wilson's law is the unconnected and underconnected rather than the newly connected. Second, it puts front and center network costs as well as benefits; collective as well as individual consequences; economic, political, and social consequences; the temporal frame within which we can expect to see consequences, whether benefits or costs; and the importance of democratic user participation in network design and operation. I argue that the factors most relevant to network inclusion and exclusion are multiple and not singular, cut across different levels of social action from individual to societywide, are nonlinear and nonbinary, and are socially constructed rather than mechanical or automatic.

Temporal Dimension

According to Wilson's law, exclusion costs will increase over time as some citizens join the network but others remain excluded offline. Costs increase over time for the excluded as more and more services migrate from the real material world of atoms to the virtual world of bits and bytes. Initially, one has access to desired services only in the "real" world. At a second stage, limited access to goods and services becomes available on Internet platforms. In a third stage, the supply of desirable goods and services is equally accessible in both worlds, and in final stage, there is a decisive shift where many desirable scarce services and goods are difficult to obtain offline. Eventually, in many (but not all) countries, the availability of banking, health, public services, and commerce will decline relatively and absolutely in the world of atoms and rise sharply in the world of bits. Anyone who is unconnected will lack access to this growing cornucopia (Price and Roger 1998). In aggregate terms, however, the negative outcomes will be partly offset by the rising number of people connected.

Economic, Political, and Social Costs

Over time, those not on the network face substantial and increasing economic costs of exclusion, including foregone consumption and investment opportunities, especially opportunities for human capital investment through lack of access to digital knowledge (whether through formal or informal education). These economic costs of exclusion for individuals include higher costs of goods and services (such as no access to "telephone over Internet" services); less information to make informed choices about employment, investments, and expenditures; fewer choices for consumer goods and durables; and ultimately, declining net income and wealth for the unconnected relative to the connected.

The political costs of exclusion include having less information about political candidates, parties, policy positions, and political alliances. Being off the network reduces the voter's opportunities to express views to decision makers and public officials, including the opportunity to vote easily (a substantial percentage of the Brazilian electorate voted online in 2000). Being unconnected might lead to a decline in the influence of the unconnected relative to the connected.

The social costs of exclusion will be reflected in declining social cohesion with others in one's community. As government's relations with its citizens come to be defined more by digital, interactive networks, effective democratic participation and full membership in the polity will equate with membership on the network. Unequal network access means that individuals are barred from the engagements and interactions with their peers that are at the heart of citizenship. Networks can become a means for re-creating elements of civil society. While there are debates over the impacts of the Internet on trust and community commitments, unequal exclusions from these opportunities probably reduce shared values among users and nonusers.

Not only are the costs of exclusion temporal and multidimensional; they also cut across different levels of society from micro to macro. Individuals suffer by being excluded from life-enhancing opportunities and choices that other connected individuals possess. This micro level is where many analysts start and end their calculation of the digital divide. But there are costs at other levels. At the intermediary meso level, increasingly isolated organizations and groups will encounter more lack of opportunity and disadvantage than connected communities or groups. Whether conceived as classes, ethnic groups, or regionally based populations, the risks of exclusion will also be calculated as a collective group disadvantage. Indeed, one of the consequences of lack of access may be weaker internal group cohesion and coordination, at least in the short to medium term as internal social connections within the organization or group fail to measure up to the connections of other groups (whether conceived as competition or cooperation). Finally, at the macro level, when people are excluded from ICT networks, there are macro-level costs and society as a whole suffers, perhaps growing more divided and unequal, risking income inequality, greater political alienation, and declining social cohesion and quality of life for all.

Taken together, these conditions can create conditions for declining social cohesion and rising levels of civil turmoil. According to Wilson's law, analysts should calculate and aggregate each of these economic, political, and social costs, expressed at macro, meso, and micro levels, over time to capture more fully the societal costs of network exclusion. One provocative report concluded that because of the exclusion of so many of the world's population from the online networked world, "this ICT-led expansion is at risk, threatening the global economy" (McConnell International 2000).

Marshall Van Alstyne and Erik Brynjolfsson (1997) remind us that networks are a human artifice constructed of people's preferences for some communication patterns over others. As such, networks develop organically over time. In the virtual world of bytes and bits, most individuals are neither completely wired with the latest technology nor completely unconnected, without access even to a radio. As Alstyne and Brynjolfsson point out, electronic communication's growth is not a straight line from a starting point of unconnected to an end point of a fully connected global village. The many intermediary points in between include subnetworks with their own architecture and affinity groups built around common concerns from Boris Pasternak to comic books. Even when access is open, individuals create their own subgroups through processes of self-selection. *Bounded rationality* means that we tend to seek shortcuts when searches are expensive and time consuming and we tend to seek out other citizens of cyberspace who share our interests and values. When geography no longer narrows interaction, people are free to select acquaintances by criteria such as common interests, status, economic class, academic discipline, or ethnic group. The result can easily be a "greater balkanization along dimensions which matter more than geography" (Alstyne and Brynjolfsson 1997, 7). Personal preferences, as well as the limits on individual mental capacities to process information, lead to bounded outcomes in technological as well as societal networks. These can either reinforce or restructure asymmetrical relationships caused by class, language, location, or other demographic conditions. The digital divide is a complicated societal reality affected by the links between the real and the virtual worlds.

Toward Action

When translated from academic formulations to policy guidelines, Wilson's law of networked inequality points to this: policy makers should act quickly to promote rapid and equitable network access immediately to sustain growth and social cohesion in the future. Government's bedrock policy goal in this area should be to promote and expand effective access to networks as rapidly as possible, while creating institutions, policies, and programs that ensure that the distribution of these resources will be more equitable than otherwise. Countries like Korea have demonstrated conclusively one can achieve fast growth and equitable growth simultaneously. But countries like Brazil and South Africa have also demonstrated that one can achieve fast aggregate growth and very low equality. National leaders must quickly learn how to achieve fast and equitable information and communication technology growth simultaneously. Data-based analysis is critical, but developing societies cannot afford to wait until every shred of evidence has been collected. By the time all the data are available it may be too late to prevent social lockout by technological lock-in, as I discuss below.

Conclusion

Access is a multifaceted phenomenon that includes physical, financial, cognitive, design, content, institutional, and political components. Effective participation in the information revolution requires that individuals be empowered to gain access to all these forms of access. Concentrating only on a single dimension of access is misleading and ineffective. These multiple dimensions should also be understood as tied to knowledge networks, to which actors have differential access determined by demographic features like their age, income, education, gender, and so forth.

This chapter identified predictions of alternative trends of future inequality. Optimistic predictions see the digital divide shrinking, pessimistic treatments see the digital divide growing, and structuralist treatments see ICTs following preexisting economic and political distributions of power. Based on the index of technological progress that I developed (with Francisco Rodriguez), I have reached the following conclusions about ICT conditions in developing countries:

• A major divide exists between poor and rich countries' access to modern ICTs. This gap exists for both ICT applications (outputs like cell phones and Internet hosts) as well as for critical inputs (like research and development spending and effective institutions).

• The rising ICT tide lifts all boats. Most developing countries, including the poorest, are increasing their access to the new tools.

• The information gap between rich and poor countries is growing. Evidence points to this being both a short- and long-term trend (Rodriguez and Wilson 2000; Norris 2000).

• It appears that both income inequality and ICT inequality are growing cross-nationally. However, we simply haven't enough data to claim a strict, definitive, causal link between the two trends.

• While ICT use is growing rapidly in most developing countries and anecdotally seems to be associated with improved economic performance and welfare, it is difficult to establish a causal relationship between ICT progress and societywide economic progress.

• Structural factors like gross domestic product per capita and sectoral makeup explain most cross-national ICT diffusion differences. There are however, important variations that can be explained by a handful of other factors like respect for rule of law and property rights protection.

• The relationship between income distribution within a nation and ICT inequality within that nation is a critical issue for all countries. There is conclusive evidence that technological diffusion has contributed to a deterioration of equality in the United States, but we lack corresponding evidence for developing nations. Gini coefficient numbers show substantial deterioration accompanying a rise in ICT in a number of countries, but we cannot claim causality.

The evidence from these tests indicates that the pessimist and the structuralist models best fit the aggregate quantitative data. The more historical and institutional qualitative analyses from Brazil, Ghana, and China also demonstrate that structure has greatly shaped national Internet diffusion patterns in those countries. Economic and social structures shaped outcomes directly through the resources that were available to potential ICT users and through the national strategies and capabilities that affected ICT development. The quantitative evidence from this chapter and the qualitative evidence from the earlier ones strongly suggest that modified structuralist models are most powerful for explaining ICT diffusion patterns and are superior to optimist and pessimist models.

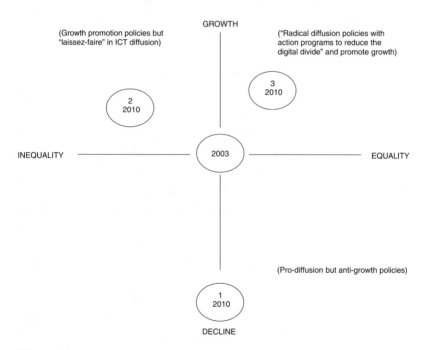

Figure 6.4
Scenario Outcomes of Equality and Development
Source: Based on Analysis 2000, with modifications.

So What?

The answer to this ultimate question hinges on the analyst's prior expectations of the future trajectory of the information and communication technologies over the long term. Usually these assumptions are left unspoken, but they are extremely important in making policy judgments. If the analyst believes that modern societies are trending toward a massive, widespread structural change toward a knowledge society, then information becomes central to the conduct of economic, social, and political life. Under this scenario, ICTs will become central to the distribution of jobs, income, and wealth in a radically restructured world and therefore deserve a lot of attention. If the analyst believes that society is unlikely to undergo such massive transformations, however, then policy makers need not give urgent priority to programs attacking the global digital divide, especially when in most poor countries today the lack of clean water kills more children than computers will save.

Figure 6.4 captures the difficult ICT options that policy makers confront—making tradeoffs between the traditional goals of growth and equality. These are not easy choices: to act is risky, to choose not to act is risky. Government inaction will almost certainly produce suboptimal outcomes—decline and inequality. This undesirable outcome is represented in the lower left quadrant. When governments pursue policies that expand diffusion but ignore distribution, they may expand ICT use (especially through the market) but simultaneously create greater inequality (upper left quadrant). There are substantial risks of social inequality in ICT diffusion. Optimal outcomes in ICT markets are found in the upper right quadrant—ICT growth with equity.

This chapter has provided an overview of structural conditions of global ICT inequality. The next chapter builds on this cross-national review by analyzing in greater detail nonstructural forces like leadership, vision, politics, and institutions as powerful international actors respond to the conditions of structural inequality by designing digital divide strategies.

7

Strategic Restructuring in the Global System

Thus far, this book has concentrated on efforts by strategically placed elites within countries to restructure their information and communication technology institutions at the national level. In this chapter, I concentrate on the parallel processes of strategic restructuring at the international level, led by elites in large, powerful international institutions. I build on the analyses of ICT inequalities and structural gaps described in the last chapter to explain the strategies pursued by public- and private-sector and nongovernmental organization leaders as they try to incorporate very different notions of equity and access into the emerging international regime. (*Regime* refers to the shared "principles, norms, rules, and decision-making procedures" that mark a particular area of international activity and are the most general "rules of the game" that govern actors' behavior [Krasner 1985, 4].) Here again the central focus is the interaction among structural and contingent factors.

The Puzzle at Hand

After being ignored for years, by the late 1990s the digital divide had become a central topic of public discourse in the Western press and on policy agendas around the world. Beginning in 1999, there was a veritable explosion of private-sector interest in the digital divide and other distributional dilemmas. These high-level expressions of private-sector interest in the digital divide were unprecedented:

• Formal meetings on the divide at the World Economic Forum in Davos, Switzerland were attended by Bill Gates, Steve Case, and other corporate leaders of great personal power and wealth.

• A new campaign on digital opportunity was launched by leading corporations under the banner of the Global Business Dialogue (Electronic Commerce). The GBD(e) assembled prominent business leaders to promote e-commerce and then extended their mandate to include e-access. Among its fifty plus members were CEOs from Vivendi, Fujitsu, and IBM.

• At the July 2000 annual Group of Eight summit held in Okinawa, the Japanese put the digital divide at the top of their agenda. One corporate CEO from each country was invited to represent the views of the private sector on this topic. A Digital Opportunity Task (DOT) Force of leading global ICT companies and other nongovernmental groups was created to provide recommendations for the 2001 meeting in Genoa, Italy.

• At its annual meeting, the Global Information Infrastructure Commission (GIIC) put the digital divide squarely on its agenda. A voice of private-sector opinion, the GIIC includes as members more than fifty top executives from the world's leading corporations.

Simultaneously, new and significant developments occurred among NGOs and governments as they also took up the digital divide anew and extended previous commitments. The World Bank created a new digital development Web portal called the Gateway project featuring important digital divide issues and also extended its experimental multidonor unit called Information for Development (*info*DEV). The United Nations Development Program (UNDP) became more engaged through several initiatives and established a high-level international advisory group. The U.S. government continued its foreign assistance program, the Leland Initiative, which brought greater Internet connectivity, training, and policy reform to Africa. The World Internet Society also trained hundreds of people from around the developing world in digital matters. The French government extended its international efforts to build French-language alternatives to the dominance of English as the language of the Internet.

That liberal NGOs and the World Bank called attention to the digital divide was not a surprise. But we would not expect the private sector to jump on the digital divide bandwagon. This is an anomaly worthy of investigation. The compelling question becomes, "How, why, and through what means did private-sector elites place distributional issues so prominently on their agenda, and what have been the consequences of these actions?"

In the previous chapter, I contextualize the digital divide by redefining it broadly and relating it systematically to global economic inequality. I extend that analysis here by contrasting the global responses to ICT inequality within the context of even more aggressive and sustained actions by powerful global actors toward other critical issues like ICT property rights, market structure, and rule making. In part, the relative importance of ICT distributional issues compared to property or efficiency issues is established by the politics of agenda setting. How is it that some topics are addressed and resolved quickly, while others are left languishing? Despite its rhetorical visibility, in the emerging ICT regime, property rights and efficiency issues have thrived while distributional ones have ultimately languished.

This progression is significant not simply as a temporal sequence. Rather, I want to make two larger points. First, I argue that when private ICT actors were faced with a need to prioritize their activities and resources, they ranked rule-making on property rights and efficiency over equitable distribution; the digital divide was last and it was least. Second, and more significant, once the basic parameters of the global ICT regime were established around new rules governing property rights, efficiency, and private-sector leadership, then efforts to address the divide equitably were considered legitimate to the degree they fit within the constraints of these new rules. This pinched conception of equity subsequently hampered more ambitious efforts to redress the digital divide.

Defined in these broader terms, the core compelling question of why property rights and efficiency have triumphed over distribution is important for scholars and practical strategists as well. The expansion of private-sector attention in the digital divide also illustrates the following:

• *The public to private shift in the global ICT regime and the rise of international private-sector governance* As we saw in chapters 2 through 5, the shift from state power to private-sector power is a fundamental element of the information revolution. Since the concept of private governance is a growing subject of interest in political science and international relations (Haufler 2001), the case studies examined in those chapters help advance our understanding of new principles of governance inside ICTs and beyond.

• *Private-public methods of handling new global ICT policy issues*   The deep involvement of private-sector actors in nontraditional areas helps illuminate the ways that unfamiliar policy challenges are addressed by new private-public coalitions.

• *Private-sector methods of achieving common business positions*   A central concern among private ICT firms is creating a common business environment across language barriers and widely divergent legal systems and markets. Such a united front is being forged to create the global network and is beginning to be used to address the digital divide.

• *Private-public methods of forming global policy networks*   Globalization has generated governance challenges for many ICT firms, and these challenges are increasingly met through global networks. (Reinicke and Deng 2000). The networks and the technologies seem to be mutually supportive.

• *The role played by individual leaders in shaping international policy*   The global digital divide reveals the role that individual leaders can play in the construction and sustainability of international policy positions.

The Structural Context of the Global Information Society

I set out the basic outlines of current global ICT distribution in the previous chapter, which examined the substantial structural inequalities that exist between North and South. In this chapter, I analyze the strategies that private corporations pursued in light of those structural inequalities. In principal, corporations could attack the inequalities vigorously to reduce the digital divide, could do nothing and leave them to be resolved strictly by the market, or could do lots of things in between.

A company's top leaders are drawn to collective action on distributional issues for the same reasons they are drawn to collective action on other issues—by assessing their short- and medium-term priorities and by calculating their material, ideological, and political interests. They respond both to deeply embedded structural factors and to shorter-term tactical, behavioral ones. The analytic challenge internationally, as at the national level, is to understand the interactions of these factors, which I try to do through the strategic restructuring model. Claire Cutler, Virginia Haufler, and Tony Porter (1999, 7) also assume a modified structuralist position to account for corporate collective action in other contexts: "Structural factors, while important, cannot tell us enough about the wide variety of cooperative institutions that exist among firms." The ingredients that normally engender market cooperation—high concentration, barriers to entry, and minimimized competition—are not present in all ICT markets. Cutler, Haufler, and Porter (1999, 7) suggest other factors that are likely to produce cooperation, including technological complexity, knowledge intensiveness, high demand for rules and order, as well as "learning processes through repeated interactions with each other and the market, and political opportunities." The possibility for learning drives cooperative behavior among corporate elites on distributional and other issues, as does the desire to define all the rules of the game in ways that advantage their firms. The point at which structure meets politics and institutions is where strategic restructuring occurs. The result is a kind of weak international ICT regime but without many of the formal elements of other issue areas like finance (Bessette and Haufler 2002).

A number of scholars have discussed the international system from a structure-agency perspective. James Caporaso (Caparaso 2000; Caporaso and Levine 1992), for example, describes this structural perspective at the global level, pointing out that actors bargain within structural settings that convey differential "structural power" to different actors within the international order. He points out that the power to govern the rules shapes bargaining power and influences the available choices and constraints. Stephen D. Krasner (1985) also reveals structural power's ability to shape North and South bargaining relations skewing benefits toward the former.

Still, Caporaso reminds us of the complementary perspective, which is actor-oriented. He argues that though the outcomes of bargaining contests may be due to differences in capabilities, they are not automatically affected by them. Outcomes can also be affected by the amount of resources available, the willingness to bear costs, and the skills of individual negotiators. Both the structural and actor-oriented perspectives are useful for understanding how distributional issues evolved over the course of the 1990s.

The Institutional Context

As we saw domestically, many institutions play critical roles in the production, distribution, and consumption of information at the international level. Some of them—institutions like the International Telecommunications Union (ITU), INTELSAT, and the World Intellectual Property Organization (WIPO)—are squarely within the sector. These and other public, intergovernmental bodies were the old regime powerhouses and once exercised substantial regulatory and standard-setting power. Other institutions, not solely within the ICT industry, also exercise influence. The World Bank, for example, is a long-term player and was once the principal capital supplier for infrastructure companies of the developing world.

Other institutions operate regionally, with power to decisively shape regional markets, as the European Union does with its competition policy directorate. These institutions have been well described elsewhere (Vogel 1996). Other less powerful but still engaged institutions include the Association of Southeast Asian Nations (ASEAN), the Inter-American Development Bank, and the Economic Commission for Africa. Yet the most novel actors are the new, private-sector ICT bodies that are assuming more and more authority like the Internet Corporation for Assigned Names and Numbers (ICANN) and the Global Information Infrastructure Commission (GIIC).

Agenda Setting in the International System

Against the structural and institutional background of this highly asymmetric international system, elites in international institutions designed new distributional strategies. Just as national economic and social structures cannot predict every ICT outcome, the international economic system cannot determine the exact pattern of diffusion. The strategic choices of leaders also matter.

Why did private-sector elites choose to take up the divide when they did? Since all issues cannot be simultaneously resolved, they must be prioritized, and in the process of prioritizing, different interests compete vigorously for an organization's attention (Kingdon 1995). Agenda-setting power has been central to choices that international institutions made between the divide and other potential priorities.

During periods of profound structural change, certain core systemic assumptions are often challenged. Actors may attempt to redefine the following:

• *Property rights* Property rights are the rights assigned for the ownership, control, and consumption of tangible and intangible resources (North 1990).

• *Governance rules* Governance rules determine who will participate legitimately in various activities, including rulemaking. These are also called constitutional issues.

• *Efficiency rules* Efficiency rules govern the most efficient way to organize production and exchange.

• *Distributional norms* Distributional issues involve access and equity.

These generic international issues—property rights, efficiency rules, governance rules, and distributional norms—closely parallel the four balances described earlier at the domestic level, and they appear with special clarity here at the international level.

Following the Reagan/Thatcher revolution that restructured public and private domestic balances and the norms that supported them, the American and British leadership aggressively pressed proprivate priorities around the world, as well (Vogel 1996). This general attack on state ownership and control and the call to restructure property rights, efficiency, and governance norms were important preludes to restructuring ICT and other economic sectors.

This constituted a clear example of strategic restructuring at the international level, paralleling the national-level restructuring experiences. The liberal agenda's construction proceeded through contested political processes that began with the fundamentals of property and then formulated particular issues to fit the new rules as they subsequently arose.

Although these principles were most directly beneficial to private firms, at critical moments they were driven by selected government officials. A brief summary of this process follows.

Businesses' first priority in global ICT restructuring was to redefine basic sectoral property rights and governance norms. Under the new norms, key U.S. corporate entities and political leaders insisted that private-sector elites must gain greater control over the allocation, use, and disposition of ICTs. While most often couched in efficiency terms, such a claim was not naïve about core political implications. This was not only a debate over property rights and efficiency but an important redefinition of the governance norms. The new doctrine indicated who would be legitimated to exercise leadership, including leadership over distributional issues.

Reform Phases of the International Level: Restructuring the International Property Rights and Governance Regime

Private-Sector ICT Leadership

Driving many of these changes was the newly elected government of the last remaining superpower, the U.S. administration of President Bill Clinton and Vice President Al Gore. Clinton and his political soul-mate, U.K. Prime Minister Tony Blair, were struggling to define a "third-way" approach of progressive social policies and market-oriented economic policies. Clinton's electoral strategy insisted, "It's the economy stupid," which continued key elements of Reagan deregulation and added a more aggressive strategy for international engagement. Clinton's backers included Silicon Valley entrepreneurs whom he and Al Gore courted during their run for office. Gore and his advisors decided that the driving force of the information revolution was the private sector. Government could facilitate certain functions like infrastructure and access, but the real energy and innovation came from private entrepreneurs. And since so many of the hot new private entrepreneurs were American, shrinking and redefining the American state would also *enhance* America's net power for the foreseeable future.

Gore stepped forward as the administration's point man on information issues. Carrying his reform message abroad in 1994, he picked the regular quadrennial meeting of the International Telecommunications Union in Buenos Aires, Argentina, the bastion of national telephone companies, as a platform to challenge monopolist telecommunications. Gore's liberal call to arms was a calculated provocation to the assembled national monopolist mafia. The core elements of that speech were private-sector leadership, market competition, market-promoting regulatory institutions, and expanding access. Gore's recommendations (1994) were controversial, particularly in this forum, but his words forced leaders around the world to reassess ICT priorities, as many developed and developing countries assembled their own national information infrastructure review teams on the heels of the U.S. challenge.

The private sector in the United States and many but not all firms in Europe strongly backed the general thrust of these reforms, even as they bargained over the details. One prominent business group, the United States Council for International Business (USCIB), issued a clarion call for private-sector leadership in June 1994. It wrote that the information revolution "should be driven by the private sector to ensure its commercial viability and sustainability over time. U.S. industry . . . has acted aggressively over the years to apply information technology to commercial activities and has spurred the development of the most advanced telecommunications networks in the world" (U.S. Council for International Business 1994, 1). As the leading U.S. business affiliate for the OECD and the International Chamber of Commerce, the Council speaks authoritatively, all the more so since this language was hammered out across four committees and working groups of the USCIB— International Telecommunications Policy, Information Policy, Privacy and Transborder Data Flows, and Intellectual Property.

These pro-private-sector positions and Gore's fundamental statement in favor of private-sector leadership were pushed unambiguously by U.S. government officials and private-sector representatives in every world forum. The American arguments drew on the irresistible logic of Moore's law (information processing costs fall exponentially as efficiency increases), the dazzle of technological innovations, and the seeming inevitability of globalization. The underlying economic and technical drivers pushed in a direction that buttressed the American position, though not always at the pace or scope desired by the administration.

Inside the Clinton administration, senior officials called endless inter-agency meetings (some of which I attended) whose purpose was to ensure that every relevant U.S. agency—the Departments of State, Commerce, and the Treasury, the U.S. Information Agency, the U.S. Trade Repre-sentative—got the four-point message and could articulate it in any international meeting. Public leaders pressing for greater private-sector leadership seems at first contradictory, as Steven K. Vogel (1996) points out in his work, since it requires that rarest of phenomena—giving up power. Beyond an ideological shift, it is best explained as the recogni-tion that full technological benefits could not be achieved through state controls and that governments were more likely to oppose rather than advance the reforms, and that U.S. firms and national interests would benefit more broadly.

Major contentious political battles occurred on other related topics and in other international forums as the new principles were articulated. Intergovernmental organizations like the ITU became less central to the emerging international regime, and private-oriented organizations like the Internet Corporation for Assigned Names and Numbers (ICANN) became more important. No longer did everyone know everyone else at international meetings where rules were designed, approved, and rejected. In such settings, commercial interests often dominated, con-joined with technical experts from developed country universities, research centers, and nonprofits. The nature of the international dis-course changed. The initial community of Internet inventors and early adopters who gave the system its flat and open architecture and its culture of participation began to be diluted.

Perhaps the most important and acrimonious episode of regime restructuring took place over the rewriting of rules governing global telecommunications markets. In 1996, a core public-private coalition in the developed world succeeded in getting other nations and firms to concede to a radical restructuring of the entire telecommunications regime (Petrazzini 1996). The restructuring would be based on three core principles—opening up national telecom markets to foreign investment and ownership, permitting telecom to be a traded service open to non-national actors' participation, and ensuring promarket regulatory struc-tures (Petrazzini 1996). These three precepts flew directly in the face of the old regime and were mightily opposed by many nations around the globe, especially by leaders of state-owned telecommunications enterprises who were at risk of being put out of business.

To achieve the concessions they did, U.S. firms and government agencies created a powerful coalition of public and private foreign allies, especially in Europe. The companies spent a lot of time and energy to press the campaign, and the U.S. government spent considerable political capital. This issue was judged to be so central to U.S. national interests that at a critical moment of the negotiations the Clinton administration declared its intention to quit the global talks if the other nations failed to adopt the three most liberal components. The other nations refused, particularly developing countries, and the U.S. representatives walked out in April 1996, stalling global negotiations for months until a deal was struck in February 1997 that the U.S. found acceptable (GIIC 1999).

This episode demonstrates that the world's last remaining superpower was willing to play hardball to get its way in implementing the vision first set out in 1994. The liberal principles of private-sector primacy and market competition triumphed.

The United States government and private-sector leaders pressed strategic restructuring beyond international treaties. They sought to create new organizational models designed to achieve their collective purposes, especially models that would advantage private-sector participants relative to public. If the WTO deal was the epitome of strategic restructuring at the legal and regulatory level, the ICANN deal was the epitome of strategic restructuring at the private organizational level. The central template for a new organizational model developed over several years. U.S. government officials decided to reduce their ability to directly allocate and register Internet domain names and numbers and took radical state action to transfer that significant power to a newly created private U.S. corporation (Levinson 2000). When I asked a senior executive of a major Japanese multinational how important ICANN was on a scale of 1 to 10, he answered it was just a 3 if measured by its narrow technical duties but a 7 or 8 as a model for future global governance.

A solid body of work on ICANN rules and regulations has developed, and some of it is quite critical. Much more analysis is needed, however, on a wider range of issues, including the struggle of individuals from developing countries (like Nii Quaynor of Ghana) to gain greater representation in ICANN. Liora Salter (1999) explains that as a regime opens to greater private power, its public participants become disadvantaged. She writes that developing countries are virtually excluded from important decision making in the international ICT standards regime. And although public entities found their authority diminished, at the end of the day the dominant players were still American.

The Unexpected Arrival of Electronic Commerce

A second major challenge to the rapidly evolving global system occurred after 1996. As private companies and governments around the world tried to set policies for international markets as they knew them, along came an unprecedented and disruptive new technology—the World Wide Web. The Web became a transformative technology to allow huge amounts of scientific and then commercial materials to be easily searched and transmitted at very low costs. Companies were eager to discover what this new technology—electronic commerce—could mean for commerce and for their markets. Soon e-commerce took center stage. William J. Drake (1995) points out that global electronic commerce has engendered more discussion and hype than any other trend in the international trade environment.

Once again the ICT hegemon, the United States, drove the process. Clinton was convinced that e-commerce would become a very big domestic and international issue and sent a strong public signal by creating a high-level post inside his White House to promote e-commerce and appointed to it Ira Magaziner, a trusted advisor to the president and the First Lady.

In brief, the developed country governments decided that the tough issues of international rules and standards for electronic commerce should not be hammered out in large, inclusive intergovernmental forums like the United Nations, where developing countries could exercise their leverage, but in a body like the OECD, which was dominated by wealthy states and also had a high degree of technical expertise and organizational capacity. The outcome of several years of many high-level meetings and consultations around the world was an e-commerce summit in Canada in 2000 that committed to a liberal, private-sector-led competitive and technology-neutral regime. These new rules were entirely consistent with the earlier Gore position. Designed mainly by company advisory commissions and sympathetic OECD governments, the summit perfectly reflected the new norms of the liberal regime then under construction. E-commerce was thereby inserted into the new property rights regime. Another potentially wild, frontier technology was thereby tamed (Spar 1999).

Intellectual Property Rights

The contentious debates over e-commerce property law reforms for electronic commerce paralleled equally contentious debates and radical reforms in the content industries over the meaning of intellectual property rights (IPR). Indeed, the two debates were deeply interwoven. Many of the themes of private property, competitive efficiency, and governance norms converged in the global debates over intellectual property, drawing on similar conceptual underpinnings and political constituencies. The outcomes are quite consequential for economic development in poor countries. IPR covers not just copyrighting records and video tapes but all forms of copyright, trademarks, and patents, including those in highly contentious areas like pharmaceuticals and bioengineering. According to Marcus Franda (2001, 118–119), "Among the many issues involved in building the international regime for the Internet, none are potentially more significant for e-commerce and a competitive framework for future world economic development than those related to intellectual property." From the mid-1980s to 1994, various private and selected public actors struggled to bring about fundamental changes in the old regime, mainly by reconceptualizing IPR as an issue of international trade.

Redefining IPR and developing new norms, rules, and institutions to govern it reflected fundamental shifts in relative power toward private actors and the shrinking power of developing country governments. Susan Sell (1998), an authority on IPR issues, wonders how a small group of U.S.-based, multinational corporations succeeded in making global intellectual property policy. She and others answer this question by showing that company power derived not only from their "sheer economic power" but because the subject matter was so arcane and technologically dense that developing country politicians and negotiators had a tough time penetrating the issues to determine their own interests. Structural power is certainly important, but so is the companies' "command of IP expertise, their ideas, their information, and their skills in translating complex issues into political discourse" (Sell 1998, 192).

Sell (1998) recognizes the structural as well as the knowledge-based cognitive and institutional sources of influence. As the political economy shifts from agriculture to industry to knowledge, intellectual property becomes as fundamental as farms, plantations, and factories were in earlier eras as a central source of wealth and power. The challenge for the global community is balancing the legitimate interests of IPR authors and vendors with the legitimate interests of poor societies. Digital divide outcomes, therefore, are analytically linked to IPR.

Finding the right balances is a major challenge under globalization and digitalization. As Catherine Mann (Mann, Eckert, and Knight 2000, 117) writes, "The architects of intellectual property protection laws must balance the need to protect intellectual property that is expensive to produce but easy to replicate with the desire to promote competition and further innovation. Characteristics of the Internet and electronic commerce—information-rich network effects, global reach, rapid technological change—accentuate the importance of and challenges to intellectual property protection."

The international accords reached in 1994 made substantial reforms in the old regime. Named Trade Related Aspects of Intellectual Property Protection (TRIPS) the new regime's key features were new standards of protection, new enforcement mechanisms and obligations, and reformed dispute settlement and sanctions (Franda 2001, 133).

Many challenges face developing countries' implementation of TRIPS. The first is that more than 90 percent of the patents in the world are held by a tiny number of highly developed nations. A second is that much of the intellectual property sold in developing countries is probably pirated and in violation of the new global standards. It is estimated that China, a major violater, had a 94 percent piracy rate in 2000 (Dedrick and Kramer 2000).

Resources Committed to Redefining Property and Efficiency

The leading powers of the world political economy took a serious interest in intellectual property, e-commerce, and related commercial matters. And although rhetoric doesn't always translate into resources, between 1994 and 1999, the resources matched the rhetoric:

• High-level executive attention was paid by presidents of countries and corporate CEOs.

• Sustained attention was focused over several years (attention was not episodic and short term).

• Political resources were committed. The United States committed its diplomatic and political power and was willing to anger foreign governments by walking away from the first WTO proposals.

• Multilateral strategies were developed. Rich country governments committed time in bodies favorable to their positions, like the OECD, the G8, and the WTO. They also banded together to attack selectively bodies they disagreed with, such as the ITU, INTELSAT, and UNESCO.

• Substantial financial investments and other economic resources were committed.

Access and Distributive Norms: The GAIT Initiative as an Example of Failure

Thus far, I have concentrated on the property rights, efficiency, and governance norms of the new regime and the success they enjoyed. Other initiatives begun in this same period were not as successful. One losing initiative was Global Access to Information and Communication Technology (GAIT). It was ahead of its time, out of phase with the earlier thinking on equity, and out of touch with the power configurations between international organizations, companies, and governments. Yet it could have made a valuable contribution to reducing the digital divide.

When the majoritarian African National Congress overthrew decades of South African apartheid, waves of enthusiasm ensued. Building on this energy, some progressive elements in the telecom sector recognized that the digital divide between whites and blacks was a major social and political issue. The South African government commissioned a study to show how universal access and service were handled in other parts of the world and how the new government could learn from these regions (O'Siochru 1996). The government believed that South Africa could host a best-practices international center that would make information available to anyone who wanted to learn about policies and projects advancing ICT diffusion. The best-practices center was discussed in conversations between the South Africans and foreign assistance officials of the Canadian International Development Research Centre (IDRC) in the mid-1990s. The GAIT idea then grew from the concerns of these few South African communication sector leaders in partnership with Canadian representatives.

For the next year and a half, an international team of experts, including the author, traveled widely to seek partners and finances. Consultations were held with multilaterals (the World Bank, infoDEV, UNDP), private bodies (GIIC), and NGOs (the Internet Society). Conversations took place among U.S. aid agencies and the governments of Canada, France, and the United Kingdom. The concept was modified so that instead of being a single "bricks and mortar" building, GAIT would be a distributed network with three nodes—one each in Africa, Asia, and Latin America—that would be responsive to local conditions and would harvest lessons and distribute them to the network.

At every turn, there was polite interest in the North but no action. However, when the team spoke to people in the South, they consistently reported that they desperately needed a repository of lessons with a training component. But the poor had their needs, and the bilaterals, multilaterals, and corporations had their priorities and money. The idea was rejected, and GAIT died.

GAIT's failure resulted from several factors. One was timing. In 1997, the digital divide was not yet the hot international issue it would shortly become. If GAIT had debuted in 1999 rather than 1997, it would have been more successful. In addition, the potential international partners believed that the need for best practices was already being met and that there was no real need for a new initiative or organization. That belief proved to be erroneous. The proposals were also met with the "not invented here" syndrome. Private-sector companies had another perspective. They were ready to back GAIT if it were based in South Africa and could support their commercial development of the South African markets. When GAIT became global, the companies were less interested. The final reason for failure was due to the South Africans' unwillingness or inability to sustain their own initial commitment. Political support came from the top two or three people in the Ministry of Communications, all of whom were loyal government stalwarts committed to equity. But below them in the ministry were holdovers from the apartheid regime who were perhaps less committed to GAIT's vision. In the third tier, committed young people had little experience, little training, and not enough political savvy to carry the project. The ministry's political "clout" could not be spared from negotiations with foreign investors, domestic ICT roll outs, or bargaining with the World Bank. Leadership was needed locally, and local people were stretched too thin. The combination of these factors was enough to doom this initiative, which originated in the global south.

The Emergence of Distributional Issues on the Global ICT Agenda

Between 1994 and 2000, ICT property rights, efficiency criteria, and governance norms were inserted into the global public agenda by a coalition of leading private firms and likeminded politicians in the United States and United Kingdom and to a lesser extent Japan and Germany. When interest in ICT equity did begin in the late 1990s, private companies engaged the global digital divide in several ways, sometimes collectively through group action and sometimes individually firm by firm.

Collective Activities: GIIC, GBD(e), WEF

Several important international business associations were formed in the 1990s to advance the private sector's vision of a global information economy. The most important were the Global Information Infrastructure Commission (GIIC) (1995–1996) and the Global Business Dialogue (Electronic Commerce) (GBD(e)) (1999). Other extant bodies with more general business purposes created special digital divide initiatives. The World Economic Forum (WEF) was one especially active group.

New ICT-specific organizations shared several things in common. They shared goals—to provide a collective, amplified voice for private-sector executives. They worked to develop common corporate positions on matters of importance to the private sector. Working hard to reach agreement internally, they then could present views to authoritative agencies of national governments and international bodies like the WTO or OECD.

These new international networks undertook the classical functions of business interest associations—lobbying and reducing transaction costs between members (Doner, Schneider, and Wilson 1998). A more implicit but equally important purpose was to provide opportunities for company CEOs and senior executives to meet their counterparts from other less familiar ICT businesses and from other countries. This mutual learning purpose was not particularly visible to outsiders but was important and should not be overlooked.

The new networks also socialized their members into evolving norms of conduct and expectations. Convergence meant that different industries—each with its own outlook, norms, and practices—came crashing together. In the wake of these head-on collisions, there could be no guarantee that the old companies or the new would share common expectations and norms. In light of the new global competitive imperatives, mutual learning was a driving motivation at the annual GIIC meetings from the very beginnings and was a key factor in Davos, home of the WEF. The GIIC annual meetings held in Tokyo, Washington, Kuala Lumpur, Munich, and Silicon Valley featured global ice-breakers that crossed cultural and corporate lines, complete with usually staid corporate executives flipping paper coasters back and forth at one another at the closing banquet, which has become a GIIC tradition.

These groups were self-consciously multisectoral, drawing their members from across the information and communication technologies industrial spectrum—telecom companies, content providers, systems integrators, and Internet service providers. Deliberately international, these groups touted members from developing and developed countries. The leading groups were led by cochairs from three main regions—Asia, Europe, and the Americas. The groups were, for the most part, comprised of CEOs and other senior executives, and each operated to influence policy content at national and international levels. Reflecting the objectives they set for themselves, they created relatively lean and transparent management operations, relying heavily on the participation of senior corporate leadership with staff from corporate headquarters providing occasional administrative support. These new initiatives were truly a mixed breed; they were not fully institutionalized bodies, and they carried more the form, feel, and purpose of an informal network.

The network socialization function was important for these bodies. Their success depended on sustaining interactions among Northern and Southern executives, hardware and software manufacturers, and private-sector executives and their public-sector counterparts. These new initiatives were both more and less than traditional institutions.

The Global Information Infrastructure Commission (GIIC)

The GIIC included among its original goals private-sector leadership, global competition, and cross-sectoral cooperation. GIIC was the first of the specialized ICT business associations, and its founding members also targeted improved north-south relations as an essential goal. GIIC's founding members, especially its founding leader, Diana Lady Dougan, believed that engaging the private sector with developing country leaders was essential for the GIIC's success and equally essential to the success of the global knowledge society (personal communication 1995). GIIC's early leadership took pains to ensure that the first commissioners invited to join the organization were selected from developing countries like Egypt, South Africa, Senegal, Malaysia, India, and Mexico.

Some of GIIC's most successful initiatives were in developing countries. In cooperation with a local India business association and through the good offices of its Indian Commissioner Parasarthy, GIIC cosponsored a high-level conference in Delhi that drew local movers and shakers in the public and private sectors (GIIC 1997) and that occurred at a time when the Indian government was considering substantial changes to its domestic regulations governing ICT industries to make them more open and competitive. Some of the suggestions offered by these captains of ICT industries appear to have been taken to heart by the Indian elites. A second contribution occurred through the participation of a senior

Chinese official, a vice minister of the Ministry of Information Industry (MII), who used the GIIC as a sounding board and learning platform for himself and his staff. A third initiative was the creation of a parallel GIIC based in Africa. This body was seen by other commissioners as a way to learn about emerging markets, to influence African governments toward liberal reform, and frankly, to sponsor a kind of "do-good" activity and had mixed successes. Despite the heroic efforts of Derrick Cogburn and other GIIC associates, the lack of local capacities and business interests made it difficult to sustain. A similar Asian effort also grew slowly and with a similar result. Along with the socialization and learning for the CEOs involved in the various initiatives, the GIIC's efforts to learn from and to educate, inform, and influence developing country officials had probably the greatest impacts of all GIIC's activities.

The GIIC employed an array of tactics to achieve its goals, including a somewhat scattershot mix of annual meetings, hearings, joint conferences, studies, and international conferences. The GIIC's strategy was to concentrate on CEOs or other senior people and use their stature to move the private sector's message out to national governments and international bodies like the World Bank, the OECD, and the ITU. The GIIC had informal, tactical ties with other groups and formal alliances with the World Bank, which hosted the GIIC's first annual meeting at its Washington, D.C., headquarters. Subsequent meetings were hosted by Cisco, Novell, Mitsubishi, Siemens, and others.

In a curious political fluke, the GIIC did not enjoy good political relations in Washington with the Clinton administration. The responsible assistant secretaries or relevant officials at the Departments of State and Commerce were especially hostile, worried because the GIIC was a new and unfamiliar Washington-based private-sector group that they couldn't control and because some officials were nervous about its founders' Republican ties. The newer and more powerful players in the U.S. government—the office of the United States Trade Representative and the Federal Communications Commission—were much more predisposed to cooperate. They viewed the GIIC as a proreform ally in the private sector. Despite this history, the GIIC was often viewed in Europe as an American creature. French companies were especially leery of the GIIC. Based on K Street in Washington within walking distance of the

World Bank and the White House, the GIIC was multinational but housed at a conservative American think tank.

Over time, as big companies asserted their organizational power, the GIIC's central concern for developing countries waned. Despite good intentions, only a few developing countries had companies that could keep up the pace with the gargantuan European, American, and Japanese corporations. The developing country companies had far fewer people to spare to track their interests in these new bodies. By contrast, multinational corporations maintained large public policy staffs to track the international dynamics of the alphabet soup of GBD(e), GIIC, WEF, and ICC and to provide guidance and presence for the international networks.

The Global Business Dialogue (Electronic Commerce)

A second business association, the Global Business Dialogue (Electronic Commerce) (GBD(e)) was created on January 14, 1999, partly as a response to the U.S. flavor of the GIIC and the U.S. administration's expansive ambitions. The GBD(e) was designed to concentrate on advancing electronic commerce, although it also was involved in other topics related to the global digitalized economy. Initially seen as the brain-child of former European Union Industry Commissioner Martin Bangemann, the GBD(e) sought to establish a liberal framework or charter that would link private and public actors in a more productive and less antagonistic fashion. Bangemann hoped to create an international constituency to blunt European governments' statist impulses. Reflecting the tenor of the times, the Americans often found Bangemann too proregulation, while the Europeans found him too liberal (Cowles 2001b). Ultimately, the EU's Bangemann Report was widely regarded as a progressive, high-powered strategy to bring Europe into the information age.

The first chair of the GBD(e) was Thomas Middlehoff of Bertelsmann of Germany, and he was followed by cochairs AOL chairman Steve Case and Time Warner chairman Gerald Levin. GBD(e) also included Jean-Marie Messier, head of Vivendi Universal (France), Cobus Stofberg, CEO of MIH Group (South Africa), Yong-Kyung Lee, chair and CEO of Korea Telecom Freetel, Gustavo Cisneros, chair and CEO of Cisneros Group

(Venezuela), and Michio Naruto, special representative of the Fujitsu Board (Japan).

The principal purpose of the GBD(e) was to remove obstacles to electronic commerce. Its issue areas and their lead companies included the following:

- Authentication and security (led by NEC Corporation),
- Consumer confidence (Daimler Chrysler),
- Content (Walt Disney Company),
- Information infrastructure and market access (Nortel Networks),
- Intellectual property rights (Fujitsu Limited),
- Jurisdiction (EDS),
- Liability (Telefonica),
- Protection of personal data (Toshiba Corporation), and
- Tax and tariffs (Deutsche Bank).

The GBD(e) eventually concentrated on alliances with regional organizations in emerging markets, especially those in Asia (such as ASEAN). Although it began with electronic commerce, the GBD(e) expanded its focus outward into other contentious issues as well, including security and the digital divide.

The Digital Bridges initiative, launched at the annual meeting in New York City in April 2000, was the GBD(e)'s first venture into distributional issues. Its purpose was to "ensure that the benefits of the Internet are more widely realized around the globe, [and] to identify and support efforts to shape policy environments that are critical to the growth of the internet" (GBD(e) 2000). The GBD(e) emphasized that all stakeholders—government, nongovernmental organizations, private foundations, and multinational institutions—must all work together in partnership: "every country should be a part of the information technology revolution." The GBD(e) also began an effort to identify best practices that simultaneously benefit both the private goals of companies and the development goals of countries. The report examined three categories of corporate activities—philanthropic, commercial, and mixed. It found that GBD(e) members were especially concerned about the sustainability of their projects and their capacity to select the most appropriate technology to contribute to commercial and development goals.

General Business Organizations

International business leaders also worked through more general business organizations to advance their interests. One of the most notable was the World Economic Forum (WEF), which during the 1990s became the premier meeting place for international wealth. The council members of the WEF are comprised of CEOs or chairmen from Royal Dutch Shell, Nestle, SAP, Itochu, Toshiba, TRW Coca-Cola, Petronas, and major companies from India, Saudi Arabia, and South Africa. At its 2001 annual meeting for example, the WEF reported that "1,000 top business leaders, 250 political leaders, 50 academic experts, Nobel Prize winners, and some 250 media leaders came together to shape the global agenda. Together they address[ed] the key economic, political and societal issues in a forward looking action-oriented way" (WEF 2001).

The WEF had a half-dozen initiatives in 2001, among them Global Corporate Citizenship, Business and NGOs: Developing a Dialogue, and The Future of the Multilateral Trade System. A global digital divide task force was created at the 2000 annual meeting, and it developed a framework for action, "From the Global Digital Divide to the Global Digital Opportunity," which was submitted to the G8's 2000 Okinawa Summit (World Economic Forum 2000). Many of its proposals were adopted during the summit and its ideas became part of the final report. This framework for action enumerated policy actions and initiatives that each stakeholder group could undertake in addressing the divide. Following the G8 Summit in July 2000, the task force continued its work, and as a result of discussions during the 2001 annual meeting, it developed concrete proposals in the domains of education, connectivity and regulatory frameworks. At their 2002 annual meeting in October in Brussels the GIIC and the GBDe, issued a joint statement committing those bodies to cooperate on digital divide matters but did not commit real resources.

Based on interviews with participants in the early meetings, the impetus for the World Economic Forum's digital divide task force grew from concerns expressed in the 2000 meeting by John Case of AOL, Bill Gates, and a few other, mainly American executives. Case and his team pressed this issue in the WEF but also in other bodies like the GBD(e). For example, in the second quarter meeting of the GBD(e) in Spain, Case argued to his fellow CEOs that they needed to concentrate on three issues of major importance rather than trying to do everything (personal communication 2000). He urged them to focus on building online trust, securing the Internet, and addressing the global digital divide.

In an attempt to expand its global influence, the WEF's leaders reached out to older organizations. The WEF partnered with the International Chamber of Commerce (ICC) in April 1999. The ICC had already cooperated with the GIIC on other international ICT issues. A venerable organization that grew from a meeting of business leaders in Atlantic City, New Jersey, in October 1919, the ICC has representatives from Belgium, France, Italy, the United Kingdom, and the United States. The ICC continues to remain active in seeking common positions for international business (Kelly 2001). One of its latest initiatives was a global compact with the United Nations Secretary General in July 2000 that brought leading multinational corporations together to agree on a set of voluntary principles on child labor, the environment, and labor union freedoms. The ICC has also produced a document on ICT that urges liberal policies and a substantial private-sector role. When the ICC took an explicit organizational position in favor of private-sector leadership in the information revolution, it did so against the background of its members' growing concern about global economic uncertainty.

In summary, the various achievements of the WEF, the GBD(e), and the GIIC and their forays into distributional issues have fallen well within the confines of core private-sector concerns. Differences were mainly matters of tactics and alliances, and intraprivate divergences were negligible.

These dynamics are not unique to ICT business associations. Writing in *International Studies Quarterly*, Xiawei Luo (2000, 149) points to the evolution of international technology organizations over long periods of time. She finds that the founding principles of these organizations have shifted from advancing the concerns of specific individual industries, solving specific technical problems, and promoting professional exchanges and profession building to broader societal goals, in which "technology should be regarded mainly as a means toward broad social development goals to advance equity as well as efficiency in the global society."

Nor is the rise of international organizations during following World War II unique to ICT groups (Salamon and Anheier 1996). Nongovernmental organization growth has been rapid across the board, and a marked acceleration of the founding of private-sector organizations has been noted in recent years (Reinicke and Francis 2000).

Private-sector ICT ideas coincided with NGO priorities in some ways: both shared skepticism about government digital divide leadership, and both believed that new innovative solutions were required. However, the two groups also had sharp differences. NGOs believed that the problems of the global disadvantaged were exceptionally urgent and politically catastrophic. This was less so for most private companies, which defined the digital divide more as an opportunity whose resolution would take years. NGO representatives often insisted that the private sector be defined as one key element in reducing the divide, although not the principal element, and some NGOs saw private firms as a big part of the digital divide problem. The greatest disagreements among governments, private companies, and NGOs revolved around NGO involvement in the global digital divide negotiations, as NGOs sought to legitimate their influence.

Differences among the private groups were overshadowed by similarities when viewed contextually within the full range of NGOs, governments, and other private bodies. Overlap among the membership of the bodies (drawn from corporations like Fujitsu, NEC, AOL, Nokia, and Siemens) indicates substantial overlap in their ideological positions. The groups differed on tactics, political strategy, and alliances but not on fundamental matters of principle.

The expectations and attitudes of the private bodies converged around their common understanding of the digital divide. According to these international organizations,

• The digital divide is partly the result of deleterious government policies of the past. It is the result of monopolies, centralization, statism, and civil pathologies, including rampant corruption.

• The private sector is best placed to resolve the inequities of the digital divide because of its superior efficiency, its investment resources, its leadership transparency, its global reach, its political neutrality, and its innovations.

• The digital divide is best defined as a digital opportunity, since *divide* has negative connotations and subverts positive action.

• Governments that become involved in the issues of the digital divide should be junior partners, restricting themselves to infrastructural activities such as fostering education, creating promarket regulatory frameworks, and designing and implementing laws and institutions that protect private property. Governments should not set targets for universal service, engage in direct ICT production, restrict international trade, or engage in redistributive activities like taxation or transfer payments.

• Intersectoral partnerships between private companies, NGOs, and government are important for sharing information and perspectives, as long as they achieve the above conditions.

A Strategic Restructuring Perspective: Global Networks in Action

Our strategic restructuring perspective reveals how interest groups work through a variety of networks and institutions to pursue common goals. The social networks created internationally through these bodies parallel those we saw created nationally among the information champions. This led to restructuring old relationships and creating new ones. For example, Fujitsu established a deliberate leadership role in the Global Information Infrastructure Commission (GIIC) and in the Global Business Dialogue (Electronic Commerce) (GBD(e)). Michio Naruto, a particularly savvy and effective Fujitsu leader, was the point man and strategists in both bodies. Backed by a capable staff in Washington and Tokyo, he exerted influence on issues like intellectual property, an issue area that he led for GBD(e). America Online chair Steve Case and his team actively pursued AOL's interests across various organizations. A rare French player was the CEO of Vivendi; Jean-Marie Messier was designated as a European leader who joined in the digital divide discussions and took a leadership position in the World Economic Forum (WEF). The business leaders, like their counterparts in the NGO sectors, operated within a highly networked international social milieu and moved easily and fluidly from one node in the network to the next. Indeed, it isn't clear whether one should treat the GIIC or the GBD(e) as a solid institution or as a specialized, amoebalike network with different nodes called GIIC, WEF, or GBD(e). The truth lies somewhere in between a network and a traditional organization—a *netstitution*. Before I define this concept in greater detail, let me suggest several complementary notions of international networking.

We can consider the GIIC and the WEF as hybrid forms for a variety of reasons. Perhaps the most important flows from their goal to create new knowledge and trust among their most senior leaders. This goal is achieved through regular high-level interactions across more fixed institutions. These bodies function with extremely thin administration and management structures and miniscule budgets. GIIC and GBD(e) have virtually no permanent structure and operate within the administrative resources of the annually rotating chair. Given their members' enormous wealth and power, one might anticipate a well-funded organization with a big secretariat and flush budget. Yet the contrary is the case. As the first administrative head of the GIIC in 1995, I spent much of the time trying to beg or borrow money to keep basic administration functioning. Today the GIIC includes companies worth hundreds of billions of dollars and yet operates with only a single permanent staff, seconded from Siemens. Annual dues of $30,000 can barely sustain the organization. The GBD(e) has no permanent staff but a small, part-time office in the tiny New England state of Vermont.

The networked nature of the new coalitions is revealed in the following GBD(e) summary (gbd(e) 2000): The organization "identified more than one hundred relevant forums in which to advocate the Paris Recommendations, and GBD(e) members also voiced [its] role on e-commerce in some thirty conferences with a worldwide or regional coverage. Special mention must be given to be GBD(e) interventions in events organized by the WEF (World Economic Forum), the OECD (Organization for Economic and Cultural Development), the ICC (International Chamber of Commerce), the BIAC (Business and Industry Advisory Committee to the OECD), the WIPO (World Intellectual Property Rights), the EU (European Union) institutions, the U.S. government, the Japanese Keidanren (Federation of Economic Organizations, Japan), and the Singapore IDA (Infocomm Development Authority). The voice of the GBD(e) was not only heard at these major organizations; it also presented a major policy paper to the G-8 nations on the occasion of their 2000 Summit in Okinawa, Japan."

At the same time, the GBD(e) and the GIIC have a curious lack of commitment to the long-term utility of the organizations. It seems as if each annual meeting has implicitly on the agenda whether the CEOs want to continue it one more year or fold their tents and move on.

There are serious debates about the meaning of these current trends in global networks. Writers like Jessica Mathews (1997) believe that there has been a major change in the world political economy and that these new, less hierarchical global networks are decisive for global society. Observers like Margaret E. Keck and Kathryn Sikkink (1999) believe that the new networks are important but are more skeptical about their inherent capacity to transform the world. A provocative study by Wolfgang Reinicke and Francis Deng (2000, 27) finds substantial increases in the number and impacts of these networks. They identify six contributions that global policy networks make for global governance, including the following (Reinicke and Deng 2000, 27):

• "Contributing to establishing a global policy agenda and offering mechanisms for developing a truly global public discourse in which to debate that agenda,

• "Facilitating processes for negotiating and setting global standards,

• "Developing and disseminating knowledge that is crucial to addressing transnational challenges,

• "Creating and deepening markets,

• "Providing innovative mechanisms for implementing global agreements,

• "Addressing the participatory gap by creating inclusive processes that build trust and social capital in the global public space by furthering transnational and transsectoral discourse."

While these two authors may be overly optimistic about the positive contributions these networks are making, they have correctly identified the potential roles that have direct bearing on the functioning and effectiveness of international ICT groups like the GBD(e).

In their chapter entitled "Capitalism, Sectors, Institutions and Performance" J. Rogers Hollingsworth, Philippe C. Schmitter, and Wolfgang Streeck (1994) identify various organizational forms that coordinate

activities in modern capitalism. They recognize these forms as a reper-
toire including associations, firms, states, and other hierarchies contributing to stable economic governance. They define informal networks
as "loosely joined sets of individuals or organizations in which transactions are conducted on the basis of mutual trust and confidence sustained
by stable, preferential,... and legally nonenforcable relationships"
(Hollingsworth, Schmitter, and Streeck 1994, 6).

Given the rapid evolution of bodies like the GIIC and GBD(e), I believe
that they represent a transitional phenomenon between formal, hierarchical business associations and more ad hoc ephemeral market engagements—a phenomenon that I term *netstitutions*. These bodies play an
important role in the strategic restructuring process by providing the
fluidity, informality, and enhanced trust for change-oriented political
coalitions that are necessary to alter norms, expectations, and decision-
making rules within an international regime that is still under construction. Some of these groups may harden and become more
institutional—with stricter role definitions, real staffs, and enforcement
mechanisms. Others may wither away. Still other business netstitutions
may remain as they are, at the level of corporate strategic alliances
(Cowhey and Aronson 1993). The degree to which they are institutions
or networks is not trivial for subsequent ICT evolution and should be
the subject of further research.

Distributional concerns were also addressed in these institutions. The
number of digital divide transactions and partnerships has grown
steadily, leading to relationships among a variety of institutions. Innovatively exploring these new relationships, Nanette Levinson (2000) identified over forty instances where new interorganizational arrangements
were formed around digital divide activities. The organizations included
NGOs, governments, and private-sector organizations, with the links
among governments and the private sector most numerous.

Levinson (2000, 6) points out that of the forty-two relationships she
surveyed through the *New York Times* archives (where she found the
term *digital divide* used 217 times between 1996 and 2001), "ten cases
involve nation-state governments, two include both nation state government agencies and the private sector, and an additional thirteen have
private-sector organizations participating without national government

participation." Of the thirteen private-sector actors, six were linked to NGOs, three to international organizations, two involved towns or cities, and two linked firms with educational institutions in developing countries. It is this actor heterogeneity that is most impressive: "Governments at all levels, private-sector organizations, nongovernmental organizations, and not-for-profits are all participants in new interorganizational arrangements related to bridging the digital divide" (Levinson 2000, 6).

Levinson's forty-two minicases had five distinct purposes, notably "promotion of access through the provision of equipment, training . . . technical expertise and funds; and sharing information" (6). She cautions that networks and their goals are not necessarily permanent; they can change the number of actors, the terms of participation, the power balances, and even their goals. Such arrangements, "can and do fall apart" (6). We should reserve skepticism about their longevity and achievement in ICT distribution until we have gathered more data.

Individuals and Netstitutions

Networks, rules, regulations, and norms do not appear automatically. International agreements and netstitutions are created and sustained by individual leaders who recognize and seize opportunities and make things happen. These are the policy entrepreneurs and early innovators that scholars have noted in other sectors (Rogers 1995). These information champions lead constituencies and create coalitions. They work through formal and informal networks to extend them from local meetings to global conferences.

The GIIC's formation, for example, was the result of an identifiable handful of individuals who brought the group together from scratch; without these individuals neither the GIIC nor the GBD(e) would have been formed. Among the key leaders were people like Diana Dougan and Martin Bangemann, who set out to create what social theorists like Frank Fukuyama and Robert Putnam refer to as social capital. The relentless driving force behind the GIIC was Dougan, who was then director of the Information and Communications Program at the Center for Strategic and International Studies (CSIS), a somewhat right of center think tank that is well regarded in Washington. She hosted public lectures and exclusive seminars for visiting ministers and top business and other leaders from Europe, Asia, and Latin America, who in turn welcomed their exposure to D.C. decision makers. As Dougan tells the story, she had arranged several meetings for visiting Japanese business leaders and another for their counterparts from Europe and believed that continuing such interactions on a more permanent basis would develop a unified private-sector leadership to advance the global information and communications revolution. Government, she felt, was more in the way than in the lead and had to be educated if countries were to take advantage of the new technologies. She believed strongly too that developing countries had to be introduced into the mix.

Dougan's own background prepared her for this position. As a child she lived in Korea, where her father was an economic advisor to the government. She worked in the private sector in the cable industry in New York and served in the U.S. State Department as the senior international ICT official, first appointed to that position by President Reagan. And she then spent years in the think-tank world of CSIS. In other words, she possessed the experience in the private, public, and nonprofit sectors that seemed especially valuable in a time of convergence. Most of all, like her counterparts at the national level in Brazil, Ghana, and China, she possessed a passionate vision for her enterprise and would not take no for an answer. She contacted large numbers of leaders to build up interest and convince industry leaders like the CEO of Mitsubishi, Harvard-educated Minoru Makihara; Les Alberthal, CEO of the information giant EDS; senior World Bank officials like Vice President Jean-François Rischard; and other global leaders to join into her vision. She soon recruited developing country visionaries like Hisham El-Sharif from Egypt who lent their experience and energy. In her own way, Dougan was the international counterpart to the national information champions we have seen in Brazil, Ghana, and China. She was creating the organizational opportunities where social capital in the ICT sector could be built up into social networks and later "invested" in technical and commercial networks (see www.giic.org).

The European counterpart to Dougan was EU Commissioner Martin Bangemann, the man behind the GBD(e). He too had a forceful personality and a potent vision that new technologies were extremely powerful but were being blocked by old rules and regulations. As

Commissioner for Industry, he had seen the new ICT firms in action and the lumbering dinosaurs that the national telecoms of Europe had become. He sought a means to open the eyes of European leaders to recognize the importance of these powerful new technologies and the commercial revolutions that would follow in their train. He was what Andrew Moravcsik (1999) calls a "supranational entrepreneur" exercising a new form of statecraft through his command of international networks.

The report that he steered through the EU on the knowledge society in Europe, called the Bangemann Report, was far reaching in its vision of a more economically liberal society served by the latest in modern ICT. Bangemann also recognized that the Americans were moving ahead to seize the lead on digital issues, especially electronic commerce, and that Europe couldn't afford to be left behind. He called on governments, regulators, and industry to start working together to create a new global framework for communication for the next millennium (European Commission 1998).

Drawing on the support of the German media company Bertelsmann and others, Bangemann made plans to gather together a group of senior private executives to address these issues of convergence and ICT innovation. Another business organization, the Trans-Atlantic Business Dialogue (TABD), was already available as a model for a private-sector-led network for policy dialogue and accelerated business-to-business communication on an international scale. Indeed, corporate leaders of the TABD from both sides of the Atlantic were instrumental in launching the GBD(e) (Cowles 2001a).

On June 22, 1998, Bangemann hosted more than 100 representatives from industry at a meeting in Brussels. While the group was mostly European and included the CEOs and board members from Nokia, Bertelsmann, Eutelsat, and others, it also included high-level executives from American and Japanese firms like MCI, NEC, and Toshiba (Cowles 2001b). Bangemann continued to push his vision of an expanded and central role for the private sector, and the GBD(e) was officially launched on January 14, 1999, drawing explicitly on the structure of the TABD.

What Bangemann and Dougan had in common was a shared vision of the potential contribution that the private sector should and could make to the information revolution and a personal commitment to create a counterbalance to government's preponderant role. Both were coalition builders as well as determined policy shapers. They were both aware of the other's work (Martin Bangemann served on one of the first GIIC-sponsored events, at the G8 ministerial meeting in Brussels in 1995). But while their vision put the private sector in the lead, curiously neither Bangemann nor Dougan was from the private sector. Rather, they functioned as policy entrepreneurs who used their institutional positions to prod and persuade private-sector leaders to form new networks and pacts that were most directly in the private sector's interest. Private-sector leadership of global profit-making companies did not always come from within the private sector.

The G8 Meetings

Leaders from the most powerful nations in the world have met annually since the early 1980s to find consensus on difficult international issues. These Group of Eight (G8) summits allow heads of government to develop common understandings on important issues. There is no permanent organization, and meeting preparations are done by prime ministerial or presidential staffs that prepare documents and escort leaders to the summit (the G8 staff have been given mountain-climbing nicknames, "sherpas"). While many issues appear on agendas, several issues are always given high priority. The host country plays a large role in selecting that year's major topics. In 2000, when Japan was the G8 host, one of the topics the Japanese selected was the global digital divide.

Why would the Japanese put this issue on the table? According to Japanese national advisory experts I interviewed, the digital divide choice reflected a compromise between powerful bureaucratic interests. Foreign aid officials saw it as a chance to gather new financial resources, while for trade experts it was a chance to highlight Japanese exports. Foreign ministry officials knew the topic would be well received in Washington and in other G8 capitals.

The Clinton administration had its own reasons for wanting this particular issue on the table. During a briefing I conducted for President Clinton and President Mbeki of South Africa at the White House in the summer of 2000, I discovered that the American president was deeply interested in and knowledgeable about ICTs in developing countries. He referred to his experience with Internet connectivity in poor Indian villages and the need for developing countries to have a central clearinghouse for globally relevant ICT experiences.

Interviews with former White House staff would later convey the sense that the time had been ripe for a digital divide initiative. When the Japanese placed digital divide issues on the agenda, the White House convened an external advisory group. The group was composed mostly of corporate representatives who suggested programs, policies, and projects that the president could announce in Okinawa. Chaired by senior economic advisor Gene Sperling and cochaired occasionally by a senior representative from the National Security Council, the advisory group was viewed by the White House partly as a way to move the Clinton-Gore ICT agenda forward and partly as a means to make their president look good by showing up to the summit with real "deliverables," not just rhetoric (personal communications with White House officials 2000–2001).

The several dozen member White House advisory group included key companies like Microsoft, Hewlett-Packard, AOL, IBM, and Intel. The group met often in the vice president's formal ceremonial meeting room and in a curious juxtaposition discussed futuristic ICT strategy surrounded by elaborate nineteenth-century chandeliers and other decorative excesses. The group included representatives from nonprofits, university ICT and development groups, the Internet Society, and more occasionally the World Bank and the Global Business Dialogue. The White House advisory group was cochaired by a senior AOL executive and by Zoe Baird, president of the Markle Foundation, a long-standing nonprofit philanthropic organization that supports progressive media and information initiatives and U.S. digital divide projects. The appointment of an NGO leader as cochair probably came about because of Baird's personal ties to the Clinton administration and because some senior staff people at the White House thought having an NGO on board seemed sensible for symbolic reasons.

Constructing this kind of mixed advisory group was not unprecedented. Company representatives and NGO leaders often serve in permanent and ad-hoc advisory capacities to the executive branch.

Interviews with former officials indicate that while the White House did want private-sector commitments and ideas in its proposals, it was concerned that too much private-sector influence would "make the whole thing look like we were shilling for the big companies. . . . We needed to get some balance and perspective for this thing" (personal communication 2001). The White House did not want the initiative to become just a platform for companies to sell their wares abroad. Still, most of the meetings were taken up by the constant search for private-sector commitments to new investments and other novel activities. Although there was virtually no interest in discussing the extent or the reasons for the digital divide, some educational, health, and other nonprofit initiatives did find their way into the package.

NGO representatives sought an independent strategy to convince others that they were more than mere symbols of grassroots viability. With Baird and her staff leading the charge, an NGO-inspired memo went to the senior White House staff, arguing that NGOs had as much concrete knowledge about ICT conditions in developing regions as corporations did and that NGO contact networks were equally extensive (personal communication 2001). The memo also argued for NGOs' legitimacy in regions where corporations are often criticized.

Two major results came from the White House meetings. The traditional result was that President Clinton took a portfolio of new programs with him to Okinawa—programs that addressed the global digital divide. The unexpected outcome was that nonprofit members of the American advisory group legitimated their ongoing and coequal involvement. They even convinced White House staffers to press their foreign government counterparts to admit foreign NGOs into the G8 discussions. Admittedly, the NGO groups were pushing against a sympathetic, politically inclined staff in Washington. It was the administration's last year, and it seemed an easy concession. But by itself, the White House would not have insisted on the new NGO status.

In early summer 2000, the White House agreed to propose unusual, nontraditional participants for July's G8 meeting in Japan. Instead of a summit attended exclusively by senior government officials or a few private-sector executives, the White House officials pressed the G8 on a new participation formula, a "constitutional" pact that proposed delegations with private, governmental, and nonprofit organizations. It was an unusual proposal. Interviews have revealed that the other G8 countries were not wholly opposed, including the United Kingdom and Canada, which supported the idea. However, the political cultures of the French and Japanese found NGOs less legitimate and a potential "loose cannon." Nonetheless, these countries decided to go along with the program.

Equally unusual was the agreement to invite a few developing countries into digital divide discussions. Nine countries were invited to attend, including Brazil, China, India, Senegal, and Tanzania. Including developing countries in the G8 process was a progressive step, even though the topic of the meeting was, in principle, closely driven by their needs. In other G8 discussions, whether of debt relief, foreign aid, or related topics, the G8 had not invited as many developing countries to participate formally. The upshot of these constitutional or governance norm adjustments was unprecedented participation by formerly excluded interests. Unfortunately, participation by the developing countries was sporadic and unfocused.

The lackluster performance of the developing countries in Okinawa and again in Genoa in 2001 reflected several factors. This collection of very heterogeneous nations had never before met on these issues as a distinct group and lacked the time to develop policies necessary to turn latent interests into international laws and norms. Second, indigenous elites were still struggling to persuade their own governments to make domestic ICT changes. Third, no nation or leader—not China, not Brazil, not Algeria—emerged as a spokesman. South Africa's Mbeki spoke out but did not and probably could not launch a sustained campaign. In contrast to developing country discussions during the oil price spikes of the 1970s, it was not obvious what benefits might flow from greater developing country cooperation.

The period leading up to the G8 meeting was defined by maneuvers to find counterparts and establish common positions. The U.S. business groups worked with overseas business groups to prepare positions on how to strategically restructure the discourse and the institutions governing distributional issues. Government representatives continued their endless dialogues with other governments. The nonprofits found creating and sustaining dialogue more difficult. They lacked the money and personnel needed to attend the many meetings and also lacked the institutionalized cross-national mechanisms and informal networks that could meet and focus on issues of common concern.

This lack of focus in the developing countries and nonprofit networks was in stark contrast to the endless strategizing and maneuvering that went into the formalization of an e-commerce grand alliance, which is a supreme example of new elite business network formation in action. Institutions like the WEF, the GIIC, and the GBD(e) were invited to solicit views from the private sector and submit a report to the G8. Knit together mainly to influence electronic commerce rules, the following organizations came together to create the Alliance for Global Business: GIIC, the International Chamber of Commerce (ICC), the Business and Industry Advisory Committee to the OECD (BIAC), the International Telecommunications Users Group (INTUG), and the World Information Technology and Services Alliance (WITSA). Their members pressed for legitimacy, seeking contacts with NGO representatives and G8 counterparts in other countries. There was no obvious counterpart in the nonprofit sector.

The other challenge was for northern NGOs, governments, and private interests to reach out to the nine developing country government representatives. The lack of previous engagement and inadequately mobilized ICT institutions made the task difficult. An opportunity for intermingling occurred in a meeting hosted by the South African government for G8 and G9 representatives. One main message conveyed by developing country delegates was that they lacked adequate resources and process knowledge. The latest meetings seemed to these leaders to represent part of the ongoing problem in international negotiations, particularly in ICT negotiations: their countries had been rarely consulted or brought into the process. Following the anti-WTO "battle in Seattle," developing country delegations had grown even more sensitive about their representation.

What Did the G8 Process Achieve?
Seen against this background of other nondistributional issues like foreign investment and IPR and e-businees, what were the year's digital

divide achievements? In 2000, the G8 leaders pledged to work together on four issues:

- To foster policy, regulatory, and network readiness,
- To improve connectivity, increase access, and lower costs,
- To build human capacity, and
- To encourage participation in global e-commerce and other e-networks.

To achieve these goals, government heads set up a task force to suggest concrete actions that could include a new institutional facility, better coordination, or more money. The World Bank was asked to set up a small two-person secretariat, and strategy responsibilities were assigned to a tripartite committee—a private company (Accenture consulting), an intergovernmental agency (the U.N. Development Program-UNDP), and a nonprofit body (the Markle Foundation).

However, by July 2001, the G8 had made very little progress. It had done little to achieve its original goals—to reduce the gap or to expand digital opportunity. In the meantime, separate institutions continued to address access problems on their own. Evidence of concrete new activities or greater coordination was sparse. Private-sector sales and investment increased. NGOs educated, trained, and agitated. Governments legislated and regulated. For Italy's G8 meeting, the Bank-based secretariat produced a document that covered basic issues—connectivity and access, wealth and content creation, e-commerce and e-government, knowledge sharing and creation, human capital development, network and regulatory readiness, and policy submissions. The document read as if written by several committees, without punch or focus and without a guiding vision or philosophy—reflecting the realities of G8 protocol.

The G8 governmental effort did mobilize high-level interest around the world, which helped legitimate the digital divide as a serious public policy concern. By creating a process with a beginning, middle, and end, it focused the attention of key world actors who might otherwise have remained sidelined. The contribution of Accenture, the Markle Foundation, and the UNDP was a document differing somewhat from the more conventional wish-lists and hortatory government statements that abound in this field. It set forth sound analytic and empirical underpinnings that had previously been excluded. In addition to national case studies and demand-side sectoral analyses, it argued that unless leadership elements reached out across sectors, national strategies were likely to fail.

The G8 process also brought legitimacy to developing countries that wished to participate in the international discourse. This is a significant achievement. However, newly enfranchised developing countries were unable to craft a coherent vision in the process. They complained of insufficient consultation and insisted on the importance of building human and local infrastructure capacity. But the G8 process revealed the structural weaknesses of those at the economic and political periphery (Krasner 1991). In the final analysis, when viewed alongside the radical changes in property rights, efficiency rules, and governance norms, the digital divide changes were modest. And the definition of the divide was often the five-point private sector version cited above. There were few serious, far-reaching equitable proposals. There has been very little material impact.

The one-year span between the two summit meetings may be too short to expect major commitments or change. We may see widespread changes in the coming years, as the seeds sown during the first year blossom. The prospects for substantial distributional change however do not seem likely. The government of Canada took up the divide mantle and struggles to maintain some forward momentum. In the absence of explicit progressive interventions, the fundamental structural dynamics will worsen developing countries' global positions. The economic downturn and the terrorist attacks appear to have undercut digital divide commitments even further. The Bush administration has shown no appetite for a multilateral ICT initiative.

These conclusions about the modest, technologically defined outcomes of the 2000 and 2001 G8 initiatives repeat expert conclusions about the one other G8 meeting that was devoted to the information revolution, a G8 ministerial conference in 1995. In a blunt assessment, Heather Hudson (1998, 16) reported that "many GII initiatives from the conference despite their sensible socioeconomic objectives . . . are technologically driven, with the major instigators being the technical ministries, telecommunications operators, and equipment suppliers. These . . . initiatives assume that converging technologies will result in . . . both social and economic benefits. Yet this assumption needs to be carefully examined." Not much collective action emerged from the 1995 meeting, nor did much collective material support build for new projects. The same was true six years later.

Responses to the Digital Divide at the Level of the Firm

Companies and firms pursued their interests through collective means, and they pursued individual, firm-oriented activities as well. The large collective activities draw scholarly attention. The actions of individual firms and trade associations are less visible to outside observers but are equally if not more important in the long term because the day-to-day practices of many firms pursuing their individual interests can become the de facto rules of the game as executives respond rationally to threats and opportunities around them. Strategic restructuring occurs slowly as companies redeploy assets, move into markets, and shift investment capital. Distinct business practices are always important and are particularly important during periods of regime decay and reconstruction.

Based on company files, interviews with digital divide leaders, and public and nonpublic documents, I found that corporate executives pursue three main digital divide activities:

• *Commercial activities* Commercial activities are initiatives designed to contribute directly to the company's bottom line. Goals include expanding market share, increasing earnings or profits, and lowering costs through sales of goods and services.

• *Philanthropic activities* Executives engage with the divide through initiatives with noncommercial goals (such as "community development" or "helping the poor"). Executives do not believe that these actions will directly help their bottom line in the short term.

• *Mixed activities* Mixed activities are efforts that combine elements of the two previous goals. Often focused on education and training, these are investments or expenditures intended to build the wider population's cognitive base. The classic case is the Cisco Academy.

Companies pursue all three goals simultaneously. They are most likely to pursue philanthropic and mixed initiatives in the country or region where they already have commercial operations. Commercial and mixed categories are not insubstantial. Microsoft in 2000, for example, contributed more than $21 million ($8 million in cash and about $13 million in software) to more than 95 community-based projects (The Journal 2001). Still, I argue that by far the greatest aggregate contribution that the private sector makes to advance ICT diffusion is through pursuit of its commercial interests; the levels of corporate philanthropy are relatively modest compared to commercial activities, which exceed several trillion dollars of world sales and investment.

Calculating developmental impacts of investment is an age-old, still imperfect art form. The International Finance Corporation (IFC) (the private investment arm of the World Bank) spends countless hours evaluating investment impacts. When a project does not demonstrate positive linkages, the IFC board rejects it.

Some will argue that *any* foreign private investments or sales will distort equitable economic growth, but that argument is too categorical. A plethora of evidence reveals that equitable growth with direct foreign investment is possible. Others claim that any investment in ICTs will automatically reduce the digital divide and enhance economic growth. The Rodriguez and Wilson (2000) findings cited in chapter 6 suggest that ICT investment alone is not directly correlated with economic growth. Collateral investments across different sectors are necessary. The solution to this dilemma is not to decrease total investments but to create ways for developing countries to attract more and more effective ICT investments from domestic and foreign sources.

Let us assume that any capital investment in the information and communication technology industries has the potential to build a country's ICT capacity and improve its development chances. The potential for positive sectoral contributions may be especially great in the poorest countries, where direct foreign investment and local investments are negligible. Until investments are made in basic infrastructures, other information revolution benefits remain unavailable. Private investments in those basic infrastructures are especially valuable. Whether capital flows to infrastructures or to mainframes and minicomputers, it can contribute substantially to poor countries' digital development.

Still, some ICT investments and sales can make better contributions than others, since each commercially viable project will affect development in different ways. One project may have narrow purposes and modest development impact. Another may even have negative societal effects through pollution or regressive income impacts and hence is less desirable locally. Other multipurpose commercial activities may have high scalability and a positive multiplier effect. In a perfect world all ICT projects would feature positive developmental and corporate outcomes. In the real world, this is unlikely to happen. Developing countries will seek projects that maximize positive development impacts, and filtering the best from the worst requires negotiations among different local and foreign actors.

In the following sections, I draw on three separate business reports (two of which I participated in) to give the reader a sense of the kinds of projects that private firms undertake to address the digital divide and digital opportunities and the ways that they articulate their purposes (Clugage et al. 2001; Global Business Dialogue 2002; Global Information Infrastructure Commission 2001). The findings are drawn for the most part from self-reported commercial activities from surveys. My purpose is not to be exhaustive but to indicate the kinds of distributional activities in which private companies engage.

Commercial Activities

In the French company Alcatel's (GBDe 2002) response to the GBD(e)'s information request, for example, the firm indicated that it wanted to give developing countries "a chance to jump ahead in their economic development thanks to rapid deployment of a powerful new kind of infrastructure—that of high-speed access to the Internet, which opens the door to the Information Society." This is difficult, the company says, since "many countries have vast isolated areas, are generally underpopulated and difficult to reach." They point out that "by forming partnerships with network operators and service providers such programs will bridge both regional and global needs." To achieve this, Alcatel pointed to such commercial ventures as Skybridge, "a low earth orbit satellite project that will provide multimedia Internet access via a small antennas linked to the global information infrastructure." At the user end of Internet access, which is largely dependent on the availability of local content, Alcatel is working in Senegal, "building African-based application domains ... by supporting a number of innovative local-content services open to the general public. Applications address traditional trade . . . [and] health care." In subsequent interviews, Alcatel managers described the importance they place on finding and working with local partners.

Philanthropic Activities

Corporations also provide charitable aid through a variety of instruments. For example, the AOL Corporation created the AOL Foundation, a private philanthropy arm of the corporation. Some companies' charitable foundations donate money, while other corporations donate equipment or staff time for charitable causes.

Almost no assessments have been made of corporate philanthropic engagement with the digital divide. Most reviews of these and other digital divide activities are not catalogued nor analyzed closely. An interesting and revealing exception by Julie Clugage, Din Heiman, Joe Schock, and Alexandra Shapiro (2001) provides more value-added analysis of corporate digital divide actions. In their *High Tech Firms and the Global Digital Divide* (also called the Haas survey, after the Haas School of Business at Berkeley, California), eighteen ICT companies were surveyed to ascertain corporate commitments to digital divide activities. The Haas survey divided the corporate activities into three categories— information exchange, education and training, and physical projects. They found company efforts that addressed the digital divide directly to be sporadic and limited. Particular initiatives were modest and publicized in a lackluster manner. In contrast to the aggressive NGOs, "most private-sector companies . . . have not yet found the way to translate the public momentum into specific strategies and programs, either as a group or as individual firms" (2). After reviewing the level of corporate involvement, the survey's authors found that "The short list of internationally pro-active companies is just that: short" (2). Better-performing companies included Cisco, HP, IBM, and Microsoft.

The survey methods were imperfect, as the authors admit, and their findings are based on publicly available information, but the survey does suggest that company-level initiatives are quite limited. Most companies still view their global digital divide initiatives more as philanthropy and less as strategy.

Mixed Categories

Not only does Alcatel claim to be active in commercial activities to reduce the digital divide, but it is also "active in the field of professional training by sponsoring and contributing to the . . . management of the Cambodia Technology Institute, . . . [which develops] local expertise in ICT and create[s] a highly skilled national workforce" (GBDe 2002). I refer to this category of training and education as the mixed category. Training may or may not target one firm, but it does create greater human capital for the whole economy.

France Telecom has adopted a program to interconnect schools, which it calls Scolagora. Its Espace, Ecoles, and Educaroc are said to provide education and training programs. Fujitsu established a Japan-America Institute of Management Science in 1972 in Honolulu, Hawaii, which is said to contribute to "the human and economic development of the Asia Pacific region by educating and training managers in the global economy." For its part, Cisco is well known for its training programs. Cisco operates in over 108 countries around the world, with roughly 10,000 trainees in class on any given day. Concentrating on training people for ICT industries, Cisco is pursuing new initiatives to provide academies for the two-dozen poorest countries in the world.

The IBM corporation in partnership with APEC, has sought "to develop and implement the APEC E-Commerce Readiness Initiative," a self-assessment guide to which IBM "provides consultation with business to develop action plans to improve the environment for e-business and electronic trade. . . . In Mumbai, India, IBM has developed a partnership with [a charitable institution and school] to start a computer center that will provide students with training in computers that will enable them to pursue advanced education and acquire gainful employment."

Grassroots Activities

A distinctive group of truly innovative companies does not fit perfectly in these three categories. These companies are driven mainly by social motives and typically do not seek maximum profits. They try to serve their members or providers and may or may not receive subsidies. They include Greenstar, PeopLink, and Souk. PeopLink, for example, seeks to expand the amount of economic surplus kept by craft producers in developing countries when they sell on international markets. The company provides small local craft persons with digital cameras, which they use to photograph their work; the photographs are uploaded onto Web sites, complemented with descriptions of the artistic process and locale so that potential buyers learn more about the context of the product. PeopLink, like Souk, tries to reduce the cut taken by middle men so that the producers can earn more (see www.peoplink.org).[1]

In Search of Explanations

How can we explain why companies engage in digital-divide related commercial and philanthropic activities? How do companies themselves conceptualize the problem at hand? Do companies from all over the world share the same interpretations?

An opinion poll commissioned by the GIIC in the first quarter (2001) to ascertain its members' views on the digital divide sheds light on these questions. The questionnaires elicited over ninety responses to twelve questions from companies the world over, providing an excellent window on the world of corporate ICT engagement in developing countries. Also, since the overlap between the GIIC and other leading bodies of corporate influence is substantial, one can capture the attitudes of more than one private-sector group. Still, this survey is far from perfect. It polled the members of a particular organization and hence is skewed toward the sectoral and geographic representation of its members. It is difficult to draw complete inferences from such a modest sample size. The GIIC has far greater representation among infrastructure and equipment manufacturers than media companies. Latin America is probably under represented. Nonetheless, the GIIC has been a leading player in the new international regime, and it is valuable to know what its members believe. This survey represents one glimpse into the thinking of some leaders among the international private-sector corporate elite.[2]

Why Does the Private Sector Care?

From every region of the world, corporations that participated in the survey stated that the search for market opportunities was their principle motivation for caring about the global digital divide. African and Latin American corporations agreed that the next most important factors were new labor sources and competitive threats. Asia Pacific respondents ranked the factors somewhat differently for second, third, and fourth, ranking social obligations, competitive threats, and new labor sources, in descending order. The differences between Asia and other developing areas may reflect political culture differences and the inclusion of Japan, a highly industrialized country, in the Asia sample. The African and Latin American countries were most skeptical that social obligations' played a major role in shaping private-sector interest.

How Important Is the Digital Divide?

The responses to the question of the importance of the digital divide perfectly tracked the relative wealth of each region, with Africans claiming it very important and North Americans ranking it lowest. In descending order, the rankings were Africa, South America, Asia Pacific, Europe, and North America.

Is the Digital Divide Narrowing?

The survey's findings about the widening or narrowing of the digital divide were unexpected, given the previous answers. Europeans and Americans were likely to answer that the divide is substantially widening, while Africans and Latin Americans were less likely to believe it was widening. This difference may reflect more accurate digital divide information among Northerners, or it may express Southern optimism about rates of ICT diffusion.

What Does the Digital Divide Mean?

When private-sector observers think of the digital divide, what comes to mind? For nearly one-third, the divide means "differential access to information and communication technologies." That was the leading response from all regions. The second most popular answer (with 28 percent of the total) was the developed-developing country gap, followed by urban-rural and business opportunity.

From Analysis to Action: Who Should Do What?

After these definitional questions, the survey turned to policy and strategy questions. In response to the question "Who should bridge the digital divide?" respondents placed the responsibilities almost equally on government and the private sector (about 18 percent and 17 percent, respectively). These two were followed by development organizations, civil society, and NGOs, each with about 12 percent of the tally, followed by foreign aid and philanthropy. The findings suggest a shared view across countries that public or private donations were not the main solutions to the digital divide.

Obstacles to Bridging the Digital Divide

The respondents concluded that the main barriers to bridging the divide were infrastructure (19 percent), poverty (16 percent), bureaucracy (14 percent), and protectionism (13 percent), with culture and corruption tied (11 percent). The companies recognized that the challenges to resolving the digital divide are truly multifaceted and that neither hard nor soft infrastructures alone were sole barriers. Culture and class conditions also had to be tackled together.

Needed Public Policy

The policies necessary to vault these several barriers were also complex. In descending order, survey respondents identified basic education, IT skills building, open investment policies, privatization, independent regulators, open access mandates, and consumer protection rules as the policy steps most needed to reduce the divide. It is striking that there was such agreement that the top solutions were "softer" capacity-building measures and rules of the game.

In the discussions that followed the release of the survey results at the Annual Meeting of the GIIC in Dublin in April 2001, there was general agreement among the commissioners that the different regional perceptions revealed important material and policy differences across regions (personal communications 2001). The digital divide was locally unique, so a single appropriate response did not exist. Solutions needed to be tailored to local needs.

Conclusion

This chapter began with the question "How, why, and through what means did private-sector ICT companies place distributional issues so prominently on the global policy agenda, and what have been the consequences of these actions?" What answers emerge from this analysis?

How and What?

The "how" question is straightforward conceptually, though more nuanced in actual operations. Companies addressed the digital divide by acting in concert with others or by acting alone through their own individual corporate programs. The latter ranged from the Cisco Academies that provide technical training to people in more than one hundred countries to one-time philanthropic activities by giants like IBM or Fujitsu. Companies sometimes join together to create a small program of three or four firms and also join larger organizations like the Global Information Infrastructure Commission or the World Economic Forum. Many larger companies engage in all three activities simultaneously. Much more work should be done on the collective action challenges that confront these groups and the ways they try to overcome them. My research identified several distinct categories of activities in which the firms engaged, including commercial, philanthropic, and mixed.

Why Are Private Actors Engaged with the Digital Divide?

Answering the "why" question is also more complicated, as we saw earlier, and both structural and contingent factors play their parts. The evidence demonstrates that companies came to the digital divide issue driven mainly by commercial concerns. The rhetorical commitments to improving global ICT access reflected the rising awareness among corporate strategists of the importance of emerging markets. One newspaper's business section announced unambiguously in early 2001 that tech firms were going overseas to China and markets in Europe in response to the slowdown in the United States (Backover 2001). The chief research officer at IDS, a well-known ICT consulting firm, predicted hardware and software spending would grow by 11 percent in Europe to $310 billion and by 10 percent in Asia to $190 billion (Backover 2001). The numbers are even higher for individual companies. Cisco was showing 100 percent to 150 percent annual growth in customer bookings in China, South Korea, and Japan. ADC Telecommunications said its foreign-derived revenue in 2001 were expected to jump from 22 percent to 30 percent, exceeding its U.S. home-based growth for the first time. European and Japanese ICT firms reveal similar success in overseas markets, in the United States, and in developing countries.

This positive perspective was also expressed in the views of trade associations. The body representing large U.S. electronics companies (the American Electronics Association) produced a wide-ranging study of major overseas markets that found that while the current computer use per capita was highest in the United States, Australia, Norway, and Canada, the per capita *growth* was highest in emerging markets (1991–1996): China (497 percent), Russia (452 percent), Ukraine (470 percent), Brazil (371 percent), and India (355 percent). The top two countries in cellular phone growth were Brazil (363,000 percent) and China (34,000 percent) (AEA 1997).

Emerging markets' importance is unequivocal according to corporate leaders (personal communications), the GIIC survey, and published materials. Company spokespersons have interpreted the digital divide as a rallying cry to expand market share, reduce costs, and enhance profits. They want to sell ICT services and goods in developing markets and buy low-cost inputs from developing markets. They have sought better intelligence concerning emerging digital markets and have tried to establish a strong brand presence. Corporate strategists are starting to see that among leading firms growing proportions of their current investments and sales have been in Asia, Latin America, and even Africa. The trends suggest that overseas markets will be even more significant in the future. Resolving the digital divide could be very good for international business.

Corporate leaders also became interested in the global digital divide through their earlier investment in domestic programs. The chair of the board of one of the world's largest companies confided to me that his company's interests in the international dimensions of the digital divide grew from its experiences with the domestic digital divide: "It wasn't much of a jump for us to see the same problems were coming up in other countries where we operate." The company is now deeply engaged in educational initiatives at home and abroad. Once several large, visible companies are engaged, others are likely to imitate.

There is some but not much evidence that company executives were worried that governments might unilaterally impose distributional requirements. Developing countries have already demonstrated they can get companies to achieve additional equity outcomes. Brazil and India, for example, require companies to show how they will meet teledensity and distributional targets when they bid on telephone licenses. Executives sometimes worry that down the road the ICT gap may create social unrest, turmoil, or even violence, but this does not appear to be a major preoccupation.

We are our brother's keeper, whether he lives next door or in the next country. Corporations give money to charitable causes in local communities around the world. By the late 1990s, more and more corporate executives, including Bill Gates, began to define the global digital divide as one of those deserving causes that required them to become more engaged. Furthermore, one found among these corporations an almost naïve belief in the transformative potentials of technology. Top executives in the field spoke with genuine almost joyous enthusiasm about technology's ability to make a difference in the lives of the less privileged. Ethical considerations thus played their part, though a secondary one.

These are the underlying incentives that led companies to engage with the digital divide. However, they fail to explain the exact *timing* of their involvement, which I believe hinges on two additional factors. The first was the 2000 and 2001 G8 meetings. Company executives saw collective actions by political leaders of the world's most powerful states as an opportunity to seize or as a risk to protect themselves against. Governments needed companies involved; companies needed to be involved. The G8 process was very much an action-forcing event on the digital divide.

Second, I believe elites in the private sector took up digital divide issues when they did because they were following a logical policy sequence driven by their own internal corporate priorities. Their first priority was to lay down bedrock property rights, efficiency guidelines, and governance norms in this new information era. Once these basic principles were in place and securely applied to commercial matters, companies had the luxury of expanding their policy portfolios to consider secondary matters, including equity and access. This was the most rational sequence to follow from their perspective, and they sought to make solutions to distribution problems consistent with the new property and efficiency principles. Market solutions were their optimal answers to the divide. Other more progressive or radical proposals might have undercut competition and property rights. Companies wanted to ensure that non-commercial approaches to global ICT inequality did not clash with the new regime's macro precepts. The timing of the G8 topic expressed and reinforced this logical sequence.

Yet few serious students of political economy would be surprised by a simultaneous shift toward commercialization *and* equity in a market. Modern capitalism has always advanced fitfully along two fronts. Karl Polanyi (1944) referred to this as "double movement"—capitalist zeal for cost-cutting micro efficiencies and worker and consumer commitment to protect their incomes and ways of life from market excesses. The tangled discussions of equity, legitimate participation, efficiency, and property rights are not unique to ICTs. From Seattle to Senegal, these issues are at the core of modern political economy. They will continue to be at the front and center of the global political debate over ICT diffusion.

Digital Divide Balance Sheet

The material and political commitments to reducing the digital divide have been modest, especially when we draw the distinction between reducing the digital divide and enhancing digital opportunity. Reducing the divide requires a conceptual framework to define the issue in a particular way. Such a redefinition would require leading institutions—the World Bank, the bilaterals, the G8, and private-sector leaders—to admit a growing structural gap, to measure that gap, and to estimate the costs needed to narrow the gap. However, little consistent effort has been made to quantify the gap. Instead, the term *digital divide* is defined more narrowly to be more acceptable to conventional thinking. The gap becomes an "opportunity," a space between a country's current ICT status, its status a few years ago, and its potential for future growth. Success becomes defined in simple terms of expanded ICT use. Neither conception of "gap" or "opportunity" has brought forth a serious effort to set targets or goals to be measured against future performance. If there have been halting efforts to redefine access beyond infrastructure in order to include content, training, and political consultations, as I suggest in chapter six, they rarely have been integrated into an approach to increase effective access that includes goals and timetable. (There are some modest efforts under way to link ICT diffusion with the U.N.'s millennium goals).

The political will and financial investments directly committed to the digital divide outside the market have been modest in their own terms and extremely modest when compared to private-sector (and governmental) commitments to other aspects of regime and market creation—property rights, efficiency rules, and governance norms. Rhetorical commitments to reducing the divide were less than ambitious; material commitments did not even match the modest language. It is not clear that any *net* resources have been added to combat the digital divide beyond what individual institutions would have done anyway.

The more the private sector sells its goods and services in developing countries, the more the current opportunities grow. The more they sell goods and services, the greater the likelihood that the gap between information haves and have-nots will also grow, at least in the short to medium term. Certainly, the absolute levels of ICT use in developing nations will continue to rise above their current miserable levels. But evidence from chapter 6 points to a continuously growing gap, at least until price, ease of use, education, familiarity, purchaser income, and other factors change sufficiently to let poor countries start to catch up through truly effective access.

The gap becomes a particularly acute problem because of a parallel shift in global responsibilities—the expulsion of state agents from central international ICT roles. The international ICT regime has shifted decisively toward privileging private initiatives. The once commonly heard term *universal service* is less prominent today.

To date, the leading initiatives have been inadequate for going beyond the immediate requirements of the market to meet the broader necessities of society. The strategic restructuring that international corporations pursue will enhance digital opportunities, but will not reduce digital divides in the short term. The efforts of the private associations like the GIIC and the GBD(e) have been unable to seriously address, much less stop, worsening e-inequality. These sharply skewed inequalities are growing worse. The anomaly I identified is apparent: there have been radical restructurings of rules governing property, efficiency, and governance. There have not been radical restructurings of rules governing access and equity. The commitments have been more rhetorical than real.

Another analytic challenge is whether the restructuring of the four policy balances will actually enhance or reduce equity. There are contradictory trends—a rising floor and a rising gap. The floor will almost certainly continue to rise. We are only 2 to 5 percent into the information revolution; the excluded constitute 99.5 percent of Africa and 98 percent of Asia and Latin America. The real question is whether the restructuring of property rights, efficiency, and governance will be sufficient to slow the digital divide as it raises the floor. Will the targeted digital divide activities be enough to raise the "poor floor" as the distance between poor and rich grows? If the answer is no, the need for distributional programs will remain urgent. The risk is that what in the last chapter I called Wilson's law (the costs of network exclusion are multidimensional, increase over times, and are borne by the excluded and society) at the national level will also assert itself at the international level. The stark realities and complexities of growing international inequality contradict the compelling simplicity of Metcalfe's law (the power of the network increases exponentially by the number of computers connected to it).

The world community now confronts a deficit of collective goods, collective will, and collective action. None of the actors is doing particularly well in this regard, and failures abound among private markets, public agencies, and nongovernmental organizations. The NGOs in the south and north lack the unity and the clout to turn the situation around. The private sector has the resources and clout but does not have enough at stake to compel the imaginative solutions that the world community requires. High-level cross-sectoral leadership that is willing to bring the key actors together to expand digital opportunity and reduce the divide is not yet well developed. The poor countries themselves have failed to come together to seize the issue and make it their own by defining clear policy options and promoting them internationally. Their domestic institutional weaknesses and lack of familiarity with the quick-changing issues undercut the prospects for successful prosecution of ICT distributional issues globally. It is unlikely that developing countries, especially poorer nations like Ghana, can do it alone. Yet until they seize the moment and define the challenges more effectively, the efforts of the G8, private companies, and Northern NGOs will make little headway to reduce the global digital divide.

8
Conclusion

This exercise in comparative political economy has led me to several conclusions about the nature of the information revolution in developing countries. Some of these conclusions conform to my original expectations of what I would find in Brazil, Ghana, and China. Other conclusions disconfirm my expectations, while still others grow from answers to questions I did not initially pose. But in the end, all the conclusions emerged from the logic of the strategic restructuring framework and the ways that it organized the comparative materials to explain interactions among structure and agency in the remarkable sequential invention of the information revolution in many locales around the world.

The most important findings of my research can be summarized as follows:

• Remarkable similarities exist across all countries in the direction, pace, and sequences of ICT evolution.

• Structures and their links to institutions play a determining role in ICT development.

• Individual ICT champions have had an unexpectedly major influence on Internet diffusion, and multinational corporations have had a surprisingly modest influence.

• The underlying distributional realities of ICT resources are complex, and achieving effective access to ICTs is more difficult than achieving formal access.

• Thus far ICTs have very limited effects on developing countries as a whole but are centrally important for the small national elites. Countries vary widely in their capacities to create an indigenous culture of knowledge innovation in support of the wider diffusion of the information revolution.

• The strategic restructuring model is a robust characterization of the complex causal processes of political, institutional, and policy changes that have occurred across the ICT sectors.

Strategic Restructuring

The strategic restructuring framework that I applied to Brazil, Ghana, and China argued strongly against technodeterminism and instead built on the assumption that ICTs were scarce resources introduced into these societies by different actors that each had very different interests and asymmetric capabilities to use ICT. Because these different groups usually had different interests and perspectives, they argued and negotiated with one another about the optimal path of Internet and other ICT diffusion. Diffusion was thus a difficult *process of negotiation*, with different interests preferring different channels and pursuing different goals and possessing different understandings of the ways the technologies should be used. In each country, some groups seized onto new ICTs and sought to embed them deeply in large formal structures like state-owned enterprises or ministries that they themselves controlled. Other groups employed less hierarchical, more distributed channels, like nongovernmental organizations or small enterprises. Other interests tried to quash the new ICTs altogether, fearing their political and commercial disruptions. And various people wanted to use the ICTs for their own unique purposes: start-up entrepreneurs wanted to deliver new services and goods in new ways; local policy advocates wanted to use ICTs as the means to advance their agendas; others wanted to help the poor, do research, or get rich.

Whatever their purposes, most eventually discovered that these technologies could be subversive because they required their users to reform existing institutional rules and regulations in order to use them most effectively. Pursuing some goals with ICT often meant making tradeoffs with other desired organizational ends, and this pursuit was always contentious. The result was the clash of contending visions within and between institutions. But slowly, over the course of the 1990s, we see the restructuring of some old institutions and the creation of new ones. Two large alternative discourses eventually emerged in most countries—a liberal diffusion model (more bottom up, transparent, and controlled by individuals and small organizations) and a more authoritarian model (more top down, embedded in big powerful institutions, and less consultative). For the moment, in this period of transition, the information revolution remains a highly contested terrain that is not easily tamed by any party (Wilson 1997). Over time, these institutional changes may alter the basic structures of the societies; but not yet. The strategic restructuring model helps us capture these ongoing dynamics more effectively than the techo-deterministic model.

There Are Many Similarities and Continuities among Developing Countries

The Direction of ICT Changes   In every single developing country that I visited, the direction of change was away from a centralized domestic state monopoly and toward a decentralized network with greater private and foreign competition. Without exception, nations' information and communication technology industries were becoming more liberal. No country moved from the then-current statist monopoly regime toward even greater state ownership, greater state control, more monopoly, and reduced foreign ownership. Whether in Communist China, mixed-economy Ghana, or nationalist Brazil, after fierce political contention among the interested parties, the core group that held decisive political power agreed to liberalize. Brazil and Ghana even recanted the holiest of holies and permitted foreign private firms to compete in the mainline telecommunications markets. Of course, the three countries' national political, economic, and educational leadership groups had their own priorities and chose to resist and embrace ICT changes in different ways, at different paces, with different winners, and with different consequences. But the direction of their compromises and victories was toward institutional and economic liberalism. These commonalities reflect and are partly shaped by the broader trends in globalization, which pushed accelerated liberalization in all markets, not just ICT markets.

The Sequences of ICT Changes   Each of the countries went through an identical sequence in which the pressures for information and communication technology reforms (especially for the Internet) began in the education and research community and moved to a new firm that offered the first open, nonexclusive networks available to all who could pay; to growing competition among many firms within the market; and finally toward even greater turbulence with consolidation as well as competition as the dot-com frenzy collapsed. These sequences occurred in most countries between the late 1980s and 2000. In each of the four stages, the national elites had to meet similar policy challenges. An early challenge for Brazil, Ghana, and China was to convince senior officials to pay serious attention to the Internet but to keep them from becoming so involved that they stifled the new medium. Also, governments around the world had to resolve conflicts over whether the state PTT would be allowed into the new ICT markets and on what terms. Another early challenge was determining how to design a national Internet backbone and deciding who would own, manage, finance, and build it. Different elites took different positions on these challenges, generally reflecting their own institutional status.

The Pace of ICT Changes   In all countries, the pace of technology diffusion was extremely rapid and remained so throughout the 1990s. Internet growth rates in China, for example, have shown a doubling every six months. Not nearly as rapid but still accelerated have been the institutional and policy changes that must occur if technological diffusion is to be sustained.

The Limits of ICT Penetration   My research also reveals a curious duality that partly accounts for the ongoing debates over the importance of the Internet in developing countries. On the one hand, the Internet's direct impacts on citizens are extremely limited in breadth and depth, and the impact of telephones is only slightly greater. (Broadcast media impacts are demonstrably larger.) Internet penetration rates of less than 1 percent are common in the developing world, and these low numbers greatly limit the possible influences that ICT can have overall.

On the other hand, the Internet is having substantial impacts on the organizational and political capacities of the privileged groups in these countries—on their professional and personal ties overseas and on some elements of national economic performance. The result is a huge domestic disjuncture between the high access enjoyed by the very few privileged and the low access permitted to the population at large. Maintaining a sense of proportion between the relationship of ICTs to these two different demographic groups is essential for accurate reporting (and theorizing) about ICTs and developing countries: the impacts on the many are low, while the impacts on the few are much higher.

Structure Is the Primary Determinant of Diffusion Patterns; Structure-Institution Relations Are Also Important
This book began with the assertion that structure determines most of the diffusion of information and communication technologies. The richer a country, the more ICT it possesses. By the end of the book, the strength of this assertion was still robust. In the main, the hypothesized relationship between structure and ICT held consistently.

If the big structural relationship is incontrovertible, detailing the exact relationships among structure, institutions, and outcomes was more difficult, analytically and theoretically. As Peter Hall (1999) argues, the principal dilemma facing structuralist and institutionalist approaches is to specify precisely which variables have the most impact on strategy and economic outcomes, including ICT sectoral outcomes like diffusion. The power of focusing on the structure-institution nexus is to be able to identify broad patterns of cause and effect that flow from structures to institutions, which by their nature are difficult to specify precisely. In this study, I was able to identify some structure-institution performance linkages. For example, in a very poor country like Ghana, with its classically underdeveloped structures, the ICT institutions work very poorly. Institutions that should provide incentives for people to lead the revolution have failed, and they lack the material resources and authority necessary to succeed. Universities have poor facilities and poor resources. Coordinating bodies coordinate poorly. Diffusion rates are respectable, but all other things being equal, the sector has performed more poorly than it would have in a less poor country with more resources.

By contrast, middle- or upper-income developing countries like Brazil have institutions that are more efficient and resource-rich. They can (though they do not inevitably) reduce transaction costs and uncertainty more effectively and efficiently than in poorer nations. Brazil's CNPq and the Ministry of Communications under Sergio Motta are two examples. The availability of skilled middle-class people in the Brazilian social structure, like the parents of many of today's information champions, have greatly shaped the demand and supply of that country's ICT and also the demand for and supply of institutions. Analytically, we can point to structure-institution links and describe them in some detail. Conceptually, we can define and delimit them. Theoretically, we can argue how institutions and structures interact to shape particular outcomes. Empirically, it is more difficult to pinpoint exactly the causal paths, reflecting, in part, the reality that considerable autonomy exists across different levels, that institutions are not merely the pale expression of structure, and that structure does not shape every aspect of institutional structure or personal behavior.

The fact that poor countries have poor institutions at a moment in history when, perhaps more than ever before, human volition and institutions can shift comparative advantage, is a sign of hope and despair. There is hope for nations whose political authorities and policy entrepreneurs can pull together the coalitions necessary to accelerate decisive institutional adjustment and create incentives that lead people to launch and sustain structural reforms. But if the poor institutions associated with poverty are determinative, then even buying the best ICT technology off the shelf and shipping it to Accra or Dacca is not going to produce sustainable institutional or structural reforms. Here the optimists need to hope that the technodeterminist approach is correct and my strategic restructuring model is wrong. The *Economist* implicitly supported my approach, however, when it concluded its own survey of "the New Economy" by writing that "the East Asian economies are likely to benefit more from IT than Africa or Latin America. Africa lacks many of the economic and legal institutions needed for a thriving information economy, and Latin America is well behind Asia on educational standards. East Asia has . . . adopted many of the right policies to enable it to gain from the use of IT" ("Survey of the New Economy," 2000, 38).

As important as structure is for determining ICT outcomes, when viewed cross-nationally it cannot be seen as a major determinant of rapid *change* in individual sectors, since the underlying economic and social structures are not changing as rapidly. The events I have analyzed over the past decade and a half resulted not from domestic structural changes but from intrastructural change. In the period under review, no country goes from quadrant one to four of our original illustration (see figure 2.1) or even from quadrant three to four. It would be interesting to sketch alternative near- to medium-term scenarios that might lead toward the structural changes among agriculture, industry, and services associated with development of a knowledge society. Can we imagine the sequences and paths over which ICTs diffuse as people seek to solve particular industrial or policy problems? Might these eventually lead to the creation of a culture of knowledge and innovation and eventually to the institutional reforms necessary for a developing country knowledge society to emerge?

Individuals and Leadership Made a Greater Than Expected Contribution to the Initial Structuring of Internet Diffusion in Developing Countries, and Multinational Corporations Made a Smaller Than Expected Contribution

The complexity of relationships between structures and institutions in determining ICT outcomes was reproduced again and again in the complexity of the relationships at the other end of the macro-micro spectrum—between individual actors and institutions. In this light, two important and related surprises emerged in all three countries studied. First, the influence of individual policy entrepreneurs—and later commercial entrepreneurs—was much greater than anticipated. Local leadership made a big difference. Second, the influence of multinational corporations was lower than I thought at the beginning.

A large body of theory and evidence suggests that the considerable economic power of elites in multinational corporations operating in developing countries should play a big role in Internet diffusion. However, in none of the three countries analyzed here did corporations exercise much influence in Internet markets, especially in the early years. By contrast, the influence of local leaders was much greater than many social science models anticipated, especially in the early stages of market structuring. Individual women and men, sharing similar characteristics of social background, behavior, and political networks, made choices as policy brokers and commercial entrepreneurs that proved decisive in the evolution of the Internet industry.

I conclude that the interactions among structure and agency are important to understand, and these emerged with special clarity in the case studies. Structure and agency were mediated in part through the medium of political culture—the norms, values, and patterns of behavior that characterize a national population. In Brazil, for example, the heavily skewed social structure was linked with a national political culture that facilitated interactive elite networks and devalued mass mobilization, which yielded highly skewed ICT distributional and competition outcomes. China's contemporary Communist system retains elements of the earlier Confucian political culture and interelite cooperation and competition and has facilitated the state-enforced norms that accelerate digital commercial networks and repress networks used for political purposes.

Concentrating on structure and agency relations allows one to ask how much freedom of action potential innovators have to pursue their interests in the ICT sectors. There is perhaps a paradox. The weaker the institutions (and the poorer the country), the greater the influence individuals have to construct singlehandedly a true information initiative, since fewer institutions and groups are available oppose it. But the very absence of institutions makes such transformative efforts difficult to sustain. Even if a benevolent dictator should try to construct the perfect information society, he or she cannot do so in the absence of enabling institutions, especially enabling institutions across the three critical sectors—private, public, and nonprofit.

Critical intermediation occurs between institutions and individuals through the formation of new social networks, yielding new patterns of sustainable social interaction that form the basis for the subsequent technical networks. The evidence is sufficiently compelling and different from the prevailing technodeterminist paradigm that I have come to think of these network effects in axiomatic terms: "Social networks determine technical networks." Or more precisely, a strong iterative relationship exists between social networks and technical networks. I argue that the social predates and trumps the technical. But the precise story in any given national setting depends in part on where one enters the dialectic.

The role of local agency and social networks is so important that it suggests a need to reconceptualize how we explain the origins of the information revolution. The diffusionist model defines the information revolution as a process by which information and communication technologies spread outward in concentric circles from a core to the global peripheries. Linda Garcia (2001) refers to this as a top-down deployment model. In this model, agency and innovation are originated at the global center; these standards are then exported and applied locally. I have concluded that this deployment model misses the main underlying societal, institutional, and individual dynamics that are driving forward the information revolution around the world.

Certainly, deployment is occurring. Certainly, organizational, commercial, and policy frameworks are developed in Silicon Valley and then exported or carried abroad by firms. At the same time, these exported forms of ICTs represent only potential and not inevitable realities. China and India chose very different ways to structure their local ICT markets, reflecting deep differences of culture, history, and institutions. My point here is that social scientists should start their investigations by reviewing deeply rooted indigenous practices and institutions. They should study the way in which local social forces that grow from those practices and institutions selectively restructure local conditions to take advantage of some aspects of imported knowledge, even while resisting others.

But a diffusion model concentrating on how the applications spread from Silicon Valley to Bangalore or Beijing through the movement of trained individuals does not fully capture the importance of indigenous initiative and context. We can regain local context if we define the information revolution as a global process of *sequential local innovation and restructuring*. This reconceptualization is compatible with the strategic restructuring approach and suggests that local innovators—often but not exclusively with overseas training—restructure their local environment through local networks. In the process, they create a local

information revolution that selectively borrows some but not all lessons
and resources of leading-edge nations.

The Digital Divide Is Important, Complex, and Difficult to Overcome in Developing Countries

There is a difficult conundrum at the heart of the global information
revolution: developing countries are demonstrably and rapidly gaining
much greater access to the fruits of the information revolution, but at
the same time, they are being left further and further behind the developed countries. Digital opportunities are fast growing, *and* digital divides
are fast growing. (One is reminded of the old folk saying, "The hurrier
I go, the behinder I get.")

The long-term implications of this double dynamic are not clear. First,
it is not clear how the dynamic will affect the development process as a
whole. We have some preliminary ideas, some provisional evidence, and
a lot of anecdotes. It is especially unclear how this double dynamic
between greater opportunity and a growing gap will affect the medium-
to long-term relationships between developed and developing countries.
Optimists point to the digital opportunity (implicitly conceptualized as
the gap between where a country was a few years ago and where it is
today). They can point to Internet increases of 50 percent every six
months in some developing countries. It is difficult to conceptualize a
faster rate of growth. Pessimists point to the 18–23 figures: developing
countries' ICT use is growing by 18 percent annually, and developed
countries' use by 23 percent annually. Will this ICT gap reinforce the
growing income inequality gap? Within countries, will this translate into
lower social cohesion? Greater social tension? The answers hinge mainly
on the political interpretation given to these trends by politicians in
developing countries and the policies they pursue to address gaps and
opportunities. But optimists and pessimists should be clear about the
empirical realities underlying their claims. It does a real disservice to conceptual clarity and remedial action when apologists for one side or the
other claim that the digital divide does not exist or that digital opportunities are not advancing.

Curiously, in none of the case study countries did I find strong evidence that the institutions at the center of the information revolution had

been significantly reformed in their openness to nonstate actors. Policy making still resembled the closed iron triangles of the past, though there was some evidence of greater transparency. Some groups were better able to make their preferences known to those responsible for ICT allocation as in Brazil. Also, democratization in many developing countries brings greater legislative leverage over executive agency operations, including ICT diffusion, as elected legislators press civil servants and other officials to serve the poor. It isn't yet clear how increased legislative power has translated into greater state responsiveness to popular communication needs. Liberalization of state-owned monopolies and new competition certainly has greatly increased the incentives and opportunities for private companies to seek out more consumers on their own; market responsiveness is much greater. But market responses are only part of the overall challenge of *effective* access, which still requires much more grassroots public education, careful regulation, and R&D funds, just as it requires support for hard infrastructures.

Capital Investment Is Not Enough; Countries Need ICT Politics

Adequate capital investment is a requirement for rapid ICT growth and for rapid economic growth more generally. But poor countries need more than financial capital; they need politics. The political logic of causality in the strategic restructuring model is supported by the economic findings in chapter 6. The conventional neoclassical logic (which is followed by many ICT enthusiasts) is that a dollar invested in ICT will lead easily to more than a dollar return in economic development. They insist that greater investment in ICT produces greater economic competitiveness and growth. In fact, the data show that is not the case. Greater investment is a *necessary but not sufficient condition* for economic growth. To transform an investment stream from a dollar of investment into one dollar and fifteen cents of growth requires that the stream of dollars, pesos, or rubles first pass through the dense elite networks and interlocked institutions described in chapters 3, 4, and 5. Notably, the interaction among the private, public, and nonprofit institutions stimulates and guides the capital flows so that the right resources reach the right needs, in the right amounts and forms, at the right time. In developing countries, this process is especially problematic, and intersectoral coordination is difficult. In all countries, this coordination requires the right kind of leadership and politics. Winners from the new patterns must be rewarded, and losers compensated or neutralized.

Nourishing a Knowledge Culture

The strategic restructuring framework found that the information revolution in general and diffusion more specifically results from the intersection of complex factors to create what I call a knowledge culture in which political actors pull together incentives, education, innovation, and resources into new institutionalized relationships. A developing country's capacity to create a knowledge culture hinges not on keeping politics out of the picture but on bringing the right kind of proreform, proinnovation politics *into* the picture and creating an ensemble of values, expectations, norms, and incentives that impels more and more individuals to want to create and become active, engaged members in a knowledge society. Again and again in this book, we have seen energetic and visionary individuals coalescing into networks and coalitions and then into political forces whose purpose is to neutralize the old antireform political coalitions that favored state-owned centralized monopolies and to create the necessary new norms, expectations, and incentives that support innovation.

Political forces in China and Brazil have been able to create coalitions that preferred more distributed and competitive ICT industries. Other coalitions of politicians, civil servants, and others opposed them. In China, for example, some coalitions wanted a much greater role for private companies, and they were only partly successful. In the end, however, more so than in Brazil, the state companies remained the most powerful in the Chinese information and communication markets and their staff and supporters have been able to block large-scale privatization. Still, politics in Brazil, Ghana, and China formed the glue that held together the component elements of technology, capital, training, and regulations so that the seeds of the information revolution could be sown and take root in local soil. The politics of strategic restructuring created the new relationships, norms, and expectations that allowed new political forces to protect the slow buildup of the new culture across several sectors over a number of years.

Taken together, the strategic restructuring perspective that emerges in this volume is at odds with the conventional wisdom on Internet diffusion. The widely accepted view is that the information revolution began in Silicon Valley or Cambridge, Massachusetts, was bolstered in Los Angeles and New York, and is now spreading outward in concentric circles from the northern hemisphere to the southern. But information technologies do *not* have an autonomous life of their own that drives them ineluctably forward. The motor forces of the modern technological revolution are not defined in cross-border flows of modern technology and money.

These assumptions are simplistic, reductionist, and misleading, however appealing they are to a certain diffusionist logic and a U.S.-centric view of the world. This volume shows that the central resource of the information revolution—the Internet—was not parachuted into poor lands from "out there." It was not brought into emerging markets by multinational corporations. The Internet was not the gift of the World Bank or other international bodies. Instead, my evidence shows that the information revolution is a local work of local construction. Local women and men in Brazil, Ghana, and China prepare the soil for change, plant the seed, and tend and cultivate the growths. Local people prune the institutions and nurture new expectations. The information revolution is created inside countries by handfuls of local people who construct social ties with one another across many institutions and sectors over many years. As they come to recognize their common interests and operational concerns, these Brazilians and Chinese develop common ICT strategies aimed at bottom-up liberalization. But once they start to act on their strategies, the information champions discover that they are opposed by others with very different interests and preferences, and their strategies are contested at almost every step—from beginning to end, from within the state and from within the market. The opponents fight tooth and nail to block restructuring of state-led monopolies. They struggle to block the liberal vision of the information revolution, and out of this struggle between the liberal information champions and their conservative opponents, the information revolution is born. In every country I examined, champions are eventually able to gain enough leverage to restructure ICT institutions and policies, and the revolution is launched.

This book provides less evidence of the detailed sectoral adjustments and reforms beyond the confines of the ICT industries. Strategic restructuring contention over scarce ICT resources in other sectors like agriculture, health care, transportation, or education has not been a central focus, though this is important work that remains to be done. The structuralists like Bell, Castells, and more recently Hardt and Negri all rightly insist that the real revolution is to be made in those secondary sectors, through the application of codified, modern knowledge to more and more human activities and reflection. As this occurs, the strategic restructuring process will be less elite-dominated and more open to restructurings by the ordinary man and woman in the street.

My findings suggest that the sequential ICT innovations of contending elites around the world that create the information revolution can be best accelerated through national and international support to build up the emerging ICT networks and "netstitutions" that link government, private, and nonprofit institutions. Without these social networks in place and performing well, the technical networks are not likely to deliver the goods that the information revolution promises, especially to those who are already undereducated, poor, and undernetworked.

Where international institutions and rules are radically changed, this too occurs through an analogous process of conflict, cooperation, and struggle in recognizable places and moments—in Brussels and Washington and Seattle. When old international rules are overturned and new ones shoved into place, when rules and institutions are restructured, they all emerge out of political contests between competing coalitions inside and around big important institutions like the World Trade Organization, the Internation Telecommunications Union, and the World Economic Forum. It is not yet clear how the global alliance patterns among technocrats, businessmen, politicians, and mass constituencies will emerge. But the emergence of these new elites in the technostructure, in politics, and in the entrepreneurial economy will almost certainly create new political dynamics in and around the critical knowledge industries (Dalpino 2001, 45–48).

Ultimately, ICT innovation comes down to a matter of freedom. The challenge for analysts and practitioners is to help people discover the far outer limits of their freedom of action to make their place in a chaotic and confusing world of rapid globalization and the information revolution. People everywhere want to know how much space they have to create meaningful and authentic lives. They want to know their local and global opportunities to enhance their communities' positive growth, equity, and democratic possibilities, while minimizing the serious risks of inequality, cultural estrangement, and the corruption of political life. People everywhere understand there are trade-offs to be made and want to know enough about ICTs to make those judgments for themselves. Women and men can make things better or worse for themselves through their human agency, even to roll back some of their structurally imposed limits. More so than in the past, today's dispossessed and their allies can truly widen their choices—*if* they are able to mobilize the vision, political will, and human capacities necessary to achieve greater freedom and the good life in our globalizing world.

Notes

Chapter 1

1. I use *analytic framework* or *paradigm* interchangeably to describe intellectual strategies that guide research problems (White 1994). Dependency theorists predicted that Indian firms would remain stuck in low-level markets. They did not. Indian entrepreneurs were able to carve out more space for themselves in the international division of labor.

Chapter 2

1. An important exception is the work of Wolcott and Goodman (2000) and the MOSAIC team.

Chapter 3

1. See the instructive collection of essays Schmitz and Cassioloato (1992) and Villaschi (1994).
2. See also Wall Street Journal, 7/11/2000, p. A1, "AOL's Big Assault on Latin America Hits Snag in Brazil."
3. See Abears's (2000) discussion of significant participation in her study of grassroots politics in Porto Alegre and Romero (2000).

Chapter 4

1. Research by the author in Ghana, Senegal, and Kenya in 1997 found no one making money at that time, but the companies were staying in.
2. Personal communication, interviews with Ghana government officials later in the decade.

3. This is where the concept we developed in chapter 2 of the Total Computer Costs (TCC) comes in. One quickly recognizes that buying the hardware is only a small part of creating information systems—there are also the hardware costs for the LANS and the salaries of the systems administrator and the technicians who repair and de-bug everyone's machines.

4. March 29, 1999.

5. Interviews.

Chapter 5

1. I began my research in China, fearing that my efforts to identify individual "Information Revolutionaries" would turn up dry, not least because of the geographic and demographic immensity of a 960-million square-mile country with 1.2 billion people. Finding ten revolutionaries in a population that large seemed like finding the proverbial needle in a haystack. I was also worried that the closed nature of the Communist system would make it very difficult to get the information I needed. Both fears were confirmed during my first research visit to China in May 1998a, which was a fruitless effort. However, during the second (and better-organized) visit to Beijing, Hong Kong, and Taipei in February and March 2000 I was able to get data to disconfirm my own original fears. Chinese colleagues were indeed willing to share detailed information about Internet diffusion in China, including on individuals and institutions. Out of the potentially huge population of leaders, the dozens of knowledgeable people interviewed were able to identify a handful of early Information pioneers. A substantial number of the names appeared on most lists of those interviewed, suggesting an underlying common agreement on the information pioneers in China.

2. The most appropriate date is either the moment of legal establishment or the date when the company actually started its operation. Where possible, I note both dates but emphasize operations. By 1995 and 1996, the market barriers to entry for creating an ISP seemed relatively low in light of the anticipated pay-offs.

3. See Ming-Jer Chen (2001).

4. For these and other tactics, see "Big Brains limited" (1999), section 2, p. 32; also Geoffrey Taubman (1998).

5. The Chinese government seems to be relying on "surrogates" in these markets, to get a feel for their commercial dynamics and then report back. Government agencies, which seem to enjoy a high degree of autonomy for experimentation about what is permissible, are able to seek surrogates to test the market.

Chapter 6

1. I want to emphasize here, as I did at the opening of this chapter, that the evidence available to scholars and policymakers is woefully thin. Our findings on

these critical relationships are somewhat at odds with our original expectations and much of the current theoretical thinking and conventional wisdom. It is quite possible that our findings are faulty. But they should challenge other scholars to pursue these questions as more evidence becomes available.

Chapter 7

1. For descriptions of these and others see <www.iicd.stories.org>, <www.PeopLink.com>, <www1.challenge.stockhold.se.challenge.html>, and others. They are the most focused on reducing the Divide directly.

2. In this sample, media and content industries are underrepresented, and traditional infrastructure companies are over represented. In terms of global ICT distribution, Latin America is relatively underrepresented relative of Africa. As Senior Advisor to the GIIC, I made modest contributions to the survey's design and interpretation.

References

Abbate, Janet. 1999. *Inventing the Internet*. Cambridge, MA: MIT Press.

Abears, Rebecca N. 2000. *Grassroots Politics in Brazil*. Boulder, CO: Lynne Rienner.

Adler, Emanuel. 1985. "Ideological Guerillas and the Quest for Technological Autonomy Brazil's Domestic Computer Industry." *International Organization* 40(1): 684–685, 684.

Afonso, Carlos Alberto. 1996. "The Internet and the Community in Brazil: Background, Issues and Options." *IEEE Communications Magazine* 34(7): 62–65.

"AISI-Connect National ICT profile." Available at <http://www2.sn.apc.org/africa/countdet.countries_ISO_code=GH>.

Aizu, Izumi. 2000. "Cultural Impact on a Network Evolution in Japan Emergence of Netizens." <http://www.glocom.ac.jp/publications/Aizu/nete&c.html> (December 2, 2001).

Alford, Roger R., and Roger Friedland. 1986. *Powers of Theory: Capitalism, the State and Democracy*. Cambridge: Cambridge University Press.

Almond, Gabriel A., and Sidney Verba. 1989. *The Civic Culture: Political Attitudes and Democracy in Five Nations*. Newbury Park, CA: Sage.

Alstyne, Marshall Van, and Erik Brynjolfsson. 1997. "Electronic Communities: Global Village or Cyberbalkans?" Paper presented at the International Conference on Information Systems.

American Electronics Association (AEA). 1997. *Cybernation*. Washington, DC: AEA and NASDAQ.

Anderson, Stephen. 2000. "China's Widening Web." *China Business Review* (March–April): 20–25.

Arquilla, John, and David Ronfeldt. 2001. *Future of Terror, Crime, and Militancy*. Santa Monica, CA: Rand.

Asia Cyber Atlas. 2001. <http://asia.internet.com/cyberatlas/2001/> (December 6, 2001).

Aufderheide, Patricia. 1997. "In Search of the Civic Sector: Cable Television Policy Making in Brazil." *Communication Laws and Policies* 563–593.

Backover, Andrew. 2001. "Tech Firms Go Overseas to Expand: U.S. Sends Firms in Search of Hotter Markets in China, Europe." *USA Today,* February 13.

Baird, Zoe. 1999. *Improving Life in the Information Age.* New York: Markle.

"Bangalore and Hyderabad: A Tale of Two Cites." 2000. *India Today,* March 6. <http://www.indiatoday.com> (March 6, 2000).

Barro, Robert, and Xavier Sala-i-Martin. 1995. *Economic Growth.* New York: McGraw Hill.

Bastos, Maria Ines, and Charles M. Cooper, eds. 1996. *Politics of Technology in Latin America.* New York: Routledge.

Baumgartner, Frank R., Bryan D. Jones, and Michael Macleod. 2000. "The Evolution of Legislative Jurisdictions." *Journal of Politics* 62(2): 321–349.

Bell, Daniel. 1973. *The Coming of Post-Industrial Society: A Venture in Social Forecasting.* New York: Basic Books.

Bendix, Reinhard. 1956. *Work and Authority in Industry.* Berkeley: University of California Press.

Beniger, James R. 1986. *The Control Revolution: Techological and Economic Origins of the Information Society.* Cambridge, MA: Harvard University Press.

Benton Foundation. 2000. "China Issues Stiffer Internet Rules on News Reports and Chat Rooms." November 8. <http://interactive.wsj.com/articles/SB973603418226699576.htm> (November 10, 2000).

Bessette, Randi, and Virginia Haufler. 2002. "Against All Odds: Why There Is No International Information Regime." *International Studies Perspective* 2:69–92.

"Big Brains Limited." 1999. *China Economic Quarterly* (second quarter).

Botelho, Antonio Jose Junqueira, Jason Dedrick, Kenneth Kramer, and Paulo Bastos Tigre. 1999. *From Industry Protection to Industry Promotion: IT Policy in Brazil.* San Francisco: Center for Research on Information Technology and Organizations.

Branscomb, Anne Wells. 1994. *Who Owns Information?* New York: Basic Books.

Bratton, Michael, and Nicholas Van de Walle. 1997. *Democratic Experiments in Africa.* Cambridge: Cambridge University Press.

Brazilian Embassy. 2000 Report at <www.brasil.emb.nw.dc.us?secom/econovr.htm>.

Caporaso, James, ed. 2000. *Continuity and Change in the Westphalian Order.* Malden, MA: Blackwell.

Caporaso, James, and David P. Levine. 1992. *Theories of Political Economy.* New York: Cambridge University Press.

Castells, Manuel. 1998. *The Rise of Network Society.* Malden, MA: Blackwell.

Cha, Ariana Eunjung. 2001. "Software Free-for-All." *Washington Post,* September 5: E1.

Chandler, Alfred, 1977. *The Visible Hand.* Cambridge, MA: Harvard University Press.

Chang, Leslie. n.d. "China Releases an Entrepreneur Convicted of Internet Subversion." *Wall Street Journal Interactive,* Issue: Internet/Political Discourse. <http://interactive.wsj.com/articles/SB952284245377547038.htm>.

Chen, Ming-Jer. 2001. *Inside Chinese Business: A Guide for Managers Worldwide.* Boston: Harvard Business School Press.

China Computerworld. 1997. November 17.

China Computerworld. 2000. January 10.

China Education and Research Network (CERNET). 1999. <http://www.edu.cn/english/statistics/edu/edu_99_06.php>.

China Electronic Commerce Association (CECA). 2001. *The Research Report on China's E-Commerce.* Beijing: China Electronic Commerce Association.

China Foresight Project. 2000. *China's Internet in 2005: Six Scenarios.* Silicon Valley, CA: Center for the Future of China, Institute for the Future.

China Internet Network Information Center (CNNIC). 2001a. *Annals of China's Internet Development.* Beijing: CNNIC.

China Internet Network Information Center (CNNIC). 2001b. *A Brief Introduction of CNNIC 2001.* <http://www.cnnic.net.cn/e-about.html> (July 16, 2001).

China Internet Network Information Center (CNNIC). 2001c. *Semiannual Survey Report on the Development of China's Internet.* January. <http://www.cnnic.net.cn/develst/e-cnnic200101.html> (January 15, 2001).

China Internet Network Information Center (CNNIC). 2001d. "Timeline of China's Internet Development." <http://www.cnnic.net.cn/internet.htm> (January 4, 2002).

China Netcom. Company Brochure. n.d. Beijing.

China Online. 2000. <www.chinaonline.com>.

CIA. 1999. "Ghana." *The World Factbook.* Washington, DC: CIA. <http://www.cia.gov/cia/publications/factbook> (July 26, 1999).

CIA. 2000. *The World Factbook.*

CIA. 2001. *The World Factbook.*

CIA. 2002. *The World Factbook.*

Clugage, Julie, Din Heiman, Joe Schock, and Alexandra Shapiro. 2001. *High Tech Firms and the Global Digital Divide.* Berkeley: University of California, Haas School of Business.

Cogburn, Derrick. 1998. "Globalization and State Autonomy in the Information Age: Telecommunications Restructuring in South Africa," *Journal of International Affairs* 51 (Spring): 583–604.

Council for Scientific and Industrial Research (CSIR). Available at <www.csir.org.gh/establishment.html>.

Cowhey, Peter. 1990. "The International Telecommunications Regimes: the Political Roots of Regimes for High Technology." *International Organization* 44(2): 169–200.

Cowhey, Peter, and Jonathan Aronson. 1993. *Managing the World Economy.* New York: Council on Foreign Relations Press.

Cowles, Maria Green. 2001a. *Who Writes the Rules of E-Commerce? A Case Study of the Global Business Dialogue on E-commerce.* Washington, DC: American Institute for Contemporary German Studies, John Hopkins University Press. Available at <www.aicgs.org/publications/PDF/cowles.pdf>.

Cowles, Maria Green. 2001b. "The Transatlantic Business Dialogue: Transforming the New Transatlantic Dialogue." In Mark Pollack and Gregory Schaffer, eds., *Transatlantic Governance in a Global Economy.* Lanham, MD: Rowman & Littlefield.

Cutler, Claire, Virginia Haufler, and Tony Porter, eds. 1999. *Private Authority and International Affairs.* Albany: State University of New York Press.

DaCosta, Eduardo. 2001. *Global E-Commerce Strategies for Small Business.* Cambridge, MA: MIT Press.

Dahlman, Carl and Jean-Eric Aubert. 2001. *China and the Knowledge Economy.* Washington, DC: World Bank Instute.

Dalpino, Catharine. 2001. "Does Globalization Promote Democracy? An Early Assessment." *Brookings Review* 19(4): 45–48.

Dedrick, Jason, and Kenneth L. Kramer. 2000. *China IT Report.* Irvine, CA: Center for Research on Information Technology and Organizations.

Diebold, William, Jr. 1980. *Industrial Policy as an International Issue.* New York: McGraw-Hill.

Doner, Richard F., Ben Ross Schneider, and Ernest J. Wilson III. 1998. "Can Business Associations Contribute to Development and Democracy?" In Ann Bernstein and Peter L Berger, eds., *Business and Democracy*, 126–150. London: Pinter.

Drake, William J., ed. 1995. *The New Information Infrastructure: Strategies for U.S. Policy.* New York: Twentieth Century Fund Press.

Drake William J., Shanthi Kalathil, and Taylor C. Boas. 2000. "Dictatorships in the Digital Age." *ChinaOnLine*, November 9. <http://www.chinaonline.com/> (November 10, 2000).

Durkheim, Emile. 1897. *Suicide.* Reprint, New York: Free Press, 1951.

Dzidonu, Clement K. 2003. *An Integrated ICT-Led Socio-Economic Development Policy and Plan Development Framework for Ghana.* Accra, Ghana:

Institute for Scientific and Technological Information, Council for Scientific and Industrial Research.

Easter, Gerald M., ed. 1989. *Restructuring Ethnic Relations in the Soviet Union: Debates on the Draft Nationalities Program.* Washington, DC: American Committee on U.S.-Soviet Relations.

Econet Wireless. 1996. "Econet Zimbabure," profile July 29, 1996. Available at <www.econet.co.zw/profile/history-fly291994.htm>.

Economist Intelligence Unit Limited. 2000. "Can't Stop Loving You." *Business China,* February 12.

Elmer, Laurel. 1999. "Education for All in the Information Age: The Potential of Information Technology for Improving Educational Access and Quality in Developing Countries." Report of an International Meeting on Telecentre Evaluation, Quebec, Canada, September 28–30. <http://www.idrc.ca/telecentre/> (March 2, 2001).

European Commission. 1998. "Globalization and the Information Society." *Communication from the Commission.* Brussels.

Evans, Peter. 1979. *Dependent Development, The Alliance of Multinational, State, and Local Capital in Brazil.* Princeton: Princeton University Press.

Evans, Peter. 1995. *Embedded Autonomy.* Princeton, NJ: Princeton University Press.

Faiola, Anthony. 2000. "Poor in Latin America Embrace Net's Promise." *Washington Post,* July 9.

Ferreira, Francisco. 1999. "World Income Equality: Is Technological Progress to Blame?" Paper presented at New IT and Inequality: Resetting the Research and Policy Agenda, College Park, Maryland, February. <http://www.bsos.umd.edu/cidcm/>.

Fine, Jeffrey C., and Rostenne, Jacques. 1998. *Connectivity, Commerce and Growth: Uganda and Tanzania.* Washington, DC: World Bank.

Fontaine, Mary, and Dennis Foote. 1999. "Ghana: Networking for Social Development." *TechKnowLogia,* September/October. <http://www.TechKnowLogia.org> (April 2, 2000).

Foster, William, and Seymour E. Goodman, 2000. *The Diffusion of the Internet in China.* Stanford, CA: Institute for International Studies.

Fountain, Jane E. 2001. *Building the Virtual State: Information Technology and Institutional Change.* Washington, DC: Brookings Institution Press.

Franda, Marcus. 2001. *Governing the Internet.* Boulder, CO: Rienner.

Friedman, Thomas. 1999. *The Lexus and the Olive Tree.* New York: Farrar, Straus, Giroux.

Garcia, Linda. 2001. "Inequality, Cooperation, and the Global Political Economy of IT." Paper presented to the Social Science Research Council Research Seminar, Berkeley, CA, July 15–21.

Geddes, Barbara. 1990. *How the Cases You Choose Affect the Answers You Get: Selection Bias in Comparative Politics.* Berkeley: Institute of Governmental Studies, University of California.

Gerschenkron, Alexander. 1962. *Economic Backwardness in Historical Perspective.* Cambridge, MA: Harvard University Press.

"Ghana at a Glance." 2000. <http://www.healthnet.org/hnet/ghana.html> (July 12, 2000).

Ghana Economic Commision for Africa NICI. 2002. <www.uneca.org/aisi/nici/ghana/ghanpol.htm>.

Giddens, Anthony. 1979. *Central Problems in Social Theory.* Berkeley: University of California Press.

Gilder, George. 1993. "Metcalfe's Law and Legacy." *Fortune*, September 13, 158–167.

Global Business Dialogue (GBDe). 2000. "Electronic Commerce." Report found at <http://digitalbridges.gbde.org/origins/html>.

Global Information Infrastructure Commission (GIIC). 1997. *The WTO Telecom Agreement: Engineering the Global Information Highway.* Washington, DC: Center for Strategic and International Studies.

Global Information Infrastructure Commission (CIIC). 1999. *GIIC Report on E-Commerce in Developing Countries: Enabling E-Commerce in India.* Washington, DC: Center for Strategic and International Studies.

Global Information Infrastructure Commission (GIIC). 2001. "Digital Divide Survey Results." Washington, DC.

Gore, Al. 1994. "Remarks to the International Telecommunications Union Development Conference." In W. Russell Neuman, *Toward A Global Information Infrastructure.* Washington, D.C.: U.S. Information Agency.

Granovetter, Mark S. 1997. "Economic Action and Social Structure: The Problem of Embeddedness." In Barry Wellman and S. D. Berkowitz, eds., *Social Structures: A Network Approach.* Greenwich, CT: JAI Press.

Greenwood, Jeremy. 1997. *The Third Industrial Revolution: Technology, Productivity and Income Inequality.* Washington, DC: AEI Press.

Guice, Jon. 1998. "Looking Backward and Forward at the Internet." *Information Society* 14(3): 201–211.

Guillen, Mauro F., and Sandra L. Suarez. 2001. "Developing the Internet: Entrepreneurship and Public Policy in Ireland, Singapore, Argentina and Spain." *Telecommunications Policy* 25(5): 349–373.

Guobin, Yang. 2001. "Information Technology, Virtual Chinese Diaspora, and Transnational Public Sphere." <http://www.nautilus.org/virtual-diasporas/paper/Yang.html>.

Haggard, Stephan. 1990. *Pathways from the Periphery.* Ithaca, NY: Cornell University Press.

Hall, Peter A. 1999. "The Political Economy of Europe in an Era of Inter-dependence." In Herbert Kitschelt, Peter Lange, Gary Marks, and John D. Stephens, eds., *Continuity and Change in Contemporary Capitalism*. New York: Cambridge University Press.

Halperin, Morton, David Scheffer, and Patricia Small. 1992. *Self-Determination in the New World Order*. Washington, DC: Carnegie Endowment for International Peace.

Hamelink, Cees. 1997. *New Information and Communications Technologies: Social Development and Cultural Change*. Geneva: United Nations Research Institute for Social Development.

Hargittai, Eszter. 1999. Weaving the Western Web: Explaining Difference in Internet Connectivity among OECD Countries. <www.sscnet.ucla.edu/soc/groups/ccsa/CD1999.html>.

Hartford, Kathleen. 2000. "Cyberspace with Chinese Characteristics." *Current History* 99 (September): 255–273.

Haufler, Virginia. 2001. *A Public Role for the Private Sector: Industry Self-Regulation in a Global Economy*. New York: Carnegie Endowment for International Peace.

Hechter, Michael, Karl-Dieter Opp, and Reinhard Wippler, eds. 1990. "Introduction." In Michael Hechter, Karl-Dieter Opp, and Reinhard Wippler, eds., *Social Institutions Their Emergence, Maintenance and Effects*. New York: Aldine de Gruyter.

Herbst, Jeffrey. 1991. *The Politics of Reform in Ghana*. University of California Press. Oakland, CA.

Hollingsworth, J. Rogers, and Robert Boyer, eds. 1997. *Contemporary Capitalism: The Embeddedness of Institutions*. New York: Cambridge University Press.

Hollingsworth, J. Rogers, Philippe C. Schmitter, and Wolfgang Streeck. 1994. *Governing Capitalist Economies: Performance and Control of Economic Sectors*. New York: Oxford University Press.

Horwitz, Robert. 2001. *Communication and Democratic Reform in South Africa*. Cambridge: Cambridge University Press.

Hu, Angnang. 2002. *Knowledge and Development; A New Catch-up Strategy in the 21st Century*. Beijing: Peking University Press.

Hudson, Heather. 1997. *Global Connections: International Telecommunications Infrastructure and Policy*. New York: Van Nostrand Reinhold.

Hudson, Heather A. 1998. "GII Project Initiatives: A Critical Assessment." Paper presented at the Twenty-sixth Annual Telecommunications Policy Research Conference, Alexandria, VA.

Huntington, Samuel P. 1991. *The Third Wave Democratization in the Late Twentieth Century*. Norman, OK: University of Oklahoma Press.

Inglehart, Ronald. 1990. *Culture Shift in Advanced Industrial Society.* Princeton: Princeton University Press.

Institute for Scientific Information. 1999. Available at <http:www.csir.org.gh/insti.html>.

Inter Media. Available at <www.intermedia.org/news_and_publications/publications/internetuse.pdf>.

International Chamber of Commerce (ICC). Report found at <www.icc.org>.

International Finance Corporation. 2002. <http://www.ifc.org> (February 2, 2002).

International Telecommunicatin Union. 1985. The Missing Link. ("Maitland Report"). Geneva.

International Telecommunication Union (ITU). 1998. Executive Summary. <http://www.itu.int/ti/publication/WTDR_98/index_htm> (July 6 1999).

International Telecommunication Union (ITU). 2000. <http://ww.itu.int/ITU=D/ict/statisties/at_glance/Internet00.pdf>.

International Telecommunications Union. 2001. *Effective Regulation Case Study: Brazil.* Geneva.

International Telecommunication Union (ITU). 2002. <http://www.itu.org> (February 6, 2002).

Johnson, Ollie. 1998. "Racial Representations and Brazilian Politics: Black Members of the National Congress, 1983–1999." *Journal of Interamerican Studies and World Affairs* 40 (Winter): 97–118.

The Journal. 2001. "Editorial." *The Journal Online* (May). Available at <http://www.thejournal.com/magazine/vault/articleprintversion.cfm?aid=3442>.

Kahin, Brian, and Ernest J. Wilson III. 1997. *National Information Infrastructure Initiatives: Vision and Policy Design.* Cambridge, MA: MIT Press.

Kahn, Gabriel. 2003. "What's Old Is New: A Chinese Internet Company Has Thrived by Focusing on a Seemingly Obsolete Technology." *Wall Street Journal* (September 23): R4.

Kalathil, Shanti and Taylor C. Boaz. 2003. *Open Networks, Closed Regimes.* Washington, DC: Carnegie Endowment for International Peace.

Katz, Jon. 1998. "U.S. Centrism on the Net." *Wired,* June 29. www.wired.com/news/business/0,13,67,13280,00.html>.

Keck, Margaret E., and Kathryn Sikkink. 1999. *Activists Beyond Borders: Advocacy Network in International Politics.* Itheca: Cornell University Press.

Kedzie, Charles. 1997. "The Third Wave," In Brian Kahin and Charles Nesson, eds., *Borders in Cyberspace.* Cambridge, MA: MIT Press.

Kelly, Dominic. 2001. "Markets for a Better World? Implications of the Public-Private Partnership between the International Chamber of Commerce and the United Nations." Paper presented at the International Studies Association Meeting, Chicago, March.

Kingdon, John. 1995. *Agendas, Alternatives and Public Policies.* New York: Longman.

Kingstone, Peter R. 1999. *Crafting Coalitions for Reform: Business Preferences, Political Institutions and Neoliberal Reform in Brazil.* University Park: Pennsylvania University Press.

Kornai, Janos. 1995. *Highways and Byways: Studies on Reform and Post-Communist Transition.* Cambridge, MA: MIT Press.

Kowack, Glenn. 1997. "International Governance and the Emergence of Global Civil Society." *IEEE Communications Magazine* 35 (May): 52–57.

Kraemer, Kenneth, Jason Derrick, and Eric Shih. 2000. *Determinants of IT Investment at the Country Level.* Irvine, CA: Center for Research on Information Technology and Organizations.

Krasner, Stephen D. 1985. *Structural Conflict: The Third World against Global Liberalism.* Berkeley: University of California Press.

Krasner, Stephen D. 1991. "Global Communications and National Power." *World Politics* 43 (April): 336–366.

Krugman, Paul. 1995. *Currencies and Crises.* Cambridge, MA: MIT Press.

Kyabwe, Samuel, and Richard Kibombo. 1999. "Buwama and Nabweru Multi-purpose Community Telecentres: Baseline Surveys in Uganda." In Ricardo Gómez and Patrik Hunt, eds., *Telecentre Evaluation: A Global Perspective.* Ottawa: International Development Research Centre. <http://www.idrc.ca/telecentre/evaluation/nn/_00Cov.html> (May 30, 2002).

Landreth, Jonathan. 2000. "Interested in a Ton of Ethylene from China?" *Virtual China,* January 12. <http://www.virtualchina.com/trade/tviews/011200-tv.html> (January 15, 2000).

Lapres, Daniel Arthur. 2000. "Legal Dos and Don'ts of Web Use in China." *China Business Review* (March–April): 26.

Levinson, Nanette S. 2000. *The ICANN Case: International Affairs in an Information Era.* Washington, DC: School of International Service, American University.

Levinson, Nanette S. 2001. "Interorganizational Approaches to the Global Digital Divide." International Studies Association, Chicago, February 2001.

Levy, Brian, and Pablo Spiller, eds. 1996. *Regulations, Institutions and Commitment.* Cambridge: Cambridge University Press.

Lieberthal, Kenneth. 1995. *Governing China: From Revolution through Reform.* New York: Norton.

Lieberthal, Kenneth, and Michel Oksenberg. 1988. *Policy Making in China: Leaders, Structures, and Processes.* Princeton, NJ: Princeton University Press.

Lima, Maria Ilca, and Ivan Alcoforado Jr. 1999. "Electronic Commerce: Aspects of the Brazilian Experience." *Electronic Markets* 9 (February). Available at <http://www.electronicmarkets.org/netacademy/publications.nsf/all_pk/1347> (March 2, 2000).

Lindberg, Leon, ed. 1977. *The Energy Syndrome: Comparing National Responses to the Energy Crisis.* Lexington, MA.: Lexington Books.

Litan, Robert E., and Alice M. Rivlin. 2001a. *Beyond the Dot.Coms: The Economic Promise of the Internet.* Washington, DC: Brookings Institution Press.

Litan, Robert E., and Alice M. Rivlin, eds. 2001b. *The Economic Payoff from the Internet Revolution.* Washington, DC: Brookings Institution Press.

Lovelock, Peter. 1996. "Asia Meets the Internet." *China Business Review* 23 (November/December): 26–28.

Lu, Xinkui. 2001. "Active Participation in Narrowing Digital Divide." Global Information Intrastructure Commission Forum, Dublin, Ireland.

Luo, Xiawei. 2000. "The Rise of the Social Development Model: Institutional Construction of International Technology Organizations, 1856–1993." *International Studies Quarterly* 44(1): 147–175.

Lyon, David. 1995. "The Roots of the Information Society Idea." In Nick Heap, Ray Thomas, Geoff Einam, Rubin Masare, and Hughie MacKay, eds., *Information Technology and Society's Reader.* London: Sage.

Mann, Catherine L., Sue E. Eckert, and Sarah Cleeland Knight. 2000. *Global Economic Commerce: A Policy Primer.* Washington, DC: Institute for International Economics.

Mansell, Robin, and Uta Wehn, eds. 1998. *Knowledge Societies: Information Technology and Sustainable Development.* New York: Oxford University Press.

Maran, Murasoli. 1999. <siliconindia.com>.

Masuda, Yoneji. 1981. *The Information Society.* Washington, DC: World Future Society.

Mathews, Jessica T. 1997. "Power Shift," *Foreign Affairs* 76 (January/February): 50–66.

Mathiassen, Lars. 1998. "Out of Scandinavia: History and Contributions of an IS Research Tradition." <http://www.icis98.jyu.fi/abstracts.htm> (June 16, 2001).

McConnell International. 2000. *Risk E-Business: Seizing the Opportunity of Global E-Readiness.* Washington, DC: McConnell. <http://www.mcconnellinternational.com/ereadiness/EReadinessReport.htm>.

McDermott, John. 2003. "Technology: The Opiate of the Intellectuals." Originally published in *New York Review of Books*, July 1969. Republished in Albert Teich, ed., *Technology and the Future.* Belmont, CA: Wadsworth.

McDonough, Peter. 1981. *Power and Ideology in Brazil.* Princeton: Princeton University Press.

McKendrick, David G., Richard F. Doner, and Stephan Haggard. 2001. *From Silicon Valley to Singapore: Location and Competitive Advantage in the Hard Disk Drive Industry.* Stanford, CA: Stanford University Press.

McKnight, Lee, and Antonio J. J. Botelho. 1997. "Brazil: Is the World Ready for When Information Highways Cross the Amazon?" In Brian Kahin and Ernest J. Wilson III, eds., *National Information Infrastructure Initiatives: Vision and Policy Design.* Cambridge, MA: MIT Press.

Metcalfe, Robert M. 1999. Quoted in report found at <http://whatis.com>.

Mills, Quinn D. 2001. *E-Leadership: Guiding Your Business to Success in the New Economy.* Upper Saddle River, NJ: Prentice Hall.

Mintrom, Michael. 1997. "Policy Entrepreneurs and the Diffusion of Innovation." *American Journal of Political Science* 41 (July): 738–770.

Moravcsik, Andrew. 1999. "Supranational Entrepreneurs and International Cooperation." *International Organization.* 53, 2 (Spring): 247–307.

Mueller, Milton, and Zixiang Tan. 1996. *China in the Information Age: Telecommunications and the Dilemmas of Reform.* New York: Praeger.

Nanus, Burt. 1989. *The Leaders Edge.* Chicago: Contemporary Books.

National Academy of Science. 1999. *Being Fluent with Information Technology.* Washington, DC: National Academy Press.

"National Information and Communication Infrastructure Country Proposal: Ghana." 2001.

National Research Council. 1996. *Prospectus for National Knowledge Assessment.* Washington, DC: National Academy Press.

National Research Council. 1998a. *Fostering Research on the Economic and Social Impacts of Information Technology.* Washington, DC: National Academy Press.

National Research Council. 1998b. *Internet Counts: Measuring the Impacts of the Internet.* Washington, DC: National Academy Press.

National Research Council. 1999. *Lighting The Way: Knowledge Assessment in Prince Edward Island.* Washington, DC: National Academy Press.

Negroponte, Nicholas. 1995. *Being Digital.* New York: Knopf.

NGO and Academic ICANN Study. 2001. *ICANN Legitimacy, and the Public Voice: Making Global Participation and Representation Work.* <http://www.naisproject.org> (June 3, 2002).

Norris, Pippa. 2000. "The Global Divide: Information Poverty and Internet Access Worldwide." Paper presented at the Internet Conference, International Political Science World Congress, Quebec City, Canada.

North, Douglass C. 1990. *Institutions, Institutional Change and Economic Performance.* Cambridge, MA: Harvard University Press.

Nua Internet Surveys. 2000. <http://www.nua.ie/surveys>.

O'Brien, Rita Cruise, and G. K. Helleiner. 1980. "The Political Economy of Information in a Changing International Economic Order." *International Organization* 34 (Autumn): 445–471.

Olson, Mancur. 1971. *The Logic of Collective Action: Public Goods and the Theory of Groups.* Cambridge, MA: Harvard University Press.

Organization for Economic Cooperation and Development (OECD). 1999. *OECD Science, Technology and Industry Scoreboard 1999.* Paris: OECD.

Organization for Economic Cooperation and Development (OECD). 2002. Statistical Information. <http://www.oecd.org/dsti/sti/it/stats> (January 2, 2002).

Osiakwan, Eric. n.d. "Ghana's Internet Industry." Internet Research Education and Consulting. Manuscript.

O'Siochru, Sean. 1996. *Telecommunications and Universal Service: International Experience in the Context of South African Policy Reform*. Ottawa: International Development Research Center.

"Overview of Ghana Telecom." n.d. <http://www.communication.gov.gh/telecomstraoverview.gt.htm> (April 2, 2001).

Paschoalino, Christiane. 2000. "Brazil." <www.american.edu/carmel/cp8809a/landscape.htm>.

Pearson, Margaret M. 1997. *China's New Business Elite: the Political Consequences of Economic Reform*. Berkeley: University of California Press.

Pennings, Paul, Hans Keman, and Jan Kleinnijenhuis. 1999. *Doing Research in Political Science*. London: Sage.

Petrazzini, Ben. 1995. *The Political Economy of Telecommunications Reform in Developing Countries: Privatization and Liberalization in Comparative Perspective*. Westport, CT: Praeger.

Petrazzini, Ben. 1996. *Global Telecom Talks: A Trillion Dollar Deal*. Washington, DC: Institute for International Economics.

Pitroda, Satyan (Sam). 1993. "Development, Democracy, and the Village Telephone." *Harvard Business Review* (Nov./Dec.).

Polanyi, Karl. 1944. *The Great Transformation: The Political and Economic Origins of Our Time*. Boston: Beacon Press.

Porat, Marc U. 1977. *The Information Economy*. Washington, DC: Office of Telecommunications, Department of Commerce.

Price, Monroe Edwin, and Roger G. Noll, eds. 1998. *A Communications Cornucopia: Markle Foundation Essays on Information Policy*. Washington, DC: Brookings Institution Press.

Pritchett, Lant. 1996. "Forget Convergence: Divergence Past, Present and Future." *Finance and Development* 33(2). <http://www.worldbank.org/fandd/english/0696/articles/090696.htm> (May 30, 2002).

Putnam, Robert D. 1999. *Bowling Alone: The Collapse and Revival of American Community*. New York: Simon & Schuster.

Pye, Lucien W., with Mary W. Pye. 1985. *Asian Power and Politics: The Cultural Dimensions of Authority*. Cambridge, MA: Harvard University Press.

Pyramid Research. 2000. *Will the Internet Close the Gap?* Washington, DC: World Bank.

Quaynor, Nii N. 2001. *Ways and Ways: The Future for Accessing the Internet in Africa*. Connect-World. <http://www.ncs.com.gh/pub/> (December 21, 2001).

Ranis, Gustav. 1979. *Growth with Equity: The Taiwan Case*. J. C. H. Fei and S. W. Y. Kuo. Oxford: Oxford University Press.

Raymond, Susan U. 1996. *Science-Based Economic Development*. New York: Annals of the New York Academy of Sciences.

Reinicke, Wolfgang, and Francis Deng, eds. 2000. *Critical Choices: The United Nations, Networks, and the Future of Global Governance*. Ottawa: International Development Research Centre Press.

RITS. 1999. "The Information Network for the Third Sector." Descriptive Summary. <http://www.rits.org.br>.

Robinson, John P., Meyer Kestnbaum, Alan Neustadtl, and Anthony Alvarez. 2000. "Mass Media Use and Social Life among Internet Users." *Social Science Computer Review* 18(4): 490–501.

Rodriguez, Francisco, and Ernest J. Wilson III. 2000. *Are Poor Countries Losing the Information Revolution?* Washington, DC: World Bank. <http://www.bsos.umd.edu/cidcm/papers/ewilson/worldbank> (March 18, 2002).

Rogers, Everett M. 1995. *Diffusion of Innovations*. New York: Free Press.

Rohozinski, Rafal. 1999. *Mapping Russian Cyberspace: Perspectives on Democracy and the Net*. New York: United Nations Research Institute for Social Development.

Romero, Simon. 2000a. "Brazil Group Protests Two Banks' Free Web Access Plans." *New York Times*, January 8.

Romero, Simon. 2000b. "Internet Takeovers Fuel a Big Surge in Acquisitions in Brazil." *New York Times*, April 11.

Romine, Traci. 1998. "On the Road to Modernization: Privatizing Brazil's Telecommunications System." *Inside Brazil* 57 (March 20): 1.

Rosenau, James N. 2002. "Information Technologies and the Skills, Networks and Structures that Sustain World Affairs." In James N. Rosenau, and J. P. Singh, eds., *Information Technologies and Global Politics: The Changing Scope of Power and Governance* (pp. 275–288). Albany: State University of New York Press.

Sadowski, George. 1996. "The Internet Society and Developing Countries." *On the Internet* (November/December). Available at <www.isoc.org/ontheinternet>.

Saich, Tony. 2000. "Negotiating the State: The Development of Social Organizations in China." *China Quarterly* 161 (March): 124–141.

Salamon, Lester M., and Helmut K. Anheier, eds. 1996. *Defining the Nonprofit Sector: A Cross-National Comparison*. Manchester, UK: Manchester University Press.

Salter, Liora. 1999. "The Standards Regime for Communication and Information Technologies." In A. Claire Cutler, Virginia Haufler, and Tony Porter, eds., *Private Authority and International Affairs*. Albany: State University of New York Press.

Sartori, Giovanni. 1997. *Comparative Constitutional Engineering: An Inquiry into Structures, Incentives, and Outcomes*. New York: New York University Press.

Sauve, Pierre, and Robert M. Stern, eds. 1999. *GATS 2000: New Directions in Services Trade Liberalization*. Washington, DC: Brookings Institution Press.

Saxenian, AnnaLee. 1999a. *Regional Advantage: Culture and Competition in Silicon Valley and Route 128*. Cambridge, MA: Harvard University Press.

Saxenian, AnnaLee. 1999b. *Silicon Valley's New Immigrant Entrepreneurs*. San Francisco: Public Policy Institute of California.

Schiller, Dan. 1999. *Digital Capitalism*. Cambridge, MA: MIT Press.

Schiller, Herbert I. 1996. *Information Inequality: The Deepening Social Crisis in America*. New York: Routledge.

Schmitz, Hubert, and Jose Cassiolato. 1992. *Hi-Tech for Industrial Development: Lessons from the Brazilian Experience in Electronics and Automation*. New York: Routledge.

Schumpeter, Joseph A. 1943. *Capitalism, Socialism and Democracy*. London: Allen & Unwin.

Schwartz, Peter, Peter Leyden, and Joel Hyatt. 1999. *The Long Boom*. Reading, MA: Perseus Books.

Seligson, Mitchell A. 1984. "The Dual Gaps: An Update of Theory and Research." In Mitchell A. Seligson, ed., *The Gap between Rich and Poor: Contending Perspectives on the Political Economy of Development*. Boulder, CO: Westview Press.

Sell, Susan. 1998. *Power and Ideas: North-South Politics of Intellectual Property and Antitrust*. Albany: State University of New York Press.

Shapiro, Carl, and Hal Varian. 1998. *Information Rules*. Cambridge, MA: Harvard Business School Press.

Sheff, David. 2002. *China Dawn The Story of a Technology and Business Revolution*. New York: Harper Collins.

Singh, J. P. 1999. *Leapfrogging Development? The Political Economy of Telecommunications Restructuring*. Albany: State University of New York Press.

Smith, Craig S. 2000. "Web Sites' Merger Signals Consolidation of China's Internet Industry." *New York Times*, September 16, C13–C14.

Spar, Deborah L. 1999. "Lost in (Cyber) space: The Private Rules of Online Commerce." In A. Claire Cutler, Virginia Haufler, and Tony Porter, eds., *Private Authority and International Affairs*. Albany: State University of New York Press.

Sprague, Katherine L. 1994. *Latin America's Information Revolution*. Mid-Year Proceedings of the American Society for Information Science.

Steinfeld, Charles, and Jerry Salvaggio. 1989. "Toward a Definition of The Information Society." In Jerry Salvaggio, ed., *The Information Society: Economic, Social and Structural Issues*. Hillsdale, NJ: Erlbaum.

Stern, Nicholas. 2000. "Fifty Years of Development." Paper presented at the Annual Meeting of the Latin American and Caribbean Economics Association, Rio de Janeiro, Brazil, October. <http://www.worldbank.org> (April 4, 2002).

Stremlau, John. 1996. "Dateline Bangalore: Third World Technopolis." *Foreign Policy* 102 (Spring): 152–169.

"Survey of the New Economy." 2000. *The Economist*, September 23, p. 38.

Talero, Eduardo. 1997. "National Information Infrastructures in Developing Economies." In Brian Kahin and Ernest J. Wilson III, eds., *National Information Infrastructure Initiatives*. Cambridge, MA: MIT Press.

Tan, Zixiang, William Foster, and Seymour Goodman. 1999. "China's State-Coordinated Internet Infrastructure." *Communications of the ACM* 42 (June): 44–53.

Taubman, Geoffrey T. 1998. "Ideas, Interaction and the Political Intrusion of the Internet: The Unease of Non-Democratic Regimes and the Construction of China's 'Golden Bridge.'" <http://www.ciaonet.org/abs/conf/tag01.html> (April 2, 2001).

Tavares, Ricardo. 1998. "Brazil: Telecommunications Regulation After Privatization." Paper presented at the Institute of the Americas, November 16–17.

Tilly, Charles. 1984. *Big Structures, Large Processes, Huge Comparisons*. New York: Sage.

Tipson, Frederick S. 1999. "China and the Information Revolution." In Elizabeth Economy, Michael Oksenberg, and Lawrence Korb, eds. 1999. *China Joins the World*. New York: Council on Foreign Relations.

Toffler, Alvin. 1980. *The Third Wave*. New York: Morrow.

United Nations Development Program. 1999. *Human Development Report*. New York: Oxford University Press. <http://hdr.undp.org/reports/global/1999/en/pdf/hdr_1999.pdf>.

United Nations Development Project. 2000. *Human Development Report*. <http://www.undp.org/hydro/statistics.html> (August 16, 2001).

United Nations Educational, Scientific and Cultural Organization (UNESCO). 1997. Records of the General Conference, twenty-ninth session. Vol. 3. Paris.

United States Council for International Business. 1994. *Private Sector Leadership: Policy Foundations for a National Infrastructure*. Washington, DC: U.S. Council for International Business.

United States Office of Technology Assessment (OTA). 1990. *Critical Connections: Communication for the Future*. Washington, DC: U.S. Government Printing Office.

Villaschi, Arlindo. 1994. *The Newly Industrialized Countries and the Information Revolution: The Brazilian Experience*. Aldershot: Avebury.

Vogel, Ezra F. 1991. *The Four Little Dragons: The Spread of Industrialization in East Asia*. Cambridge, MA: Harvard University Press.

Vogel, Steven K. 1996. *Freer Markets, More Rules: Regulatory Reform in Advanced Industrial Countries*. Ithaca, NY: Cornell University Press.

Walder, Andrew G. 1986. *Communist Neo-Traditionalism: Work and Authority in Chinese Industry*. Berkeley: University of California Press.

Wallis, Joe. 1999. "Understanding the Role of Leadership in Economic Policy Reform." *World Development* 27(1): 39–55.

Wang, Honying. 2000. "State and Networks in a Transitional Society." Paper presented at the Annual Meeting of the American Political Science Association, Washington, DC.

Weaver, Kent, and Bert Rockman, eds. 1993. *Do Institutions Matter?* Washington, DC: Brookings Institution Press.

Webster, Bruce. 1999. *The Y2K Survival Guide.* Upper Saddle River, NJ: Prentice Hall.

White, Wendy. 1994. "Growing the Internet in Africa." *Internet Society News* 3, no. 2. Quoted in *Bridge Builders: African Experiences with Information and Communication Technology.* 1996. National Research Council. Washington, DC: National Academy Press.

Williamson, Oliver. 1986. *Economic Organization: Firms, Markets, and Policy Control.* New York: New York University Press.

Wilson III, Ernest J. 1990. "Strategies of State Control of the Economy: Nationalization and Indigenization in Africa." *Comparative Politics* 22 (July): 401–420.

Wilson III, Ernest J. 1997. "Introduction: The What, Why, Where and How of National Information Initiatives." In Brain Kahin and Ernest J. Wilson III, eds., *National Information Infrastructure Initiatives: Vision and Policy Design.* Cambridge, MA: MIT Press.

Wilson III, Ernest J. 1998. "Inventing the Global Information Future," *Futures* 30(1): 23–43.

Wilson III, Ernest J. 1999. "Organizing Foreign Policy: A Pragmatic Approach to the Information Revolution." *Information Magazine Impacts* (May). <http://www.cisp.org/imp/may_99/wilson/05_99wilson.htm> (July 6, 2001).

Wilson III, Ernest J. 2000. "Wiring the African Economy." *EM Electronic Markets* 10 (2).

Wilson III, Ernest J. 2001. "Taking Us from Here to There: The Role of Leadership in the Transition to a Networked Society of 2020." *Information Magazine Impacts* (February). <http://www.cisp.org/imp/february_2001/02_01wilson.htm> (April 12, 2002).

Wilson, Richard. 2000. "The Many Voices of Political Culture: Assessing Different Approaches." *World Politics* 52 (January): 246–274.

Wolcott, Peter, and Seymour E. Goodman. 2000. *The Internet in Turkey and Pakistan: A Comparative Analysis.* Stanford, CA: Stanford University, Center for International Security and Cooperation.

World Bank. 1999. *World Development Report: Knowledge for Development.* Oxford: Oxford University Press.

World Economic Forum. 2000. *From the Global Digital Divide to the Global Digital Opportunity.* Davos Switzerland.

World Economic Forum (WEF). 2001. Annual meeting. Found at <http://www.weforum.org>.

Index